Literature at War, 1914–1940

Literature at War, 1914–1940

Representing the "Time of Greatness"
in Germany

Wolfgang G. Natter

Yale University Press

New Haven and London

Set in Adobe Garamond type with Stone Sans display by The Composing Room of Michigan, Inc. Printed in the United States of America.

Library of Congress Cataloging-in-Publication Data

Natter, Wolfgang, G.
Literature at war, 1914–1940 : representing the "time of greatness" in Germany / Wolfgang G. Natter.
    p.   cm.
Includes bibliographical references and index.
ISBN 0-300-05558-7 (alk. paper)
    1. German literature—20th century—History and criticism. 2. World War, 1914–1918—Literature and the war. 3. War in literature. 4. Nationalism and literature—Germany. 5. Literature and state—Germany—History—20th century. 6. Germany—History, Military—20th century. I. Title.
PT405.N285 1999
830.9'358—dc21   98-39029

A catalogue record for this book is available from the British Library.

Dedicated to my parents,

Wolfgang Ludwig Natter, 1919–1954
   Ensign, 1938–1944
   Prisoner of War, 1944–December 27, 1949

"Und seid vor allem lieb zu einander," December 13, 1954

Dolores Hornbach Whelan, 1928–
   BDM Trench Digger, 1944–1945
   Tuberculosis Patient, 1945–1955
   Widowed 1954, emigrated 1956
   Ph.D., 1977

Ross Edward Whelan, "Take your child and bring him into safety," Caucasian Chalk Circle

In memory of

Otto Natter, 1889–1955, Artillery Captain, 1914–1918, Captain of the Reserves, 1939–1945

Ella Weigel Natter, 1889–1986, married August 2, 1914

Hermann Natter, born 1920, Captain, fallen 1943

Georg Hornbach, 1898–1963, Artillery Soldier, 1916–1918, 1939–1942; Information Corps, 1942–1945

Mattilde Schmid Hornbach, 1903–1962, Owner, Zum Rössel, Speyer

Contents

Introduction

In this book, I examine the relationship between culture and warfare in the context of German texts written about the First World War. This book is not a military history of the war in the traditional sense of providing an assessment of the strategic and tactical decisions taken by the German High Command or of their consequences on the battlefield. It is instead concerned with how the German military orchestrated efforts to write its own history, what value literature and culture acquired as part of the war effort, and how the institution of literature participated in and was altered by this cultural mobilization.

The military effort to shape literary depictions of the war extends well beyond 1918. Although most scholars have studied war literature of the Weimar Republic and the Third Reich in isolation from this effort, I argue that the information flows and cultural memories that resulted from them during the war itself are central to subsequent attempts at reordering the lost war's "meaning" during the Weimar period or for understanding the successful appropriation of *das Kriegserlebnis* (the war experience) by National Socialism. I shall address this serious shortcoming in existing scholarship by analyzing what literature meant to the war and what the war meant to literature and its institutions.

The study reflects on nationalistically oriented literature (in some cases accorded canonical status after 1933) that was once widely read but is now largely forgotten by scholars. Its reassessment is predicated in part by a concern that ignoring such texts misrepresents the relation of forces competing within the institution of literature. From the critical literature that represents this period in the contemporary canon of German literature, we might assume that every citizen of the Weimar Republic was a democrat, Marxist, or pacifist. But for every novel like Edlef Köppen's *Heeresbericht* (Army communiqué), or every novella like Bruno Vogel's *Es lebe der Krieg! Ein Brief* (Long live war! A letter), four others that affirmed the war effort became best-sellers.[1] Each chapter of this book therefore analyzes such published literature in conjunction with previously unexamined archival materials to contextualize how *die große Zeit* (the time of greatness) came to be represented in literature and history in an overwhelmingly affirmative manner. Thus the study presents an account of how meanings were generated and disseminated during the war, how literary culture participated in that project, and what the consequences were for subsequent war depictions during the Weimar Republic and the Third Reich.

I do not pretend to have seized my subject matter "as it actually occurred" (as Leopold von Ranke defined the aim of historical research), not least because the conditions that led to the constitution of salient "events" between 1914 and 1918 and, furthermore, their passage into narration belong to this study's ongoing concerns. The study thus emphatically links both meanings of *Geschichte* (history and story) in connecting past events with the storytelling of these events. I seek in examining this linkage to contextualize the question of narrative authority with the force exercised by institutions in making and disseminating pertinent facts about the war. The voices that "speak" loudest in this study are thus not only the works categorized in libraries today by the proper names of "authors" but also those agencies, institutions, and individuals who attempted during the war to organize the reading, writing, and distribution of texts.

To uncover the dimensions of the forces exercised through and upon literary culture is to come to grips with the enabling limits that frame representations of the First World War and to renounce a reading of war prose as the unmediated expression of any given author's "experience" of the war. This study suggests a way of reading that demands an understanding of the text itself as the product of a host of institutions attempting to shape its meaning and reception. Its orientation fosters an appreciation of the role of the state and social relations within the institution of literature during this period, instead of seeing both merely (or at best) as distanced objects of reflection presented at the level of content in any given work.

Factors to be considered in the analysis include the relation between the state and the arts at the end of the Second Reich, the administration of wartime censorship, and the interaction of publishing, academic, and military agencies in actively constructing an authoritative, state-sanctioned interpretation of the ongoing war. The conditions that guided the efforts of the Imperial Army, the state, and select mainstream publishers to organize reading culture and public discourse about the war also provide a clue to the unequal footing on which the left and right stood after 1918 in their respective attempts to appropriate or deny the language generated during the war and assign it a specific meaning consistent with their political imperatives. The "ideal" narrative cultivated by various state agencies during the war—not to mention an impressive body of accumulated evidence to support it—retained a unique power after 1918 despite the "unhappy outcome" that prohibited the full exercise of force envisioned for this narrative.

The crisis that played out during the Weimar Republic regarding the war's "meaning" seems significantly a result of the cultural battle between the officially generated but damaged paradigm constructed between 1914 and 1918 and competing narratives that largely lacked the authority of the former. Recent theories regarding the relation between, on the one hand, the state, the law, and historicality, and, on the other, the authority to narrate, offer compelling grounds for assessing the impediments that a general legitimation crisis confronting the Republic posed to a democratic rendering of the lost war.[2] The wholesale failure of (anti)war novels of the democratic left in Weimar to be taken seriously—even initially to be published and read—demonstrates the continued authority of an earlier narrational scheme. For various reasons, National Socialism was best able to appropriate the language generated during the war and to offer the promise of undoing the rupture brought about by defeat. The essential, recurring elements of National Socialism's appropriation of this narrative maintain the earlier heroic tone while recasting the defeat of 1918 as the seed of national rebirth. The *Frontgemeinschaft* (warrior's community) of the trenches, much celebrated during the war as the German people's partial realization of its essential identity beyond particularities of class, religion, and region, would be repositioned as the cradle of a new Germany, the first installment of a process leading to the realization of a class-surmounting *Volksgemeinschaft* (folk community). Hitler himself would be stylized as the embodiment of the ideal German soldier at the front, and thus as the incarnation of the "new man" reborn in the trenches. In practice, the realization of this idealized folk community under the leadership of some part of a generation "reborn" in the trenches would be defined by the exclusion of (and attempt to annihilate) a series of racially, nationally, sexually, politically, religiously, and biologically defined others.

Thousands of volumes about the war were written between 1914 and 1940 in Germany. The extraordinary proliferation of volumes and genres to which I refer can be observed in the neatly organized system of classification in a well-ordered library of war literature, where texts are categorized by place, event, academic discipline, author, and Gattung (type, genre)—the latter in both its military and literary sense.[3] The recently unified Kaiserreich quickly stylized the continuing war as the "time of greatness," and numerous individuals and institutions embarked on a multilayered enterprise to preserve its greatness. The enterprise begun in 1914 continued well into the Nazi era, albeit with the significant exclusions that mirrored the regime's racism and anti-Marxism. By 1933 the contributions of virtually every imaginable particular grouping— designated by occupation, military unit, region, or religion—had been singled out as part of this expansive textual commemoration celebrating a people supposedly unified as a nation by war.

The textual presentation of the war illustrates above all the effort to forge— despite the very particularities singled out in the titles themselves—a sense of realized nationhood in which particularity had been subsumed in an overarching national narrative. This "forging" of a nation is strikingly related to how the war was framed between 1914 and 1918, both in the sense of that ironwork that serves as the contemporaneous metonymy for the union between industrial capitalism and nationalism and in the term's additional sense of fabrication of a fictitious story. The latter sense invites analysis of the tools and craftsmanship, the agencies and institutions at work in shaping national identity during the period. If I have chosen not to center such analysis on the inner-genre logic of belletristic texts, it is not because such analysis is without merit but because I believe its undertaking is predicated on an analysis of the interinstitutional frame that not only generated the raw materials for these stories but significantly circumscribed their mode of presentation as well.[4] The relation between the regulations guiding the writing of official regimental *Kriegstagebücher* (war diaries) and the form and content of critical war books written during the 1920s in the New Objective style is suggestive. Ignoring the effects of the wartime frame on such later representations too easily suggests an order of things that tautologically reenacts many of the categories employed by military officials and academics who produced and collected "authentic" materials during the war under the influence of the German High Command, which claimed the prerogative of writing the definitive history of the war upon its conclusion.[5]

An equal danger is that the seemingly well-ordered and settled identity of cataloged works too readily veils the violence wrought upon individual identities and bodies at work in the constitution of public memory about the war. So, too, soldiers' cemetery landscapes in Belgium and France, whose spatial structuring as well-ordered symmetries with individualized "plots" in which everyone is "in his place" likewise convey an illusory harmony. This semblance of order and peacefulness—a veritable "second nature"—not only contrasts with the violent manner in which those thus remembered lost their lives but also often disingenuously suggests the preservation of a specific identity of place, name, and corporeal remains. The names on the cemetery markers often enough bear a suspect relation to the remains below.[6] Both practices nonetheless suggest an ordering in which individual identity and historical coherence are preserved, such that even the most tragic social reality achieves a storylike comprehensibility. Both obfuscate the social production of public memory and the reason that the language of nationhood had to be so incessantly invoked to begin with.

Though constrained by a chronological frame, this study treats the First World War as anything but contained by its reference marker as the "Great War, 1914–1918." In spite of the wartime efforts to fix its events into a particular narrative, the war has in principle and often in practice been subject to multiple interpretations by novelists, poets, literary critics, and historians of various schools. Each fragment becomes significant—events, dates, documents, and texts—and the meanings attributed to each are analogous to the process of *Nachträglichkeit* (belatedness) considered by Sigmund Freud in his analysis of the relation between *Geschehen* (event) and *Geschichte*. Relating the concept of belatedness to the problems encountered in thinking about the works that fictionalize or historicize the war, one might think of the undeniably real event as being less an origin from which interpretation proceeds, as it is already its result. To continue the analogy, fragments that could not be integrated or that were censored from integration into a context of significance at the time of the event were, after a period of forgetting, reordered according to later experiences.[7] The concept of belatedness suggests an ongoing rewriting of experience, impressions, and memory traces in the context of new phases of development. An overview of the works written in Germany between 1914 and 1940 about the First World War offers evidence of the rewriting of experience and history.

We can distinguish among three distinct phases characterizing the conditions of any given *seizing* of war events deemed "significant" and the conditions directing their representation in literature: the period between 1914 and 1918 and, belatedly, under different conditions during the Weimar Republic and in the Third Reich.[8]

War literature published during the first and third phases is remarkable for what it reveals about how the frame of the potentially significant was created, yet works written during the Weimar Republic were published under conditions permitting an inherited order of understanding to be contested (or affirmed).[9] This allowed such literature to participate in an interdiscursive process in which the meaning and memory of the war could be rewritten.

To be sure, the primal scene is the war period, whose rendering in prose was contested during the Weimar Republic. But in this study the return to the war years is undertaken not to uncover the irrefutable grounds that would finally delineate the war "as it really was" and subsequent factual distortions between 1919 and 1940, but to consider how dislocation is already at work in what is appealed to as the point of origin. By focusing on the veiled presence of social relations and the state found in war novels, letters, and other texts (constituted by the relation between authority and narration), this study invokes the forces that will be seen to mediate an individual "voice" or "experience."

The archival materials analyzed below elucidate the convergence of both primary meanings attached to the word *Geschichte* as it pertains to the First World War. The German word enjoins against a hasty separation between its meanings as the "events of the past" and the "telling of stories about the past." Once these meanings are thought of as fragmentary products of a state-administered mechanism of *Entstellung* (dislocation),[10] the texts become valuable as does a dream to a Lacanian analyst. For the analyst, the unconscious is understood as a translation without an original or as a representation without a represented. The texts I have analyzed similarly represent the departure point for the public memory of the war in Germany. They do not, however, stand in a univocal relation to the objects they signify; they might better be thought of as "original translations" framed within the state-administered mechanisms that engendered the illusion of a seamless national identity and will, covering up incoherence or contradiction. For that and other reasons, the administration of censorship between 1914 and 1918 is noteworthy. For Freud, as registered in a postwar edition of *The Interpretation of Dreams,* its enactment provided belated vindication of his choice of the term *Zensur* (censor, censorship) as a key concept explicating the mechanisms at work in dream displacement. His discussion of the effects of both *präventiv* (preventive) and *nachträglich* (belated) censorship on the political writer "who has unpleasant truths to tell those in power" provided an apt analogy for him to the censoring mechanisms in the dream work whose results were various forms of *Verkleidung* (disguise). In a footnote, Freud comments on a dream reported by Dr. Hug-Hellmuth that "is better suited than any other to justify my choice of nomenclature. In this example, the dream-dislocation adopted the same methods as the postal censorship for expunging passages that were objectionable to it. The postal censorship makes such passages unreadable by blacking them out; the dream censorship replaced them by an incomprehensible mumble."[11]

Like most of his contemporaries, Freud had ample occasion to reflect on the import of the First World War. His 1915 essay "Reflections on Death and War" found meaning in the reality of mass death caused by the war, which sheared from dying the appearance of the accidental, and in the revelation that the prohibition against killing was not absolute but a matter of state authority.[12] In his interpretation of death dreams, meanwhile, censorship was found to occur "in order to prevent the development of fear or other forms of painful affect."[13] As I show in Chapter 3, Freud uses language that is uncannily echoed by military censors.

If Freud's reflections caution us against assuming that censorship can ever be completely successful—were that so, we would have no consciousness, however distorted, of certain impressions or events—he also offers a highly suggestive way of thinking about the effects of censorship on the individual and collective constitution of memory.[14]

A reading of war literature written after 1919 must take into account an understanding of how meaning was generated and disseminated during the war and how literary culture participated in that project. In Chapter 1, I present a temporal and methodological framework appropriate to the three contexts of reception analyzed by the study. The chapter situates the production and reception of war literature within a larger social and cultural struggle to determine the commemorative value of a language generated between 1914 and 1918, thus demonstrating how and why the signs and codes used to represent the war were contested after 1918. National Socialism successfully appropriated specific aspects of this language and purged others; in 1933 the Nazis expunged "incorrect" literary renderings of the war, thus permitting the war literature sanctioned by the regime to become a bulwark of their cultural and educational policies.

In Chapter 2 I examine various ways the army and the state sought to direct the public's acute interest in the continuing war, beginning with the sloganization of the ambivalent expectations with which Germany went to war as "der Juli-Geist" or the "spirit of 1914." One salient feature of these activities was the effort to frame a paradigmatic representation of the ongoing war, actively— through such agencies as Walter Bloem's Press Agency and the institution of frontline war reporters—and reactively in the form of literary and informational censorship. German military censorship had many aims: the prohibition of published accounts that threatened military security or endangered the *Burgfrieden* (domestic peace), control over the framing of what will become pertinent facts about the war, and, most expansively, control of the media disseminating these (or undesired) facts.

Within these parameters a language manifesting *Frontgeist* (spirit of the trenches) was forged; after the war this language buttressed the ideology of soldierly nationalism against the political left. My analysis of Bloem's writing between 1911 and 1940 also considers the continuities between the uses of nationalist war literature during the Kaiserreich and the Third Reich to erase particularities of class, region, and religion and to shape a collective sense of national identity. The chapter concludes by juxtaposing such efforts with those of Köppen, who in his 1931 novel *Heeresbericht* used montage to emphasize the making of history.

In Chapter 3 I illustrate the process of document production and its entry into narrative by examining one characteristic genre of war prose, the war letter, and the anthologizing of such letters. Far from simple, authentic "mirrors" of any given individual's war "experience," these letters, like other war prose, are shown to be embedded in a mediated process of social signification and, as such, are revealed as participants in a highly contested colloquium of public memory formation. The most influential collection of such letters was *Kriegsbriefe gefallener Studenten* (War letters of fallen students) edited by Philipp Witkop in several volumes published between 1915 and 1942. I examine the value ascribed to war letters by the army and state before and during the war, the aesthetic-political categories that informed Witkop's selection process, and the shifting grounds of commemoration that underlined their reception between 1914 and 1942.

In Chapter 4 I consider the role of reading during the war, with reference to the efforts to direct this activity undertaken by the army, the *Volksbildung* (popular education) movement, and publishers. In addition to documenting reading practices at the front, I argue that reading, far from being an innocent activity, served the war effort as part of a broader cultural mobilization. The chapter situates the state-supported endeavor to quench the *Lesedurst* (thirst for reading) at the front by portraying the war as a *Kulturkrieg* (war of culture) waged against the nation's external and internal enemies. The war reportedly schooled a generation of readers. The primary question, from which others ensue, is: what literature was made available to these readers and how did they respond to it? Within this context, I also consider a wider debate on *Schund-literatur* (trashy literature) and the highly modern activities of individual firms (particularly Ullstein and Reclam) in producing inexpensive literature at home and for the troops.

Chapter 5 offers an analysis of how the Cotta publishing house—arguably the most tradition-rich publisher in Germany of the modern period—sought to frame the war consonant with the "spirit of 1914." The analysis, based on publication theory and company records, establishes a profile of the works on the topic chosen or rejected by the firm throughout the war and in the 1920s. Of Cotta's Weimar-era works, the memoir of Crown Prince Wilhelm receives particular attention as it is representative of the company's editorial stance in commemorating the war.

The final chapter confirms the perseverance of a particular understanding of the role of literature in the eyes of the state and select mainstream publishers as an anodyne to the cultural and spiritual malaise brought about by Germany's defeat. The war of culture unleashed in 1914 continued to direct the self-understanding of prominent publishers despite its "unhappy" outcome in 1918. The limits confronted by publishers, authors, and works that did not conform to this credo are suggested by the reception and trial of Bruno Vogel's text written in the Weimar period, *Es lebe der Krieg! Ein Brief,* which has been analyzed as an attempt to intervene against a commemoration of the war, and again targeted its meaning as an ethical, national pursuit.

Throughout this examination, I include texts usually subsumed as documentary evidence (or "context") in studies of literary criticism—institutional appeals, military edicts, and proclamations—for the language encountered there signifies an intentionality that pointedly reveals the traces of social production and circulation in which the wartime institution of literature participates. The effacement of this circulation is the illusion on which rests the claim for literature as a purely poetic, autonomous realm of creation, an aesthetic construct that I reject.

In formulating the questions that propel this book, I have profited from discussions among German and intellectual historians, literary critics, and social theorists. It is a pleasure to thank Lieselotte Kurth, Rainer Nägele, Peter-Uwe Hohendahl, Frank Trommler, Tom Childers, Fritz Hackert, Sam Weber, Tom Laqueur, Vernon Lidtke, Eberhard Jäckel, the late Bernard Bellon, Klaus-Peter Fillipi, Russell Berman, Martin Jay, and Richard Macksey for reading various versions of the book as it progressed. A number of archives, libraries, and individuals have greatly facilitated my access to the primary materials on which I have relied. I should particularly like to thank the following institutes and individuals: the *Hauptstaatsarchiv* Stuttgart and Dr. Helmut Cordes of its *Militärarchiv,* the *Landesbibliothek* of Baden-Württemberg, Dr. Jürgen Rohwer and the staff of the *Bibliothek für Zeitgeschichte* in Stuttgart, Wilhelm Deist and the *Bundesmilitärarchiv* in Freiburg, the staff of the *Literaturarchiv* in Marbach, the *Generallandesarchiv* in Karlsruhe, the *Stadtarchiv* in Wuppertal, the *Stadtbibliothek* in Dortmund, the Hoover Institution Archives at Stanford University for use of their postcard and poster collection, the *Universitätsarchiv* Tübingen, the *Landesarchiv* Koblenz, the Bavarian *Hauptstaatsarchiv* and the Bayerische *Staatsbibliothek* in Munich, my editor at Yale University Press, Joyce Ippolito, and finally Mrs. Anna Witkop, Freiburg, who generously permitted me the first scholarly access to the private papers of her late husband, Philipp Witkop. Ross Whelan, Bärbel Hornbach Schäefer, Ramona and Alan Ungar, Bertha Gartner, and Brigitta Hornbach Balint gave support and assistance of many kinds, as did Dolores Hornbach Whelan, who, with tired eyes, additionally helped translate. My German studies and social theory colleagues at the University of Kentucky have offered an ongoing colloquy for testing several of this study's guiding ideas. The University of Kentucky additionally provided a fellowship, permitting a summer of research and writing on the war series published by Ullstein, while the German Academic Exchange Service funded two years' stay in the Federal Republic of Germany, without which the archival research that underlies the analysis would not have been possible. Finally, Elizabeth Ungar Natter, a kindred and generous spirit whose counsel breathed wisdom on many pages, saw this project through with me from its inception; Joseph Ross Natter gave his father the gift of laughter in its final phase.

Chapter 1   What Is War
Literature and Why Does
It Merit Study?

One of the most compelling challenges faced by German writers during the First World War and in the interwar period was how to structure an interpretation of meaning upon the events of the war. Whether they viewed the conflict as a moral-cultural mission or a defense against imminent territorial invasion, a struggle of culture between German *Geist* and Western materialism or an imperialistic battle waged solely for the benefit of national ruling classes, an event tragically devoid of meaning or, finally, as the birth of the new Germany, the issue of how to interpret and represent the war pricked deeply sensitive assumptions regarding virtually every facet of German civic life.

I describe in this chapter many of the issues that a reader must weigh in determining the meaning of the war in the literature, particularly between 1914 and 1940. The chapter also discusses why it is necessary to pursue the general question of how—through the interaction of military, academic, and publishing agencies—a particular knowledge about the First World War was created and disseminated. In this collaboration between political, military, and literary institutions, the guiding framework emerged for what became a war aesthetics. A consideration of the ongoing consequences of this interaction informs the analysis of each focus in the following chapters.

The textual object from which this analysis proceeds is the war book—principally books of prose, written both during the war and afterward, that deal with the war experience. This definition of the subject as "war prose" replicates the hybrid character evidenced by the source material and its reception. Moreover, while functioning as accounts of battlefield events or, more broadly, of a nation at war, these war books often not only are accounts of the fighting that took place in Verdun or on the Somme but perform the function of social commentary, expressing views of German society and nationhood from within a teleologically oriented, though shifting, historical framework. In them (and alongside them, in the institutional mediation that frames them), an imagined community is being forged.[1]

Within this broad categorization, proximity to the front—and to the front line of combat—is the ultimate ground of authenticity for the genre as a whole. Such a framing of war for the purposes of literary depiction is hardly inevitable; the lives of women munitions or textile workers or public and private practices outside the workplace during the war might as readily serve as the material for the narration of war experience. And the First World War in Germany also provided some access for women volunteers to the *Etappen* (support zones) in proximity to the front—as trench diggers in Alsace, for example, and news service personnel.[2] But because the *Erlebnis* (experience) of the front—this most "sacred space," in the language of much commemorative literature written during and after 1918—was fundamental in Germany and because direct experience of this space remained generally off-limits to women, what contemporaries in Germany took to be the war book is almost exclusively a male genre.[3] Indicatively, nationalist critics of Erich Remarque's *All Quiet on the Western Front*, the most widely read war book of the Weimar period, challenged its success by asking whether the author had really been at the front and, in particular, the combat zone. Could he personally authenticate the experiences that his narrator had made his own? These critics thus employed a code of spatially defined legitimacy that equated authentic and privileged masculinity with the front and femininity with less sacred spaces of cultural practices and memory.

Despite such assertions of masculinist privilege, this hardly means in theory that the wartime division of labor along gender lines—most generally, front and home front—ought provide only (male) soldiers with a war experience to narrate, or, as importantly, precludes a recognition that masculinity and femininity are not equally under construction during wartime (and, thereafter, in books that thematize the war) both "at home" and at the front.[4] In war books about the First World War published during it and the periods of Weimar and Nazi Germany, however, the gendered character of "experience" that emerged during wartime overwhelmingly separates men and women physically along binary zones of activity and create norms among gender roles and attributes according to a masculine martial code.

Given the difference in settings available to subjects during the war, it should not be surprising that a chasm separates the war experience for men and women. An absolute divide is, in fact, insisted upon by many soldier-poets and their interpreters who deny the possibility of communicating battle experience to those who have not been there, thus again privileging that "sacred space" of combat. But in spite of that binary cultural coding, the social truth remains that gender by itself is anything but homogenous or fixed; in pre–Second World War Germany a multiplicity of possible subject positions developed in tandem with particularities of class, religion, gender, and region.[5] In the German context of the First World War, moreover, a cultural struggle to align the lived experience of its participants with the prospect of an official national history is particularly fragmented because after 1918 the war is a lost war. The character of this loss complicated passage toward a common, that is, national, memory of it. Such fragmentation is precisely what much National Socialist rhetoric offered to stamp out by promising to deliver the closure to German national history that had been promised but deferred during the war years. Between 1919 and 1939, the domain of experience anchoring what will come to pass as national history is increasingly and emphatically not multiple or fragmentary but rather masculinist, racialized, and self-contained. This is particularly true after 1933, when combat and the front are again reified as the site of character rebirth essential for the reemergence of the nation.

Direct experience of rebirth, consequently, is available only to combatants, not to those kept from the front by sex or age. What is given to women within this construct is knowledge of the spaces of experience that follow from a front versus home front divide, the noble virtues of sacrifice, nurturing, and service to the combatant. The idealized subject position being called for (including writing by middle class women during the war—for example, Gertrud Bäumer and Thea von Harbou) embodies "quiet preparedness for sacrifice," "women's service," and "quiet heroism," both "good" and nationalist at the same time.[6] This nationalization of femininity calls for a subject who will share (with nation-

Fig. 1.1 Wartime poster: "German women, work in the home army!"

alized masculinity) the ethic of self-sacrifice while transforming attachments from personal to "higher" forms of love, independent of individuals and, of course, class interest.[7] The model of development for fighting men in this construct makes their war experience the mutually reenforcing grounds linking the *Bildung* of masculine self and nation.[8]

The war and its retelling in war books thus crucially marks the linkage of experience and history, (gendered) subjects, and national identification. Not coincidentally, several antiwar narratives written during the Weimar Republic widened the frame of the war book to include wartime experiences at the home front and among civilians precisely to provide an expanded context for an effective social critique of war mobilization (and experience).[9]

In contextualizing how war books enact these various functions, moreover, this study simultaneously examines a constellation of issues affecting the production, distribution, and reception of literature between 1914 and 1918. Books have a substance and materiality without which their messages cannot enter circulation—an important practical consideration given the regulation of paper supplies during the war. More generally, a number of institutions will be shown to mediate the materiality of the book, what is and is not contained in it.

As Michel Foucault and Roland Barthes insisted, the book (or, in Barthes' case, the text) is not simply the object that one holds in one's hands. Writers and their intentions form only one part of this social process. No text exists outside of the support that enables it to be read; any comprehension of a writing depends on the forms in which it reaches its readers.[10] Implicated in this understanding of literature as a social process are the activities of publishing houses, booksellers, states, academies, libraries, and archives, which have all promoted and inhibited the parameters of the iterable on this subject. The concept of "war book" will therefore here also refer to the general expectations designated for and particular institutions of "the book" in a society at war.

In several significant regards, the First World War manifests the symptoms of the "end of the age of the book" in Germany in the powerful sense that an entire support system and cultural program was mobilized in its name for perhaps the last time.[11] The presumed "Germanness" of book culture, from Gutenberg and Luther through the aesthetic *Bildungsprogram* (program of education and development) of the Enlightenment, to the comparatively high levels of book production and readership in 1914, all became "facts" of German cultural superiority usable in the war effort.[12]

For some thirty years after the Second World War, study of German literature of the Great War—as it is still referenced by scholars working from other national perspectives—lay largely dormant. A recent article has appropriately characterized the (non)treatment accorded this facet of German literature by noting its status as a "stepchild of literary criticism."[13] Reasons for this neglect are in one sense conveyed by the changing concepts used in German to designate its subject. The designation as the "First World War," now in usage, became necessary after the "*Second* World War" linked the lapsed singularity of the first to a catastrophe that all the more marks a limit of understanding. That designation, in turn, had replaced "der Weltkrieg" used in Germany during the interwar period, which itself was a replacement of the label *die große Zeit* used by contemporaries in the first phase of the ongoing war. The First World War has not been the "time of greatness" for some time now for those few scholars of Germanistics who addressed it following the Second World War.

The limited attention paid the topic until recently also reflects the history of such treatments during the Weimar Republic and, more portentously, during the Third Reich. In writing about literature of the First World War today, one is not only writing about "the war" but also engaging this tradition of its reception. Few issues were as highly contested in Germany between 1918 and 1933 and beyond as the question of how to render "meaning" unto a war that had left nearly two million dead and nearly five million wounded and furthermore had left Germany the vanquished opponent charged by the Treaty of Versailles with being the sole culprit for the war's outbreak and devastation. There were no material spoils of war for the German Reich, none that even remotely postulated that the nation had made a good exchange for the resources expended. Any cultural capital to be forged from the war in Germany after 1918 would necessitate a dramatic reordering both of the war's events and of the society interpreting them. As we shall see, both would be forthcoming.

Unlike writers in France, the United States, and England, who after 1918 could at least represent the war as a victorious campaign for self-preservation, democracy, or expansion permitting the expense of life and material to appear justified, if costly—those in Germany could offer their readers little tangible solace, profit, or glory for four and a half years of suffering and loss. To begin with, the high casualty rate virtually ensured the personification of loss in Germany. A reminder of such total, private, and collective loss and of loss despite survival was omnipresent via the wounded, sometimes maimed or limbless survivors present on the streets of Weimar Germany.[14] More numerous, dependents of the war dead, especially widows' children, "paid the cost of World War I in installments of their daily lives."[15] Commenting on another aspect of this exposure to loss, Walter Benjamin remarked that language itself offered telling insight on how total the loss of a war was in the collective life of a nation. Not without some recognition approaching empathy, Benjamin analyzed a collection of essays edited by Ernst Jünger as indicative of the severity of that trauma for these veterans. Jünger's volume pointed to the unflinching demand for another (total) war as the sole means to regain the "entire substantive and spiritual substance of the people" that had been invested and lost in the First World War.[16]

Belletristic renderings of the meaning and significance of the war in Germany, as well as criticisms of such literature, consequently entered into a highly charged public arena in which issues directly tied to the war's legacy (and thus its interpretation) and the specific forms of its public commemoration were a matter of unresolved dispute. Any writing about the war immediately "mobilized" positions regarding war guilt, the Kaiser's abdication, the status of the 1918–1919 revolution, attitudes toward the Republic's legitimacy, veterans' compensation, war memorials, and rearmament—to name but a few—that were daily matters on the political and journalistic palette.[17] Post-1918 writings about the war can thus be perceived as engaged in a wider, belated, and

Fig. 1.2 A mass-produced commemorative plaque made of paper. The blank spaces to be filled in by the group or individual posting it with the names of "our comrades who died in the World War, 1914–1919."

interdiscursive battle for control over the war's events, dates, and symbols— that is, as individual efforts to authorize specific competing narratives and their attendant "lessons" for the present.

Those German writers who sought to represent the events of the war in literature could be assured, particularly after 1928, of a broad audience interested in a set of issues whose narratization unmistakably related the questions of aesthetic representation to issues of politics, history, and public memory construction. At the same time, journal reviews appearing during the Weimar Republic that reacted to the flood of publications following the unexpected success of Remarque's novel *All Quiet on the Western Front* generally focused on the presumed moral, political "lessons" offered by the work, and this in terms that set up a simple binary opposition. One was either "for" Remarque or "against" him. The heated debate over the "true" meaning of the war (and to a lesser extent the "proper" literary form that such meaning should assume), which became particularly acrimonious as sides were drawn for and against

Remarque, engaged a surprisingly broad audience. An individual work of literature rarely provokes the type of reaction that leads, as with Remarque's book, to mass-circulation newspapers printing reader responses for nearly half a year after its initial appearance.[18]

What is at stake in this unprecedented public literary reception—nearly one million copies of the novel were sold within a year—is more than a misunderstood notion of aesthetic enjoyment and aesthetic judgment: for contemporary audiences, the debates surrounding war literature brought questions of interpretation on a nexus that one could regard as *the* genealogical issue for a republic born out of defeat and revolution. The categories of aesthetic and political discourse, often separated, are explicitly united in this discussion.

Any analysis that would do justice to the phenomenon of German war literature would do well to consider the contemporaneous conditions affecting the unusually public reception of these works and therewith a host of reception-theoretical implications. Because it was of significant interest to readers outside the German university, the institutional setting of the discipline called *Germanistik,* it will not do to be content with a consideration of the reactions of a few vociferous *Germanisten* toward this new type of literature.

That would be difficult in any case, because with some notable exceptions examined below, institutionalized Germanistics remained largely silent during the Weimar Republic about contemporary literary treatments of the war, a situation that would change dramatically after 1933. Moreover, in thinking about the literary complex that one critic in 1931 would sloganize as the "literary return of war" it becomes pertinent to consider the conditions affecting the production and reception of these works in the context of a mass market.[19]

If the intersection of literature with other forms of social and political discourse is unusually animated by the reception of war literature during the Weimar Republic, any present reading of such works is further affected by the use and abuse of war literature and the mythology of the front by the National Socialists. The unusually young generation of leadership that assumed power in 1933—former corporal Hitler and the last leader of the Richthofen Staffel, Hermann Göring, being two salient examples—was strongly influenced both by its experiences during the war and, after 1918, by the war's interpreted legacy. Although it would clearly be reductionist to attribute the complex nature of National Socialist cultural politics to the personal tastes of Hitler, it is still worth bearing in mind that the Iron Cross recipient took a personal interest in the memoiristic and belletristic literature written by fellow combatants and indeed took time to write endorsements of any treatments he found particularly admirable.[20]

The bitter campaign waged by the party against Remarque's book and the film inspired by it was a harbinger of the May 1933 burning of that book along with other similarly undesirable literary interpretations of the war. The so-called *Feuerspruch* (tribunal) in Munich on May 10, 1933, singled out the war novels of Remarque, Gläser, and Renn for condemnation with the following proclamation: "Against their besmirching and insulting of our fallen soldiers, against the defilement of our national honor, on behalf of the nation's will to resist, I consign to the flames the writings of E. M. Remarque, the writings of Karl Renn and Ernst Gläser."[21]

Having thereby been expunged of any "incorrect" renderings, the war literature sanctioned by National Socialism became a bulwark of the regime's cultural and educational politics. By the time the next world war had begun, the "best" of this "literature of soldierly nationalism" had been canonized in the curricula of German high schools and universities, made available in inexpensive editions for all readers, and become one of the preferred objects of analysis for National Socialist Germanistics.[22]

As the introduction to *Weltkrieg und Deutsche Dichtung* (World war and German poesy), a school textbook published by the firm of Schönigh, noted, the *nationale Erhebung* (national uprising) had placed new demands on teachers and students. With selections from Walter Flex, Werner Beumelburg, Joseph M. Wehner, Hans Carossa, Paul Alverdes, Ernst Dwinger, Hans Grimm, Paul Dörfler, and the war letters of fallen students edited by Philipp Witkop, the textbook offered current students the "best, and best known" of the war poets. It was expected that in reading them, "the new generation of youth will stand in admiration before the immeasurable achievements of the German people during the World War, grateful to their boundless love of the Fatherland, and their unconditional fulfillment of duty. They will be deeply moved by this heroism that is demanded by our own age again as well."[23] A well-received (and, thereafter, frequently cited) literature dissertation published in 1937 aptly summarized and articulated the necessity of reordering the war's events and meaning to allow for their "correct" meaning to again generate cultural capital: "We recognize that in the trenches of Verdun an era was buried and that from Verdun's graves a new epoch of German history was born. Only a mode of understanding that is able to see in the German people's fight for existence the demise of the outmoded and the unfit and the birth of a new community of our people—that is, a mode of understanding that grasps the unique dynamic of the events of the World War—will be able to understand the inner value of World War poetry and will help us to hear the testament of the dead."

Consistent with the "unique dynamic of the events of the World War," the aesthetic categories elsewhere identified by Walter Benjamin as "creativity and genius, eternal value and mystery" were to remain largely paradigmatic for the literary movement that dominated the literary and academic marketplace during the Third Reich and whose "uncontrollable application" of these categories is enacted in the war literature of Werner Beumelburg, Heinrich Lersch, Ernst Jünger, Börries von Münchhausen, Hans Grimm, and Hans Friedrich Blunck, among others.[24] After 1933, the above-named authors became cultural icons of the new regime, enthroned in the newly re-formed Academy of Arts in Berlin.[25] Beumelburg's career is particularly symptomatic of how (properly written) war literature intersects with the cultural politics of National Socialism. He began his literary career as a semiofficial military writer and went on to write four best-selling war novels during the Weimar Republic before becoming corresponding secretary of the Academy of Arts.[26] The soldier-poet, in turn, whose moral and aesthetic mission derived from his wartime experiences, became a model for the next generation of aspiring soldiers and authors.

Soon after the beginning of the Second World War, a noteworthy volume appeared that focused solely on writings about the First World War as the inspiration for those beginning to fight the Second. Published in 1940 in the Nordland-Bücherei, the title, *Wie die Pflicht es befahl: Worte unserer Weltkriegs-dichter* (As duty commanded: Words of our world war poets), crystallizes the lesson its selections present. As the foreword by Matthes Ziegler ("At war, 1940") amplifies, the writings selected for the anthology (several by Jünger, others by Beumelburg, Flex, Thor Goote, Groch Fock, and Hans Steen) were meant to steel the resolve of a new generation of fighters to risk death for a greater good, the good of the German *Volk*. For Ziegler, the combatant (addressed with the familiar *Du* form) learns that death is not the destroyer but the preserver of life, "embodied" in the *Volk*. Furthermore, this generation of soldiers was told that they owed a debt to past ones and were thus required to share the same commitment to this greater good, comforted in the certainty that their sacrifice would in turn be similarly honored. "The reverence that we accord to our forefathers will in time be accorded to us by those who follow. Just as we take up the duty which the blood sacrifice of the World War laid upon us, our children will one day need to draw their faith in Germany and the strength to fight from our commitment and our sacrifice."[27] Within this logic, an economy of debt (*Schuld*) owed the fallen necessitates reciprocity. After 1939, the words of canonized war poets of the First World War (particularly those who had died in combat, such as Walter Flex) were often included in the mourning services of the newly fallen.[28] Within months of the appearance of *Wie die Pflicht es Befahl*, the first publications by the new generation of thus inspired "soldier-poets" began appearing, including volumes that joined two generations of combat soldiers in topical literary anthologies.[29]

For those literary critics inclined to a misunderstood classic-idealistic view of art as an autonomous realm of aesthetic reflection or, alternatively, who differentiate between authentic works of art and endless recyclings by the culture industry, study of war literature leads to thorny questions. First, from a critical perspective informed by the search for "beautiful appearance," there appears little literary merit in much of this writing. Most of the novels, and particularly those of greatest interest during the Third Reich, are formulaic, stridently nationalistic, and permeated with resentment. A formalist reading of these works will find little to affirm—unless read against the grain and through the optic of an aesthetic of terror or pain.

Second, the manifest impact of state and market structures on this art would seem to doom it to the Germanistic limbo of so-called trivial or tendentious literature. Even worse, the scenario of utopian redemption that underlies some current interest in likewise-forgotten popular authors will hardly find much to laud in the dystopia of the nationalist battlefield. Characteristically enough, the few studies of war literature in general and Remarque in particular that appeared in the West during the immediate post–Second World War period seemed most interested in asking whether Remarque's book was aesthetically sound and deserving of inclusion in university canons of literature. The answer in most cases, due perhaps to a discomfort with Remarque's status as a best-selling author, was a resounding no.[30]

Despite such discomfort, Remarque is today probably the most remembered of all the best-selling authors who wrote war narratives during the Weimar Republic. What characterizes the scholarly treatments of his war and postwar novels, however, is also true of the several hundred others published immediately before and after the success (and immediate translation) of *All Quiet on the Western Front*.[31] Nonetheless, the works penned by Remarque along with those by Ernst Jünger, Edlef Köppen, Arnold Zweig, Werner Beumelburg, Josef Magnus Wehner, Bruno Vogel, Ludwig Renn, Adam Scharrer, Philipp Witkop, Walter Flex, and others, have come to stand for the range of experiences and understandings of millions of German soldiers who fought during the war.

Fig. 1.3 Typical commemorative church plaque, following the names of parish dead. The inscription reads "Honor their memory! With proud bereavement and deep gratitude we remember our fallen comrades. May their spirit of duty serve as a model for later generations!" (Author photo)

It has become an accepted truism that the First World War was an overwhelming experience for the veterans who survived it. Reading their war novels, supplemented perhaps by memoirs and letters, might therefore seem ideal for getting at the transformation in consciousness that so many contemporaries had noted as the war's legacy. Doing so would appear all the more valuable because these novels are some of the few available sources through which to approach the war's primary victims. The *Frontschweine* (common soldiers who served in the front lines), in fact, have largely been silenced in the official histories and literary histories of the subject. Rather like Africans in Georg Hegel's use of the continent in his *Philosophy of History*, their voices—at least judging by the treatment accorded them by scholars—have not counted in spirit's self-actualization.[32]

Although reading best-selling war books published between 1914 and 1945 leads to a more accurate understanding of what constitutes "representative" works of literature for the period, simply lamenting the absence of such works on current university reading lists, or, conversely, making such "voices" accessible through their inclusion in the contemporary canon, does not in itself do justice to the voices silenced before their time by bullets or disease—or by the operative parameters of the iterable. For as later chapters will demonstrate, precisely the relation between the textual order found in letters, diaries, and works of literature written by soldiers on the one hand, and the mediating institutional forces that frame this order on the other, encourages reconsideration of any presumed self-identity or sovereignty attached as a property to the writing subject in question.

Exploring the history of the reception of war literature, however, does invite interest in the interrelated problems of disciplinary history and literary canonization. For here is a genre of literature, representatives of which had at one time been canonized with the ideological vehemence of midcentury German Germanistics and that furthermore had contributed a significant number of the best-sellers sold in Germany between 1914 and 1945, all but forgotten some fifty years later by the same discipline. Literary tastes obviously change, as do the ways critics read literature, and a history of the reading (and nonreading) of works about *die große Zeit* immediately confirms the recognition that any attempt to portray the enterprise of literature and its critique as subject to unchanging and eternal laws of value is a disingenuous and ideological, not to mention ahistorical, veiling of its operation. Treating the period between 1933 and 1945 as an exception (a *Betriebsunfall* [company accident], as it were), however, tends to enure the rest of the post-enlightenment institution of literature in Germany from such critique.[33]

What has been glaringly missing from scholarly treatments that seek to come to grips with the "experience" of the First World War on the basis of the extant literature is a concomitant reading of these works viewed in the context of the institutions that mediate them.[34] Regarding the difference in the literary language used in these works as a violence wrought on everyday speech is a necessary first step in overcoming this lacuna. Equally important, however, is a consideration of the dimensions of violence implicated by the process whereby language interpreting the war was created, disseminated, and received in Germany.

I attribute such importance to this question for many reasons, the first involving the already-mentioned broad reader reception during the war and, under different conditions, thereafter. As a type of hybrid, but not technical, writing whose implied reader after 1918 was one remembering (and perhaps reinterpreting) recent experience, literature about the war commanded national attention; it was discussed in newspapers, by veterans' organizations, in parliament, and even in churches beginning in the middle period of the Weimar Republic. Erstwhile combatants and those whose lives were affected by the war found in these works a medium through which to reflect on "what had really happened." This Weimar-era reception is informally connected to academic institutions of art and is largely propelled by the perceived and actual vicissitudes of the book market.

Furthermore, most of the individuals who received attention as writers of war novels or published diaries were newcomers to the literary marketplace. Jünger, Remarque, Köppen, and Wehner each either had no literary ambition before 1914 or had no success. Hans Carossa, already a well-established author of the well-known Insel Verlag a decade before publishing his war diary, *Rumänisches Tagebuch,* in 1924, and Walter Bloem, who was one of the best-selling German authors well before he wrote his *Kriegserlebnistrilogie,* are the exceptions rather than the norm. Many of these new authors received their literary training during the war, as poets or writers of short stories or letters published for the first time in army or civilian newspapers. The shift that Benjamin observed affecting the relation between authors and readers, and therewith the fundamental status of both reading and writing—more readers at the same time becoming authors—was accelerated by the First World War. As he noted, "The facts today are such that there exists hardly any European engaged in the working process who could not find opportunity for publication based on a work experience, a grievance, a report, or similar event. Therewith, the fundamental differentiation between author and audience becomes less distinct."[35]

Although the constellation of economic, educational, and social developments underlying this fundamental shift in reading and writing practices already had begun to be felt in the wake of the printing press and then the Enlightenment, and more rapidly so after the mid-nineteenth century, the First World War dramatically accelerated and consolidated development of a mass reading culture in Germany. The forms that this development took at the end of the Wilhelminian period lend considerable credence to Theodor Adorno and Max Horkheimer's thesis that the aesthetic ideology articulated under the aegis of Enlightenment reason would by the middle of the twentieth century reify into the production of material of subjugation.[36] Following chapters will show that the type of reading and writing encouraged during the war by state structures informed by instrumental reason demonstrates an overarching intention to provide a palliative for real suffering. This intention was carried out with the cooperation of an affirmative culture industry whose technological capacities for production and distribution incarnate a modernization that is in stark contrast to the manifest content of the works disseminated. Editions of more than 500,000 became commonplace during the war for the most successful of these books. The resistance previously encountered in the book trade—in particular, demands for inexpensive books by proponents of the *Volksbildung Bewegung* (popular education movement) dissolved as part of a national imperative to provide "our fighting men" with textual evidence of the culture they were fighting to defend and to provide civilians with a taste of *Frontgeist* as written by contemporary soldier-authors.

Not only did numerous collecting agencies, including the Imperial Army, actively encourage soldiers to record and submit their letters, poems, songs, and prose narratives for publication, but civilians too felt compelled to add their voices to the chorus celebrating *die große Zeit* in forms and numbers that astonished (and sometimes dismayed) contemporary observers of the literary scene. For beginning with the mobilization of August 1914, the war was constantly described by leading politicians, government officials, and cultural authorities as a *Volkskrieg* (war between the nations, but also a people's war) and thus linkable in rhetoric to those earlier manifestations of a *Volkserhebung* (uprising of the people), particularly in 1813 (not 1848) and from 1870 to 1871. In an era of mass readership, the voice of *das Volk* authenticated such a characterization of this "große Zeit." Staying within Benjamin's categories, contributions chronicling the nature of soldiers' "work experience" (and their socialization as participants of a national German culture) were particularly encouraged by collecting agencies, unlike reports of complaints.

At the same time, the audience for this new generation of writers would reach beyond academically trained or other middle-class readers to new groups for whom reading would become a relatively novel use of their free time. According to many contemporary observers, this new readership in Germany (at least among those doing military service) was in part schooled by institutions (like *Feldbibliotheken* [soldiers' field libraries]) that the army developed. On the home front, burgeoning organizations tied to the Popular Education Movement and worker education likewise saw their facilities and their readership actively supported as part of the war effort. For some readers-become-writers, the import of the types of books encountered in such facilities cannot be underestimated in accounting for the literary form and rhetoric perpetu-

Fig. 1.4 First World War postcard, featuring three cultural heros (Jahn, Arndt, and Fichte) from the "Wars of Liberation" (1812–1813) often referred to between 1914–1918. Arndt's poem reads: "That God who made iron grow / wanted no vassals. Therefore he provided sabre, sword and spear / to the man asserting his rights."

ating Wilhelmine-era aesthetics, which one finds in many war books published after 1918.

During the Weimar period, readers of war literature often commented on the value of war books for their veracity, or *Wahrheit*. This phenomenon is interesting for at least two reasons. It first confirms the difference affecting the reception of these literary works from other more obviously "fictitious" genres. Even those written as reflections on, not chronicles of, events of the recent past that self-consciously recognized the passage of time and authorial standpoint since the war's end nonetheless were read by most readers as if from within a frame that had closed in 1918.[37] It secondly points to a condition of uncertainty regarding the vital questions affecting the meaning of the lost war.

There was a crippling absence of social unity in the Weimar Republic on this issue, reflected in the inability to find a common public language or set of symbols (and monuments) bespeaking a basic consensus regarding the war's meaning. The inability of the Weimar Republic to implement a unified day of mourning is one symptom of this absence. The same conflictual configuration applies to the reception of the language and symbols employed in war literature. The usage of the term *Denkmal* (monument) in the subtitles or prefaces of many war books is not coincidental: though the Republic's legislature could not agree on a specific date (which, after all, would bespeak an interpretation not acceptable to all regions or parties) to commemorate the war (which aspects, which virtues were they to be?), an individual writer could, on his or her own authority, create a monument to elicit reflective thinking about the attributes that seemed to him or her most compelling and constitutive of the war's place in civic memory. These literary interpretations were in turn subject to the same analysis regarding their "veracity" as were proposals for other commemorative monuments.[38]

The questions of how to represent the war, in literary language and in other signifying languages—stone and bronze monuments, plaques, public holidays—were seen in the context of the Weimar Republic as interrelated issues understood as fundamental matters not of certitude but interpretation and political struggle. This condition is predicated on the conceptual abyss and loss of grounding (for meaning) entailed by the German collapse in November 1918, the attendant (if temporary) exhaustion of an officially sanctioned grammar of heroism, coupled with the demise of the Hohenzollern regime that had chosen such language to represent the war's meaning. These consequences of defeat were spared the Allied nations.

Literature published during the Weimar Republic about the lost war is engaged in an effort to create a rubric of understanding capable of filling the abyss caused by defeat, abdication, and the social experience of mass death. Any narrative about the war, even in the form of diaries, memoirs, or letter collections characteristic of much of the war literature published during the Weimar Republic, is not only a chronicling of a given individual's experiences while serving (for example) along a section of the western front. It is also, among other things, a judgment of the Kaiserreich, the military and civilian leadership between 1914 and 1918, and an expression of one's attitude toward the republic. The codes, slogans, and signs that are activated in this process of judgment were well known to a contemporary reading audience. "Langemarck," "Verdun," "Kameradschaft" (comradeship), "Juli-Geist" (spirit of July, 1914), "Etappe" (support zone), "Heimat" (homeland), and "November 1918," to name but a few, resonate with significance, albeit not as neutral elements employed in an equally neutral narrative but as objects of contestation. What these signs were to signify, as a focus of struggle and contradiction, is what is at stake in the charged reception of war literature during the 1920s.

Is, for example, Langemarck understandable as a glorious symbol of the willing self-sacrifice of Germany's academic (and other) volunteers? Or does Langemarck connote a tragic tactical blunder, an early manifestation of the military leadership's ineptness that cost the lives of thousands of poorly trained recruits? An army communiqué published in German newspapers on November 11, 1914, claimed that the preceding day had brought "good progress" for the Imperial Army. The report also provided the material for the subsequent dissemination of the Langemarck myth: "West of Langemarck, young regiments penetrated the first line of enemy positions and took them while singing 'Deutschland über alles.' About 2,000 French infantry were taken prisoner and six machine guns were captured."

In this official report, there is no hint that the German offensive against the West was already acknowledged by the High Command to have failed, or that the "young regiments" were young not only in age but in terms of the limited military training received, or, finally, that the tactical objective was never taken.

As such, the report is a witness to and participant in a conscious strategy of deception practiced by the German High Command following the failure of the Marne offensive.[39] A tactical (and costly) military failure was with this strategy transfigured into a glowing example of willing self-sacrifice, nationalism, and heroism, whose symbolic capital increased in proportion to the growing recognition of the absence of tangible gains resulting from the war.

Two examples from writings of the 1920s illustrate how this capital might be invested or, alternatively, declared bankrupt. Hitler's narration in *Mein Kampf* of his wartime experience is careful to mention his participation in the singing of the song in Flanders. Under attack, surrounded by the first casualties and in man-to-man fighting, he hears the song: "From afar, the sounds of a song approached and came closer and closer, catapulting from company to company, and then, just as death reached busily into our ranks, the song reached us as well, and we passed it further along: Deutschland, Deutschland über alles, über alles in der Welt!"[40] Hitler's account replicates the message imposed by the *Heeresbericht* on the battle for Langemarck—no mention of the tactical defeat, instead, a celebration of soldierly heroism, death-defying comradeship, and nationalism—and his writing simultaneously serves to envelope Hitler (as a participant) with the symbolic power of the Langemarck legend.

For Ludwig Renn, the author of *Krieg* and *Nachkrieg*, Langemarck connotes not only a tragic tactical blunder but, worse, a pernicious legend, which his short story "Deutschland, Deutschland, über alles," published in 1929, is meant to demystify. In writing from the perspective of an infantryman, he, like Hitler, emphatically uses the pronoun *we*, but this is a "we" with a different message.

For Renn, the song was sung in desperation that November day to alert the German artillery that it was firing on its own troops: "We were singing for our lives: But we were lying on our stomachs and the grenades penetrated the ground—Fatsch-Bumm. Over and over again when they hit they took our breath away. I roared as loud as I could. But our artillery had heard nothing of it. They fired and fired. The wounded whimpered. Here and there the song bubbled up again, ever more despairingly: Deutschland, Deutschland über alles."[41] In retelling the story, Renn is not only offering an alternative perspective to an isolated battlefield event, he is simultaneously attacking one of the central elements of a front mythology created by wartime cultural propaganda, whose power to redefine memory is displayed in the Hitler text.

There is, I would argue, a connection between the street battles waged in the Republic's cities and the battle of signification raging in the various subinstitutions of literary culture over the "proper" rendering of the war. The latter was a battle between conflicting individuals, discourses, and social groups, to appropriate the generated language of *die große Zeit* and fill it with specific meaning. Following Mikhail Bakhtin, and in an epistemological approach taken up by many subsequent language schools, one can think of this (like other) available language as a battle for control of the social world.[42] In this view, language generated during the war is in principle inherently multiaccentual, certainly anything but natural or univocal, making it impossible to assume a relation between word and object/event as given or outside their social constitution. Although language (also as instantiated by a poem or novel) in this view is a socially constructed sign system, the mediation of various forces seen to reduce the polymorphous character of war (and other) language to univocity in support of the dominant likewise warrants analysis.

The participants in this contest did not stand on equal footing. As Hayden White's study of the relation among law, historicality, and narrativity suggests, "The truth claims of the narrative and indeed the very right to narrate hinge upon a certain relationship to authority per se."[43] The "ideal" narrative set in process by the discourse production of the state during the war, not to mention an impressive body of accumulated evidence to support it, retained a unique power after 1919 despite the ruptured ending precluding the closure envisioned in 1914. After 1918, the ambiguity over the status of Germany's legal system following the Kaiser's abdication in one sense stymied the impulse to "moralize reality" in the way envisioned during the war for postwar society, but no other lasting social center (with its attendant authority to create narrative) coalesced during Weimar to redirect this ambivalence with any authority.

The general relation that White postulates is borne out in the particulars of this study: "Where there is ambiguity or ambivalence regarding the status of the legal system, . . . the ground on which any closure of a story one might wish to tell about a past, whether it be a public or a private past, is lacking. And this suggests that narrativity, certainly in factual storytelling and probably in fictional storytelling as well, is intimately related to, if not a function of, the impulse to moralize reality, that is, to identify it with the social system that is the source of any morality we can imagine."[44] Furthermore, as regards another essential ingredient for the exercise of narration as political power (control of the archive), what was available to answer the genealogical question of the Republic—how to represent the lost war—was an archive generated to celebrate *die große Zeit* as a victorious "people's war," in the sense not only of having defeated the Allies but of having finally instantiated what was only portended for the nation in 1813 and 1871 regarding Germany's becoming a united and unified people.

The general failure of (anti)war novels of the democratic left in Weimar to win the battle of signification, or for that matter initially even to be published and read, arguably bespeaks the continued power of an earlier narrational scheme, one that National Socialism appropriated and provided with a convincing telos. The essential recurring elements of National Socialism's appropriation of this narrative maintain the earlier heroic tone while recasting the defeat of 1918 as the seed of national rebirth. "We had to lose the war in order to win the nation," is the oft-stated formula transforming apparent tragedy into comedy.[45] Moreover, the *Frontgemeinschaft* (community of warriors at the front) much celebrated during the war is repositioned as the cradle of a new Germany, the first event leading to the realization of a full *Volksgemeinschaft* (folk community). Finally, Hitler himself appears as the embodiment of the ideal German front-soldier, and as such the incarnation of the "new man" reborn in the trenches. At other times, his rebirth acquires totemlike qualities in his guise of the "unknown soldier" miraculously returned from the dead and ready to avenge those who have been betrayed by Germany's defeat.

Given the contested reorders of significance engaged in by war narratives, the temptation might loom large to seek out an alternative to such "merely" subjective texts by appealing to a more certain ground from which to give them an order. Such temptation, however, will find little succor by appealing to the "facts" lifted from their embeddedness in historical discourse, even if numerous strands of literary criticism unraveling the sock of new criticism have been content to do so. Defeating such unreflective usage of the important insights and oversights that historians of various schools have contributed to understanding the war and its literature is the consideration that history no less than literary criticism is engaged in an ongoing (though, as with literary criticism, often merely implicit) debate involving interrelated epistemological, political, and methodological positions that provide the enabling limits to the activity of practitioners in any given place and time.

Such an understanding of historical writing, as bound over time to numerous and variable epistemological and methodological issues and practices, is now more readily acknowledged in the wake of recent disciplinary self-examinations, not the least of which have been occasioned for German historians and historians of Germany by the controversy surrounding Fritz Fischer's analysis of the First World War and the more recent *Historikerstreit* (historians' dispute).[46] Each has focused on the seemingly extradisciplinary social processes constituting and mediating the discipline's methods and objects in its varied articulation as an enterprise generating national self-understanding, while additionally (particularly true of the Fischer controversy) causing some consideration of the disciplinary procedures that govern variable norms for the identification and understanding of pertinent facts and evidence. For some commentators, by contrast (for example, Thomas Nipperday, who therefore dismissed Habermas's intervention), it is less any new facts or even particular interpretations of events (as the Fischer controversy provided) that remain the legacy of the historians' dispute.

The importance for historians, however, lies in the recognition of the relation of one's standpoint to the past and its implication for the present and future. It is this caution that Saul Friedlander addresses in probing some of the epistemological stakes involved in calls of the past decade to "historicize" and hence encapsule National Socialism. Perhaps, he offers, this past is still much too contemporary for working historians—especially Germans and Jews of the first or even third generation—to be easily conscious of their assumptions. It is then less a choice "between facts and facts, but rather varied interpretations, which are anchored in different value judgments and therewith outside of the circle of proof and counter-proof."[47] Efforts to historicize *die große Zeit* are clearly affected by these remarks, both because of the thesis offered here regarding the strong relation between the legacy of the First World War and National Socialism and because of the stakes and conduct of the war-guilt debate waged by German historians (against, doubtless, the similarly nationalistic perspectives of former combatant countries) that mark the findings disseminated during the interwar period. Further, as Fischer and his students learned, answering questions raised in the controversy involved a paradigm shift away from diplomatic history and toward a new method of social-historical research and writing.

Even this brief exegesis suggests that a mode of literary analysis that relies on a positivistic rendering of "context" in books written by historians (misunderstood as articulating a transcendent or objective ground separable from subject positions), with which one can then put the "fictional" narrative "in its place," misses a great deal, including the point of what Hayden White has aptly called the "fictions of factual representation." Further, as Dominick LaCapra has argued, the preferential position accorded seemingly direct informational documents in the "documentary" model of historical knowledge additionally "diverts attention from the way 'documents' are themselves texts that 'process' or rework 'reality,'" easily leading to the abuse of a notion of objectivity that decouples the notion from the process. Such caution need not deny the quest for objectivity, but rejecting foundational or absolutist versions of it does entail a reconceptualization of the presumed relations between objects, objectives, subjects, and objectivity. For example, in criticizing a notion of historical writing that posits the possibility of representation that stands in direct relation to its object—in effect, if not in principle, immediate and unaltered—White has suggested the notion of a middle voice for historians, modeled on Barthes's intransitive writing, and LaCapra has offered psychoanalytic categories to enable a dialogical voice.[48] Both models suggest the need for continual rethinking and renegotiation rather than the sealing of boundaries (for example, object-subject) seemingly constituted once and for all by synthetic closure. Such an understanding may productively unsettle synthetic efforts to historicize events too hastily, to emplot them into preexisting national narratives or other a priori positions (conscious or not). That concern is registered again in reaction to efforts of the past decade in Germany to historicize—that is, to synthetically render—National Socialism and the Shoah.

Although pertinent facts may be thought of as subject to similar processes of narration as in the literary work, it becomes equally pertinent to consider also the constitution and status of those documents and "facts" narrated in war prose. It has seemed most useful in my analysis to consider pertinent facts given in documents of various kinds as being the outcome of prior interpretative narratives and inseparable from them rather than the objective stuff (in the sense of self-sufficient) from which historical narration only then proceeds. Although attention to narrative may still retain a distinction between facts and their interpretation (for example, by equating narrative and interpretation), the view of pertinent facts presented here undermines their clean separation. As we will see, what is at stake in several key instances is not the accuracy of the facts recorded but the value of the frame that generated these while precluding the generation of others.

What I am arguing is that the standard against which to assess, for example, the value of interwar official or quasi-official German military history is not the accuracy or inaccuracy of the facts recorded in them—the effort involved, for example, to accurately compile the numbers and movements of all units is quite prodigious—but rather their correspondence to the narrative guidelines that produced them and that they in turn substantiate. The task of a reader of war literature, it has seemed to me, must therefore be to work through the construction process that generated pertinent facts of a particular kind to thereby remove the attributes of timelessness, objectivity, and monumentality with which many historians and literary critics of the war and interwar periods clothed their arguments.

Rich materials are available to study war literature from many social perspectives. There are first the voluminous numbers of war books themselves, published, roughly speaking, under three sets of conditions: during the war itself, during the Weimar period, and during the Third Reich. Less accessible but equally numerous are documentary sources that point to the traces of social circulation otherwise concealed by the texts themselves.[49] This investigation focuses on aspects of the attempts to organize public discourse and particularly reading culture during the First World War in conjunction with a consideration of their belated effects thereafter. With reference to the period from 1914 to 1918, this will entail consideration of such factors as the relation between the state and the arts at the end of the Second Reich, the administration of wartime censorship, the interaction of publishing houses, academic institutions, and military agencies in constructing a state-sanctioned interpretation and language for the war, and finally, consideration of the literary marketplace as a determinant of belletristic content.

The crisis sketched above that played out in Weimar regarding the war's meaning seems largely a result of the battle between the officially generated paradigm, damaged by the unanticipated outcome of the war though still powerfully present, and other competing narratives, which, however, largely lacked the authority of the former. The works published after 1918 are in turn either affirmations or critiques of the codes developed before them, and it seems essential to me to view them in terms of this relation. One should not read the *Frontromane* of the 1920s simply as private expressions of meditation "given" and accessible today in an act of empathetic understanding, or only within the context of literary production during the Weimar Republic.[50] The later mode, of course, is sustained by the proclivities of much literary and political history that in the interest of conveying the impression of an epochal divide between the old and the new has separated Wilhelmine society and its cultural institutions from those of Weimar and the modernism that purportedly represents it. In this scenario, the war years function as the transformative passage between the two epochs. Though familiar, this neat chronological divide is problematic.

Reading instead the way I am suggesting involves a shift away from reading the text "itself" to an understanding and problematizing of "the text" itself as being already the product of a host of institutions attempting to author meaning and its reception. Undecidability notwithstanding, decisions are taken, power is exercised, traces are instituted.[51] Further, in Germany during the First World War, the interlinkage of army and academic institutions is pronounced. The following chapters consider the decisions taken and the traces thereby instituted with reference to the reading, writing, and dissemination of texts during and about the First World War.

The lingering effects of the efforts of these mediating agencies during the First World War in propagating a specific aesthetic and social program would have lent, had they known of these efforts, considerable evidentiary support to Horkheimer and Adorno's characterization of the tautological effect of reality production in the understanding at work in *Aufklärung* (enlightenment/propaganda): "The senses are already determined by the conceptual apparatus even before perception can occur. . . . Kant intuitively anticipated what Hollywood first made routine: pictures are precensored during their production in accordance with the faculty of understanding's standards, according to which they will also be seen afterward. Public judgments meant to be substantiated by perception were already rendered before perception could take hold."[52]

Chapter 2 Establishing the Paradigm: Censorship, *Frontgeist,* and Walter Bloem's *Kriegspressestelle*

The efforts of various military agencies both to censor information about the ongoing war and, more actively, to collect and generate stories and documentary evidence to support the military's rendering of it had important consequences in establishing the parameters of war representation for literary and political discourse both between 1914 and 1918 and thereafter. As the war dragged on, the parameters of what could be published as determined by government and military censors grew ever more restrictive. The regulation of all communications in German territories preceded the *Belagerungszustand* (state of siege) of August 1914, but both the orbit and apparatus of censorship took on a new character during the war years, particularly following Erich Falkenhayn's replacement as head of the military High Command (OHL) by Erich Ludendorff and Paul von Hindenburg in August 1916. If Germany's military and government offices were unprepared for the implications of mass media, reading, and information flows in the conduct of war, they took increasingly significant steps to homogenize and centralize information, print, and visual media.[1] Additionally, following the tactical stalemates in the West and the decline of morale at the front and at home, military informational services, including several created during the war, took active steps in disseminating a type of writing imbued with what, both then and after defeat, would be labeled *Frontgeist*. In this chapter I examine these developments to assess the contents and pertinent facts generated by this framing of the war's significance.

Walter Bloem (1868–1951) was a pivotal figure in these efforts, which included the institutionalization of the *Kriegspressestelle* (War Press Agency), centralization of army newspapers, and the establishment of *Offizierkriegsberichter-statter* (officer war reporters). Though largely forgotten today, Bloem was taken seriously by the nationalist circles that propelled him into literary fame as one of the most popular authors of the Wilhelmine period. In some accounts—certainly his own—he was *the* best-selling author in Germany between 1912 and 1922. It is not coincidental that the writing that likewise made him one of Wilhelm II's favorite authors centered on the events culminating in the 1871 founding of the Kaiserreich, and this prewar prominence positioned him to become director of the War Press Agency, where he could with some authority establish the narrative guidelines for rendering the value of combat in the life of the nation. Consideration of his wartime activity leads us back to the beginning of the war and the first flurry of literary activity that accompanied it.

MOBILIZATION, 1914

Shortly after hostilities began in August 1914, the reading public was inundated by a flood of publications that sought to explain "what the war is about" from ethical, military, religious, philosophical, commercial, and political vantage points. Most of Germany's best-known intellectuals, both inside and outside of academia, joined in a literary "mobilization," writing popular scientific treatises as well as essay and poetic texts almost uniformly welcoming the war, though often for starkly conflicting reasons. These texts were augmented by poems whose total number was estimated to have exceeded one million in the first few months of the war alone.[2] Whether or not such estimates can be documented satisfactorily, the role extension of readers into writer-readers brought about by the war was, as observed by numerous contemporaries, unprecedented.

In the imaginations of many, the war was a welcome opportunity to implement changes desired but hitherto stymied, affording the necessary push to overcome the blockage cemented by a static and self-serving status quo. War was often greeted as "factor X," a bridge to the imagined goal of achieving an authentic national identity in moral, political, religious, and aesthetic terms.

The content of "factor X" differed widely and conflictingly among the various ideological groupings, but most authors shared a readiness to affirm the possibility of change the war seemed to present. Lending respectability to this readiness was an almost universally accepted premise that the Reich was fighting a defensive war. Publicly, few doubted the Kaiser's assertion that Germany had been forced "to take up the sword"and was merely fighting to defend its territorial integrity.[3]

Beyond that cause, though, what any individual believed the fight was for varied considerably. Many expressionists offered the hope in the early months, for example, that the war would destroy a corrupt and bankrupt bourgeois order, permitting a "new man" to develop, freed from that order's grasp, while pan-Germans saw the war finally manifesting the nation's deserved place under the sun as a world power. Wartime letters collected and published by different agencies proclaimed that socialists were fighting to improve labor conditions and achieve political equality, Jewish soldiers were fighting to speed their full acceptance into society, Catholics were fighting to dispel any lingering suspicions from the *Kulturkampf,* and students were fighting to preserve German culture or to surmount class differences. For Adolf Hitler, writing ten years after the war had begun about the events that so decisively affected him, "factor X" was more a symptom of a general malaise—and an adolescent one at that—to which a war promised to put an end. "God knows the battle of 1914 was not forced upon the masses, but rather coveted by the entire *Volk.* One wished to put an end to a general condition of uncertainty," Hitler wrote in *Mein Kampf.* "Those hours appeared to me then personally as a redemption from the irritated sentiments characteristic of youth."[4]

Despite dissimilar aims and motivations (distinguishable at least by class, region, and religion) the attitudes that accompanied the outbreak of the war— sloganized thereafter as "der Juli-Geist" or "die Augusttage" (days of August)— confirmed and subsequently served as a readily quotable reminder of the possibilities the war afforded in propelling the German nation toward the actualization of a telos of unified social identity, recognized as having begun only in 1871. Suddenly, everything seemed possible as the barriers between social groups and their political agendas seemed to melt into insignificance. "I no longer recognize party divisions, only Germans," proclaimed the Kaiser, and most Germans—including, to the surprise of many, those labeled *Vaterlandslose Gesellen* (apprentices without a Fatherland, that is, with socialist sympathies)—chose at least briefly to embrace (and quote) this new, if wildly indeterminate, spirit of harmony and unity.[5] Accounts of men and women from

„Ich kenne keine Parteien mehr, kenne nur noch Deutsche!"
(Wilhelm II.)

Fig. 2.1 Wartime postcard. The caption quotes Kaiser Wilhelm's famous line during the days of mobilization in 1914: "I no longer recognize political parties, only Germans."

different classes, of different religious faiths, and from different regions embracing one another and singing songs fill the newspapers and the war books written by contemporaries. A friend-enemy distinction is at work, reframed at an international scale; the threat posed by enemies outside Reich borders constitutes a redefined boundary enclosing (new) friends.

Early best-selling war books such as Paul Oscar Höcker's *An der Spitze meiner Kompagnie* (At the head of my company) or Paul Grabein's *Im Auto durch Feindesland* (By car in enemy territory)—two of the forty-five-volume war series published by Ullstein—display this dynamic in an account that employs both technology and distance as significant elements of its narration of experience.[6] In the narrative, being transported by train across Germany to the front becomes a journey consolidating national and collective identity in spatial terms. As passing panoramas are registered by the soldiers in the train cars, the concept of *Heimat* expands to encompass the entire Reich for those from various regions of Germany. The crystallizing moment in the narrative is the crossing of the Rhine River. This crossing of the border demarcates a definitive inside-outside topography, separating friend from enemy. The now-collectivized soldiers sing "Die Wacht am Rhein," ceremoniously acknowledging their new consciousness of this demarcation. This pivotal moment—the border crossing—is recalled in many of the later volumes in Ullstein's series (and elsewhere), recalling that "spirit of 1914" long after its mobilizing power had weakened.

One can regard this initial, often euphoric, literary and journalistic output as a projection screen, interesting for having sublimated competing visions of society that when presented stirred strong debate in parliament months before. A common feature of much of this early wartime writing—as widely varied as the suggested correctives one encounters in them—is the hope that the war would redefine social and political identity in Germany. Yet viewed in a way that distinguishes between war affirmation and the reasons for it, this writing should not be solely read as saber-rattling intoxification with battle or as an expression of deep attachment to the status quo but as an articulation of both a utopian hope for the transformation of German society and disappointment with it as found in 1914.[7]

The euphoria of the early war days passed, however. For many Germans, "factor X" had become hardship, suffering, and loss. The war of attrition that characterized the western front from 1915 on, the rationing of food, clothing, and housing at home, and the continued unequal distribution of benefits and burdens, demanded new explanations of "what the war was about."[8] Even though much German writing continued to include references to key attributes and gestures of the "spirit of 1914" throughout the war, the inescapable fact of its waning power to mobilize the spirit intensified the state and army's imperative to censor words and information.

CENSORSHIP

Military censorship, first activated following declaration of a state of siege, created an informational chasm between a small group of well-informed, policymaking insiders and the vast majority of civilians and most military personnel, dependent on newspaper reports subject to this censorship mechanism. Terse army communiqués, revealing little tangible information, relied markedly on a language of suggestion, increasingly so after September 15, 1914, when it became necessary to disguise the fact that winning with the planned strategy had become extremely problematic with the failure of the Marne offensive.[9]

Given the elevated expectations aroused by the "Juli-Geist," leading poli-cymaking circles found it impossible to acknowledge the offensive's failure, and concomitantly the miscalculations that had occasioned the imperial govern-ment's willingness to declare war. To do so would probably have meant at least the fall of the government, if not a concerted restructuring of the form of government. The war continued, stalemating along the western front into a war of attrition after 1915. Ludendorff and Hindenburg restructured Germany's resources to mount something approximating a total mobilization. This also included increased attention to the dissemination of communications in all media that might affect morale. The mechanisms of this dissemination are of interest both for their contents and for their organizational forms. None of these efforts could stave off defeat. Following the failure of the final German offensive in spring 1918, Ludendorff had no choice but to acknowledge defeat in October of that year, given the threatened collapse of his front line. Luden-dorff's petition surprised most of the Reichstag and even government minis-ters, who, following official communiqués, had perceived no more than a momentary setback at a time when the whole front was in hourly danger of total collapse.[10] An increasingly efficient administered network of information control had perpetuated the expectation of ultimate victory to the very end.

The way Ludendorff left office during the last days of the war, moreover, set the stage for the *Dolchstoßlegende* (stab-in-the-back thesis), an explanation that would have ominous consequences: it "explained" that responsibility for the inexplicable defeat lay not with strategical and economic miscalculations of the German High Command, and certainly not with the fighting troops, but with the parliamentarians at home, particularly the socialists and their discontented supporters (and in the National Socialist version—the Jews), who had "given away" the *Siegfrieden* (peace through victory) while the army bled at the front.[11] At public hearings after the war and in their own memoirs, Ludendorff and Hindenburg continued to insist that the army had been "unbeaten on the battlefield"; the blame for Germany's collapse was to be placed on the home front, which had not adequately supported the army's efforts to gain victory.

Expressions of resentment directed against the *Heimat* by nationalist vet-erans became quite explicit in writings of the 1920s. In them, the international casting of a friend-enemy distinction, which had enabled the articulation of the "spirit of 1914" and its redefinition of a collective of friends constituted by enemies outside Reich borders, returned home with a vengeance to scapegoat the enemies within. Hitler, for example, voiced this resentment graphically, connecting it to a ghostly fantasy of revenge in describing his feelings when told that Germany had lost the war: "Must not the graves of all the hundred thousands who had once marched into battle with faith in their Fatherland only never to return not open up now? Would the graves not split open and send the silent, mud- and blood-covered heroes as vengeful ghosts back to the homeland, which scornfully had cheated them out of the reward due the highest sacrifice a man can make in this world for his people?"[12] The lingering power of this explanatory model, never dispelled by professional German historians during the Weimar Republic and not to be demystified until after the Second World War, was a major obstacle to providing a legitimating ground for a democratic order during the Weimar Republic. Never disarmed, the stab-in-the-back thesis would enter the ideological arsenal of National Socialism.

The explanatory power of this phantasmic thesis can be accounted for only by government and military censorship, which effectively charged the High Command with narrating the war. Until October 15, 1918, the military constituted an increasingly autonomous, unchecked news and censorship apparatus.[13] Its forms are particularly noteworthy following Ludendorff's restructuring of it, when the proactive dimension of *Vaterländischer Unterricht* (Patriotic Instruction) was added to the mix. But Ludendorff built on many previous initiatives that had gradually developed during the High Commands of his predecessors Helmuth Moltke and Erich von Falkenhayn.

When Kaiser Wilhelm II declared war on July 31, 1914, the "Gesetz über den Belagerungszustand" (law pertaining to a state of siege) of June 4, 1851, became effective. Thus military authority was entrusted with preserving public security. The first "catalog regulating communication," promulgated by Chancellor Theobald von Bettman-Hollweg, consisted of twenty-six items. Among other things, it specified that the *Burgfrieden* (domestic truce) be preserved: "Maintenance of the spirit of devotion and unity is of great importance. Therefore everything must be prevented that might tend to disrupt the unity of the German people and the press." A later amendment added that "in discussions regarding questions of peace, it is essential that the *Burgfrieden* be guaranteed and that any impression that the people's unified resolve to attain victory has wavered be prevented."

With this directive, government censorship was given a new and explicitly political criterion (as distinct from previous moral or religious categories).[14] Attitudes toward the war that appeared in print were thereby constrained to adhere to the general parameters of a discourse of national unity and individual identity. The decree's amendment is a reminder that censorship was directed not only at the Left, for the prohibition of a public discussion of war aims incensed pan-Germans and other conservatives. In late 1917, this prohibition was lifted when Ludendorff wanted to permit public discussion to remobilize support for the war effort (though, obviously, not from the far Left).

This prohibition of a discussion of war aims, initiated by Bettmann-Hollweg, is part of the "spirit of 1914" and its enabling limit. The indeterminate appeal to a broad national collective fundamentally relied on the notion of a supplement that would manifest the "missing ingredients" for the realization of an authentic national identity. Yet given the extremely varied expectations of what "X" was thought to consist of, any broad public discussion of its contents could reveal only unchanged social antagonisms and the limits that even a victorious Germany would inevitably set for some of these social aspirations.

With the beginning of the war, competence for censoring military depictions was given to the individual military commanders (that is, the *Generalkommandos*) with the twenty-six points serving as the guiding framework.[15] In the recognition that the press was an "unentbehrliches Mittel der Kriegsführung" (indispensable means in the pursuit of war), Commanding General Moltke established a press service within the competency of Section III B, whose director was Major Walter Nicolai. Daily press conferences took place in Berlin, while the official reports took the form of terse *Heeresberichte* (army communiqués). In addition to the official reports, a limited number of civilian war reporters were permitted access to the front (but generally only to the main headquarters [*Grossen Hauptquartier*]) to provide newspaper reports in Germany about the experiences of the troops at the front. The October 1914 directives regarding these war reporters defined the following grounds for their selection: "Only such individuals are to be considered who are of recognized patriotic sensibilities, who as officers have belonged either to the army or to the reserves or otherwise have made themselves known to higher authority as reliable individuals."[16]

In the early phase of the war, competitions between Reich, army, and Prussian offices created loopholes and regional variations, compounded by the growing difficulty of separating "military" from political or economic news or information. Regional differences manifested themselves according to the proclivities of the individual press liaison and the state government they represented. Alfons Falkner von Sonnenburg in Bavaria, for example, pursued a policy that, given Bavaria's particularism, appeared more liberal than that practiced in Berlin. Censorship laws continued to evolve, however, arching toward uniformity and affecting fewer or more types of publications at different stages of the war. The initial guidelines were quickly replaced by an eighty-page

Fig. 2.2 The Hornbach family, 1915; photograph taken in Speyer during leave of the three men in uniform. From left to right, Rosa, Georg, Auguste, Kaetchen, Ludwig, Richard, Valentin. (Author family heirloom.)

blue book that grew longer each month.[17] The "Merkblatt für die Presse" (press directive) was not given to "untrustworthy people" (for example, at various times, editors of *Der Sozialdemokrat* and *Die Gleichheit*), and in reading them, one can see good reason for the military's sensitivity, because—read today— the list of prohibitions offers a telling gauge of the attitudes and norms of the population that were of concern to the military and government. On one hand, except for those newspapers and publishers deemed unreliable *an sich,* these regulations point to a mechanism of cooperative, self-imposed censorship, based (as often stated in them) on trust. On the other hand, newspapers, publishers, and authors were fined for a wide range of objectionable communications. By the March 1918 edition, there were 954 ordinances in effect regulating the parameters of the iterable. Each circumscribed to a greater or lesser degree the possible representation of *die große Zeit.*

The censorship initially applied to indigenous and foreign newspapers, but by April 1915 it was extended to the import and export of all books and printed matter including pamphlets, catalogues, or advertisements. By the time somewhat uniform norms had been established with a more rigorous mechanism for their enforcement—accelerated following March 1915, and again after the initiation of Patriotic Instruction in summer 1917—the fact that any books read in Germany might at the same time be sold in neutral or enemy countries legitimated enforcement of censorship standards in compliance with a state of siege as a precondition of its publication. From the beginning, censors were aware that the distinct reception contexts of inner German and international readership at times created unique censorship demands. Although reports of acts of cruelty toward wounded German soldiers or prisoners, for example, were to be encouraged for consumption abroad, it was recognized that the same reports might cause "disquiet," not to mention "despondency," for domestic readers.[18] Alleged atrocities committed by Catholic priests in Belgium are an example from the early part of the censorship war's "split consciousness"; these atrocities were given a domestic reception context in which the bitter *Kulturkampf* waged against Catholics was still in memory.

In several regions, such as Württemberg, a voluntary prepublication censorship was arranged in cooperation with the local publishers' union, then formalized by order of the Thirteenth Regional Army Command before it too became nationally mandated. For book publishers, preventive censorship meant that manuscripts would be reviewed, approved, prohibited, or ordered changed before publication rather than having the decision made after books were already in print. Württemberg military authorities were able to quote in their reports the favorable attitude of Peter Hoffmann, head of the publishers' union in Stuttgart, who in February 1916 had written that "preventive censorship lies in the interest of publishers, since its exercise protects them from penalty and great economic damage."[19]

"Military security" was used as the key to determining censorship needs, but as the war continued and the military assumed more and more responsibility for the day-to-day running of Germany, more types of writing could occasion censorship. The Regional Army Command of Württemberg found its decision to exercise prepublication censorship well justified by the end of 1915 because of the increasing difficulty of separating "military" reportage from publications that could be categorized as "political" or "economic" but without military significance.[20]

Censorship was several times the focus of debate in the Reichstag. Debates during the winter of 1915–1916 and in 1917 were prevented from being published in pamphlet form, despite the norm of unencumbered reporting of Reichstag proceedings but in accord with the censorship regulation of October 3, 1914, which stated that any criticism of the censors that may threaten public confidence was forbidden. These debates demonstrated the limits of civilian governmental control over the issue and therewith any control over the High

Command's depiction of war events. Reichstag factions, particularly the Social Democrats, the party most effected by prohibitions, could do little but voice their complaints and accept reassurances that the "domestic truce" was not being unevenly administered.[21]

Wartime censorship considerably affected publishing house activity, as this study further demonstrates. Fear of transgressing these censorship regulations, which carried penalties including fines and the suspension of publishing rights, caused most firms and newspapers to exercise a cautious self-censorship. As the examples above also suggest, the enactment of censorship policy was perceived by most publishers and the military as a two-way affair, dependent on the willingness of the publishing press to internalize and even anticipate regulations. Otherwise, as numerous memoranda of individual press liaisons reminded other responsible military offices, publication would have to cease in Germany, and an indispensable weapon serving the nation would be lost. Most of the established publishing houses—apart, at times, from the organs associated with the Social Democrats—were amenable to this policy. The army consequently pursued a policy that tried to work with those publishers willing to cooperate, sometimes fining or warning, but rarely suspending publication,[22] while simultaneously undertaking new initiatives to ensure that its own message was directly received by Germany's readers.

The High Command, though initially surprised by the power of the printed word, soon registered that a controlled press was essential to maintaining morale at home and in the army. Efforts to control wartime civilian publishing with censorship decrees were then supplemented by its own publication initiatives, and both combined to generate a paradigm of sanctioned war representation. A General Staff directive from September 29, 1914, laid down the policy linking the two: "A prohibition of the publication of individual, private reports must be avoided. On the other hand, military agencies ought to secure for themselves a greater influence regarding the selection of reports to be printed, not only in regard to the elimination of unsuitable material, but more importantly in the procurement and diffusion of reports that are especially valuable because of their form and content and whose publication supports the national cause. Therefore, the purposeful gathering and sorting through of this rich material is recommended." Further, on Christmas Eve, 1914, the Army Chief of Staff announced that the Kaiser had decreed the creation of a *Kriegsnachrichtenstelle* (war news agency) attached to the field command. Its mission was not to write an official account of war events but rather to prepare treatments of skirmishes and combat situations for the public, particularly emphasizing "outstanding achievements of units or individuals." The form these were to take became more concrete in a further directive dated January 15, 1915, which encouraged the generation of material for so-called *Ehrentafel* (tablets of honor) in which "individual depictions of remarkable heroic deeds by individual soldiers would be published in order to honor the heroes, to instill pride in their relatives, and to spur on the younger troops."

The popular author Walter Bloem played a strategic role in subsequent army implementations of these directives to narrate the war. In analyzing the import of Bloem's activities here, I consider him as an author in two senses: first as a writer of war books, about both the Franco-Prussian War and the First World War, and second as a coauthor of decrees and military guidelines that greatly affected the parameters of representation for *die große Zeit*. In this latter capacity, Bloem's activities will be situated within a social context of institutionally fostered authorship.

WALTER BLOEM, FORGER OF THE FUTURE

Walter Bloem enjoyed dizzying fame as an author. Even before the first shots were fired in 1914, he had garnered a commanding reputation as a writer of war books. His popular success principally bespeaks the attitudes and ideals of nationalistic, conservative middle-class readers. Inasmuch as Bloem—as well as any of his literary contemporaries—did not experience the war with neutral eyes, the optic through which he narrated its events is best understood with reference to his earlier works. In them, one sees a narrative and its telos that his "authorship" of the war's events sought to bring to conclusion.

Bloem's trilogy about the Franco-Prussian War (1870–1871), *Volk wider Volk* (Nation against nation), *Das eiserne Jahr* (The iron year), and *Die Schmiede der Zukunft* (Forgers of the future) made him one of the most widely read authors of the early twentieth century and brought him the accolades of Wilhelm II's court. *Die Schmiede der Zukunft*, published in 1913 by Grethlein in Leipzig (which along with Ullstein published most of his prose works), had sold more than 50,000 copies before the war broke out. *Das eiserne Jahr*, published in 1911, had sold in excess of 140,000 copies by 1914, and, as Bloem later registered with pride, even Wilhelm II read aloud from it to his family. More than 120,000 copies of *Volk wider Volk* had been printed by 1914. By 1941, the total trilogy was listed at 734,000 copies.[23]

Although he was a lawyer by training, Bloem's passions centered on his life as a reserve officer and on the theater, for which he dramatized those virtues he saw embodied in military life: duty, comradeship, and love of country. In 1913, Wilhelm II awarded him the *Roter Adler* medal for his contributions to the arts. He frequently lectured throughout Germany, often reading from his works, and it was he whom the Kaiser chose to deliver the dedication address for the *Völkerschlachtdenkmal* in Leipzig, commemorating 1813 and the "Wars of Liberation." His call to arms in 1914 came just after planning the autumn season of Stuttgart's Court Theater, where he had been director and *Dramaturg* since 1911.[24]

As much as any Wilhelmine writer, Bloem perpetuated in his work a normative, paradigmatically nationalistic view of war's virtues, complete with attendant vocabulary, ethical purpose, and dramatic development. As recorded in his unpublished diary, he felt that these poetical achievements were to be valued even higher because his best-selling novels published before 1914—praised by critics, incidentally, for their realism—were completely works of imagination, written without the experience of having been involved in combat.[25]

Buoyed by imperial favor and high levels of popular sales, Bloem enjoyed a sense of self-worth that did not shy away from comparing himself to Goethe and his productivity and life; like his townsman Rudolf Herzog (another enormously successful and unusually egocentric author), he was able to purchase a small *Ritterburg* (knight's castle) with his earnings, which allegedly exceeded one million Goldmark in 1918.[26]

Bloem's trilogy culminates with *Die Schmiede der Zukunft,* in which France is vanquished and the Second German Reich established. It is noteworthy not only as an example of the type of writing that enjoyed popular success in late Wilhelmine society but also for its revelation of the narrative structure on which Bloem's fashioning of *die große Zeit* would be based. The work is thoroughly imbued with the "great man" view of history. The reader encounters kings, cabinet members, and generals; above them all as the hero of the novel is a fatherly and sage Fürst Bismarck, whose foresight and diplomatic skill orchestrate the events that culminate in the proclamation of the Second Reich in Versailles. Neither women nor working-class characters play significant roles (apart from providing romantic entanglements, loving support to husbands, or phrases in regional dialects extolling love of king and country) in the "forging" of these great events.

Although Bloem does not entirely shy from depicting battlefield violence in his epic (besides the predictable glorious cavalry charges, some ten of the five hundred pages portray a third-person narration of man-to-man fighting) his characters fight valiantly, expressing no doubts about the ethical, divinely sanctioned purpose of their cause. Such bravery is amply rewarded with Iron Crosses by Wilhelm, a compassionate and personable king (soon to be Kaiser).

The novel's telos, the proclamation ceremony in Versailles, begins and ends with the hearty singing of Christian chorales, while an army minister speaks a benediction joyfully celebrating the reestablished trinity of (a Christian) God, Fatherland, and Kaiser. In epic fashion, the plot depicts the would-be nation fragmented at the outset by individual and regional dissention, then overcoming self-interest to develop a united will toward national unification. The only obstacle inhibiting the manifestation of the general will is the *leadership* of the Social Democratic Party, August Bebel and Wilhelm Liebknecht, whose refusal to join in the jubilation provokes one of the few unresolved threads of an otherwise univocally resolved narrative. Yet even while faithfully recording the actual position taken of Bebel and Liebknecht, Bloem's narrative simultaneously hints that the party's leadership is out of sync with the "true" desires of German Socialism's rank-and-file.

The becoming of a nation is both the content and the integrating principle of the novel, which ends with a paean to a "united, reborn, elevated" Fatherland, now a unified Reich with one Kaiser whose remaining challenge it will be to utilize the hard-won "concord" to unite its people. "May the concord that now circles your tribes grow and mature into a unity of the heart. . . . May it help to fill the chasms—relics from the past—that still separate the estates, social strata, and the hearts. Let us become one people. . . . All have helped achieve it . . . may it belong to all!"[27]

Although the novel leaves unexplained what concrete political gains should compel those social groups hitherto disenfranchised to join in this general harmony—apart from the intrinsic pleasure of being part of a Völkisch community—Bloem's ending identifies an agenda that would be of some consequence very shortly. With all else thus put in place, this final desideratum— truly becoming a united people—would, one year after Bloem's novel was published, animate his and other nationalist celebrations of the "spirit of 1914" and later of the "community born at the front." Both of these are portrayed as core moments in which the process of becoming a unified people displays itself. Bloem's writing during the First World War consequently seeks to situate and narrate its events as the continuation and culmination of a three-pronged process begun a generation earlier.

In light of war books published after 1918, Bloem's novel is noteworthy as well for its celebration of the Prussian military spirit, and the narration leaves no possibility for doubting that the army and its leadership—and not a civilian-dominated parliament—should be viewed as the guardians of the new German spirit.

One of Bloem's characters, Clemens Müllenseifen, articulates and incarnates this position. He is the ideal embodiment of an educated, middle-class subject in the novel, a battle-tested university professor of history and a member of parliament who is not uncomfortable using the familiar *Du* in speaking to his fellow privates. His most important deed is to deliver a speech to the North German Confederation condemning fellow parliamentarians not unequivocally supportive of Bismarck's model for unification. Having just returned from the battlefields, wearing (at Bismarck's request) battle-frayed clothing and displaying his Iron Cross, he is appalled by the "pettiness" he hears in the speeches of civilian representatives. "Here, where the elected spokesmen of the people were gathered, here a dry bureaucrat stood up to speak . . . and not one sentence was enunciated about the glorious victories of the people-in-arms, not one sentence about the mountain-moving faith of a nation in its national future. . . . Here one heard only the dry rustle of paper documents" (75–76). As he rises to speak, his dramatic appearance lends considerable force to his speech, which includes a threat to those assembled should they not do as Bismarck demands: "A scream of outrage will shrill through the German lands. The old, disgraceful lamentation, the old misery, the old dishonor! That which the soldier had done so well—and for once the diplomats also—that was being spoiled and denigrated by the phrase-mongers and the pedants" (80). The men of mere words, the quibblers and dissenters, are antinomically juxtaposed in these passages to the men of deeds, who, by contrast, are united by their shared vision of nationhood. That shared vision is predicated upon the transformative experience of victorious combat, something civilian "rhetoricians" seem precluded from understanding. Without hesitating to use the plural "we" in speaking for the multimillion member army, Müllenseifen tells parliament what the "people-in-arms" desire: "Germany's unification into a national state under one common leadership. We do not wish to have fought and bled for our goal in vain." The army's sacrifices invoked by Müllenseifen, as well as his equation of dissent with betrayal, convinces his audience (except for Bebel and Liebknecht, of course) to set aside their differences and endorse Bismarck's proposal. Chancellor Bismarck, for his part omnisciently aware of all relevant activities, rewards Müllenseifen for the speech with a promotion to full lieutenant.

The polar categories evident here seem remarkably prescient of anti-Republic war narratives written during Weimar and after 1933: the front versus civilian perspectives, army versus parliament, united will and duty versus "rhetorical" self-interest and betrayal; these antinomies would resurface with a vengeance for those writers who after 1918 sought to maintain a nationalist, soldierly understanding of the changed circumstances brought about by Germany's defeat.[28]

That nationalist authors were able to do so is premised in part on the preexisting schemas and vocabularies available to them that were articulated before 1914 in such works as Bloem's trilogy. The literature about the period from 1870 to 1871 is evident throughout works published between 1914 and 1918. One wrote about *die große Zeit* in the way this earlier literature had taught one to think about and narrate war and nationhood. The language and categories of understanding displayed in Bloem's trilogy, intensified after Germany's defeat with a further valorization of the front experience as an end in itself, would in turn recur in countless texts written after 1918.

Equally important in preserving a structural continuity between normative Wilhelmine categories and the rhetoric of the national Right in Weimar was the interaction of educational and army institutions, including the press agency in the field under Bloem's command, in collecting and preserving material "for the later writing of the history of *die große Zeit,*" as military ordinances described this collection effort. As is true for the literature published between 1914 and 1918, the suitability of materials deemed appropriate for inclusion in this national project were thus judged on the basis of a narrative model derived from 1870 to 1871. Recognition of this institutional frame is thus important in accounting for the puzzling perpetuation of "traditional" alongside "modernist" forms of remembrance in Germany.[29]

What changed, however, for those writing about the war after 1918 and before 1933 (after its passage from being *die große Zeit* to becoming "der Weltkrieg" but before it became "der Erste Weltkrieg") was the possibility of inscribing recent history within a teleological framework culminating in victory—that is, the realized presence of a process of continuous (and hence necessary and determinate) national self-development. Authors like Bloem who wished to continue writing about their ideal of Fatherland as the subject of a national *Bildungsroman* were forced to emplot November 1918 as a moment of passing negativity whose contingent truth was the *Systemzeit*, as some of its enemies would loathingly call the Weimar Republic. Unlike some of them, Bloem did not embrace anti-Semitism as part of the package of betrayal. Indeed, in 1922, the same year, he published *Der Weltbrand: Deutschlands Tragödie, 1914–1918*, an overview of the war written in the same spirit described above, he also authored a novel (*Brüderlichkeit*) that offered a severe criticism of

Fig. 2.3 Early wartime postcard, linking the beginning of the Franco-Prussian War to the first year of hostilities in 1914. "Forward, let the flags fly. We will and we must be victorious!"

the unnecessary intolerance that prohibited individuals (including those of "Jewish blood") to realize their desire to become German. His vision of a German national community, articulated in the *Frontgemeinschaft* of the battle-field, retained a commitment to the spirit of 1914 that was not necessarily embracing but was nonetheless tolerant of differences within the community (differences, however, that *Brüderlichkeit* presents as obstacles that perhaps in time and with effort on the part of the educated middle class will be overcome). Following the novel's largely negative reception, the author devoted his energies fleeing from *Zeitgeschichte* into the timeless vision of an eternal Germany, rich in medieval tradition, which was a more fitting subject perhaps for history as it ought to be and whose temporal scope permitted the outcome of the war to seem an even more fleeting moment of contingency.[30] After the "awakening" of 1933, Bloem would become active in party affairs despite suspicions regarding his racial views, joining the party in 1938.

A WAR OF WORDS

Bloem's activities extend to his role as a policymaker and administrator and as a major figure in generating the guidelines for officially sanctioned writing about the war. In exploring this institutional dimension of authorship, it is necessary to consider simultaneously the larger institutional complex in which Bloem's activities in Belgium, and later the *Feldpressestelle* (army field press agencies), are situated.

Bloem began the war training a regiment, then briefly saw combat before being wounded. He was appointed as an assistant to General Bissing, the overseer of occupied Belgium, which was designated a *Generalgouvernemount* after its conquest. In many ways it was an enviable assignment; two other prominent men of letters, Rudolf Alexander Schroeder and Anton Kippenberg, needed to fully exploit their connections before finding similar positions in Belgium. Like Schroeder before him, Kippenberg requested the intervention of Krupp Steel Works' director Eberhard von Bodenhausen to secure a position. Reacting to Bodenhausen's initial recommendation that he would best serve the war effort by continuing his activities with Insel, Kippenberg pleaded (successfully) that a post in Belgium would not create a conflict: "I can now take my distance from Leipzig without harm to the publishing house, and my most ardent desire is to be given a suitable military or military-political position in Belgium. The excellent postal connections would make it possible for me to direct the publishing house from there."[31]

All three men are examples of the mobilization of literati for the war effort. Attending to the day-to-day details of administering an occupied territory, each also contributed to the strategy designed to wean the Flemish population from its French-speaking countrymen. Schroeder did so as an adviser assigned to the political department, where he cultivated contacts with German- and Flemish-speaking educators and authors, some of whom he translated for, others whom he put in contact with his publisher, Kippenberg. Kippenberg became editor of a particularly important soldier's newspaper (*Kriegszeitung der 4. Armee*) and later succeeded in gaining approval to edit and publish the journal *Der Belfried: Eine Monatsschrift für Geschichte und gegenwart der südlichen Niederlande*. The journal, which appeared between July 1916 and December 1918, was expected to play a useful propagandistic role in realizing German policy in Belgium and in explaining occupation politics to a home audience. According to a memorandum dated March 3, 1916, the journal was not supposed to look like an official organ of the occupation forces.[32] "Rather, it will take on the appearance of a private enterprise underwritten by a German publisher. It will be printed and appear in Germany, but the leadership of the [military] Press Agency will retain the right to influence its direction in concert with the interests of German politics."

In late 1916, Kippenberg also became a regional director of the propaganda campaign known as Patriotic Instruction. Kippenberg's role in this concerted effort, directed at the troops to defuse the Bolshevist threat of revolution and inspire unmitigated battle resolve, was apparently a considerable success.[33] For his part, Walter Bloem could rightfully consider himself General Bissing's right-hand man in Belgium.

Bloem's code of honor and his literary ambitions as an author renowned for writing war books drove him to seek an active field command, and he was successful in convincing Bissing to allow him to return to his regiment in time for the Somme offensive. There, he was wounded for the second time. He spent his convalescence writing what was to be the first volume of his trilogy of novels detailing his war experiences, an autobiographical chronicle of his activities during the first year of the war. Like his earlier war books, *Vormarsch,* published in 1916 by Grethlein in Leipzig, became a best-seller, with sales of over 60,000 copies before the end of the year.

After his recuperation, Bloem was appointed to a position that matched his talent as a popular author loyal to his protector, Wilhelm II. In March 1916, he was appointed head of the *Feldpressestelle* (FPS) and thus became a direct subordinate of Major Nicolai, head of the information services of the army. The *Feldpressestelle* was organized at a propitious moment in the war's development. By the beginning of 1916, visions of swiftly defeating France and England had bled to death in the trenches near Verdun. As the promises and expectations elevated during the heady days of August 1914 had turned into increasing deprivation and hardship at home and devastating casualties at the front, the War Ministry realized the need to offset the allied propaganda that, it was feared, was gaining credibility both at home and with neutral countries.

Bloem's new appointment was one reflection of a widespread attitude that had developed by winter 1915–1916 in many military and government circles, that the particular power of the press had not been fully utilized from the beginning of the war. Indeed, numerous books written after Germany's defeat, including Bloem's own memoir, reiterate the feeling that the imperial government had not been prepared for this aspect of total war. A work published in 1916 already warned that as a consequence the very nature of war had drastically changed: "More than any other conflict hitherto, this is a war of words and with words, a war which is about the power of words."[34]

An army memorandum of 1917 used language that bespoke a belated but similar recognition. "In the course of this war, probably for the first time in Germany, the recognition of the tremendous importance of the press has

Die Allerärmsten.

Von allen Losen, die der Krieg verhängt,
Ist dies mir stets als bitterstes erschienen:
Gefangen in des Feindes Frohnde dienen,
Den Nacken krumm, den Blick in Scham gesenkt.

Verlacht, in jedem Heiligsten gekränkt,
Verachtung und Triumpf in allen Mienen —
Und Feige sind doch selten unter ihnen,
Die auch einst opferfroh ein Schwert geschwenkt!

Wie viele waren übermannt von Grauen,
Wie viele lagen wund, gelähmt, zerhauen,
Als sie der Feind von blut'ger Walstatt las —

Sie tragen Erdenjammers Übermass
Schmach, Fremde, Knechtschaft —
                              lasst für sie mich bitten,
Die auch für euch gestritten — und gelitten!
                              Walter Bloem.

Kornsand & Co., Frkf. a. M.

Fig. 2.4 Wartime postcard with a poem about prisoners of war by Walter Bloem titled "The Poorest of the Poor." The poem offers a catalog of the sufferings endured by German soldiers and prisoners of war and extolls the reader to be mindful of their extraordinary sacrifices.

gradually surfaced. Certain circles who previously visibly avoided every contact with the press, or who contemptuously judged its tasks and significance, have realized as a result of this war what mighty power the press represents, and how prudent it is to secure the support of the press."[35]

Not only did traditionalists within the military have to rethink their attitudes toward the press, they also had to reconsider the type of language they used in communicating with the public. In the battle of words, some technical military words, like *Menschenmaterial* (human material), had public meanings that were better avoided: "A letter to the editor points out that people often take offense at the description of troop replacements by the press as human material. The writer asks that the expression be used as sparingly as possible."[36]

Bloem describes his work with the FPS and his first meeting with Nicolai in *Das ganze, halt!* which was published in 1934 as the final volume of his trilogy of the First World War.

[Nicolai] told me that the failure of a greater success at the Verdun offensive forces High Command to prepare the German people for a provisionally undetermined duration of the conflict. To this end, High Command will need to exercise another order of psychological influence on the nation and army and with different means than have hitherto been used in the conduct of this war. . . . The area of competence for the office to be entrusted to me within the parameters of Department IIIb would be fostering the General Staff of the Field Army's ability to participate in promoting the nation's spiritual fitness to defend against the spiritual offensive being mounted by the enemy.[37]

Within the overall structure of Nicolai's information service, the FPS was assigned three areas of competency: 1) the centralization and organization of the army newspapers, 2) contact with and influence of the press at home, and 3) the discrediting of Allied propaganda, particularly in reference to the ongoing reports of alleged German atrocities in Belgium and France.[38]

The first of these tasks was the most pressing. By 1916, there were nearly two hundred army newspapers, several of them with circulations of fifty thousand (like Kippenberg's *Kriegszeitung der 4. Armee* and the *Kriegszeitung der 7. Armee*, where Philipp Witkop was an editor), and one, the *Liller Kriegszeitung*, edited by the best-selling author Paul Oscar Höcker (*An der Spitze meiner Kompagnie*, December 1914), boasted a circulation of 115,000 by November 1916.[39]

Before the FPS was assigned control over them, the newspapers had been overseen by the individual army corps or divisions, allowing some differences in the form that each assumed. Some, like the *Kriegszeitung der 4. Armee*, joined battle news with cultural feuilletons to entertain the troops. As controlling editor of Insel, Kippenberg drew upon his circle of renowned authors to fill the *Beilagen* (supplement pages) of the newspaper. Several first printings of poems and essays (as well as reprintings) by R. A. Schroeder, Hugo von Hofmannsthal, Felix Braun, Stefan Zweig, and others, were joined by inspirational quotations taken from Goethe (whom Kippenberg revered above all other German writers), Otto von Bismarck, Karl Moritz Arndt, Heinrich von Treitschke, and other cultural luminaries to underline the spiritual message of each particular issue. Other army newspapers saw their purpose as providing a forum for the troops within their units to exchange humor (sometimes quite black) and literary accounts of recent skirmishes or experiences, while still others communicated nothing more than the military news affecting their immediate area.[40]

Once Bloem took over the FPS, meetings were held with the editors of the papers to unify publishing policy in the interest of using the papers more consciously as forums to generate, for example, support for war bonds and to maintain élan in the trenches. As decreed by the Field Army's General Staff, this required a mechanism to provide the front newspapers with suitable articles and depictions from the battlefield and from home that would affect the attitude of the troops positively.[41]

Bloem further elaborated the newspapers' goals in discussions with the editors as the "awakening and satisfying" of the spiritual needs of the soldier. "They should reveal secure paths to the seekers, shore them up for the uncertain, sustain the wavering, teach the ignorant, cheer the assiduous, and lead the intellectually motivated upwards." Bloem's FPS was furthermore assigned the duty of feeding the army papers with the correspondence of numerous Berlin authorities (like the Foreign Office), but only after these reports were recast by the FPS in a form approved for the men at the front.[42] The High Command hoped this measure would be an effective step in countering the news coverage of some of the civilian (most notably the socialist newspaper, *Vorwärts*) and neutral presses among the troops.

At first, several editors of soldier newspapers resented this intrusion into their authority. The newspapers lost much of their individuality during the last two years of the war as army High Command came to perceive them as far too influential not to be better utilized and directed: "[For] with competent leadership, they seem in increasing measure capable of positively affecting the troops and working against pernicious influences."[43] Indeed, the homogenization and centralization of information, which occurred following their restructuring, became another instance of how whatever particularity had been possible for expressing *Frontgeist* within this medium prior to Patriotic Instruction became more circumscribed, even as its consolidation of a purported authentic voice from the trenches served as further material to sustain élan at home.

Bloem wrote countless essays that were subsequently circulated in the army newspapers and (in line with the second major task of the FPS, to contact and influence civilian newspapers) throughout Germany as well. He also gathered a group of writers around him whose productivity and influence swelled as the war went on. As verified by internal army opinion takers, their influence on combat troops was enormous despite soldierly access to the civilian press.

Local newspapers in Germany were happy to print these articles, which typically were introduced with the heading "It is reported by General Headquarters . . . ," perhaps implying to its readers that their newspapers had a direct line to the front. The FPS also became a clearinghouse for reports written about battlefield conditions from the perspective of the individual soldier. This activity directly bespoke a memorandum of Falkenhayn's, entitled "Chief of the General Staff of the Army in the Field and dated November 3, 1914–August 29, 1916," that the official army communiqués needed to be supplemented to preserve the "elevated mood of the German people and its participation in war events."[44]

No doubt impressed by widespread interest and the success of publishing war letters written by soldiers in the field (which I explore in the next chapter in detail), the German High Command continually encouraged soldiers to submit letters and *Erlebnisberichte* to their archives. Advertisements for such documents were regularly printed in the newspapers, and announcements on heavy cardboard were placed prominently just behind front lines. The general staff had come to realize that its initial impulse to prevent the publication of these materials until after the end of the war, when its "complete history" could be written, ignored a potentially powerful weapon to be forcefully employed in the battle for public opinion.[45] Such texts, it was argued, became attractive and useful supplements to the army communiqués once properly censored by the FPS. "Official news reporting must not stray from sparse, purely factual depiction. It must be complemented by other publications which by means of a richer and more colorful language can bring to people's consciousness the great and small successes of our men at arms."[46]

To appreciate sharply the difference of the supplemental language developed by the FPS, it is necessary to examine closely whose writing they intended to supplant: the *Kriegsberichterstatter*, professional civilian writers, and journalists who had petitioned and received permission from military authorities to write about military events from slightly behind the front. But their activity, despite great initial interest in such reports, gradually fell into disrepute. Some were criticized both in the Reichstag and among soldiers for exaggerating or distorting events. In many cases, that criticism would have been more properly directed at the censorship policies of the army and not at the individual correspondents themselves because their work in one sense reflected evolving phases of the censorship code. This is not to suggest, however, that most of these reporters constantly tested the limits established by the censorship code, for a consensus on general aims and narrative strategies united them with their censors. These individual writers would not otherwise have been given access to the front.

But despite this general consensus, military authorities still found it necessary to issue various censorship regulations. The *Kriegsberichterstatter* were, for example, expected from the beginning to refrain from any criticism of military operations in their writing and were warned "to refrain from critical observations in their publications." Similarly, the reporting of heavy German casualties was not permitted. Although the army took steps to veil its censoring—a decree of October 3, 1914, specified that the "stamp of approval applied to articles written by war reporters is not to be duplicated in print," critical readers began to realize that the correspondents' writings more frequently mirrored the perspective of the support-line strategists than that of the frontline troops.[47]

During a session of the Reichstag in which the issue of precensorship of the literary work of soldiers in the field was addressed, Ludwig Haas, a parliamentarian from Baden, cited a fatuous example of the bombastic tone used in 1915 by one of the correspondents, "a man who otherwise justly enjoys a good reputation as an author." His report read: "Württemberger troops lay opposite the French, at one stretch only thirty meters apart. At that spot, the regimental band played before an attack, and after the last sounds of the regiment's music had faded, the whole company fell in to attack." The reaction to Haas's anecdote was "amusement," as recorded by the Reichstag proceedings, and "amusement" again as Haas continued: "Now I know that the Württembergers are brave soldiers. . . . That they, however, would have their regimental band play only thirty meters away from the enemy's trenches—even the courage of the Swabians doesn't go that far."[48]

Haas expressed the common complaint that the officially sanctioned war reporters themselves never actually went near the trenches. He could furthermore point to letters he had received from soldiers in his district "which complained that the nonsense and tastelessness produced by some war reporters—certainly not all—is almost beyond endurance."[49]

The anodyne to the loss of credibility of such writings—as it seemed in January 1916—was to encourage publication of "authentic" reports that frontline soldiers had written about their own experiences: "The cooperation of the troops is indispensable. Experience speaks a powerful language. Details thereby come to the fore which elude the knowledge of more distanced individuals. Also, voices from the front ensure a welcome diversity. Since they address relatives and friends, colleagues and like-minded persons from their home environment, they continue to uphold the connection to it and thus to strengthen the patriotic spirit of all social strata."[50]

These are, as we will see, precisely the attributes—immediacy, ability to seemingly speak directly to a local, private audience, and the personalization of events—that also accompanied military support for the publication of letters written by soldiers. The same persuasive intent underlies interest in both kinds of writings. The language of experience and authenticity employed a powerful rhetoric, one that the military intended to harness effectively in efforts to overcome an acknowledged credibility gap.

The appeal of such writings lay in that nonprofessionals seemed more trust-worthy to simply "mirror" events as they experienced them, without literary artifice, particularly because they utilized a language that was anchored in everyday experience. Furthermore, different from the reports of the officially sanctioned civilian war reporters, as, for example, Ludwig Ganghofer (whose *Reise zur deutschen Front,* published in 1915 in Ullstein's war series, sold 239,786 copies), these other writings contained the promise that the author using the first-person narrative voice had indeed been in the front lines.[51]

AUTHORITY AND NARRATION

Falkenhayn's directive acknowledged the unique power invoked by such a "personalization" of events, particularly in communication with specific, smal-ler audiences, an audience that could more readily recognize itself as the in-tended readers in the letter or report written by a townsman or another peer than in the most general language of the army communiqués. But it also sought to contain that power, creating a border beyond which the appeal to authen-ticity relinquished its claim to verity in the interest of military security. The arbiter of this limit was, of course, the office of the military censor. "Where in particular the borders lie may be judged accurately solely by the censor at General Headquarters. Therefore, all reports of commandoes and troops in the fields will have to be examined prior to any kind of publication."[52] Although permitting, indeed encouraging, more individuals to write about the war and be published, and thus potentially opening the doors to criticism and inter-pretation, Falkenhayn's decree explicitly reiterated the prerogative of the OHL to write the definitive history of the war. Any accounts from the trenches published before this definitive history was finished were to limit themselves to the "rendering of personal experiences" and were ready for public consumption only after complying with the various censoring agencies. The place of "experi-ence" thus conceived was as a harnessed rhetorical effect, carried by individual voices who explicitly were not to function as autonomous authors in a tradi-tional sense. Instead, the role foreseen for their usage was to provide persuasive evidentiary support to be situated within the ideal narrative envisioned by the OHL.

The rhetoric used to explain the OHL's prerogative had first been employed in a decree in December 1914 necessitated by the frenzy unleashed when publishing houses began approaching high-ranking officers to write descrip-tions of their campaigns. According to this edict, which remained in effect into the 1920s, historical objectivity dictated that the writing of a definitive history of the war could be attempted only after all information had been collected and properly evaluated, and that only the perspective of the OHL permitted such objectivity: "Military operations cannot be viewed from the perspective of a single army but rather only from the perspective of the OHL with respect to its context and effect. Any intended publications that might perhaps awaken erroneous understandings and lead to disagreeable public discussions must await the prior completion of a summarizing account to be undertaken by this agency."[53] These decrees are crucial in considering what form the prose representations of the war, particularly before 1918, were to assume. The relation they create between authority and authorship is doubly significant: the decrees circumscribe the scope wartime publications could aspire to and simultaneously create the expectation that a work was forthcoming that would narrate the war's import with total authority. What might be written before its appearance could be assigned only contingent value. As we have seen, this framing of the war as a narrative in progress decisively affected the content (as pertinent facts) of its form.

Establishing the prerogative of the OHL to write such a total history and to censor all prior publications did not in the short term, however, solve the army's problem of how to impress its point of view most effectively on the civilian population. Neither the army communiqués nor the officially sanctioned civilian reporters were completely satisfactory means of doing so.

A secret communiqué of the information officer assigned to the Crown Prince's army corps from the summer of 1917 recounted the problem: the institution of civilian war reporters generally benefited only those newspapers that were wealthy enough to support sending their own reporters into the field. It seemed necessary, therefore, to create a supplementary reporting agency within the military. This supplementary informational service was the FPS, supervised by Walter Bloem. The agency was formed to ensure that all of Germany's readers were provided the type of information the army thought appropriate, without having to rely on civilian reporters or the spheres of influence that early-twentieth-century newspaper monopolization had created.[54] The military's policy for the dissemination of information, which accepted and worked with the major power relations to be found within the media in the summer of 1914, had hitherto allowed a virtual monopoly by several major newspapers (such as those associated with Ullstein), thus squeezing the small regional presses out of the competition for major war news.

The manner in which the civilian war correspondents were regulated by the military had also strictly limited their number permitted at the front, and none but the major newspapers were given access to these desirable posts. The presence of an official correspondent at the front not only benefited the newspapers, inasmuch as the news they conveyed guaranteed sales, but also virtually guaranteed well-paying publishing contracts for the writers—for example, Ludwig Ganghofer, Bernhard Kellermann, and Karl Rosner. Collections of their articles published in book form often reached circulations of more than 200,000 copies, particularly at the beginning of the war. But even after 1917 the books of Kellermann and Robert Michel, both published by S. Fischer, and Rosner, an editor at Cotta, to name only three, continued enjoying excellent sales.

The directives guiding Bloem's agency, by definition, put him and his subordinates in direct competition with the war correspondents of the major newspapers, and although on a personal level he sought to maintain good relationships with individual correspondents, he did not think highly of their work. They were, as shown above, limited in the types of information they could communicate in their "letters from the field of battle." But that limitation in itself was not a source of criticism. Bloem thought it proper that these journalists should be subjected to restrictions. Rather, what he found missing in their reports was a particular standpoint—namely, the perspective and stance of the fighting soldier schooled in military tactics and thoroughly familiar with the conditions in the trenches. Too often, he wrote in his diary, the newspaper accounts of the war correspondents betrayed their distance from frontline events, to speak nothing of their civilian, unmilitary private backgrounds. Although this method of reporting had worked well enough in 1870 and 1871, he wrote, "to impart to the newspaper reader a vivid, personally tinted and often almost poetically transfigured picture of war events" (Bloem refers specifically to Theodor Fontane and Hans Wachenhufen) the strategic conditions of the First World War—including the factor of speed in the deployment of men and material and in the dissemination of communication—had created new imperatives.[55]

OFFIZIER-KRIEGSBERICHTERSTATTER

To counter this deficiency and to represent the war "truly," Bloem established an agency within the FPS whose special task was to provide both the army and civilian newspapers with frontline journalism. Bloem personally selected a number of writers who had distinguished themselves with their reports for army papers or as authors of early war literature: "A push of the button, and a few days later the person contacted reported to my office in Charlesville" (152).

These specialists became known as *Offizier-Kriegsberichterstatter* (officer war reporters, OKBs), and to facilitate their work, they were given access to battlefield locations and staff strategy sessions behind the front. With them was born a new breed of war writer and a new mode of recording war itself. OKBs were first of all soldiers, and as such no strangers to the battlefield, but more important, they could be relied on to write within the parameters of the guidelines they were given, minimizing the time necessary for censorship correctives and speeding dissemination of that news throughout the Reich. Furthermore, informed of impending troop movements, they could report "on location" completely in sync with High Command strategy and were able to authenticate their representation by personal observation. To the extent that army (and later navy) High Command could know where a reportable combat situation would occur, these reporters could be deployed to record events occurring within the frame structured through this strategy.

With regard to the motivation of the military in informing the civilian population, the OKBs had made the reports of the civilian war reporters obsolete. Unfortunately, perhaps, from the perspective of the army, the newspapers still had to be cultivated, and the OHL insisted that at least the appearance of good relations be maintained with the civil correspondents and their newspapers.[56]

Each army corps was assigned its own OKB, while Bloem himself became the first officer-reporter, establishing the paradigm of representation in a number of essays by which he had gained approval for his plans. He describes his aims and the manner that the OKB reports were disseminated in his *Kriegserlebnistrilogie*. These were "special reports and descriptions of certain moods similar to those of the civilian war correspondents, except these were seen from the close-up perspective of the front and of martial life. I disseminated these reports through our correspondence channels for the army newspapers or through the channel newly created by the War Press Agency for distribution at home, or sent them directly to the leading civilian newspapers at home."[57] The reports thus continued to perform the function the OHL had assigned to the production of "mood pieces," but with them the focus had changed. Hereafter, the voice of the man fighting in the trenches was to speak to readers. As such, the reports became the authorized source giving content to *Frontgeist*.

Bloem's careful records of the reprinting of his agency's articles make it possible to reconstruct their dissemination. From January 1 to July 1, 1918, the

OKBs distributed 2,883 articles and sent 234 shorter telegrams to newspapers. In June alone, 1,941 newspaper clippings were returned to the FPS, confirming publication in various presses. Bloem's idea was so popular that during the last year of the war, even an initially reluctant admiralty established its own corps of officer–war correspondents.[58]

Bloem was not shy in giving himself credit for his splendid solution; in 1943 he wrote, "I found a solution that represents a first realization of the thought from which sprang everything later realized in the Second World War that goes by the name war reporter, propaganda company, weekly film news, etc."[59] Bloem retrospectively took pride in his service to the Third Reich for his role in providing National Socialism with the "factual" documentary material that led to the myth of a community born at the front, and also in establishing the prototype of a new kind of war reporter.[60]

To account for the recurring elements that are noticeable in all writing by Bloem's OKBs, one need turn only to the service manual authored by Bloem in 1917 that delineated the tasks and methods of his subordinates. "The task of the OKB is: to maintain and strengthen the connection between front and homeland by continuous reporting which will solidify the understanding of all for the war events and so to strengthen the uniform will for victory on the part of our people. . . . The OKB is not a war correspondent but rather a war journalist who is capable of describing the events in such a manner as is advantageous for the purposes of the General Staff. His description must be engaging and should not be addressed only to the highly educated, but particularly to the average German."[61]

Clearly then, their writing was intended to be a form of Patriotic Instruction, which by putting the best spin possible on military events would attempt to strengthen the will of the population to demand military victory. Furthermore, evident here is the military concern that civilian resolve in the *Heimat* was crumbling, as events later that year confirmed. Equally telling is the audience for whom the reports were intended and the style of communication that this intent prescribed.[62]

Bloem's service manual in essence established the paradigmatic framework for subsequent literary representations of the army's *Frontgeist* by defining seven categories of reports to be written by the officers. These included 1) articles intended for a nationwide audience about skirmishes or limited excerpts of larger battles, 2) articles intended for specifically designated regional audiences, 3) articles destined for publication abroad, 4) articles consisting of so-called tablets of honor, stressing heroic deeds of individuals with the intent of awakening pride for the achievement of heroes and the readiness for one's own sacrifices, 5) depictions of larger battles, once they were over (these reports carried the rubric "We have received word from general headquarters," implying their finality and veracity), 6) poems and novellas sent in by soldiers, and 7) depictions of battles still underway.[63]

In large part, these guidelines represented a consolidation of both the functions and guidelines developed between 1915 and 1916. The stress on the activities of localized units filled the void felt by the provincial press without their own war correspondents. No longer would the army unit singled out for praise be from only the readership areas of the major papers. The OKBs were instructed that it was "desirable to capture a local tone, such that the special peculiarities of the particular regions be given consideration in the reports." Thus, at least in the composition of war events reported in any regional press, readers from any province could feel included in the mainstream of events as part of a larger, national collective, while this representation served to further homogenize the reading public.

The seventh category was perhaps the most important addition. Hitherto, the FPS had been allowed to report on battles only once they were completed, and/or after the High Command had imposed narrative order and closure, as well as a teleology, on transpired events. But with the tactical stalemate that characterized the war on the western front in mid-1917, battles—if one could still label them as such in a traditional sense—could hardly be inscribed within a sweeping teleology. A war of attrition—the OHL's strategy with and after Verdun—lacked the spatial and geographic markers to which one could attribute beginnings and conclusions. Therefore, without necessarily having to promise imminent or complete victory, this new type of reportage depicted bigger battles that could be transmitted to the homeland immediately after or even during the battle. This provided a picture of the battle that did not yet claim total and detailed historical accuracy but that offered those at home an impression of the force and meaning of those battles that were the focus of general interest.

These "fragments" were intended to portray the spirit of the frontline troops (their *Frontgeist*) as a goal in itself in order to impress "those at home" with the heroism of its defenders and presumably, by example, to strengthen civilian resolve to match the spirit of Germany's soldiers.[64] Meanwhile, the phrase "historical exactness" left open the possibility that any of these reports as elements of a historical narrative could be reentered into a suitable teleological framework, or, for that matter, cast out, once that became possible or appropriate in light of the final total and detailed to-be-written history of the war.

A communiqué explaining the activity of the OKBs to the field officers in the "Crown Prince's Army Corps" made the first point graphically. The new task of depicting battle action, even though not suitable to confirm an imminent telos of victory, served a specific purpose, which was

> to give an image of the actual process of individual battles. Such images can provide those at home with an idea of the severity of the fighting, the merits of our leadership, the spirit of our troops, and the entire terrible and touching gravity of those actions taking place far away from home. These descriptions are intended to steel the spirit of sacrifice and brave endurance on the part of civilians who will be inspired by the example of their soldiers, constantly reminding them how tiny and ridiculous their own sacrifices in daily comfort are compared with the achievements and sacrifices of the front.[65]

The communiqué strikingly conveys the sense of antipathy that festered among the army command toward a recalcitrant *Heimat.* Such sentiments, stated so directly, as they were in letters from the field, were always censored before publication during the war as not being in the interest of domestic peace, but in the war literature of the 1920s and 1930s, the publication of this antipathy became common. The *Heimat,* seedbed of sedition, needed concerted instruction designed to instill respect for the authority of the military leadership and intended to teach the civilian population the (to-be-applied) virtues of *Frontgeist.* What matter that by the summer of 1917 food rationing had limited adult per person consumption of meat, sugar, and butter to half a pound per week, three ounces per week, and half a pound per month, respectively?[66] A spirit of total mobilization for the conduct of war informs the imperative for this sharpened focus on troops in combat as models to be learned from in a society at war.

Although a new tone of "realism" versus the "poetically transfigured language of the civilian war correspondents" was being called for, quite discernible limits circumscribed the types of situations and the kind of language allowable for the OKBs to describe the "terrible and touching gravity" of battle. The extent to which these parameters and the basic formula (outlined above) were adhered to are evident in a number of the reports, some of which will be examined here.[67] These reports written under Bloem's direction are curiously reminiscent of many of the elements in his prewar novel *Schmiede der Zukunft.*

One report, "Ein Zugführer, wie er sein soll" (A model noncommissioned officer), depicted an event that demonstrated why "Sergeant First Class of the Reserves Eichenhofer, from the town of Au near Illereichen" was a "distinctly determined and circumspective leader of special courage." Another, written by Friedrich Loofs on the occasion of King Luitpold's birthday (celebrated with free beer and extra rations for the troops), conjectured that "anyone who suffers at home because of the war would have been refreshed and convinced that no one out here is thinking of a smelly peace." Loofs, whose influential war novel *Der Hauptmann* is examined in Chapter 5, conveyed the desired intonation by ending his report in dialect: "Aber mir sannoa net firti! Es san ihrer z'vüll! Aber mir wern's scho derkraft'n! Macht nur ihr dahoam euer Sach! Sonst könnt ihr uns . . . !" (But we are not finished yet! There may be too many of them! But we will manage! You at home be sure to do your share! Otherwise you can kiss our . . . !).

The report "Bayern weisen eine Amerikanerpatrouille ab" (Bavarians rebuff an American patrol) singled out individual members of a company who had repelled American infantry "right after lunch, between 1 and 2 o'clock. The sun shone on Corporal Hartl, a leather worker from Walchshofen near Aichach, who incessantly peered over toward the enemy." Each soldier involved is introduced ("occasionally the comrades exchange words . . .") and has his profession and his hometown mentioned (Sergeant First Class Hecht, a gymnasium high school student from Munich . . . Private Krönner, a mail carrier from Landshut . . . Lotterschmid, a laborer from Oberlaufenbach near Pfaffenhofen . . ."').

Quite consciously, then, the report stages an example of *Frontgemeinschaft* in which representatives of the various classes are shown working together toward a common aim: the front appears as that place where class and occupational differences are overcome, where the third goal of Bloem's novel—the realization of a unified nation—will be realized. Furthermore, once this report was published in the local press, any reader could see that this was truly a genuine people's army, in which the everyday heroism of each individual, made stronger by his actions within a collective, mattered significantly.

Another report, "The Battle for Selenoy," written by Joachim Freiherr von der Goltz, uses the mist shrouding a battlefield to envelop the soldiers with a mythic aura, a literary technique that readers encountered again in 1934, when he wrote his best-selling war novel *Der Baum von Clery:*[68] "In the meantime, the fog lifted over a near lying elevation, and in the disappearing mist one could see several deeply staggered lines of marksmen who marched toward the summit with deliberate steps. . . . The village, gray and homely a moment ago, whose streets and alleys had appeared virtually empty among the piles of rubble, now swarmed with troops and vehicles." In this report, weather itself becomes material heightening soldierly activity as a form of *Frontmythologie*.

In another article, "Moyen," Goltz used his sighting of a field strewn with bodies as an occasion to point out what these "signs" expressed about the culture from which they originated. Even the dead cannot escape their instrumentalization by the literary war effort:

> While until now the brown tunics of the Englishmen were barely visible contrasted with the soil, now the blue-gray tails of the French coats gleamed brightly over the freshly plowed soil on both sides of the roads. Even the dead testified to the difference between the nations. Most often alone, or at most in groups of three, lie the Englishmen in the ditches. Solitude reigns in the nature of the proud islander. It is different with the Frenchmen, who crave company and are trained in skillful tactics. As is well known, the over-civilized Napoleonic epigones shy away from the shiny bayonet— one fights and dies more easily in company.

Selectively depicted, no German bodies litter this literary field, where instead the antinomies of *Kultur* versus *Zivilisation* are projected on the dead and where the death of (enemy) soldiers is placed within an organic cycle of seeding and harvesting.[69]

These examples are only a few from the hundreds written by Bloem's OKBs and subsequently disseminated throughout Germany. OKBs were explicitly instructed to ask the troops who were the subjects of their stories for names of local newspapers to which the reports should be sent, thus ensuring the most direct and effective communication of an individual soldier's *Frontgeist* to his local community.[70] This personalization of war events for specific home communities marks an additional nuanced stage of propaganda dissemination.

The reports also enjoyed a considerable afterlife during the 1920s being selectively reprinted in the hundreds of regimental histories published during the Weimar years, and in such histories sustained their "authentic" version of what the war "truly" had been like. Furthermore, among the OKBs who served under Bloem were many who continued writing about the war during the Weimar Republic and beyond, producing some of war literature's most well-received volumes.[71] Bloem's subordinates included Fritz Bubendey, Joachim Freiherr von der Goltz, the playwright Hans Fritz von Zwehl (who authored the report on the first use of tanks by the English at Cambrai; Bloem considered this report to be his agency's finest), Walter von Holländer (see his essay on *Kriegsliteratur* cited below), and Friedrich Loofs (who wrote under the pen name Armin Steinart), author of *Der Hauptmann,* published in 1916 by Cotta and considered by many cultural conservatives (like Friedrich Avenarius) to be the finest war book ever written.

Despite the many commendations he received, Bloem was not happy either with the obstacles that he perceived had been posed by the government (particularly the Foreign Ministry) or the lack of understanding of the realities of their tasks evinced by his superior, Nicolai. For Bloem, Nicolai was a "thoroughly well meaning man of comradely disposition and purest intent" who lacked a proper understanding of the methods needed in modern political propaganda, even though he fully understood their importance. According to Bloem, whose criticism would be echoed by other nationalist veterans following the war, Nicolai failed to understand that to combat Allied propaganda effectively, one needed to be equally adept at caricatures: "The methods that the enemy employed against us on the psychological level appeared to him, as they would to any decent German, unchivalrous, unsoldierlike and disgusting. But he never understood that one can counter an enemy who fights with such weapons only by employing parallel methods."[72] For Bloem, the level and tone at which Nicolai directed his coworker's efforts of persuasion was much too high, presumably unlike that expressed in Bloem's own OKB guidelines.

Bloem furthermore resented the fact that in winter 1916–1917 an area of his competency was transferred to the War Press Office of the Foreign Ministry. The rhetoric Bloem used in 1934 to condemn this curtailment of his authority is instructive both as an expansion of the perspective in which Bloem saw himself and his own activities and as a reminder of another level of institutional conflict through which his intentions are mediated. Furthermore, the structure of antinomies (front lines versus support lines) is symptomatic of much of the nationalistic war fiction of the 1930s. About the War Press Office, he proclaimed, "This creation of the war . . . had soon developed in accordance with bureaucratic self-promotion and aggrandizement into an elephantine organization which had not only its seat in Berlin, but also took its spiritual nourishment from there. Within it, there ruled not the spirit of the front lines but that of the reserve battalion. Every trench soldier knows what that will mean" (143). It is this same *Frontgeist* whose absence Bloem deplored in civilian war correspondents' reporting, and the symbolic capital attached to the concept was to be reserved only for those who had been in the trenches: "As nonsoldiers, they lacked a deep understanding of the trench soldier's nature, lacked final knowledge of leadership, comradeship, obedience, fear of death, and readiness for death" (147).

These were the virtues signified by his understanding of *Frontgeist,* and they are essentially identical to the meaning that National Socialism imposed on it.[73] But, in a sense, Bloem had not needed the First World War to define these virtues; he had already depicted them in his character Clemens Müllenseifen in *Die Schmiede der Zukunft.* As Bloem had made plain with Müllenseifen's speech to the parliament, only those who had been under fire themselves at the front could be expected to be animated by its *Geist.*

SOLDIERLY NATIONALISM

The relation among Bloem's writings before, during, and after the war demonstrates a continuity of thought linking the uses of nationalist war literature during the *Kaiserreich* and the Third Reich to shape a sense of national identity. Bloem's activities in this regard acquire character in relation to later representations of the First World War authors. When Bloem's final chronicle of his First World War experiences was published, he was still four years away from becoming a member of the National Socialist Party; but there is little in the previous quotations that he had not said and written since before 1914. What does speak through these words is an expression of what has aptly been characterized *soldatischer Nationalismus,* a view of the world that found its most celebrated expression in the writings of Ernst Jünger. While Jünger, no doubt in considerable part because of his longevity, continued a literary career as *cause célèbre,* most of the other exponents of this worldview are all but forgotten today. Yet writers like Bloem, Werner Beumelburg, Walter Flex, Franz Schauwecker, and Hans Magnus Wehner belonged to the group of authors most widely read in Germany between the wars.[74] The sales figures between the wars of Ernst Jünger's edition pale in comparison.

Although many of those who subscribed to this worldview actively placed their literary services at the disposal of the National Socialist party early on and were, after 1933, handsomely rewarded (Beumelburg, for one, became *Schriftleiter* [executive director] of the Deutsche Akademie der Künste), it needs reiteration in light of recent scholarship that the soldierly virtues extolled by *soldatischer Nationalismus* were not exclusively paraded in fascist literature. For one thing, many military authors felt bound by the code of military honor—to which they were also legally bound by the Weimar constitution—to "remain above" politics. The German slogan "political song, nasty song" applied to all manners of political organization. For another, there existed a broad sphere of antidemocratic, cultural conservatism for which National Socialism was just a little less detestable than that most hated enemy, bolshevism.[75]

Beyond the need to remember the strong discomfort toward National Socialism felt by various groups generally at the right of the political spectrum during the 1920s, it is important to consider also the extent to which the vocabulary of soldierly nationalism had entered the political and everyday language used by many groups in the 1920s. First, as with many issues—apart from Hitler's radical anti-Semitism and the drive for *Lebensraum* (living space) in the East—it is indeed extremely problematic to identify an irreducible political and cultural program that would exclusively differentiate National Socialism from some of its political rivals. Particularly in the cultural realm and regional administration, one is hard-pressed to identify policies created by National Socialism. Second, the reception of Ludwig Renn's *Krieg* and Witkop's *Kriegsbriefe,* as well as the heated debates surrounding Remarque's *All Quiet on the Western Front* by a broad spectrum of cultural journals and newspapers, indicates how widespread this language remained a decade later. Of course, the commemorative, ceremonial rituals of the various veterans' organizations of the KPD, SPD, the Catholic Center, and the Right particularly used the vocabulary that was derived from a wartime military code throughout the years of the Republic. After all, roughly 13.2 million males were mobilized at some stage during the war, and more than four years of exposure to the vocabulary and concepts described in the present study would not have vanished after November 1918. Although on average 465,600 German soldiers were killed during each war year (according to the official total of nearly 2 million), the sheer number of surviving war veterans ensured a continuing interest in defining what the experience had meant and would continue to mean. This should not be surprising. At stake, of course, in the conflicting usage of a term like *Langemarck* was the question of what it would signify and who was authorized to appropriate it.[76]

That the individuals who remained committed to a view of soldierly nationalism helped to forge a vocabulary and mythology that was eagerly subsumed by the cultural politics of the National Socialists is beyond question, even if individual authors subsequently felt betrayed by "the revolution" or, like Jünger, took steps to distance themselves from the movement once it gained power.

In the case of Walter Bloem, in his writing during the war and more critically after 1919, when he no longer felt bound by a code of silence, Bloem perceived himself as a carrier of that *Frontgeist* which he, like many other representatives of a nationalistic conservatism, felt had been betrayed while the soldiers bled in the trenches. In addition to the alienation, shown above in reference to *die Heimat,* that nationalist veterans felt toward the civilian population, the *Frontgeist* legacy includes two further salient motives embodied in Bloem's depiction. The first is an overriding contempt for the "political" arms of the imperial government. Bloem's lambasting in *Das ganze, halt!* of the handling of correspondence for the civilian press summarizes its criticism by stating that the organization was "subject to the paralyzing effects caused by consideration given to allow cooperation with the rest of the pertinent offices—the Foreign Office, the Prussian War Ministry, and all the other innumerable offices—which ought to have cooperated in the conduct of a total war of the German people but did not cooperate because the political leadership had a totally different mindset than did the military" (145).

Although *Frontgeist* as represented by Bloem involved overcoming peculiarities of class, region, and confession in the process of becoming *one* nation, the political leaders of the nation had crucially undermined the possibility of this unity. Parenthetically, this sentiment resonates with the tension already encoded in his *Schmiede der Zukunft.*

Critics writing in the vein of soldierly nationalism share with Bloem a distrust of the army's leadership behind the lines. A generational conflict between predominantly younger frontline officers and a generation of elders established at the top of the *Kaiserreich's* military hierarchy also shows itself here: "I encountered a number of extremely gifted, strong-willed personalities—but not among the actual commanders-in-chief. These, almost without exception, were overaged, usually merely ceremonial performers, providing cover for their chiefs of staff."[77]

These elements are constants in much of the war literature written before 1933 and are found not only in the literature of the Right—with different accentuation, the three elements identified above also occur in the antiwar novels associated with the Left. Remarque's *All Quiet on the Western Front,* though without the pronounced perspective of the frontline officer that informs works—for example, by Ernst Jünger—radiates generational conflict, a sense of alienation between front and *Heimat,* and a distrust of the leadership behind the front, all the while extolling the virtues of "comradeship." These not easily harmonized elements go a long way toward accounting for the ambivalent interpretations of the novel as well as its popularity. Bruno Vogel's *Es lebe der Krieg! Ein Brief,* discussed in Chapter 6, also contains all three elements, with a significant change in focus regarding the alienation between front and *Heimat.* As with Remarque's accentuation, the latter is too bloodthirsty, too distant from war's reality, to know what the words *honor* or *God intended* inevitably entail for those who suffer the meaning of these expressions on their own bodies.

Writing in 1934, Bloem's *Das ganze, halt!* offered his audience the lessons of his experience with the Office of Information. Each conclusion underlined his central assumption of the importance of maintaining a "spiritual bond between the general staff and those at home." Altogether, his lessons are an expression and affirmation of the widespread sentiment among the antidemocratic Right in Weimar that victory had not been lost on the battlefield but in the battle for public opinion on the home front: "Propaganda is one of the most important means of conducting war. Its organization for wartime must already be established during peacetime such that it can be made operational at once. Doing so requires harnessing and instructing all intellectual forces of the nation already in peace time" (160).

Bloem's remarks are, of course, first of all a polemic against specific superiors (like Nicolai) who failed to give him free reign in designing the German propaganda effort during the war. Beyond that, however, they reflect a commonly held view in military circles during the 1920s that the power of the press and propaganda more generally had not been fully exhausted during the war. Too little "guidance"—for example, censorship, incentives, cooperative publishing ventures—had been applied to specifically cultural affairs. As such, this view fits neatly into the doctrine that combatants, while valiantly fighting a two-front war, were "stabbed in the back" by the internal enemies of the Reich—the parliamentarians, the socialists, the liberal press, the Jews, and the old men who commanded them from behind the lines.[78]

Bloem's evaluation of Germany's morale and propaganda efforts may have a certain validity in characterizing a relative state of unpreparedness in August 1914, but not when viewed against the mammoth organization of "spiritual matters" by the end of the war. It is difficult to view Bloem's assessments as anything but wish-fulfilling repressions, especially in light of the massive efforts organized under the name of Patriotic Instruction: the publishing ventures supported by the Foreign Ministry, the army and other agencies, the financial support for influential publishers to print books sympathetic to the war effort, the direct and indirect forms of censorship applied to every war book (and, after 1916, retroactively to every book published since 1914), and, to mention only one more aspect, the activities coordinated with such institutions as the "Organization of German Artists and Scholars."[79]

The successes of Bloem, the Office of Information, and allied agencies were indeed considerable, though obviously not when measured against the principal goal toward which they were directed—military victory. During the war years a mechanism of oversight had been established that inhibited the generation of an antiwar literature as well as the reception of such published in other countries. No novel comparable to *Le Feu* was published in Germany during the war years, and the best-known German language pacifist works, Leonard Frank's *Der Mensch ist gut* and Andreas Latzkos's *Menschen im Krieg*, were published in Switzerland and immediately prohibited; they could reach German readers only by adventuresome means. The literature giving meaning to the war in a spirit of affirmation, by contrast, was voluminous. The fruits of that success, moreover, became apparent belatedly in the debates surrounding the lost war as a subject of history and literature in the years of the Weimar Republic. The failure of German historians during the 1920s to unveil critically the myths created and disseminated by the military during the war is matched by the lack of success of the critical war novel—with a few notable exceptions—during the last years of that decade.

Let us consider some lines of continuity that link the paradigm of iterability established by the censorship code and the literature written during the war to subsequent literary depictions of the war.[80] When hundreds of war books appeared immediately preceding and following the success of *All Quiet on the Western Front*, the overwhelming majority of them reinscribed the narrational scheme characterized here.

Among these best-selling war books, one will rarely find a depiction of what caused the war (the *Kriegsursachen*). Equally rare is a criticism of the strategic leadership of the OHL in any but the most general terms. The narrator of such fictional accounts typically limits his perspective to a depiction of the battlefield conditions in which his group of characters is involved. In the novels of "soldierly nationalism," in which this microcosmic spirit of the front is most pointedly expressed, the war is simply "there," like a law of nature, a phenomenon that recalls the censorship directive of 1914 that a soldier should limit (*beschränken*) himself to recounting personal experiences. The author can, at most, accommodate himself to (or glory in) war's necessity. Furthermore, in these novels, the war rarely ends in defeat. The condition of "being at war" simply ceases. This absence of closure bespeaks the perpetuated myths of a military that was allegedly unbeaten on the field.[81]

The regimental histories that flooded the market in the 1920s (the most expansive of which was the series "Erinnerungsblätter deutscher Regimenter," numbering two hundred volumes) are of necessity marked by the same characteristics because they relied exclusively on the official "war diaries" of individual regiments, supplemented by reports of the FPS and letters from the field (which were also circumscribed). In these accounts, the narrative strategy and rhetoric, as regulated by the wartime censorship and war book directives, returns again. A stipulation issued by the *Reichsarchiv* in February 1920 addressed to the "coworkers on the Memorial Books" established the following ground rules for using the archival material housed there for publication: "Their content is limited to excerpts from regimental war diaries which reflect in chronological order the respective place of an event, participation in combat, losses, issues regarding personnel, etc. They will abstain from any critical position taking."[82] As during the war itself, the reason given for this measure was the prerogative of the OHL (through the *Reichsarchiv*) to write the "Gesamtdarstellung des Krieges" (complete depiction of the war), a project, however, that was not finished until after the Second World War. Thus, until the collapse of the Third Reich, a linchpin of National Socialist ideology—its interpretation of what the First World War "really meant" for Germany—could cloak itself behind the "objective" authority ostensibly contained in these works.

One notable war book published during the Weimar Republic attempted to draw conclusions from the situation described here. In *Heeresbericht* (Army communiqué), published in 1930, Edlef Köppen found a narrative strategy that presupposed the by then well-developed and acrimonious public debate regarding the war's meaning. The novel above all centers on the question of the givenness of historical certainty by focusing on the mediation and construction that had bequeathed this particular war legacy. What is ultimately at stake in the novel is how memory is collectively organized, disseminated, and received in the public sphere.

Köppen pursues this question by framing three levels of narration. On one level, like *All Quiet on the Western Front*, it employs a first-person narrator recording the personalized front experience of its main character, Adolf Reisiger. On another level, the narrator ironically distances himself from and comments on the wartime experience of his protagonist. This narrator is clearly reflecting on those wartime experiences from a later (post-1918) temporal perspective. Finally, the work's omniscient narrator analyzes the institutional forces that had shaped public knowledge and memory about the war—that is, its history—presented as material for reflection to a contemporary audience whose capacity to judge the war's meaning assumes it is reading yet another novel about the war during the waning years of the Weimar Republic.

By the time *Heeresbericht* appeared, the literary marketplace had been inundated by nationalist prose reacting to the success of Remarque's novel. Critics of that work had railed against it by appealing to an aesthetic of immediacy and authenticity that Remarque's novel was accused of violating. In addition to privileging the frontline combat zone, this aesthetic also insists on the primacy and ontological givenness of the war experience, as it "really is," and contrasts the experience "itself" with the belated reconstructions of primary impressions undertaken by "Literaten" such as Remarque. Köppen's three-leveled narrative strategy becomes meaningful in the context of this aesthetic-political debate. His use of dialectical and montage techniques testifies to his familiarity with the literary implications of radio and cinema, but, as importantly, he was able to utilize previously confidential source material housed by the German national archives, and he weaves this material together with contemporary edicts, proclamations, and the official army communiqués lending the novel its title.[83] The model experience of the protagonist is thereby juxtaposed with the larger context of a nation at war, including the conflictual perspectives of civilians, combatants, and the High Command.

Köppen's strategy of deconstruction is signaled on the novel's first page in a quotation of the edict from March 1915 that prohibited statements by people who "by reason of their occupation and lack of experience could not possibly be in a position to take comprehensive views." We have seen how the right of authorship on war matters was reserved for proper authority by this "comprehensive view," moreover, the place of "authentic" and "spontaneous" reports in the narration of a nation prescripted by its institutional "authors." Köppen's *Heeresbericht* uses wartime documents and letters not (as with nationalist fiction) to provide an aura of authenticity for his book but as critical commentary on how public opinion had been manipulated. The presentation of the facts in the novel are generally accompanied—within the third narrative frame—by a reference to the mediation that produced them. At all times, but particularly where montage juxtaposes levels of memory, the reader finds that public perception as well as individual memory of the war are the products of a continuing mediation between "event" and its historicizing narration.

Having judged the wisdom disseminated by professional historians as largely abetting the enemies of democracy and the Republic, Köppen's narrative strategy therefore entailed exploding the objectivist mask of this institutionally constructed truth, opposing it with a technique of montage intended to reveal history's selective omissions and distortions. The sinking of the *Lusitania,* for example, is presented with three accounts of the event: a rendition from the (censored) press, an official military communiqué on the event, and finally, an advertisement for a popular vaudeville act that toured Germany performing the event. In a later section, a chauvinistic proclamation signed by two hundred German university professors in 1914 is quoted in full, reminding readers of the role of the university system in actively encouraging student volunteers like Reisiger and commenting generally on the apologetic role of the social and other sciences in legitimating governmental policy. Another example is that military edicts proclaiming the need for enlisted men to maintain an iron will and spirit of sacrifice are montaged within the text with a reprinting of a lavish menu from an upper-class New Year's Eve supper in Berlin. Additionally, the mythology of collective unity and soldierly comradeship evidenced in wartime documents is juxtaposed to a polar perspectivism contrasting the optic of the trench soldier with the "comprehensive view" of the High Command. An event that for one is a matter of personally felt horror and shock is for the other an abstract question of military science and mathematical planning. Finally, instead of the united voice of the nation speaking as one, *Heeresbericht* shows as many "wars" as there are characters in the novel. One vainglorious officer views war as a means of gaining the Iron Cross. For another, the front provides a convenient escape from domestic life, and for yet another, it is a matter of mere survival.

Given both the fragmentation of perspective unraveled by the novel and its epistemological questioning of knowledge about the war, it ends as it must, with Reisiger's transport to an insane asylum. His *Bildungsgang* ends with the declaration that war "is the most horrific crime that I know of"—of that alone he is certain. His refusal to continue killing in the name of a higher collective meaning underlines his rejection of the false harmonies of recorded history, of history's proclivity to embue nonsense with affirmative national meaning.

Köppen's democratic montage asks for a reader who will interact with the text, who will critically distance himself from a (now so understood) constructed experience and memory of the war. Regrettably, only ten thousand copies of the book were sold before it was banned two years later, despite being warmly praised by the Left liberal press. A review by Axel Eggebrecht, published in *Tagebuch,* resonates today with the stakes of this nonreception: "How little hope can one extend to the near future of a mankind for whom such a book comes too late, is no longer in fashion, a little-considered straggler. Sometime in the future, however, it might experience its great chance. After the next world war, namely. Astonished and shocked people will read there how much we know and how little we wanted to know."[84]

The novel's afterword, a statistical numbering of this war's casualties, represents the outcome of those wartime activities and events that I have narrated in the preceding pages. *Heeresbericht* contradicts the view that war is an essentially natural, or at least unavoidable, stage of social development. As its narrator stresses, wars, like accounts of them, are constructed. Köppen himself died in 1938, a consequence of a collapsed lung he had suffered in the trenches.[85]

The reverberations of what can rightfully be considered a "hindered debate" reverberated again during the so-called Fischer controversy, and since then, whenever that controversy is a marker for subsequent related ones.[86] As I have also suggested, this hindered debate had significant consequences for public and literary discourse after Germany's surrender in 1918.

Chapter 3 The Use and Abuse
of *Feldpostbriefe* for
Cultural Life

Letters of soldiers at the front were powerful instruments of self-expression and, simultaneously, public representation. In this chapter I examine the forces that fostered the value that was attached to the genre of *Feldpostbriefe* (letters from the field) viewed in the context of the military's efforts to collect and preserve "authentic" materials for its depiction of the war. The form and content of the literature disseminated during the war is considered in conjunction with the role of war letters in subsequent war commemoration during the Weimar period and after 1933.

As in the previous chapter, a particular "author," Philipp Witkop, looms large in my discussion of the genre, although I will likewise view his authorship in an inter-institutional sense. Witkop was a prominent Germanist, virtually forgotten today, who between 1916 and 1933 published several editions of the student letters he was authorized to collect. The various versions of his anthology played significant roles in each of the three principal periods in which war literature was published and received, and I examine each period to describe the shifting constellation in which the volumes participated. Like Walter

Bloem, Witkop "went to war" with an aesthetic that influenced his editorial decisions. I therefore examine his other works and the aesthetic that informs them in relation to the war letters. As with my discussion of Bloem, I refer first to the expectations for their dissemination and to the prewar context that informed their collection.

PRESERVING *DIE GROßE ZEIT*

Against the backdrop of sparse official information, letters written by individual soldiers to family, friends, and acquaintances were a crucial source of information and communication between those at the front and those at home. Almost immediately, most major German newspapers began publishing letters from soldiers that had been forwarded to them by private correspondents. Even before the first volumes of what became multivolume war series were published, these letters were eagerly disseminated sources of information. By October 1914, one-quarter of a newspaper's space might be filled with *Feldpostbriefe*.[1] Such letters were quoted often at civic functions in the Reichstag and also read aloud and discussed in classrooms during the war.[2]

These letters appeared in newspapers and were subjected to censorship regulations, although the absence of unified enforcement (particularly during the first year of the war) caused discrepancies in the types of information considered objectionable. Often, though, it was precisely the publication of a particularly revealing letter that became the cause instigating further censorship regulations.[3] Nonetheless, it proved impossible for the military to foresee and regulate every objectionable statement (despite the ongoing revisions of the blue book), particularly because shifts in the strategic or political spheres would belatedly affect what was deemed publishable and what was not.[4]

Even before August 1914, a well-organized structure for collecting letters from the field from previous wars had been established in Prussia through the cooperation of policy, academic, and administrative agencies. In 1911–1912, a committee headed by privy councillor Dr. Ubisch, which included the historian and later minister Hans Delbrück, required that the Prussian Ministry of Culture collect letters and diaries from previous "wartimes" before such documents were lost. The committee's appeal reflected the development in historiographical thinking that was predisposed to extend the borders of subject matter viewed as suitable for writing history: "Is it possible today to know exactly what most deeply moved and motivated our people despite the seemingly abundant source materials of newspaper reports, copies of letters, war testimonies, and other remembrances?"[5]

Ubisch's committee promised answers to such questions from letters "that contain the innermost thoughts and feelings of the people as a whole," written "without consideration for publication." The committee's appeal expressed the hope of (re)discovering (and "scientifically" grounding) the "authentic" history of the German people at war on the basis of these "spontaneous" expressions of the "mood of our people."[6]

Twelve libraries in Prussia and the Rhineland were established as collection centers. Correspondence from Minister of Culture and Education Naumann to each district president communicated local guidelines. Naumann's instructions were directed to every community and thereafter to every organization that might have veterans as members. Lists reaching back to 1848 of surviving veterans were compiled, whereupon requests for material were conveyed. In addition, announcements were published regularly in local newspapers to promote continued interest in this project.

With the declaration of war in the summer of 1914, civil and military agencies were able to build upon this recognition of the value and potential usage of war letters. In the early months of the war, public and private organizations intent on collecting *Feldpostbriefe,* soldier newspapers, and other war memorabilia mushroomed throughout Germany.[7] The *Kriegsministerium* in Berlin (and thereafter the regional war ministers) kept a close eye on the competitive market for material that developed among academic, army corps, and private institutions. The ministry's primary interest was to ensure control over the material for a later writing of the history of *die große Zeit,* as the war was touted by September 1914 in official communiqués and newspapers. Soldiers were encouraged to make copies of their letters and other writings to be deposited in the Library of the General Staff.

Publishers solicited such materials in newspaper announcements and with posterboards displayed at the front. The Ninth Army Corps, for example, posted announcements informing the troops that its Lieutenant Lorenz had been assigned to collect such texts "to prepare the project of writing the history of the present war by editing war letters, diaries, and other memorabilia of war participants of all ranks and educational levels. He who has special experiences to relate is herewith urged to write down his memories so they can be preserved by the General Staff. Everything is to be reported honestly and nothing needs to be concealed (as is the case with the newspapers)."[8] Thus all soldiers, regardless of rank or education, were invited to participate in this commemoration by

Kriegs-Karte der „Lustigen Blätter" Nr. 1.

Der erste Soldatenbrief.

Kinder, so fing's damals an,   Wie ich euch versichern kann:
Und so weiter und so weiter!   „König Wilhelm ist ganz heiter!"

Fig. 3.1 Early wartime postcard, titled "The First Soldier Letter," recalling similar letter-writing activity during the Franco-Prussian War, thereby linking the two generations of German soldiers.

contributing accounts of unique experiences. The communiqué's reference to newspaper censorship indicates that its operation was not assumed to have escaped the attention of potential contributors.

At first, the use of *Feldpostbriefe* for war depictions in books and newspapers was liberally supported by the war ministry. Letters with the "right" spirit were seen as a useful supplement to the reports of civilian war correspondents or the *Heeresbericht*. But by December 1915 the government had decided that sterner measures than prepublication censorship were needed to prevent possible "misuse" of letters; by then, many letters were found to be lacking in the "Juli-Geist" that pervaded the early letters that had been published in newspapers and anthologies. The Prussian War Ministry informed the Interior Ministry "that it has become necessary to place the deputy of the General Staff exclusively in charge of collecting letters from the field and other sketches by war participants because of the serious potential harm to important military interests these documents might cause if they became public."[9]

By mid-1916, however, there were legal complaints by other organizations who objected to the ministry's demand that their materials be handed over to the army library. These complaints caused a policy reformulation that permit-

Berichte über den Krieg.

Vom stellvertretenden Generalkommando des IX. Armeekorps in Altona ist Oberleutnant **Lorenz** beauftragt worden, die Geschichtschreibung des gegenwärtigen Krieges durch Bearbeitung von Feldpostbriefen, Tagebüchern und sonstigen Denkwürdigkeiten von Kriegsteilnehmern aller Dienstgrade und Bildungsstufen vorzubereiten.

Wer besondere Erlebnisse zu erzählen hat, wird hierdurch aufgefordert, seine Erinnerungen niederzuschreiben, damit sie im Generalstabswerk aufbewahrt bleiben.

Es ist alles wahrheitsgetreu zu berichten und nichts braucht, wie in den Zeitungen, verheimlicht zu werden.

Die Aufzeichnungen müssen mit Angabe des Namens und Truppenteils auf losen Blättern, die nur auf einer Seite beschrieben sind, im Geschäftszimmer eingereicht werden.

Der Inhalt der Mitteilungen wird als Vertrauenssache behandelt und nicht eher dem Großen Generalstab zur Verfügung gestellt, bis die Krieger oder ihre Angehörigen es erlaubt haben.

Der Name bleibt ungenannt.

Altona, den 29. Dezember 1914.

Stellvertretendes Generalkommando
IX. Armeekorps.

Fig. 3.2 Appeal posted on heavy cardboard asking soldiers "of all ranks and educational levels" assigned to the Ninth Army Corps to submit "letters from the field, diaries, and other memorabilia" as contributions "for the writing of the history of the current war." The appeal notes that "everything is to be reported truthfully and need not be kept secret as in the newspapers." Kriegsarchiv, Stuttgart.

ted nonmilitary institutions to maintain and continue their collections. To vitiate the danger that unreliable persons ("whose collecting activity gives sufficient reason for suspicion that it endangers or might endanger military security") might use the rhetorical power of the *Feldpostbriefe* to "misrepresent" the war, however, the Ministry empowered local army corps to impound such collections. The decree continues, "The unwanted but legally unpreventable fragmentation of these writings, as well as the worrisome loss of *Stoff* (material) valuable for war-historical and other imaginable contexts, can thereby perhaps be prevented (and redirected)."[10]

At the same time, because of the "particular value that the General Staff accords to the collection of such writings for the history of the great war," all army agencies were directed to intensify efforts to encourage writers of *Feldpostbriefe* "from the widest circles of the population" to donate their letters to military agencies.[11] These guidelines remained in effect through the war's end, and regular ministry directives and advertisements in soldier and civilian newspapers continued to appeal for letter donations.

WAR LETTERS BETWEEN FRONT AND *HEIMAT*

Publishing firms quickly recognized the marketability of *Feldpostbriefe* and began compiling and printing anthologies of such letters. This was by no means a radical change in publishing strategy. Collections of personal letters had become an important staple of literary publication in the eighteenth and nineteenth centuries. "The nineteenth century," writes Fritz Schlawe in his monumental compendium *Die Briefsammlungen des 19. Jahrhunderts: 1815– 1915,* "is the florescence of epistolary literature." Not surprisingly, Schlawe ends "his" nineteenth century in the midst of the First World War, which countless contemporaries would belatedly see as the beginning of a new age. For Schlawe, this beginning was evident in the significance that letters had lost since the previous age was ended. "The present has no idea about the importance that letters played in the past. . . . Letters, that is, as *the* medium of human communication."[12]

Technological innovations and extensions serving the war effort, such as the radio and the telephone, caused letter writing—to extend Schlawe's organic metaphor—to lose its bloom in the public realm. But the importance attributed to letter writing between 1914 and 1918 attests to a reading public that went to war schooled in this eighteenth- and nineteenth-century tradition.

An inestimable number of war letters were written between August 1914 and November 1918. The massive outpouring of verse that Julius Bab remarked on at the war's outset—approximately 50,000 poems per day during the first months—is completely overshadowed by the number of *Feldpostbriefe* written during that period. The number reproduced in the numerous war letter anthologies is quite small in comparison. Regrettably, only limited evidence remains of the intensified collection efforts undertaken by state and military agencies, private individuals, and the recipients of letters themselves. In the interwar period, however, the archival preservation of these collections (principally in the Reich archive) lent authority to the editions of letters actually published because of the archival promise of completeness. The largest such holdings apparently were destroyed by bombing in the Second World War. Today, only a fraction of the wartime collections can be found in archives.[13]

Letters published during or after the war, however, remain numerous. Apart from their ubiquitous appearance in daily newspapers and in various journals, at least fifty anthologies were published in Germany during the war, several dozen volumes more were published by individual letter writers, and another dozen anthologies appeared in the two decades following the armistice. In addition to anthologies, individuals used the epistolary form to compile an impression of war events. For example, Paul Oscar Höcker's *An der Spitze meiner Kompagnie,* which inaugurated "Ullsteins Kriegsserie" and sold 400,000 copies by the end of the war, originated as a series of self-contained *Feldpostbriefe* written for the *Berliner Lokal-Anzeiger* before being printed in book form in December 1914.[14]

Some anthologies of war letters were compilations of previously printed letters, as, for example, *Hundert Briefe aus dem Felde: Der große Krieg* 1914–15 *in Feldpostbriefen,* three volumes edited by Hans Leitzen, and *Von Flandern bis Polen: Feldpostbriefe der täglichen Rundschau aus dem Weltkriege.* Other volumes were compiled from the collections of professional associations, such as *Lehrerbriefe aus dem Felde.* The German education ministries of various states promoted the publication of several collections, including *Das Erlebnis unserer Jungen Kriegsfreiwilligen: Nach Feldpostbriefen,* edited by Willi Warstad, an aesthetician of photography. Confessional organizations also published collections of "their" soldiers' letters. The noted theologian Georg Pfeilschifter edited three volumes of *Feldbriefe katholischer Soldaten,* and Eugene Tannenbaum and Adolf Plessner were the first to edit volumes of letters written by Jewish soldiers, in *Kriegsbriefe deutscher und österreichischer Juden* and *Jüdische Feldpostbriefe aus dem großen Weltkrieg.* Finally, numerous collections of letters written by individuals, like Walter Heymann's *Kriegsgedichte und Feldpostbriefe* or Friedrich Witte's *Kriegsbriefe eines deutschen Studenten,* appeared during the war years and were followed thereafter by others.

In an era in which *media* still referred primarily to the written or printed word, at a time when public discussion of war aims and tactics was forbidden by law (until 1917), *Feldpostbriefe* were the prime sources of information for the public about the war. These letters consequently were important in framing the tone and structure of literary representations of the war in the following two decades.

Hermann Hesse, himself using the form of the *Feldpostbrief*—and reversing the roles of addresser and addressee—pointed to the significance of these letters in his aptly titled *Brief ins Feld:* "In the beginning, your life out there was so unknown, strange and uncanny to us. Since then, we have heard a great deal about that life, the best of it from your letters." Walter von Holländer, in "The Development of War Literature" in *Die neue Rundschau,* wrote that in the first year of the war the *Feldpostbrief* was the dominant and most appropriate form of literature, before being supplemented by the essay: "The war needed to become recognizable in its exterior forms. The language of war needed to be taught to all noncombatants. *Feldpostbriefe* were the appropriate dictionary."[15]

The preface to the first book of what became a ten-volume series of letters published by Georg Müller, *Der deutsche Krieg in Feldpostbriefen* (The German war in letters from the field), is relevant to many of the early anthologies. Describing the collection, General Imhoff, the volume's military adviser, used language that was echoed by numerous commentators: "The terse official news probably said much too little to many people. . . . All the more anxiously, families waited at home, and received the news from the battlefield that brought news of life out in the distance." Imhoff thus invoked the privileged status of the letters within the general dearth of information. The general then cast the special power of these letters in a heroic mold: "Thus for the duration of the war, letters are the only means to stoke that warlike fire which by itself has kept alive and will keep alive shining examples and actions."[16]

Published war letters sensualized and personalized the war. Sanctioned by the communicative, public purpose superimposed on them, these letters bespoke the public's desire for "true" and "authentic" accounts portraying soldierly existence and battles, and also the military's direction of such interest.

Although the official army communiqué utilized language stylized to invoke an oblique, epic perspective, the letters provided immediacy in perspective through an individualization of events. The subject (or hero) of the army communiqué was a supraindividual entity—"the German army"—encompassing millions, whose activities were nonetheless described to suggest a uniform volition. The primary subject of the letters, on the other hand, was generally an individual describing events that he himself had experienced. Author and narrator converged in these letters, creating the impression of immediacy and authenticity that made them so dramatic for their readers. The attributes "authentic," "immediate," and "true" subsequently became extremely important in debates in the 1930s over the presentation of the war, and often these collections were held up as carriers of the true spirit of the trenches over and against the "merely" fictional treatments by novelists.

CENSORSHIP AND AUTHENTICITY

From the beginning of the war, then, these letters were sanctioned and thus presented by numerous editors as the realm of the "subjective" voice of individ-

ual soldiers: a medium in which the individual could "divulge" his thoughts—
as long as they fell within the boundaries of censorship regulations and met the
intention of the anthologizing collector.

Specific censorship regulations clearly framed the limits of publishable material,
creating a sieve that most successful letter publishers—if not many letter writers—
internalized. Forbidden topics for published collections included certain weapons,
some types of violence, manner and place of death, and political beliefs.

Four examples of these regulations suggest how concretely censorship policy
affected the parameters of literary representation during the war. By October
23, 1914, the army censor was forced to address the problem of how to represent
depictions of battles:

> In many *Feldpostbriefen* that have been submitted to Deputy General Command for
> censoring, there are to be found more or less drastic depictions of the horrors of combat.
> Even if these reports do on the whole bespeak the facts, it nevertheless does not seem
> desirable to publish them with all their upsetting details, because the fears and cares of
> those left behind, especially wives and mothers, are only further elevated. Therefore,
> until further notice, the Deputy General Command requests editors to suppress such
> depictions in the letters they receive even prior to submitting them to the censor.[17]

This decree is remarkable for many reasons. It explicitly differentiates between
facticity and its effects on a reading audience. Thus, the presumed effect of a
description on the public rather than its veracity was to determine its suitability
for public consumption. This is noteworthy because army directives most often
indicated that the primary reason for censorship was to gain historical objectivity by avoiding the "premature" release of certain types of information. But
now the authorities were acknowledging that censorship was needed for more
immediate reasons—the depiction of violence and death, particularly when
presented in the first-person narrative of the *Feldpostbrief,* was unsuitable for a
home audience. That an unaware civilian population, depicted as being on the
verge of hysteria, should be personified by women in this decree is also telling in
regard to the gendering of war zones, discussed in Chapter 1. Equally telling, in
light of subsequent comments by Hitler and others cited in Chapters 1 and 2, is
the likely concern that letters from home communicating such sentiments
potentially diminished the heroism of the warrior.[18] Further, the decree points
to the self-censorship that the censor expected individual publishers to practice.
Freud's contemporaneous observation that individual and social censorship
occurred "in order to prevent the development of fear or other forms of painful
affect" aptly described the situation.[19]

Fig. 3.3 Advertisement for Beyer ink, targeted to writers and recipients of soldier letters.

After January 23, 1915, editors were informed that they were not allowed to print references to the new "close-combat weapons" or to the physical effects of such weapons, and they were asked again to practice self-censorship. These weapons were specified as "mine-throwers, hand grenades, rifle grenades, incendiary mines, flamethrowers, etc. The editors are requested to erase all such references in those letters they intend to submit for censorship."

Following the tacit truces that evolved on many sections of the western front between Christmas and New Year's Day, 1914–1915, "reports of scenes of fraternization between friend and enemy in the trenches" found their way into newspapers via *Feldpostbriefe*, yet soon enough the censors forbade such reports (January 28, 1915). Although these scenes recurred, no mention of them was allowed to be printed in descriptions of the Christmas seasons that followed during the war. To this day, such fraternization is generally thought to have occurred during only that first holiday season, testimony to the lingering effectiveness of such censorship.

As of February 23, 1915, it was forbidden to list the geographical location where a soldier had been killed: "Even general information, such as in the Argonne region, is prohibited. In such a case what may be said is only that the person has fallen on the field of honor for the Fatherland, or some such language. Mention of a geographical location is to be omitted." Specificity of place was thereby transformed into the place of abstract euphemism, the field of honor.

Thus by mid-1915 these four censorship decrees ensured that one could not publish a letter describing a soldier who fraternized with the enemy, was subsequently attacked with a close-combat weapon, then died in a geographically identified terrain of French mud—unless the regional censor granted special permission. Of course, this exemplification applies only to *published* letters. As with other aspects of cultural mobilization, a full-blown policy and apparatus for more efficient censorship did not exist in August 1914. During the war, particularly after Erich Ludendorff and Paul von Hindenburg assumed command in 1916, this mechanism became increasingly extensive, but even so, the pure volume of mail hampered efficiency. Nonetheless, fear of being "caught" was a further inducement to practice self-censorship, even for letters written with no thought of publication.[20]

Quite explicit, on the other hand, was the imperative to reduce the violence depicted in all wartime publications—and not only in *Feldpostbriefe*. Even well-intended portrayals of battlefield violence in literary depictions were of great concern to the censors, as will become evident in my later comparison of the galleys and the final print copy of Friedrich Loofs's *Der Hauptmann,* the novel that many conservative intellectuals considered the finest one written during the war. Self-censorship, however, whether due to the demand for voices expressive of "silent heroism" or out of fear of reprisal from letter control, is equally an issue in considering the content and tone of letters mailed from the front.

For many wartime editors, creating an anthology of war letters was conceived as a matter of finding representations of the objective universal, inscribed paradigmatically in the language of the army communiqués. Prefaces to virtually every anthology address the (unstated) question of the grounds for the collection's representativeness. Many anthologizers represented their efforts as the attempt to reveal and discover the fusion of the singular and the universal in their letter selections.

For General Imhoff, heroism was the universal to be individualized. Although attributed constitutively to the entire German army, soldiers individualized heroism in recounting their exploits: "The people want to see their heroes."[21] In a culture whose normative values at war's outbreak were firmly rooted in a heroic ideal, personified models of heroic conduct were essential, more so because the heroic was characterized by its aristocratic individualism. The hero, while acting for the good of the community, did so as an individual. Traditionally, the hero had been represented as the purest member of his people, as a man (rarely a woman) of action, a performer of great deeds, a confronter of the unknown, someone who redeems his people through his actions or death.[22]

Seeing the need for heroes, and in compliance with the Kaiser's decree to compile accounts of heroic deeds for broad dissemination, the Thirteenth Army Corps in Württemberg began keeping files of *Heldentaten* (heroic deeds) in 1915. Officers at the front were asked to submit the names of candidates who had exhibited meritorious valor. Individual cards listed a soldier's name, religion, unit, heroic deed, and medals awarded. These cards provided the material for reports and letters published again in local newspapers.[23] After the war, many of these *Heldentaten,* along with *Feldpostbriefe* collected during the war, were published in the regimental histories that began appearing in the early 1920s.[24]

The army communiqués, whose epic tone suggested a people united by a single volition, necessarily overwhelmed individuality and the hero.[25] Anthologies of war letters provided individualistic answers to the questions, "How does a hero act?" and, by inference, "How should I act?"

Stated in language outside the heroic metaphor, most of these published letters used first-person narration to perpetuate the illusion that the single individual could influence the outcome of the war and should not be viewed as a passive victim of war technology or tactics commensurate with a war of attrition. German heroism offered proof of cultural superiority in spite of the massive technology arrayed against the "encircled" German nation. The imperial army, moreover, extended the social parameters of the heroic to make it a nationwide attribute. Although being awarded an Iron Cross first class remained largely the prerogative of officers, common soldiers were honored and named as recipients of the Iron Cross second class as evidence that all Germans, regardless of social differences, were united in a common purpose.

In his preface, General Imhoff conveys his belief in a heroic worldview in which loyalty, bravery, and self-sacrifice figure prominently, and discusses the process involved in memorializing these virtues for ensuing generations. He ties this commemorative function of the anthology to a pedagogical mission: "The duty of us all is to instruct our youth in this thought [heroism] and to vaccinate them with the idea that Germany can and will assert its proper place forever only because of these characteristics realized by the combatants fighting in the war."[26]

PHILIPP WITKOP

Philipp Witkop, professor of modern literature at the Albert-Ludwigs University in Freiburg, was the editor of the most significant collection of wartime letters. He felt as strongly as Imhoff did that such letters were destined to play an important pedagogical and cultural role. Witkop's activities reveal the discipline of literary criticism as another component of the interinstitutional setting out of which war literature emerges. The optic through which Witkop wrote about and anthologized the war reflects this disciplinary site.

In 1914, Witkop began collecting letters written by students at the front. The collection and editing of these letters was a twenty-year project that resulted in the publication of four distinctly different anthologies, published in 1916, 1918, 1928, and 1933. Though Witkop completed numerous other projects between 1916 and 1942 (the year of his death), he returned to these collections again and again. His anthologies in turn garnered him his greatest critical acclaim in scholarly and popular journals. His anthologies made Witkop probably the most influential constructor of a public view of the student *Kriegsfreiwilliger* (student volunteer), which became one of the most popular and evocative symbol legacies of the war.

The genealogy of Witkop's anthologies illustrates the constellation of conditions and expectations that governed the publication and dissemination of war literature between 1914 and 1935. A study of the evolution, reception, and subsequent influences exercised by Witkop's volumes provides a paradigm for analyzing other war literature. Journal and newspaper reviews, private correspondence reacting to the war letters, and correspondence with publishers, as well as the use of these letters in other forms of commemoration, are important in addressing how this type of war literature interacted with other cultural forces of the period and, more specifically, what need and meaning Witkop's anthologies fulfilled between the wars. Furthermore, an analysis of Witkop's project illustrates the process by which textual knowledge about the war was formed and rewritten, a process that links power and language as discourse to an academic discipline's institution of a literary genre.[27]

Witkop's anthologies mark the evolution of a genre that emerged from the

First World War, solidified during the Weimar period, and entered the canon of national literature in the 1930s. Because of the enthusiasm for Witkop's 1928 collection, every subsequent comparable anthology measured itself against it. The genre was perpetuated during and in the wake of the next war, with due reverence for Witkop's founding efforts. Since then, groups of individual letters from Witkop's collection have resurfaced in various guises, sometimes joining letters from the Second World War in postwar commemorative books.[28]

Philipp Witkop affected the store of knowledge about the First World War in three capacities: as the anthologizer of student war letters, as a professor of modern literature, and as an editor of a soldier newspaper. Witkop's aesthetic position and its related political stance should not be viewed solely as a matter of personal predilection, but with reference to the institutional limits that constrained and enabled this important neoromantic strain of thinking.

Academic Career

Witkop's biography, even as encapsulated by contemporary compendium accounts, is characteristic of German academic and intellectual history. He achieved some prominence in public life, enjoying the accolades that accompanied the position of professor. His short biographical sketch appeared in volumes 5–10 of the German version of *Who's Who,* spanning the years 1911 through 1935, the final year of publication. *Kürschners gelehrten Kalender* likewise gives Witkop's biography and a listing of his works—the most extensive list in the 1928 edition, updated in the *Gelehrten Kalender* 1935. Such encyclopedias as *Meyers Lexikon, Der grosse Brockhaus,* and *Der grosse Herder* included Witkop and his works during the 1930s; the last also included Witkop in its first postwar edition, in 1952. Witkop's international profile is evident from his inclusion in the *International Who's Who* until 1942, the year of his death.

Witkop was born in 1880, and as a young man at the turn of the century he was involved in the Munich circles that included Thomas Mann, Michael Conrad, Carl Muth, and the young Arthur Kutscher.[29] His first publications were of his poetry. Significantly, his first academic degree was in political economy, before he earned a doctorate of philosophy. His first published work was his dissertation, *Die Organisation der Arbeiterbildung* (the organization of worker education), 1903, which addressed the "social question" from the perspective of education.[30] He offered an overview and comprehensive plan to organize *Volksbildung* (popular education) in the form of libraries, reading halls, and adult public schools.

In this study, whose thesis resurfaced in his wartime activities, Witkop expressed the topical view that *the* social issue must be solved before Germany could realize its national potential: "Only through a general uplifting of workers' education (*Arbeiterbildung*) will we achieve that national unity which is the basis of every free state, which in turn is the guarantor of Germany's future." But the goal he envisioned betrays no self-consciousness in separating *Bildung* from bourgeois conceptions of it. Nowhere does he consider that his notion of *Bildung* might itself be ideology. The language of an idealistic *Aufklärung* (enlightenment) pervades his analysis of the issue in bluntly phrased antinomies: "The goal of the social question is to help the working man reach an existence worthy of human dignity. What else does this mean but to elevate him to a state of conscious existence; to lift him from a condition of dullness and animal urges toward a clear, conscious way of life that would enable his full participation in the achievements of human culture and education?"[31]

A paternal sense of noblesse oblige, common to the idealism associated with the youth movement and the Carl Muth *Hochland* circle, permeates Witkop's program. These sentiments reveal an attitude that agitated during the war for the promotion of reading and self-education facilities at the front and glorified the concept of comradeship as the vehicle through which class barriers would be resolved. The war appeared to some as a powerful opportunity to raise the level of *Bildung* in the nation, a kind of *Volkshochschule* (people's educational facility) where students and workers, members of lower and middle classes would overcome class differences and presumably socialism as well.[32]

Witkop affirmed this hope in 1917, writing about Walter Heymann and war poetry. The war had in his view created a new task for poetry and the poet that bespoke a reawakened collective sense of aesthetic and social wholeness caused by the events of July and August 1914:

> Just as it seemed that the German people had disintegrated socially and politically into classes and parties who no longer understood one another, so too had they seemingly become chasmatically separated in the realms of art and poetry. . . . The differences between education levels, which had precipitously accelerated since the epoch of humanism, appeared to have hardened into harsh, unbridgeable oppositions. But just as the days of mobilization proved that these political separations were not really so antagonistic or alien to each other, so too did it happen in the realm of poetry, as surface appearance gave way to recognition of a deeper common ground that had been made visible.[33]

Many of the means that Witkop had suggested in organizing the *Arbeiterbildung* were extensively adapted to frontline conditions, a project that Witkop himself was actively involved in. Furthermore, Witkop amplifies both the notion of war as a *Bildungsstätte* (site of education) and the concept of comradeship by letters included in his first anthology, marking a continuity of ideas throughout his career.

Witkop became a Lecturer (*Privatdozent*) at the University of Heidelberg in 1909 and associate visiting professor at Freiburg in 1910, but he did not become Ordinarius there until 1922, despite a recommendation in 1913 by his predecessor, Roman Woerlin. Witkop's nomination had become the object of a methodological dispute. His initial appointment to Freiburg had been as a professor for aesthetics and German literature, not for literary history. Witkop was an oft-published poet during these years, and his methodology was viewed as inimical to historical philology.

In a letter to the Ministry of Culture of the state of Baden in which he sought to overturn the decision, Witkop noted that the same arguments against his unscientific method by his major opponent, Professor Kluge, had already been disputed during the defense of his *Habilitation* between the chair of his committee, Wilhelm Windelband (a noted philosopher and aesthetician), and culturrat and professor of Germanistic Theodor Braune. Witkop's letter to the Ministry of Culture, which quotes from recommendations written by Mann, Richard Dehmel, and Hans Thoma, reformulates his teaching methods in opposition to the philologists: "The purpose of my teaching activity is art. For my purposes, science is only a means to that end, just as for the historian, art is used as a means to supplement his scientific results."[34]

Witkop acted as the editor for new editions of Friedrich Schiller's complete works, several of Gottfried Keller's *Novellen,* and the poems of Friedrich Hölderlin. He also wrote full-length monographs on Heinrich von Kleist, Goethe, Tolstoi, Keller, several studies on German poetry, including a three-volume anthology and commentary "from Luther to Nietzsche" as well as several analyses of developments in contemporary literature.[35] These volumes suggest the contours of a literary aesthetic complementing his interest in the social question.

His prolific output ceased after 1933, doubtless because he was one of the few professors in Freiburg after 1935 who had not, despite pressure from many colleagues, Martin Heidegger reportedly among them, joined the Nazi Party. Reputedly, in those years he thought often of resigning.[36] When the Second World War broke out, he wanted nothing to do with the collection efforts for a new generation of student letters. The "ideas of 1914" that continued to animate Witkop's conservative idealism did not allow him to be happy with the regime that used the symbols Witkop had helped to create for its own aims.

Witkop spent the first two years of the First World War relentlessly writing in Freiburg, where he frequently heard cannon thunder from the west. He wrote for Germanists and educators about the newest (war) literature and the teaching of such literature. His correspondence of the period with Mann, Dehmel, and Karl Henckell most often revolves around the special role that literature and culture might play in forming the new spirit of the day.[37]

After being called into the army in April 1916, Witkop actualized his ideas at the front. Like Anton Kippenberg and Robert Musil, Witkop became the editor of a soldier newspaper, the *Kriegszeitung der 7. Armee*. From this post he solicited poems and essays from his many literary acquaintances. Readers at the front (and, through subscription, at home) were treated to regular four-page supplements, including his articles on, for example, "Young Goethe," "Lilliencron," "Heinrich v. Kleist," "Walter Flex," and recurrently, "War Letters by Student Soldiers."[38] In book review columns he recommended reading material for the troops, and as an editor he supervised the flow of books in the *Feldbuchhandlungen* (field bookstores).[39] In December 1917, under the auspices of the Seventh Army Corps, Witkop organized classes for front soldiers, who were given two-week furloughs to attend. This program continued through April 1918, when the final German offensive dissolved the stability of the front lines. In accord with his concept of *Bildung* at the front, Witkop explicitly advertised that some accommodation would be made for soldiers without prior academic training. In addition to these activities, he also made himself available as a speaker for the home front as part of a lecture service organized by the Organization of German Scholars and Artists, a service coordinated with the program of Patriotic Instruction. These activities indicate that Witkop gave himself entirely to the war effort. Near war's end, Thomas Mann congratulated Witkop for having received the Iron Cross in recognition of his educational and literary undertakings.[40]

Witkop first announced his intention to collect student letters in a fifteen-page pamphlet published in 1915 by the Panther Verlag.[41] Witkop's first published anthology of letters (W16) appeared early in 1916 and was published by the Perthes Verlag in Gotha. The 114-page softcover text bore the title *Kriegsbriefe deutscher Studenten* (War letters by student soldiers). In the preface, Witkop asked his readers to send additional letters to him for a more extensive anthology at the end of the war.

In 1918 the second Witkop anthology (W18) was published, this time by the Teubner Verlag in Dresden. It too was a softcover book, printed on flimsy war paper, encompassing 153 pages. The letter dates indicate that the anthology portrays the war through the winter of 1917–1918. Again the preface stated his plans to publish a more thorough two-volume collection, of which this was a provisional rendering. Significantly, the title and a fundamental organizational principle had changed: the anthology was entitled *Kriegsbriefe gefallener Studenten* (War letters by fallen students).

Ten years elapsed before Witkop found a publisher for anything close to the expansive anthology he had envisioned during the war. But finally, in 1928, the Georg Müller Verlag in Munich printed a hardbound book on excellent wood-free paper, retaining the title *Kriegsbriefe gefallener Studenten* (W28). Three hundred fifty-three pages of letters described the war until October 1918. Critical acclaim and public response carried this anthology through four printings before it was rereleased in modified form by the newly constituted publishing house of Albert Langen–Georg Müller. Witkop's 1933 anthology (W33) was a hardbound *Volksausgabe* (people's edition), 345 pages long, and it too was reprinted several times—though with significant changes after 1937.

KRIEGSBRIEFE DEUTSCHER STUDENTEN (1916)

Having now briefly described the genealogy of each of the four anthologies, I return to the first of them to situate it with reference to Witkop's aesthetic reflection on the status of such letters. Two separate anthologies, both published by the Perthes Verlag (which also published W16) and concerned with the relation between war and culture, included essays by Witkop. By 1914, Perthes had gained renown for its geographical publications as well as for its works on cultural life and pedagogy. Like other major German firms, Perthes issued a special "war series," its *Schriften zum Weltkrieg,* initiated early in 1915. Academic authors like Hermann Oncken, Wilhelm Goetz, and Heinrich Scholz wrote on *Das alte und das neue Mitteleuropa* (1917), *Deutschlands Geistiges leben im Weltkrieg* (1916), and *Der Idealismus als träger des Kriegsgedanken* (1915). Fifteen volumes had appeared in that series by 1917 and, in addition, several anthologies combined shorter writings of authors who had become prominent "politicizing academics."

Contributions by Witkop appeared in anthologies entitled *Der Weltkrieg im Unterricht* (1915) and *Der Kampf des deutschen Geistes im Weltkrieg* (1915). In these essays, entitled "German Instruction in the Classroom" and "Poetry," Witkop explicates his conceptual grounding for the importance attributed to wartime letters in the framework of German wartime literature. Furthermore, the essays provide a context for the expectations attending his first anthology, as it was published by Perthes not long afterward. Finally, these essays and the pamphlet "War Letters of 1915" go beyond the preface of W16 in grounding the aesthetic that guided Witkop's selection and editing of student letters during the war.

In these essays, Witkop first considers the effect of war on the reading public. Two years before Flex's evocation of the triad in *Der Wanderer zwischen beiden Welten,* Witkop noted the extraordinary popularity of the New Testament, Goethe's *Faust,* and Nietzsche's *Zarathustra* among soldiers, and he interpreted this reception as a sign of spiritual preparedness. The desire for cultural and spiritual life among the soldiers, as well as the necessity to support such sentiments, was equally validated. Furthermore, he suggested that it is precisely the conditions of the front that enabled reader-soldiers to experience the "sublime soul" of *Zarathustra.*[42]

Second, he considered the effect of the war on individual writers. The examined authors (the core of which remained constant in later essays written during the 1920s on German poesy) include Mann, Dehmel, Stefan George, Rainer Maria Rilke, Gerhard Hauptmann, and Rudolf A. Schröder. For Witkop, Mann was at the center of German poesy. Mann's enthusiasm in greeting the outbreak of the war ("War! It meant purification, liberation from our sensations, and an enormous optimism") was therefore recalled, along with Mann's citation of the letters he had received from soldiers recounting how important his novella *Death in Venice* had been for them. Witkop concluded the essay with his hope that Mann would someday write the great epic of the war.[43]

Fascinated by the outburst of poetic activity that the war occasioned throughout all strata of society, Witkop greeted the war as the forger of a new art: "Thus for the entirety of our spiritual and intellectual life—certainly for art and poetry—war means a new and fruitful rapprochement, penetration, and union, consciously and joyfully greeted, of all the life forces of our people."[44] Furthermore, in Witkop's analysis, war had reinstated the poet as the prophet and seer of his people, ending his painful isolation: "Grateful and deeply moved, the poet learns again that feelings and opinions that he poetically expresses are not shared only by the few, that is, a related and educated minority who experience with him and sing along, but rather that he is again the poet, the prophet, of an entire people. A religious meaning pulses through his songs" (58–59).

The war had thus reunited the artist with his community and re-created the grounds for a new epic art, thereby forging a solution to the problem of "merely" subjective and ultimately decadent art so painfully experienced by the modern artist. The dilemma posed by modernism was overcome by a new poesy created by the war, "which puts an end to a period of individual over-refinement, arbitrariness and chance, and empty formalism."[45] The possibility the war had created in aesthetic terms was viewed as a challenge: "Shouldn't we, the people of lyric poetry, of subjectivity and bipolarity, not have at last matured into becoming epic human beings and poets?" (121). Witkop embraced the hope that art, proclaimed dead by Hegel, might be resurrected through its return to Elysium.

The theory of the epic was central to Witkop's project and therefore deserves analysis, particularly because it is the establishment of the possibility of epic art that guided the theory behind the letter project during this period. I refer here to Hegel because the theory of the epic that Witkop developed closely follows a particular, if debatable, understanding of Hegel's analysis.

The sustaining antipode to the modern romantic novel (in which "mere contingency" and "subjective caprice" are seen to reign) is the constellation of conditions seen by Hegel to have enabled the "beautiful harmony" of Greece and Greek art embodied in the epic. Subsequent historical developments have made the epic impossible; according to Hegel, the adequate grounds and *Weltzustand* (condition of the world) for epic art no longer exist in the bourgeois age. Epic art remains a sadly unrealizable aesthetic model.

In the third part of his *Aesthetic,* Hegel states: "In general, the conflict presented by war may be considered as the situation most appropriate for the epic." Hegel reasons that "it is in war, after all, that the entire nation, which is set in motion and which experiences, in all its circumstances, a fresh impulse towards activity, finds occasion to be responsible for itself as a totality and to stand for itself as such."[46] Hegel had earlier specified the substance of that totality: "The entire *Weltanschauung* and objectivity of a people's spirit, presented as a real event in its objectified *Gestalt,* determines the content and the form of the epic, properly defined" (121).

Witkop interpreted the First World War as reestablishing the conditions necessary for the epic and the heroic virtues of the epic sensibility, overcoming the malaise of Wilhelmine Germany. He renders his theory in terms similar to Hegel's formulation: "Wars are the appropriate periods and tasks of epic art, because they demonstrate all vital forces of a people in the most distinct way."[47] Regarding whether the grounds for epic art (specified by Hegel as the "general epic condition of the world") could be established, Witkop suggested that an enabling transformation had indeed occurred in 1914: "Only since this war has our people become a unity and totality, matured enough to take on the greatest epic task, an art form in which the people's spirit consciously and lovingly recognizes its nature and fate and relentlessly produces it totally in action and image" (120).

Hegel had written of the epic poet: "For the sake of the objective totality, the poet as a subject must step back behind the object and disappear in it," as it is the object and not the "inner world of the poeticizing subject" that forms the epic.[48] Witkop repeated this aesthetic of epic objectivity: "The epic poet steps back behind the world, dissolves into the world, insofar as he surrenders all personal demands, all will for individualization, he can become everything. For the sake of his total-love, his total-justice, he sacrifices his own self for the world."[49]

Although the epic should "organically" express a nation's spirit, Hegel's aesthetic insists that "a people as a totality does not write poetry, rather only individuals." The *Geist* of a time or a nation first enters the reality (*Wirklichkeit*) of the work "when it summarizes itself into the genius of one poet, who then leads this general spirit and content to consciousness and performance as his own."[50]

On the other hand, the mode of presentation utilized by an epic style, despite all claims to the objectivity representing "the object" itself, rests upon a fundamental "as-if illusion." What Hegel called the "subjective dimension of production" has to disappear in the background: "In this regard, great epic style consists in its giving the appearance of singing forth for itself, independently, without an author guiding it" (121).

In his wartime essays, Witkop held out the promise that someone (perhaps Mann) would someday write the great epic of the Great War. In 1915 and 1916 it was still impossible: "Only when the war has ended, perhaps a long time afterward, will it be possible to see and shape it as a *Weltbild* [total picture]."[51] Until then, the materials for that epic existed in the letters of soldiers. Witkop's essay "Die Dichtung" used the same language as the earlier essay to make this point: "The war, however, has already provided and continues to provide an abundance of epic evidence and materials in the letters of our soldiers. Nameless they appear in our newspapers, magazines, and anthologies, a sign that not one single individual is seeing and interpreting subjectively, but rather that *die große Zeit* is speaking through the single voice" (119).

In Witkop's analysis, the conditions of epic objectivity established by Hegel are thereby met; the object itself, the *Geist* of the time, "speaks" through the writers who as subjects have disappeared behind their object, their depiction of what is. The singular and universal fuse in the coveted voice of epic style.

"Without the letter writer's effort, by the sheer force and power of facts, the letters give perfect individual images, materials for future epic world paintings" (119).

Witkop thereby established his grounds for the representation of objective reality (understood in an idealistic sense) in war letters in terms of epic theory. Parenthetically, as noted in Chapter 2, the relation between such individual images and a future epic world painting mirrors the role slated for individual war reports, pending the appearance of the yet-to-be-written objective history of the war by the OHL. Witkop's claim for the veracity of the letters remained a constant throughout the various editions of his anthology. His argument became more sharply pointed, however, in W28 and W33 in response to the increasingly vitriolic debate surrounding the competing claims for represented truth in the war literature published in the Weimar years.

Witkop's analysis embraced the entire genre of *Feldpostbriefe* without further differentiation. The "terrible grandeur of the war gives to the depictions of even the simple soldier a moving power and poetical meaning."[52] Consequently, he suggested in his essay "German Instruction in the Classroom" that such letters should be taught: "The best of these letters should be read aloud to students, allowing them to experience the fertility, power, and frightfulness of the facts directly. . . . In this way they will learn the proper inner meaning and grandeur of epic style" (64).

Having thus pedagogically and aesthetically legitimated the genre of *Feldpostbriefe,* Witkop prepared the grounds for his first anthology with a pamphlet; much of the thought and language describing the genre in terms of epic theory recurs in his essay "War Letters by German Students." Once again, he expressed the idea that the epic form alone is capable of representing the war, and again he characterized war letters as the only epic material already available.

By mid-1915, a plethora of letter anthologies had appeared. The logic of epic theory demands, however, that the unified totality speak with one voice, thus raising the question of whether epic truth could be equally present in all these anthologies. Why publish or read any more? Witkop grounded his claim to the truth of his intended anthology in a notion of symbolic representativeness. Students' writings best represent an epic style: in the "incalculableness of the people as a whole," there exists one particular group that is not "without unity and singularity and yet possessing a general symbolic power."[53]

The explanation for why students should be accorded this status was reproduced in all of Witkop's anthologies (except W33, which had a slight but significant change): "In German student circles, there is an abundance of professions and social classes sprouting forth next to one another; in them past and future meet, subjective emotion and objective cognition, alertness of the sense and flexibility of the intellect."[54] Under the auspices of the symbol, then, an *organic* (*keimend*) process is initiated that portends the surmounting of class barriers. Temporality is bridged by a present that is "full" of past and future. Subjectivity fuses with objective knowledge, and the antinomy of body and soul merges.

Having thus claimed to fit the prescriptions promulgated by epic theory regarding the representativeness of his material and to have the legitimacy to articulate the voice of a nation in epic style, Witkop completed the gesture prescribed by Hegel for the self-presentation of an authorial voice. Hegel's stipulation that the epic style project the *appearance* of being authorless ("that the work appears to sing forth by itself independently and without an author guiding it") enabled (or compelled) Witkop to extend the laws of epic representation to his process of selection and editorship. Accordingly, Witkop "disappears" behind his *Gegenstand,* repudiating any "subjective" authorship at all. The task of the anthologizer of these epic materials is rendered as "solely to sort out the individual documents of this epic style from the abundance of merely circumstantial material and then to place the documents in an order such that they are enclosed in an inner unity, into a total epic image."[55] Witkop then should not be thought of as the speaker. Rather, the events seem to tell themselves; the appearance of objectivity in the epic narration is preserved by the absence of all reference to its narrator. The absence of such reference to a narrator would seem also to distinguish historical narration more generally.[56]

The preface to W16 describes the task of the editor of these "epic" documents even more modestly: "Thus I began collecting after the war began, not in accordance with thematic points of view, but rather always searching for the deepest secret expression of the spirit, for the simplest inner confession that— in the words of Goethe—makes the poet."[57]

Even as he claims the power of the epic tradition for his anthology, concomitantly invoking the concepts of immediacy, eternal value, and others, Witkop's editorship, when viewed as a twenty-year project, reveals the inherent dissembling behind this unchanged self-presentation.

Following Witkop's pedagogical articles and the positive reception of "War Letters by German Students" (it was subsequently published as a separate pamphlet), he garnered the support of the Cultural Ministries (and the OHL) to embark upon the nationwide collection he had earlier called for.

The pamphlet conveyed a message that the Cultural Ministries wanted amplified—namely, that the idealistic spirit of the students persevered even during or precisely because of the war. For Witkop himself, as he wrote in the introduction, these letters demonstrated "how in these students, the spirit rules next to things and events."[58] A letter he quoted as a sample includes a key characteristic passage: "This self-assertion of the spirit and soul safeguards the senses, too, from an early stupefaction. It alone makes it possible that the inestimable positive effects of the war—the depersonalization, the surrender of all to serve a total fateful will and substance, the deepening and renewing power of death, this daily die and become—truly take hold and grow, and do not calcify into early apathy" (7).

Had he written the letter himself Witkop could not have phrased his codex any more clearly: war as a *Bildungsstätte* (educational institution) forging a new culture and concomitantly a new type of community, the confrontation with death as the positive teacher of new values, *Bildung* itself as the protector of the soul.

In a private letter accompanying an official request for material to Karl Fuchs, his former teacher in Tübingen, Witkop described his editorial intent in greater detail. He expressed the hope that the project would achieve importance as a "national document." The key phrase describing his task as editor is contained in the concept of "creative working-through." The letters selected will, he wrote, need to be shortened and rearranged ("also within sentences") and attention must be paid to the order in which the letters appear:

> I am sending you an advertisement essay for my *War Letters of German Students,* which I intend to publish after the war and which I want to shape into a national document. This activity entails not only the work of collecting but also involves a creative working through, attentive to the certainty of the selection and then toward helping the letters to find their richest and strongest expression—without changing a word, but by cutting at the beginning and end, also within sentences themselves, and by regrouping parts of the letters. Then I consider the order the letters should follow. . . . Perhaps you own or know of beautiful student letters, which depict either the mood of the front or a combat scene particularly well. The samples I am sending you will surely convince you that in its entirety the project may attain national importance. I would also be much obliged if you were to share this request with your colleagues.[59]

The "advertisement essay" mentioned is his Panther-Aufsatz of 1915. In this letter to his erstwhile teacher and in far greater openness than in the public essays where he claimed to be merely collecting epic material in which events seem to "tell themselves," Witkop unveiled his status as an "epic-author" and his criteria for establishing a narrative.

Witkop's earliest anthology (W16) was a critical success. The number of journal and newspaper reviews suggests that Witkop had been right in his estimates of what significance a collection of student letters might have for the German reading public. Contemporary reviews give a flavor of how the volume was received during the war. The evening edition of *Germania* (July 13, 1916) stated, "This little volume belongs in the category of the most gripping of all the immeasurable literature the war has sprung forth." The reviewer of the *Sozialistische Monatshefte* (1917, p. 652) was moved by "the reflective, brooding young men for whom the war had opened a view of new and large problems. That which appears most humanly touching is the emerging inner tension between natural human egotism and devotion to the general welfare." The *Deutsche Tageszeitung* (February 9, 1916) praised the "unexpected" idealism of student thought: "What strikes one at once about this generation of youth is their renewed idealism in sensibility and desire. All pettiness and egotism, all self-importance, boredom and dissipation, all inclination for empty pleasures and enticements, have disappeared. One experiences the enormity of things, and that grants the strength to resign oneself to death."

Several other reviews manifested surprise over this development. Such reviews interestingly suggested reversals of previously held negative images of students, stimulated by the students' confrontation with the "seriousness of life." The *Steglitzer Anzeiger* (February 5, 1916) offered that "if these letters don't lie, then one can live with joyful certainty that this war has not been in vain for educated German youth; so genuine and pure sound from them words of German idealism, confessions of youthful yet combat-steeled and purified souls, who seem destined to become the carriers of the rebirth of German substance." Witkop's efforts in creating a specific public image on behalf of student-soldiers were indeed bearing fruit, as was the notion of war as an "educational institution" and the thought that *der neue Mensch* (the new human being), who in time would be ready to assume his special mission, was being reborn in the trenches.

Other reviews judged the collection "a document of our age, a testimony to persuasive eloquence" (*Berliner Volkszeitung,* May 7, 1916) or found that the letters "deliver moving and also literarily outstanding depictions of the horror of battles and the unspeakable troubles and sufferings of trench warfare" (*Propylaen Münchner Zeitung,* February 14, 1916).

The *Deutsche Zeitung* (January 16, 1915) found that the authenticity of the letters, as private expressions of emotion, compared most favorably with all previous war literature, particularly the "more or less merely poetic depictions by war correspondents or the official reports of events." The Leipzig family magazine *Daheim,* noting the crosses after some of the letter writers' names, touched upon an aspect that would find fuller expression in Witkop's next anthology (and in its reception)—namely, the consolation that the volume offered for those who had suffered grievous loss:

> Many parents, every mother to whom perhaps a son was unable to report his last and greatest experience, will be able to read from this book consolation, uplift, and deep inner tranquility. For in it, death loses its terror for us too, because its speech is so alive. As readers, we share life in the trenches, in the guardhouse, and we listen in on the last thoughts of the dying in the field hospital. They don't face death with rigid dogma, everyone resigns himself to things in his own way and according to his particular mood. Because of that, the volume as a whole seems real as life.

Attuned to such receptions, the foreign ministry took an active interest in the book and had it translated into English, French, Danish, Japanese, Flemish, Spanish, and Dutch and had the volume distributed through its consulates abroad.

Before turning to other aspects of W16's reception and the letters themselves, recall that this volume, after all, was only one of the many anthologies of war letters that appeared during the war years. Although recent scholars have come to identify the idea of student letters and indeed wartime letters with Philipp Witkop, an overview of the history of the genre demonstrates no immediate necessity for this identification. Of the more than fifty letter anthologies printed, why should Witkop's have become the most successful and thereafter the most "representative" or eminently quotable for subsequent scholarship?

Witkop's project faced stiff competition for popular and critical acclaim during the war years, even within the publishing firm (Perthes) that issued his first anthology. As discussed above, many organizations and publishing houses were interested in anthologizing such letters. Perthes published Willi Warstat's *Das Erlebnis unserer jungen Kriegsfreiwilligen* (The experience of our young volunteers) with letters selected from the collection of the "German Association for Education and Instruction" within six months of Witkop's anthology. Warstat issued a call identical to Witkop's for contributions to his collection of student letters. Like Witkop, Warstat envisioned an expansive collection, including statistical analysis, to be released at war's end; Warstat's project, however, was not extended or reprinted after the war.[60]

There are two possible reasons why Warstat's anthology did not become canonical. First, Warstat focused on letter writers between sixteen and twenty years old, an age group some years younger on average than Witkop's writers, with less claim to "representativeness," a criterion that by the last war years (and during the late 1920s) had become an issue. Furthermore, the reflective, less ubiquitously pronounced heroic tone of W16 (which in that regard adumbrates W28) and the studied reflections on death's impact were presumably more in tune with the public for whom *die große Zeit* was becoming a *Materialschlacht* (battle of matériel) with the myriad ramifications of widely experienced death and loss. Although Warstat's younger letter writers rarely addressed their own mortality, Witkop had selected letters that frequently did so, yet without losing thereby a sense of ethical and national purpose.

But clearly—and this illustrates why it is helpful to think of the influence of state institutions in producing textual memory—the benign support of the foreign ministry in promoting W16 in Germany and abroad was most decisive in establishing prestige for Witkop's anthology.

The imperial government, stung by charges of barbarism following the invasion of Belgium and aware of the possible pernicious effects on the opinion of neutral countries, encouraged academicians to counter Allied charges. Societies were formed and appeals were issued (most notably the first "Appeal by German University Professors," dated October 16, 1914, which embodied what became known retrospectively as the "ideas of 1914."[61] Such appeals proclaimed the holy mission of German culture against the partisan misrepresentations of English and French critics.

Witkop's first anthology was viewed by the Foreign Office as a useful weapon with which to offset allied charges, and both Witkop's preface and the types of letters selected squarely place that anthology in the then-current ideational battle for foreign public opinion. It is characteristic that none of the letters included in W16 mention the ugly skirmishes with Belgian "Franktireurs" (partisan fighters), quite in contrast to several other war letter anthologies of the period that mention ambushes and German retaliations. To profile the undiminished level of culture upheld or even augmented by battle, it struck Witkop (and apparently the foreign ministry as well) that few groups could better "represent" a particular image of *the* German combatant.

Chancellor Theobald von Bethmann-Hollweg agreed; in one of his letters he acknowledges the copy sent him and thanks Witkop for "the kind mailing of the war letters, which surely move every reader."[62]

Witkop's was not the only letter anthology of the war years to explicitly cite Allied misrepresentations as the provocation for its publication. The three-volume *Kriegsbriefe katholischer Soldaten* (War letters of catholic soldiers), compiled by the noted theologian Georg Pfeilschifter, was commissioned in late 1916 to offset the perceived defamation of German Catholicism, particularly by the French.[63] Pfeilschifter's letters demonstrated the undiminished religious devotion of Catholic soldiers (so he said), and letters grouped into individual chapters ("wounded enemies," "sacraments") offered documentary proof of the humane, Christian conduct of German soldiers. Like Witkop, Pfeilschifter claimed that the letters he chose from were all written without thought of publication and were thus "authentic." Pfeilschifter's anthology was, however, too inherently "parochial" to claim "representative" status or active government support. Although praised by confessional journals such as *Der Türmer*, the anthology received limited notice outside Catholic circles and was not reprinted after the war.

The principal misrepresentation that Witkop sought to correct in his anthology was the familiar Allied propaganda dualism that saw Prussian militarism swamping Weimar spirit, creating an army of thoughtless marionettes. Both alliances, in fact, enjoyed setting up the dualistic fiction of a "good" Germany or England existing alongside of a "bad" German military or naval England. Witkop's preface in W16 should be seen against the backdrop of such binary oppositions.

Individual letters in Witkop's collections by no means belied that shock and horror could result from trench experience, but in all these letters the word *terror* remains a description of a passing emotional affect and, at that, something that is overcome by *Geist*. Individual letters recount experiences of reading in the trenches, listening and playing music, and pastoral walks through the countryside. Hugo Steinthal wrote (March 5, 1915): "With special care, even love, I keep my small volume of Lilliencron poems. How often has the magnificent Detlev shook up again my tired, worn-out life-spirits! On sentinel duty, revolver in my belt, alone with my thoughts seeking out a distant homeland and loved ones, his spirit often came to me and conversed with me."[64]

Karl Wasserzieher (November 8, 1914) wrote of his leave to Ostende. "With such delight we drank the sounds of German music into our souls searching for culture. This musical pleasure—in the middle of war!" (20–21). Eduard Friedberg, having just received his Iron Cross, wrote (October 30, 1914): "If you only knew what an important part is played [out here] by the academically cultivated! Idealism, regard for duty, heroism, enthusiasm—they particularly emanate from our young people of intellect. Not only militarism, but especially our deep spiritual culture are the carriers of our success" (19).

Death (in W16) is quick and painless. Helmut Straßmann, himself killed later in the war, noted his troop's casualties in a letter dated July 24, 1915: "Our own losses were 3 dead and 11 wounded. One of the best fell next to me during the attack, just as he intoned 'Hurrah'; he was shot through the heart and had a happy death, because he fell down lifeless at once" (110).

When horror threatens to overcome a letter writer, it is blocked and reversed. Gerhard Pastors, whose letter is the most explicit in the collection regarding battlefield conditions (April 16, 1915), described such a moment: "Our clothes, a structure of mud, rained through, smacking and sucking frozen limbs underneath. Then hours worth of terrible grenade attacks, which threatened to drive one mad, and finally the attack by the French, which ended in a bloody butchery. Thus it went days on end—thousands of corpses. Trench battles are something unspeakably horrible. . . . As Frederick the Great would say, that's when the intestines become iron and the heart turns to steel. It cannot be any other way. That is the only good thing: one becomes strong" (110). The curious, seemingly redundant two-time affirmation at the end of this section becomes even more interesting when considered with the part crossed out in blue pencil by either Witkop or the censor. In the unedited letter manuscript, the following paragraph comes after the word "horrible":

> *The strains:* Always wearing boots, in a metaphorical sense. Every night out at 3-½ a.m., running (while on patrol) until one keels over, starving, thirsting. Sitting in the wet and cold for hours on end like someone nearly dead, to turn and twist like a snake because of back pain.
>
> *The dangers:* To persevere in the fire of grenades, to expose oneself to exploding shrapnel, to go through a rain of bullets as often happens. And with all of this, the terrible yearning for home and the prospect of a difficult future that awaits.[65]

Such a passage apparently did not belong to the "deepest, secret expression of spirit . . . those simple, innermost confessions" that the preface to W16 stated as determining the principle of selection. A literate censor or the volume's editor realized that the seeming redundancy above might otherwise unveil itself in light of too much physical detail.

Rudolf Fischer's letter in W16 (November 18, 1914) assured readers that things were not as bad as they might otherwise be: "I believe you imagine our lives out here to be much worse than they really are" (24). Fritz Klatt, one of Witkop's students in Freiburg, assessed battle conditions that in 1916 could easily be read to apply to the need to persevere on the home front as well: "Battle is not something that permits the individual—say in an attack, for example— to prove his courage. Perhaps that was the case in the past. For all of us today there is only that great heroism which is an endurance of things that appear insufferable to mind and heart" (72).

Other letter writers in W16 included several students of Witkop's with whom he corresponded during and after the war. Of those, Wilhelm Spengler went on to write war novels, while Walter Harich (who also edited a critical edition of E. T. A. Hoffmann, having just finished the doctoral study he had written with Witkop) became a popular playwright and novelist.[66] More than a dozen letters written by these three Witkop students are represented in W16.

From the above quotations, it is apparent how well composed most of the writing in W16 is. Far from being the "confessions of the soul" that were advertised, these letters, undoubtedly written with the expectation that they might be published, speak the language the letter writers hoped an addressee would want to hear. Witkop had corresponded with his students since they had joined their units, and W16 includes letters that are dated long after Witkop had made public his intention to publish student letters.

The censorship regulations noted above were followed without exception. No descriptions of close-combat weaponry or its effects are printed, no Christmas truce occurs in this framing of the war, not a single political utterance intrudes on the "spiritual" confrontation with war's meaning, and certainly no assessments of the strategic leadership of the war can be found. To assume, however, that any of the above topics was not mentioned at all—as was glowingly postulated by those reviewers of the book who praised the students for their experience of the war as an inner, moral battleground—would be a mistake that Witkop's later anthologies would disprove. An analysis of a sample of letters that appear in the four volumes shows further shifting stages in the state-sanctioned paradigmatic representation of the war in language.

If wartime letters strengthened morale internally, as suggested by General Imhoff, some anthologies, like Witkop's and Pfeilschifter's, also played explicit roles in combating Allied propaganda, particularly in neutral countries. Witkop's publishing efforts during the war were directed toward both goals, external and internal. The latter directive was further defined by Witkop's interest in pedagogy and in the teaching of German literature during wartime.

KRIEGSBRIEFE GEFALLENER STUDENTEN (1918)

The response that W16 received ensured Witkop the support and permission of the army High Command and cultural ministries for the collection effort for what would become *Kriegsbriefe gefallener Studenten* (W18). Witkop was permitted to send out form letters to all German universities requesting the home addresses of students killed at the front. Witkop then sent another form letter describing the project to the parents whose addresses he had received from the universities. In addition to the assistance he received from universities, once Witkop was inducted into the army he was able to publish his appeals for letters in the *Kriegszeitung der 7. Armee*. These appeals to soldiers to send letters from friends who had died were accompanied by sample texts. According to the preface of W18, Witkop received twenty thousand letters to select from during the last one and a half years of the war.

Two essays that Witkop wrote for his army newspaper reflect on and mark this important shift in the subject matter of W18. In the May 17 issue of the paper (no. 237), Witkop refers to a volume of letters of fallen students that he intends to print as the next in a series of student letter volumes. By August 1917 (no. 263) Witkop had a publisher (Teubner) and a tentative publication date (late autumn of that same year). Witkop wrote (no. 263) that the volume

> shall give expression to our yearning, love and gratitude toward those who have died young; it is to be a monument of honor, more alive than any one made of stone or metal, more moving than an artist could ever hope to create. . . . It is intended to be more than a monument, more than a sign of our yearning and remembrance; it will be a living testimony, full of life and yearning in the present. . . . Just as a painter lives on in his pictures, a poet even after death lives on and affects us in his poems by touching us and awakening in us all that is beautiful and true, so too these young heroes will live on and affect us through their letters.

The May essay had already explicitly associated his forthcoming volume with the movement then under way to ensure a "dignified honoring of the graves" for the fallen (Kaiser proclamation, January 28, 1917). The Kaiser had commissioned a standing committee of "renowned artists and landscape architects serving in the military" with the task of creating such sites in occupied territories. Numerous proposals for the architecture of the cemeteries were sent from Berlin to the individual army corps from then until the end of the war. Witkop was able to relate his own project to these commemorative efforts of public memory: "In this sense too, the 'Letters by Fallen Students' are to be a cemetery of honor, a monument of honor that these young fallen have built for themselves; a national book of edification, to which we, to which our grandchildren, will return over and over again, touched, with respect, love, and gratitude."

The organizing principle of W18 (as of all subsequent editions) is indeed reminiscent of cemetery architecture. Each letter writer is introduced by a brief heading that gives the dates and places of birth and death. The "occupation" of each student—in this case the faculty to which he belonged—is the only other biographical information provided. An individual writer, moreover, enters the narrative on the occasion of his death. The placement of each writer is thus determined by the time of death (as in cemeteries), evoking the Catholic tradition of feast days for saints, which are marked by the date of the saint's death. As in the Catholic tradition, which promises everlasting life, inclusion in Witkop's anthology promises immortality to the heroes thus canonized.

Already in W18, one discerns an organizational principle that would be highly praised by critics following the publication of W28. After the publication of W28, critics uniformly praised the letter anthology as a "substitute cemetery" and a national symbol for the fallen. Often in terms similar to Witkop's, these reviews suggested that the fallen would live on and continue to influence their community. The "missing" body of the dead returns, as it does in the Easter message, as purified spirit.

A letter that Witkop received from the parents of one of the letter writers (Friedrich Steinbrecher) included in the volume offered him their gratitude for having "erected a memorial" for their son: "We cannot have his grave decorated, since his last resting place is unknown." During the war and for many years thereafter, friends and family of dead soldiers had no opportunity to attach their mourning to a place, no grave to put flowers on. For those left behind, even the place of death, in accordance with certain censorship guidelines, could at times not be a geographical place but a metaphor, the "field of honor."

W18's appearance was noted in journal and newspaper reviews, but the volume printed on thin war paper was overshadowed by the military and social collapse that ended the war. Although Witkop's preface speaks of planned subsequent volumes and asks for further letters, Teubner apparently lost interest in a project that, after all, had been envisioned as a "monument" for a victoriously concluded war. Both this volume and W16 were, however, available and in print (at least as listed in the *Deutsches Bücherverzeichnis*) through 1922, thereby contributing to the stock of pre-1918 war books that constitute the overwhelming majority of texts on the war available during the early 1920s. Virtually none of the major publishing houses (apart from those that had a tradition of military specialization in literature like E and M Mittler) were interested in printing new belletristic accounts of the war. Firms like Ullstein did, however, continue successfully to sell copies from their war series, reprinting some of the most popular works, like Richthofen's *Der rote Kampfflieger* and Plüschow's *Der Flieger von Tsingtau*. The pervasive image of the war in available fictional accounts thereby remained the same as during the war and under the restrictions of the wartime censor.

By 1927 the *Deutsches Bücherverzeichnis* had no listing for either W16 or W18. There are no statistics on the final number of copies printed for either volume.

KRIEGSBRIEFE GEFALLENER STUDENTEN (1928)

The major popular success of Witkop's anthology began with its publication by the firm of Georg Müller. The appearance of *Kriegsbriefe gefallener Studenten* (W28) in September 1928 predated the serial publication of Remarque's *All Quiet on the Western Front* by the *Vossiche* newspaper, which began in November 1928. The anthology quickly established itself as an important rendering of the war among journal critics and was often discussed in conjunction with Remarque's book. At least forty journals ranging from *Literarische Welt, Die Literature, Die Furche,* and *Die Tat* reviewed W28. Virtually all the major Christian confessional journals reviewed it, as did numerous newspapers. A fourth expanded edition, released in the same year, listed 21,000–30,000 copies. According to the annual reports of the Georg Müller Verlag, Witkop's anthology was the only new publication in 1928–1929 to sell more than 20,000 copies, and in 1930 only one other book—also a war book, *Sieben vor Verdun*—matched that figure. The 1928 edition of the *War Letters by Student Soldiers* became Georg Müller's best-selling book of the period. By 1931, as reported in *Ausritt,* the house journal of Georg Müller (and later of Langen-Müller), Witkop's anthology had sales of 61,000–65,000. *Ausritt* listed 90,000 for the *Volksausgabe* (people's edition) of the book in the 1933–1934 report, 110,000 in 1935–1936, and 180,000 in 1940–1941. The people's edition remained in print and the 1941–1950 edition of the *Deutsches Bücherverzeichnis,* which was actually published in 1955 in Leipzig, lists the anthology's sales as 196,000–200,000.[67] At the end of the Second World War, Langen-Müller told Witkop's widow that, despite the scarcity of paper, the firm had received permission to print another 10,000 copies. W28 was one of the two best-selling nonfiction titles of the whole Hansiatische Verlags Anstalt, the publishing conglomerate to which Langen-Müller belonged during the 1930s.[68]

Witkop had not found it easy to interest a publisher in this collection. Aware of the lack of publishing house interest in war books during the mid 1920s, Witkop asked several state educational ministries in 1927 whether they might be interested in subsidizing a publication. He did indeed find support. The Prussian ministry of culture and the education ministries of Sachsen, Thüringen, Bavaria, and Baden pledged financial aid. Furthermore, the Foreign Ministry, in the person of Karl Schwendemann, took an active role in creating a favorable climate for the book. The publisher was thereby guaranteed funds to cover the cost of the first edition. The book was released on the eve of the ten-year anniversary of the armistice. Georg Müller sent a poster-sized flyer to all major newspapers to coincide with the release. The flyer included excerpts from numerous letters and acclaims of the book by Reichschancellor Müller, Thomas Mann, Kardinal Bertram, and Prinz Max von Baden.

The response of the press was as overwhelming as it had been unforeseen. Hundreds of newspapers printed selections from the flyer with a review, often running several pages. Not a single review I have read was negative, astonishing unanimity given the contentiousness that shortly greeted *All Quiet on the Western Front*. The praise accorded the volume spanned the entire political spectrum of the Weimar Republic. W28 had specific meanings for a contemporary audience, but its "message"—and therewith what the war had come to signify—varied considerably. Witkop's anthologies, like *All Quiet on the Western Front* or Renn's *Krieg*, were interpreted in many different ways by critics in the 1920s and 1930s. Axel Eggelbrecht's June 1929 comment on *All Quiet on the Western Front* might have applied to the reaction to Witkop's anthology in the late 1920s: "The political interpretation or evaluation of the book is the business of each individual reader. The book itself is as neutral as a mirror. Everybody will be able to form his own political opinions of it."[69]

A sampling of review excerpts suggest how well the book was received outside nationalist circles. Edlef Köppen, the author of *Heeresbericht,* wrote in *Die literarische Welt* (March 28, 1929):

> A volume of 345 pages: a humble place of burial—but perhaps with the one hundred twenty-one [sic] youths who lie in it slain and silenced, it is one of the most horrible mass burial sites of the years 1914–1918. Perhaps one of the most threatening accusations from those days. And certainly one of the most moving, stirring documents dictated by the war. . . . Why is everything here quoted so literally? . . . Because, therefore, with these war letters those people should be silenced who today still are capable of dismissing a Remarque, or a Renn, with an arrogant wave of the hand and

muster the courage to smilingly dismiss all depictions about the insanity of war as not half so bad, or as the deformed brainchild of hysterical literary imaginations.

For Gertrud Bäumer, the editor of *Die Frau* (April 1929), the book was the "highest affirmation of those who in it speak about war. It is not an affirmation of the war. There is no legitimation for war, even—and especially—after these testimonials. These letters are a solemn, compelling accusation against war." In 1929, Ernst Toller and Kurt Kläber, editors of the most significant collection of antiwar texts assembled in a single volume during Weimar, *Das erste große Volksbuch vom Krieg,* felt it appropriate to include one of W28's letters with other antiwar texts. Two individuals who privately wrote Witkop expressed similar sentiments. The former minister of justice Gustav Radbruch discerned a clear imperative emanating from the anthology, which he had read with "shock." To him, its message was "never again war."[70] The author Jakob Wassermann similarly recounted his grim reaction in a 1929 letter: "[I] don't know what might induce for the nation and all humanity a more healing measure of terror against the barbaric destructive insanity of war than this collection, which without exaggeration can be called a grandiose document of history." Finally, in a 1930 review for the *C. V. Zeitung* significantly titled "Nationalistic Books and a Book for the Nation," Hans Reichmann compared Franz Schauwecker's *Aufbruch der Nation* and Arnolt Bronnen's *O.=S* with Witkop's anthology. He correctly noted the absence of any racist sensibility in the anthology. Reichmann, like many others, thought he discerned immediacy and authenticity in the letters, which he believed, echoing Witkop, had been written without thought of publication. He contrasted this with the belated shaping of impressions characteristic of the former two works. For this reviewer, Witkop's anthology was a work of admonition, particularly suited for those nationalist leaders who threatened to lead the youth astray. These war letters, Reichmann concluded, were the most beautiful and the strongest work of war literature to be found.[71]

The dissemination of W28 extended beyond the borders of the German *Reich:* it was translated into English, French, Spanish, and other languages. The reaction in the English-speaking world (at least as indicated in contemporary reviews) was also almost overwhelmingly positive. The *Manchester Guardian's* review of "German War Books" attached high praise to W28: "No realism, no tragic art, no funereal eloquence could so convey that supreme enormity of the massacre of youth in a senseless war." But W28 could be as easily read in completely antonimical ways. Given the interpretations of the collection by the

German press, it is surprising how Witkop's anthology was almost universally perceived abroad as a pacifist book.

For in Germany, readers interpreted different messages in the anthology. The author E. G. Kolbenheyer, in an endorsement included in the pamphlet circulated to newspapers, made an observation that evoked fantasies of revenge. "Whosoever believes that our people is beaten and conquered should listen to these dead. A nation that possessed such youth still retains today future power." Graf Westarp, a member of the *Reichstag,* saw an evocation of "heroism, dutiful and sacrificial devotion for empire and nation." One sees a foreshadowing in these two endorsements of the kind of reading that became dominant after 1933.

Karl Schwendemann, the director of the War Guilt Department of the Foreign Ministry—an institution whose importance in shaping the perception of the war during the 1920s has been alluded to—had more than a passing interest in the use that could be made of the anthology. In his review, he delighted in the absence of political references and turned to the more substantial qualities evinced by the letters: "In them, one looks into all the depths of German nature and German disposition, into German idealism and its attitudes as citizens of the world who all are illuminated by a deeply serious sense of duty, a magnificent and touching love for their people and Fatherland. That one must sacrifice oneself, that it is a sacred duty to defend loved ones and soil at home, that compared to this goal, all the dreadfulness, care, and hardships of war count for nothing, this is the conviction that speaks out clearly and strongly over and over again."[72] Schwendemann furthermore revealed why his agency had presumably become so interested in the anthology, encouraging all readers with acquaintances abroad to send them this book: "There is no better antidote to the propaganda lies spread during the World War and their ongoing effects today than this book." Schwendemann had previously expressed this sentiment privately in a letter to Witkop.

The reviewer for the journal *Der Gral* heard a similar voice in the letters: "A noble moral attitude, heroic bravery, a belief in education and religion—all of these are irrevocably demonstrated line for line in their youthful, quickly matured idealism which proves that we were not Huns and Barbarians. Any thought about the final downfall of a nation must vanish if this generation of youth still possessed such vital forces."[73]

For another reader, who linked his appreciation of the volume to his distaste for a "certain modern war literature that wishes to deprive us of the pride of our heroic race," the letters affirmed the "spiritual" character of the war: "Not only did they withstand the most atrocious physical assaults, they accomplished spiritual achievements on an order hitherto unknown. Whichever manly virtues have been most praised, they can be found in the young academic students who wore the field gray tunic."

Another journal review believed that the volume's overriding message was the individual's (re)turn to God: "It bespeaks an inner, internal rebirth or renewal of religious conviction."[74] Regardless of the intent each reviewer attributed to the volume, the terms "true," "authentic," and "experience" recur, elevating the status of the letters beyond any belated fictional account. Equally frequent is the relation established between memory of the war, public commemoration, and the text as cemetery. For one reviewer, who like Radbruch and Wassermann saw the warning "never again war" as its message, the book was more powerful than any stone monument: "What will a national *Reichsehrenmal* (monument of honor) accomplish if we act without honor toward our dead? Why do we need another monument when we already possess a document, a monument in the shape of 'War Letters of Fallen Students'? As edited by Witkop, these call us to watchfulness much more than a monument of stone or wood, they appeal to us to exercise wisdom and humanity, memory and to gratitude, to loyalty and true honor—to peace!"[75]

The contribution the volume might make for public commemoration induced Theodor Maus, an editor of *Deutschkunde,* to suggest their pedagogical use: "For school use as well, this work represents an incomparable enrichment of reading material. . . . In German and history class presentations of the World War, our eighteen- and nineteen-year-olds will be able to look at the true face of war, which now seems to be fading slowly into memory."[76] His suggestion became a reality soon enough with the publication of W33.

Witkop himself read selections of the letters for the South German Radio Network in November 1928. The letters were also read on the radio by others in Berlin and Bucharest. Ministers read the letters from the pulpit. Ten years after the end of the war, Witkop's anthology helped to engender a national reflection on its meaning. That it did so indicates that W28 had a message for almost everyone. A number of letters that because of wartime censorship could never have been published were included in the lengthier W28; these stronger condemnatory letters account for much of the praise from those who read the volume as a pacifist statement. Witkop himself had amended his preface in W28 to guide such a reading. It concludes with a didactic hope that placed the anthology in this tradition: "These letters are intended to act as a spur for a new reconciliation of justice and understanding in the lives of the peoples. If so, then the last will and testament of these young tragic idealists will be redeemed and their deaths will not have been in vain." Still, letters of that nature were few enough that readers who, like Kolbenheyer, were inclined to find a different message could overlook them as a minor irritation.

THE *VOLKSAUSGABE*

The newly merged Langen-Müller publishing house then seized upon the popularity and availability of Witkop's anthology to publish a selection of the letters in two separate books, the first of which bears the title *Langemark: Ein Vermächtnis* (Langemarck: A legacy).[77] The letters were prefaced in this edition by Josef Magnus Wehner's speech commemorating the "Langemarck Day" sponsored by the German student union, an address that was publicly read on July 10, 1932, at German universities. *Ausritt* lists the twentieth printing in its 1933–1934 edition, the fortieth printing in 1937–1938, and the sixtieth printing in 1940–1941. *Langemark: Ein Vermächtnis* should therefore be considered along with the *Kriegsbriefe* in estimating the anthology's popular success, even if Witkop, resentful of the abrogation of his editorial authority, was less than pleased that Georg Müller published it. *Langemark: Ein Vermächtnis* marks the beginning of Witkop's loss of control over the anthology.

The second volume culled from the anthology was published in 1933 for a special schoolbook series entitled the "German Series." Edited by Walter Linden, who also edited the professional journal *Deutschkunde,* this fifty-page booklet sold 15,000 copies by 1942. With it, Witkop's letters entered the curriculum of the interwar educational system.

A not-so-curious change marks the appearance of W33. The change is signaled in Witkop's preface to the 1933 *Volksausgabe* (popular edition). The reference to international reconciliation has been purged, and instead his preface aligns the letters with the spirit of renewal that had recently enveloped Germany. The switch is symptomatic of how the *Volksausgabe* was reviewed by professional critics in journals and newspapers after the *Gleichschaltung:* "In these days, as Germany, rejuvenated and responsible, reflects upon its national dignity and renewal, a people's edition of the *War Letters of Fallen Students* becomes a national demand. It was they, after all, who first experienced and proclaimed the thought of a national and moral renewal under fire and fear and a willingness to die." This reinterpretation of the war legacy unites *Frontgemeinschaft* with *Volksgemeinschaft,* 1914 with 1933, identical in this regard to the "message" of National Socialism.[78]

This seems to be a long way from a text that, to some at least, seemed a condemnation of Germany's involvement in the First World War. At this point the anthology and its editor might readily seem to express a National Socialism that banned the war books of Renn, Remarque, Zweig, and Köppen and that elevated those texts—including Witkop's—that had "properly" rendered the war.

Yet Witkop's "national monument," as it was often referred to in both book reviews and essays, did not merge quietly into National Socialism. To appropriate this monument for their cultural politics, the Nazis had not only to silence the type of critique that had read the war letters in the manner of Köppen, Bäumer, and Wassermann, among others. There remained in the letters elements that did not conform to the legacy of the front soldier as National Socialism wanted it to be understood. Under pressure from the *Deutsche Arbeits Front* (German Labor Alliance) and the War Ministry, Langen-Müller gradually mounted pressure on Witkop to eliminate these elements.

Two examples mark this shift and simultaneously document Witkop's loss of control over the project to a form of institutional authorship. They also suggest the difference between the idealistic conservative war legacy that Witkop had sought to preserve and that propagated by National Socialism.

The first example concerns the letter writer's religion and party affiliation. In November 1932, Langen-Müller inquired whether Witkop would be willing to note the religion of each letter writer for the forthcoming people's edition. Witkop adamantly refused, writing the firm, "I am not able or willing to sort out the war letters on the basis of whether their authors are Jews, Catholics, or Protestants. In any case, that contradicts the character of the work. I would be equally unwilling to divide them according to political affiliation."[79] In Witkop's epic understanding of the "spirit of 1914," the war had (at least briefly) overcome the regional, religious, and political differences that had marred Germany's quest for unity. His vision of community included the German-Jewish population (and by inference those with left-wing political allegiances).

The publishing house relented for a while, but returned to the question in 1940. A letter informed Witkop that "independent research" by the German Labor Alliance had uncovered the fact that at least one of the letter writers, Otto Heinebach, was Jewish. Henceforth, the Heinebach letters were to be excised from all reprintings of the anthology. As the party had made clear in other contexts, the term *Frontsoldat* (front soldier) could not be used to apply to Jews.

The second example of institutional intervention occurred in 1937. Langen-Müller informed Witkop that the War Ministry had demanded the exclusion of three letters written by Karl Peterson, as well as one by Friedel Oehme. These are the letters that most radically question the purpose of the war. They are precisely the ones referred to by critics of W28 who thought the volume conveyed a pacifist message, and they had not been included in W18. Peterson's letter dated October 25, 1914, for example, contains this unambiguous passage: "Do away with war, the most hideous misbirth of human vice. Human beings slaughter one another in masses without knowing, hating, or loving each other. Damnation to those who conjure it up without having to experience its horrors themselves. Devastation to all of them, war against war. Fight against it with all possible means."

Friedel Oehme, who includes in his letter an intensely realistic description of his company's foray into enemy artillery fire, mentions the refusal of some of the men to move forward. They could be motivated to do so only after being threatened with a pistol: "A sergeant drives the men from behind with a pistol toward the front. It is terrible to be here." It is not the description of violence that made the letter unacceptable to the Nazis but rather Oehme's questioning of the purpose of the violence, as well as the strong suggestion that the army was not motivated by *Frontgeist* alone.

Witkop vehemently objected to Langen-Müller's intent to remove the letters. He reminded his editor that "until now, and especially on the part of the military, the book has been recognized and celebrated without reservation as a national monument, by von Hindenburg, by von Makinson, General Reinhard, etc. And now somebody comes along who doesn't experience the book's spirit but rather clings to details." Witkop speculated that the new military censors were concerned that individuals might read the Peterson and Oehme letters "out of context." He countered by invoking the national and international importance of the book, arguing that it was precisely the inclusion of the Peterson letters in particular that had been seen as evidence of the anthology's "originality and humanity." Should Kleist's Prinz von Homburg be censored, Witkop continued, because of the prince's weakness in front of the open grave?[80]

Witkop's lament fell on deaf ears. His editor consoled him by saying that Witkop should be happy that further cuts had not been demanded as "the War Ministry had not been nearly as drastic as apparently hoped for by other Party authorities."

Purged of the letters most contradictory to the paradigmatic view of *die große Zeit* promoted by National Socialism, the voices that speak in the volume after 1937 and 1940 are ones with which Kolbenheyer, Westarp, Linden, and others had aligned themselves in the last years of the Weimar Republic. Germany's next generation of soldiers would learn from the voice of Willi Naumann, who was killed in 1916: "It is a great joy for us to read poems that don't view war only as a destructive force, but also as an agent creating the new; not only as a heavy burden, but also as a purification" (236). They would also learn, as had the previous generation, that it is honorable to die for one's country. "Tell her," Ulrich Sarnow had written a friend before his combat death in 1917, "that I have gone to my death for my beloved Fatherland with a firm trust in God and a joyful hope in eternity" (310).

Two unresolved issues remain to be considered: the use of Witkop's anthology after 1945 and a final reckoning with the category of *Unmittelbarkeit* (immediacy).

With the broad international exposure of Witkop's anthology, it is not surprising that two works were written in the United States during and immediately after the Second World War that relied extensively on W28 to prove to Americans that there were democratically inclined segments of the German population with whom a postwar rapprochement could be reached.

Wilhelm Pfeiler's *War and the German Mind* (1941) was an influential attempt to view the rise of National Socialism against the backdrop of the First World War. One chapter of his study is devoted exclusively to the analysis of wartime letters; in this section, Pfeiler's only source is Witkop's anthology: "These letters of students at the front are simple and true accounts of events and emotions as they were reflected in the minds of the writers. Here is a vivid picture of the tragedy of war as it was experienced by individual educated Germans . . . in brief, a kaleidoscopic tableau, which in its directness and authenticity helps in gauging the character of a later literature that makes the experience of the front its basic element."[81]

Hanna Hafkesbrink's *Unknown Germany* (1948) cited several letter anthologies, but none as extensively as Witkop's, in her book documenting the "other" Germany. Hafkesbrink uses Witkop's anthology most extensively in the chapter entitled "Disillusioning Encounter with War" (51–75). Witkop's letter writers prompted Hafkesbrink to describe "another" Germany, one that reacts sensitively to the barbarism of war, is imbued with the highest moral values, and endlessly questions the war's meaning: "When under the impact of personal experience the soldiers saw that war meant not only their own readiness for sacrifice, but also the destruction of other human beings, their original enthusiasm turned first into skepticism and finally into bitter hatred of war."[82]

Both Pfeiler and Hafkesbrink use A. F. Wedd's English translation of Witkop's 1918 anthology, while Hafkesbrink supplements Wedd with student letters from W28 that his selection omits. I mention these two studies here not only as examples of an American reception of Witkop's anthology but also to raise several other issues that are pertinent to this study. For one, Pfeiler astutely suggests the genealogical effect that Witkop's letters may have had on subsequent war fiction. He facilely accepts the content value of the letters as "authentic" or "true," however, without considering adequately what would constitute their "authenticity" or "truth." For him, their status as private letters legitimates their truth value.[83]

Overall, he accords the letters the same privileged status as contemporary reviews and later scholarship, both of which treat them as unmediated and direct expressions of the heartfelt sentiments of the individual writers. Hafkesbrink's overall appraisal of Witkop's collections again leaves open the hermeneutic question of what "meaning" or intent one might attribute to the anthology and what the grounds for such an appraisal might be.

The answer invites further consideration of a central category alluded to in reference to Pfeilschifter. In the journal and newspaper criticism (as well as in the Reichstag debates between 1928 and 1933), a recurring category of evaluation regarding the war is the concept of "immediacy." The aesthetic of immediacy, most often employed by the center and the right, juxtaposes the experience of the war "as it really was" with a reconstruction of occurrences and impressions temporally distant from the event. The critical polemics against *All Quiet on the Western Front* often contrast Remarque's narrative to an "authentic" point of view, embodied in Witkop's war letters, the letters in the volumes published under the auspices of the National Archive, and the other letter collections that were published during the Weimar years.

Measured against the truth value presumed to inhere to the attribute of immediacy, any novel portraying a nationalist or *Frontgeist* perspective of the war likewise could be faulted with lacking its guarantee of truth. This standard had become so powerful that the obvious temporal distance between events and their reordering in the late 1920s and 1930s forced even right-wing authors and critics to take up and redirect the critique. The preface written by Adolf Hitler in 1931 for Zöberlin's *Der Glaube an Deutschland: Ein Kriegserleben von Verdun bis zum Umsturz* displays this necessity in the wake of the Remarque debate.[84] Hitler stresses that its author was a "simple soldier" and not a professional writer. The soldier has consequently (and presumably in contrast to such "literary types" as Remarque) not written the book to make money but to purge a "burden from the soul." This narrative, Hitler writes, is faithful to historical truth, and the evidence he offers recalls the censorship applied to the "Erinnerungsblätter deutscher Regimenter" discussed in the previous chapter. "The fighting and the battles come back to life in their historical verity, identified by day and hour, location and area." Not surprisingly, Zöberlin's novel, like the "Erinnerungsblätter," refrains from any belated critical expression regarding the spirit of the trenches.

Hitler completes his endorsement of the novel's authenticity by making belatedness the central category of judgment. The truth revealed by the work is of a different order, "not how one might perhaps see these events today, years later. . . . One hears the front's heart beating, the source of that strength which created our imperishable victories." *Frontgeist*, when emplotted in a narrative form following the OHL's directives for the keeping of regimental war diaries, thus functions as the guarantee of authenticity.

Interpreters who believe that the letters in Witkop's anthology are authentic—weren't they after all written directly at the front and without thought of publication?—succumb, finally, to the same tautological logic that secured that wartime aesthetic. They overlook the fact that these letters were written and published under conditions of censorship that defined what was allowed to be said in any given period of the war. Possible arguments from those accused of belatedly reconstructing the "real experience of war" after 1918 were thus "immediately" undermined. Censorship, however, applied via the postal service, then by publishers, the individual editor, and finally by the censors of each army corps largely contributed to a representation of the war between 1914 and 1918 that was anything but "immediate" in its framing of perspective and content. To unravel the temporal grounds securing this claim to authenticity is thus to disarm a principal weapon of the National Socialist rendering of the war.

Witkop's anthology and its different versions have undergone a twofold evolution. Apart from the evolution of the *Kriegsbriefe* between 1916 and 1940, the work has evolved into a compendium of indispensable documents of the war experience for literary critics and historians. Virtually every important study on the literature of the war has elevated this letter anthology to canonical status, as indispensable as Remarque or Jünger.

What is striking in the use of the anthology is the uncritical usurpation of individual letters treated as a source of information independent of the contexts in which these letters appear.[85] First of all, one would assume from these citations that there is only a single edition that perhaps went through a number of reprintings. Secondly, for these writers, the letters appear as the raw data for historical or linguistic analysis; they are used as a primary source to study the attitudes of German student-soldiers during the war. Whether these few letters are in fact representative, on what grounds such an evaluation might be made, or by what standards or aesthetics a letter was or was not included is never addressed.

In short, the state and censorship context of the production of a war letter anthology never enters into the discussion, nor does the suggestion that Witkop's anthology, far from being self-contained, is itself a creature of evolution that surfaces at different times to reveal a new identity. By extension, this chapter has offered reasons why a mode of analysis that attributes objective value to these cultural objects itself demands ongoing scrutiny and reflection.

Chapter 4 Literature at War: Literature for the Warrior, 1914–1918

Letters from the field were one source used to document cultural life in the trenches, and the activities organized around reading were another source that assumed new significance and value during the war. The importance attributed to reading by policymakers and commentators, moreover, persevered after 1918 as an aspect of the war's legacy. In this chapter I analyze this climate and the various functions assigned the act of reading between 1914 and 1918 in order to further contextualize an understanding of "the text" as being the product of a host of institutions that attempted to affect their meanings and reception.

Many contemporaries claimed that the war strongly affected and directed habits of reading, and not only at the front. This wartime activity is thus also relevant in considering the reception of war literature thereafter. The war reportedly schooled a generation of readers. What did these readers read, and how? What were the intentions of the individuals and organizations involved in schooling these new readers?

Furthermore, what was the value of reading for a nation at war? What types of books were published? How did publishers react to the new opportunities? What were the roles of various military and government agencies of the army in this development and what policy steps did they take? How was the system of book distribution organized to make books accessible to soldiers? What types of books were made available to the *Feldbibliotheken* (field libraries)? In exploring these issues, I also examine broader social currents that intersect with the distribution of books to soldiers. These are the so-called *Schund* (trashy art) debate, the aesthetic ideologies of organizations known collectively as the *Volksbildung* (popular education) movement, and the emergence of a modern form of publishing rationalization, exemplified by the wartime activities of two notable publishing houses, Ullstein and Reclam.

DIE GROßE ZEIT AS A WAR OF CULTURE
AND EDUCATION

> The book, whether in story or instructional form, with a tone of humor or seriousness, refreshes hearts, chases dour thoughts away, and beautifies the loneliness of the trenches and convalescence in the field hospital. In this way, books are weapons which fortify courage, and courage is victory.
> —Honorary President Erich von Hindenburg

The impassioned advocacy that marks the movement to provide books to the front as well as the number of army memos and communiqués on the subject might at first seem strange, given the pressing material demands imposed on a nation embroiled in a massive war effort. One soon realizes, however, that a nexus of ideational concerns and military needs propelled this issue to the forefront of wartime activity. Numerous individuals and institutions recognized that the soldiers needed not only weapons but also material to sustain their spiritual needs, as did the nation at large. Literature as an institution—all those agencies whose task is writing, publishing, and distributing books—took on the imposing role during the war of both legitimating claims of Germany's superior national cause and providing this spiritual succor to its citizens.

Countless intellectuals analyzed the outbreak of war as not so much a territorial conflict determined by economic interests but as a *Kulturkrieg* (war of culture), at the heart of which lay the mission of German culture to inaugurate a new age in European civilization. The proponents of what became known as the "ideas of 1914"—Werner Sombart, Johann Plenge, Friedrich Meinicke, Thomas Mann, Gerhard Hauptmann, and many others—juxtaposed in their numerous wartime essays the attributes of *Zivilisation* and materialism that they projected onto their image of the Allies with the virtues of *Kultur* embod-

Fig. 4.1 Appeal issued by Hindenburg's committee soliciting contributions for the purchase of reading materials for the army and navy. "We need books, donate money!"

ied in German life: idealism, heroism, a sense of community, and antimaterialism.[1] The thoughts of the philosopher Adolph Lasson, published in the influential and representative volume *Deutsche Reden in schwerer Zeit,* is illustrative of many like-minded chauvinistic speeches and proclamations issued in the early months of the war: "Germany is a country at the center of things. Its culture occupies a central position. European culture in its entirety, which is actually universal human culture, gathers itself like a burning point on this German soil and in the heart of the German people. . . . We Germans represent the last and the best of what European culture has brought forth; our strength and self-esteem is based on this understanding."[2]

This understanding of what the war "was really about"—namely, it was a war of culture fought by Germany in the name of the highest ideals of European culture and humanity—legislated a special obligation for those charged with disseminating German culture. Almost all of Germany's intelligentsia responded with the certitude, as phrased by the "Proclamation of Bonn Historians," that "in fighting for its national existence, Germany has been appointed to fight for the most noble possessions of European civilization."[3]

In a war of culture, the problem of *Bildung* as it related to *Volkserziehung* (national education) gained new currency and sharpened expectations of the role of literary culture and the publishing industry in disseminating the ideas of the new age. Speaking on behalf of the book trade and to its constituent members in 1914, Heinrich Lhotzky promulgated the call in the *Börsenblatt für den deutschen Buchhandel,* the journal of the German book trade, in his article "Don't Skimp on Books!": "Do you really know what books have done for Germans? They have helped us to win the great victory of becoming the most important people of the world. That we have become the first people on earth is due in no small part to the fact that we produce the greatest number of books. You will see that not the largest fleet, not the largest army, but the largest library will be victorious!"[4]

Although one cannot discount the obvious self-interest in the essay's equation of the book industry's output with military victory, its rhetoric nonetheless deserves to be taken seriously both as a symptom of the self-understanding for those engaged in wartime book production and as an idealized self-representation of the publishing industry directed to the public. Similar self-characterizations of its efforts predated and survived the First World War, but with the nation's destiny at stake, the industry claimed an even more privileged status that transcended commercial concerns and depicted its activity as a form of national service. Lhotzky's "call to arms" to the German book trade to increase its stock of "munition" struck a resounding chord of approval. The German Publishers' Association (*Deutsche Verlegerverein*) subsequently printed 110,000 copies of the pamphlet.

In August 1914 the French Academy of Science portrayed the war against Germany as a conflict between the forces of (French) civilization and (German) barbarism. German academicians countered these Allied charges by portraying German soldiers as the recipients of the finest humanistic education, and steeped, even in the midst of war, in the process of learning. "Nothing is so deeply ingrained in our youth," announced the Proclamation of German Universities, "as respect and admiration for the creations of the human spirit in art, sciences, and technology, whatever their country or people of origin."[5]

Reacting to another Allied charge, which sought to construct a notion of a "divided" German soul, academics rallied in denying any antinomy between the spirit of militarism and that of German science. The "Proclamation of University Professors of the German Empire" stated that "in the German Army rules no other spirit than rules among the German people, because both are one, and we too partake of that spirit." Similarly, Alfred Hettner, editor of the leading journal of geography, *Die Geographische Zeitschrift,* declared in the journal's first war issue that while his journal would remain faithful to the truth

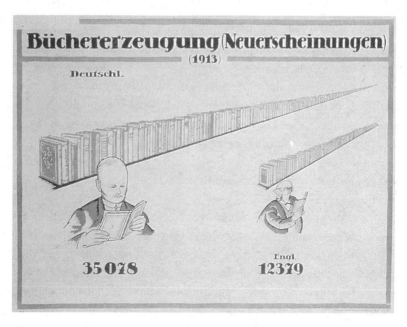

Fig. 4.2 A wartime poster contrasting the number of new books produced in Germany (35,078) and England (12,379) in 1913.

and not permit hate to color its pages, scientific objectivity would not mean a "total objectivity in the sense of regarding friends and enemies with equal dispassion; that is impossible and cannot be striven toward."[6] Instead, the fundamental ideal of universal scientific objectivity would temporarily be nationalized, since, like the English, "we Germans also must view things from our standpoint."

Gerhard Hauptmann, patriotically countering enemy portrayals of the German army as an assembly of mindless marionettes whipped into submission by Prussian drill, declared in his essay "Against Untruth" that Germany's warriors knew exactly for what they were fighting: "One will not find illiterates among them, but all the more individuals who besides carrying a rifle pack have Goethe's *Faust,* their *Zarathustra,* a work by Schopenhauer, the Bible, or Homer in their knapsacks."[7]

Hauptmann's impressive list suggested that the German fighting man was also a soldier of culture. Whether or not enough evidence exists to support his contention, "at war with Nietzsche and *Faust* in my knapsack" became an oft-quoted idea and phrase, a bit of rhetoric that became one of the war's legacies. More immediately, however, the propagandistic value of this portrayal facilitated the efforts of Germany's publishers to ensure that the nation's soldiers were sufficiently armed.

THE PUBLISHER'S MISSION

German publishers had traditionally represented themselves as spiritual hand-maidens of culture; in a *Kulturkrieg*, there was added urgency to ensure that "their" authors and works were read by the public. Publishing house wartime advertisements promoted the purchase of their products as an issue of national importance. Publishers touted writers who had joined a regiment at the front line. The *Börsenverein* (Publisher's Union) began publishing lists of the writers and their units with the suggestion that bookstores and libraries display these lists conspicuously as "tablets of honor for those poets and writers . . . who have gone to war for the Fatherland."[8] The lists included many best-sellers of the war years: Walter Bloem, Hans Blunck, Richard Dehmel, Alfred Döblin, Walter Flex, Ludwig Ganghofer, Carl Hagemann, Rudolf Herzog, Walter Heymann, Paul Oscar Höcker, Hugo von Hofmannsthal, Hermann Löns, Börries von Münchhausen, Rudolf Stratz, Heinz Tovote, Ernst von Wolzogen, and Fedor von Zobeltitz. Bookstores were asked to ensure vigorous sales of these authors' prewar works in appreciation of their devotion, and publishers were advised to seek these individuals when soliciting manuscripts about the war.

Looking back twenty years after the war, the German Publishers' Association could congratulate itself for the role it had played in sustaining the "forces of mind and soul that were required to wage a defensive battle of the greatest dimensions." The book trade, wrote Annemarie Meiner, in a *Festschrift* on the organization's activities, "recognized very well that a large part of this defensive spiritual battle would fall to them as an 'elevated and holy task.'"[9] As never before, she noted, publishers played an active role advising and influencing public policy.

This active role entailed creating a market for war-affirming works. The German book trade quickly recognized the possibilities created by the war. The first few months of the war brought hardships to the industry, reflected in annual reports by regional branches of the Publisher's Union. But while the reports from Leipzig, Berlin, and Stuttgart noted the decrease in book sales between August and November, they found satisfaction in the surprisingly strong Christmastime book market, which compensated for the previous three-month decline. These regional reports also noted the sources of the recovery: "The brisk sale of books treating the war and the beginning of what became a

Fig. 4.3 A poster testifying to the cultural superiority of Germany against comparable Allied achievements in the areas of literacy, school expenditures, book production levels, social insurance measures, and numbers of Nobel Prize winners. Busts of German cultural icons complete the poster, whose caption reads "We Barbarians!"

major wartime pattern, the sale of books intended for a readership doing duty on the front."

THE WAR BOOK AS BEST-SELLER

Virtually all the major publishing houses competed among themselves to obtain manuscripts that discussed what the war was really about. Not without irony, the curator of the newly founded National German Library in Leipzig, which had begun collecting the numerous volumes of war literature, wrote that "one finds all the faculties meeting up in this assemblage; the theologians deal with the ethics of the war, the medical people heal the wounds it has inflicted, the lawyers inquire into now-outdated international law, and the philosophers are seriously at work pursuing the history of war and compiling many profound observations."[10]

Within weeks of the war's beginning, another type of war literature entered circulation and became widely disseminated, no doubt because it addressed the public's curiosity about military conditions at the front. This framing of the war as experienced by the fighting soldier or army unit occupies the center of what became known as *Kriegsliteratur* (war literature). By December 1914, coinciding with the Christmas book market, these works dominated the new publication listings and advertisements that appeared in the journal of the book trade, the *Börsenblatt für den deutschen Buchhandel*. Individual publishing houses soon established specialized "war series," whose numbers grew in each war year, describing various aspects of military life. Often written in autobiographical or documentary style, these books encapsulated events in a style that was familiar to readers from popular literature published in the decades preceding the war. This merging of the genres of "reportage" and adventure tale now served as the form in which authors could make this frightening, unknown war accessible to readers. The response of a number of publishing houses to the war is of considerable interest in considering how the war was domesticated for the reading public.

ULLSTEIN AND NATIONALIST FICTION: INTERSECTIONS OF SPACE, TECHNOLOGY, AND NATIONAL IDENTITY

The forty-five-volume Ullstein War Series, which was widely disseminated between 1914 and 1918, is interesting for its use of spatial and technological representation in narrating the war. On the topic of the First World War, Ullstein is perhaps best known for its publication of Remarque's *All Quiet on the Western Front*. But the firm also played an influential role between 1914 and 1918 in affirming and disseminating a nationalist rendering of the war.

Individual volumes within the series addressed new forms of technological warfare—submarines, automobiles, airplanes, zeppelins—as well as combat sites throughout the globe.[11] In formal terms, these works, which were written by previously well-known authors (Richard Voss, Walter Bloem, Ludwig Ganghofer, Rudolf Herzog), military heroes and diplomats combined elements of adventure and travel narratives with contents sanctioned by the military and Foreign Ministry's censorship agencies that encouraged their dissemination. In them, both the technological and the spatial pointedly signify for the constitution of national identity. This wedding of nationalism, war technology, and heroism recurs too frequently in the series not to have been by editorial design.

The series included Paul Oscar Höcker's *An der Spitze meiner Kompanie* (1914), Ludwig Ganghofer's *Reise zur deutschen Front* (1915), Karl Doenitz's *Die Fahrten der Breslau* (1917), written by the later Admiral and Chancellor, and Manfred von Richthofen's *Der rote Kampfflieger* (1917), each of which sold hundreds of thousands of copies. Höcker's novel, which originated as a series of *Feldpostbriefe* in the Ullstein newspapers, appeared in book form by the end of 1914 and had sold 391,627 copies by 1927, the year Ullstein published *Fünfzig Jahre Ullstein,* a commemorative volume celebrating its own fiftieth anniversary. The novel was also translated into several languages, including Japanese.[12]

Even this substantial circulation is almost dwarfed by the success of von Richthofen's book, by that of Paul König's *Die Fahrt der Deutschland* written in 1916, or by Günther Plüschow's *Der Flieger von Tsingtau.* By 1927, *Der rote Kampfflieger* had sold 521,000 copies, König's book had sold 555,000 copies, and *Der Flieger von Tsingtau* had sold 610,000 copies.[13] With such production and sales capacity, Ullstein had definitively altered the standard by which effective book dissemination was judged.

The literature published by Ullstein and strategically aimed at the mass market stands out as one thread of literary modernism—less in the sense of the literary form one finds in the works bearing the firm's trademark, but all the more particularly in terms of their "modern" technological contents and the technological rationality of the firm's production and distribution practices. Ullstein's fiftieth-anniversary volume in 1927 captures and projects this modern image. It contains numerous glossy pictures of shiny, well-oiled printing machines, the modern architecture of the firm's newest buildings, and airplanes, sports cars, vending machines, and other technological innovations surrounding the speedy and efficient dissemination of its products. The First World War, however, was responsible for exposing the firm to both the contents and the production technology that enabled it to become the 1920s publisher of urbane *Unterhaltungsliteratur* (entertaining literature).[14]

In books such as Paul Oscar Höcker's *An der Spitze meiner Kompagnie* and Paul Grabein's *Im Auto durch Feindesland,* one of the first narrated experiences is one that simultaneously involves distance and technology. The train ride across Germany to the front describes a journey consolidating national and collective identity in spatial terms, whose crystallizing moment in the narration is crossing the Rhine River. The crossing of the border demarcates a definitive inside-outside topography, separating friend from enemy. The now collectivized soldiers sing "Die Wacht am Rhein," ceremoniously acknowledging their new consciousness of this boundary. The pivotal moment of the border crossing is recalled in most of the later volumes in the series, recalling as well that "spirit of 1914" long after its mobilizing power had lost force.

But the Ullstein books, bespeaking the etiquette *Weltkrieg,* did indeed encompass the world. Individual titles centered on Paraguay, Jerusalem and the Middle East, Cameroon, Greece, and Siberia. Kurt Aram's book, *Nach Siberien mit 100,000 Deutschen,* chronicled the deep-seated hatred of Czarist Russia for all things German, documenting the cruelty and barbarism he had experienced before escaping back to Germany. Major Falkenhausen's *Die Erdrosselung Griechenlands* used "official documents" to illustrate the "unprecedented rape" of Greece by the Allies. Emil Zimmermann's *Meine Kriegsfahrt von Kamerun zur Heimat* described the battle of Dualo, its plunder by the English and Allied "schwarze Gauner" (black tricksters), and of his escape through the jungle to Germany. Freiherr Gedult von Jungenfeld told of his journey through the jungles of Paraguay and through Gibraltar on his way to Germany to enlist as a war volunteer. The personalized narrative "I" telling the story in each of these books—usually a military officer, a nobleman, or both—lent authenticity to the reports. Furthermore, each author creates a connection between the German *Heimat* and the point of embarkation or destination that is thereby connected to the Reich, establishing legitimate spheres of cultural, economic, and political interest. Even where a defeat or withdrawal is the subject of the narrative, as is the case for Tsingtau or Cameroon, the narrators leave no doubt about a lingering hunger for a renewed German political and cultural presence in those countries.

In the works that are set in Constantinople, Syria, and Mesopotamia, the benefits of German expertise for local economies are benevolently linked to German interests defined by the need to counter English hegemony over the Euro-Asiatic *Hochstrasse,* (literally, high street), which (in the imaginations of contemporary geopoliticians, at least) spanned the area from the English Channel to Mesopotamia.[15]

In the five volumes depicting submarine warfare in the Mediterranean, no argument is put forth regarding a secret Spanish or Egyptian hunger for German intervention. Here, the German Reich's imperial geopolitical interests in penetrating the English stranglehold on the "connecting route" crossing Gibraltar, Southern Europe, and Northern Africa provides its own rationale. To solidify this rationale, readers are offered lengthy historical and geographical instruction on the importance of such geopolitical strategy. A relation is established linking the success of submarine warfare to the outcome of battles on the eastern and western fronts, and of course the well-being of civilians, who as a

unified collective form an *Einheitsfront* (united front), as Forstmann put it in
U.39 auf Jagd im Mittelmeer. Forstmann furthermore outlines the simultaneous
and interconnected struggle for spatial hegemony on two surfaces of the earth,
the oceanic and the morphological. In creating a German imperial space,
Forstmann's narrative begins with the German labor and engineering know-
how of the "warriors at home" who craft the submarine. He emphasizes the
"German-ness" of this technology and production over and against earlier
French advances in sub technology. Forstmann's plot continues with his submarine's departure amid salutes and music, offers occasion to remember the
comrades on both fronts following the successful torpedoing of Allied troop
and munitions transport ships, and returns the sub to home port to be wel-
comed by waving flags and cheering countrymen. Although separated from one
another by larger distances, a unity of purpose links the various sectors of the
war effort into a narrative synchronicity.

The geographic subtext of Ullstein's war series reflects the need to provide
greater geographical understanding, a view that academics like Friedrich Ratzel
had been popularizing since the Franco-Prussian War.[16] The geographer Felix
Lampe, author of an essay that appeared in *Der Weltkrieg im Unterricht,* an
anthology published in 1915, illustrates the character of this wartime reflection.[17] Lampe, whose pedagogical interest culminated in an appeal to elevate
geography from a secondary to a primary subject matter in German schools,
offers the assessment: "The World War has made us Germans into geographers.
Quickly it impressed upon us the steely names of rivers and cities that we had
heard little of until then. In the process, almost everybody came to realize how
his geographical knowledge was lacking. With fiery torches, the war illuminates
the fact that the nation must be an empire, that it needs a broader territorial
base, and a people capable of grasping greater expanses of space."

Lampe spoke from a tradition of German geography that encompassed Karl
Ritter, Friedrich Ratzel, and Alfred Hettner.[18] Lampe believed that the particular expertise of the geographer was in revealing the threads of reciprocal relations between things, where random placement had earlier seemed to be the
rule. Territories also evidenced reciprocal relations, and studying of them "in
their entirety" is the task of political geography:

> Geographical perception is based in spatial thinking insofar as the size and location
> of countries and localities is grasped and demonstrated as being in accordance with
> spatial proximity and the interactions of things near to each other. It is of course the

state's task to create an equilibrium between the developmental abilities provided by the country's size and location, natural resources, and the talents of its subjects, but the resolution of this task also demands consideration of the forces that foster and inhibit such developments exerted by the surrounding neighboring states.

The war, Lampe maintained, had also opened new spaces of analysis for the geographer: it had revealed how trains and trucks, airplanes and zeppelins, the telegraph and telephone had been interlinked in new spatial relations. The geographer's task was both to provide instruction to the populace about these interrelations and also to provide a comprehensive overview of them for the military leadership. The geographer and the military leader, he concluded, have much to teach one another. In this regard, Lampe was petitioning on behalf of a subfield of the discipline—transportation geography—which Friedrich Ratzel had begun giving a theoretical and methodological framework to in the 1890s. The extent of this subfield's utility and further elaboration during *die große Zeit* is readable in the strategic and tactical military planning of the First World War. Not without praise, R. Langenbeck suggested some correctives to Lampe's perspective for readers of *Die geographische Zeitschrift*—notably, that national perspectives should be foregrounded even more than they had been previously. Regarding Lampe's determination to elevate geography's status to that of a primary subject, Langenbeck had no criticism to offer. But the importance of Germany's colonies in regard to their value as emigration destination, source of natural resources, and export destination for German industry needed to be clarified for schoolchildren. Additionally, Langenbeck wished his colleagues to stress the "diffusion of Germanness on the earth . . . the position and the influence which the Germans exert in particular countries, especially the U.S.A., Brazil, Argentina, Chile, Turkey, and China, the work of German capital abroad, the economic and cultural achievements of Germans in almost all countries." Doing so, thought Langenbeck, would cultivate national pride and nationalist self-consciousness, "in which we have often been sorely lacking."[19]

Although the intended audience for these suggestions were schoolchildren and adolescents, the civilian and enlisted populations also needed instruction on the spatial dimensions attached to an imperial model of German national identity. As Lampe knew, the audience that a professional journal could reach was limited, even if Alfred Hettner, the editor of *Die geographische Zeitschrift*, had declared in 1914 that science and objectivity aside, the journal would serve the German war effort: "Love for our Fatherland will guide our pens."[20] In this context, Ullstein's war series, fostered by the High Command until the last month of the war despite severe paper shortages, was an exemplary effort to expand the limits of a prewar understanding of space for the volume's readers.

The wartime editions of its popular successes might have been even higher (thus Ullstein's speculation in 1927) had it not been for the paper shortages that were a general (though unequally administered) problem for German publishing after 1917. Nonetheless, the appeal of Ullstein's war series to civilian readers and its circulation among soldiers at the front via front libraries and bookstores made it one of the most prodigiously read during the war.

The commercial success of the series did not end, moreover, with Germany's defeat. In 1927, Plüschow's book had just been reissued: "Its content is effective even today," claimed *Fünfzig Jahre Ullstein,* "independent of every war mood, inspirational to youth, a true adventure book. In rare agreement among members of the school textbook selection committee, it has been recommended by them for use in school."[21] *Der rote Kampfflieger,* the autobiography of the Red Baron, Freiherr Manfred von Richthofen, was reprinted many times after 1927, once with a preface by Hermann Goering that was published after 1934. There is even a 1957 edition, albeit without the Goering preface. Both books thus continued to swell the market after 1918 while critical antiwar books were encountering great difficulty being published—including by Ullstein. Ullstein waited ten years before publishing such a book, finally releasing *All Quiet on the Western Front,* which it did with great fanfare in 1928.

Ullstein was uniquely poised to take advantage of readers' interest in the war and to direct this interest in a certain way. As a thoroughly rationalized commercial enterprise, which combined the production of newspapers, magazines, and books in one house, Ullstein had also pioneered the usage of modern advertising techniques. Equally important for its wartime success, the firm enjoyed good working relations with the military. Not only did Ullstein enjoy special privileges in establishing bookstores at the front, it also was successful in gaining lucrative government support for promoting its books once the army began administering its own bookstores.

One example of this kind of cooperation, on the level of both production and distribution, is documented by a Prussian war ministry directive from November 30, 1917, sent to all army corps. The directive announced the publication of *Wir Marokko-Deutschen in der Gewalt der Franzosen,* an inflammatory depiction of atrocities inflicted on German civilians and prisoners of war. Written by Gustav Fock, it appeared as another volume in the series of Ullstein Kriegsbücher. The book's message of what one must expect if captured by the French could only have been intended as a warning to continue fighting at all costs. The war ministry, which had solicited its publication by Ullstein, now requested that order forms for the book be sent to all regimental libraries and bookstores.

Another example of such cooperation is evidenced by Hans Grimm's *Der Ölsucher von Duala,* set in southwest Africa, which was in many ways a forerunner of his *Volk ohne Raum.* It too was a commissioned work, financed in part by the Foreign Ministry. At the request of the Foreign Ministry, it became part of the Ullstein war series, whose acquisition by bookstores was strongly encouraged by the army.

A final example concerns Ullstein's publication of Walter Forstmann's *U.39 auf Jagd im Mittelmeer,* described above. The publisher petitioned the Press Bureau of the Navy Admiralty (*Presseabteilung des Admiralstabs*) to allocate an extra ration of paper supplies, which by then had grown scarce, to ensure the prompt publication of the book. Ullstein wrote the admiralty that the book clearly stated an important point: "That the submarine participated most effectively in the defeat of Italy. We believe the book is suited like no other to renew and increase the enthusiasm in all sectors of the German population for the deeds of the submarines." The admiralty, convinced that this book was in the national interest, approved a paper allocation for 27,500 kilos.[22]

This type of active official intervention helps to explain the phenomenal success of the Ullstein series. The cooperation between the firm and government and military agencies lends an unintended irony to the innocently phrased statement in Ullstein's commemorative history that "every bit of paper was read in the field," inasmuch as the likelihood of any given book being in the trenches at all was greatly improved if the book was imprinted with the firm's owl insignia.

These specific incidents, which presumably stand for many others, direct attention to two interrelated issues of wartime book consumption. The first, involving book production, suggests how actively the army, the Foreign Ministry, and other branches of government solicited authors and publishers in their efforts to disseminate what essentially was intended as propaganda. The second, involving distribution, suggests the mechanism of control that was created to encourage the reading of the "right" kind of books. For the army took steps to ensure that only the products of those publishers deemed reliable were given access to the lucrative trade at the front.

On both counts, Ullstein was uniquely poised to capitalize on the situation created by the war. The publishing empire, which owned such daily newspapers as the *Vossische Zeitung,* the *Berliner Morgenpost,* and the *BZ am Mittag,* had (along with the Wolff telegraphic service) garnered the privilege of serving as a semiofficial organ of information disseminated to its own and other newspapers during the war. Thus, in one sense, Ullstein actually recorded the semiofficial history of the events of *die große Zeit* as they were occurring (at least one version) through its cooperation with various government agencies concerned with press matters.

Furthermore, Ullstein established a network of war correspondents that were given access to the front, and their published reports, endlessly reprinted by the provincial press, were often republished in book form. Ullstein's newspaper information service provided easy contact between the firm's book division and potential authors in every branch of military service. Emil Herz, the chief fiction editor, actively pursued authors through this network and solicited manuscripts that became almost automatic best-sellers. Arguably, the firm's war series was the most extensive of any publisher for precisely that reason. While other firms just as interested in publishing war chronicles often encountered long delays because of military censorship, Ullstein was able to publish two new war books per month, often prominently advertised on the front page of the book trade's journal, *Die Börsenblatt.* Ullstein's preeminence in establishing *Feldbuchhandlungen* (book stores in the field) was a further benefit derived from its good relation with the military. As paper supplies grew scarce after 1917, the firm continued receiving highest priority for both reprintings and new books even as its competitors suffered. Little distance separated the perspective of the High Command from the Ullstein's volumes, and the firm's technological capacity had markedly diminished the distance between production and consumption. In this sense too, the activities of the publisher record the history of *die große Zeit.*

This is not to say that other publishers who had taken a similar nationalist stance suffered shutdowns. On the contrary, firms like Georg Müller, with its war series of fifty titles; Albert Langen; S. Fischer, with its publication of the war correspondence of Kellermann, Michels, Ludwig, Requadt, Bahr, and Madelung; as well as the Inselverlag, with its editions of war poetry by Schaeffer, Schröder, and Winkler, and new editions of the poems of the freedom fighters from the War of 1813, Arndt and Geibel, were all able to continue printing through the end of the war. Their books also became widely accessible through the *Feldbuchhandlungen* administered by the army itself. But no firm matched Ullstein's production numbers during the war.

Ullstein was of course not alone in responding to the public's interest. Georg Müller in Munich likewise published some fifty entries in its series that include a ten-volume war letter collection, soldier songs, war poetry, essay reflections, and novels.[23] The sales of the most popular books in the Georg Müller Verlag, though not as overwhelmingly high as its competitors in Berlin, occasionally approached the six-figure levels achieved by Ullstein.

Georg Müller's publication of Walter Heymann's *Kriegsgedichte und Feldpostbriefe* (War poems and letters), for example, in print shortly after he was killed in action on January 9, 1915, helped to elevate that author (along with Hermann Löns, who was killed a few months earlier) to one of the early archetypes of the soldier-poet of the Great War. Carl Hagemann, who before the war had been the director of the Hamburg Theater, published his manuscript *Mit der fliegenden Division* with Georg Müller, who advertised it as filling an important opening in the market. An advertisement noted its contrast to other early war books, which were "written for the most part by infantrymen, generally only dealing with combat and related matters from that perspective. This is a book about artillerymen; the war seen not from the viewpoint of the trenches but from above, on a horse."[24] As this curious book and its advertisement indicate, virtually no branch of military service was overlooked by publishers.

Notably, editors for Georg Müller were also among the most popular authors in the series. Karl Ettlinger's *Lustige Kriegsberichte* were continued in three separate volumes, the first, *Kriegsberichte der Herren Grandebouche und Lausikoff,* selling 150,000 copies by 1915. Heinz Ewers, like Ettlinger, one of the firm's editors, assembled *Deutsche Kriegslieder.* Both men continued to play influential roles in determining what books carried the Georg Müller signet well after Müller's death in 1917, even through their takeover by the *Hanseatische Verlagsanstalt* in 1927 and the merger with the Albert Langen publishing house in 1931.[25]

Samuel Fischer inaugurated the *Schriften zur Zeitgeschichte* (texts about present events) in which Thomas Mann's war essays complemented the war literature penned by (among others) Bernhard Kellermann and Robert Michels, who were war correspondents, and Richard Dehmel, one of the war's oldest volunteers for military service.[26] The publishing houses Insel, Albert Langen, and Beck contributed to this list as well, confirming that the established publishing industry in Germany by and large aligned itself solidly behind the war effort.

LITERATURE FOR THE WARRIOR

The publisher's wartime mission entailed not only producing volumes that addressed the civilian population's curiosity about front conditions but also actively supporting the movement to provide troops with reading material. To seemingly lend the assertions made by Gerhard Hauptmann and others about Germany's reading soldiers even greater credibility, the imperial army and numerous publishers and private organizations began a partnership to provide books to soldiers on the front.

Portable libraries were specially designed by Insel, Diederichs, and the Reclam Verlag, among others, who created the most elaborate of what came to be called portable field libraries. Each firm made its classics available along with topical essays on cultural and political life. According to a contemporary *Börsenblatt* account, Reclam initiated the practice, following the suggestion of several field officers, to put together one hundred volumes of their Universal-Bibliothek, or U-B (Universal Library) series in a lightweight container.[27] These efforts were quickly praised by numerous private organizations concerned with "national education" as well as by soldiers at the front.

The *Börsenblatt* of the war years is sprinkled with such testimonies (often used thereafter as advertisements) thanking individual publishers for making particular books or series available in this format. Meanwhile, Friedrich Avenarius, in the annual "War Adviser" published by his *Dürerbund*—one of the most influential groups to articulate a program of *Volksbildung*—offered practical advice for those at home wondering what literature to send to quench the "reading thirst" at the front. He gave high praise to the inexpensive volumes published as *Die Tat-Bücher*, those published by Perthes in its "Texts about the World War," and particularly the books in the series published by Insel: "The Insel publishing house has accomplished a remarkably fortunate deed by making available for the duration of the war unbound volumes of their excellent works which are otherwise only available as hardbound editions. One finds among them glorious works at the lowest price possible and yet printed beautifully and on good paper."[28]

The production of inexpensive books for "our fighting men" became a battle cry of many cultural luminaries. The long-standing resistance of publishing houses to the inexpensive book format melted under the imperative of the national cause. Anton Kippenberg, the director of the publishing house praised here by Avenarius, and by then wearing a captain's uniform in Belgium, was among those most responsive to the calls that the treasures of German culture be made accessible to those fighting to defend it.

RECLAM AT WAR

Reclam offered yet more inexpensive volumes (at twenty Pfennig a volume), continuing a tradition honed in the decade before the war. By 1917, Reclam offered the buyer (or sponsor) a choice of six separate *Büchereien,* each consisting of one hundred volumes and costing twenty marks. In addition, one could also buy the more expensive "Library for Officers," the "Novella Library for the Field," or two separate libraries in "lasting clothbound volumes."[29] Reclam's selection is testimony to the degrees of consumer specialization the market afforded.

Having made the inexpensive book its calling card, Reclam was uniquely poised to react to the movement to provide books to the troops. Since the inauguration of its U-B series following the change in copyright law in 1869, the firm had weathered the criticism of the established book trade thanks to the fulsome praise received from the incipient *Volksbildung* movement. The firm was also the first to recognize the suitability of lightweight, inexpensive books to the millions dug into trenches along the front. In a single year (1917), Reclam sold 20,000 of its portable field libraries. By January 29, 1918, Philipp Reclam announced that over fifty million copies from its universal library had been sold since the beginning of the war. He could furthermore document hundreds of letters written by soldiers, politicians, and cultural luminaries praising the valuable contribution to the war effort made by his publishing enterprise.[30]

Such letters stood the firm in good stead when paper shortages began affecting production during the winter of 1917 and 1918. The allocation of the scarce paper supplies to individual publishing firms marks yet another facet of army and governmental censorship intervention in the publishing industry. Publishers who produced unwelcome books were simply denied paper and glue rations, while those firms deemed *kriegswichtig* (important for the war effort) were allocated the necessary raw materials. Philipp Reclam mounted an ambitious and successful advertisement campaign to ensure the continued consignment of adequate raw materials for his books.

In January 1918, Reclam sent a twenty-page prospectus to Freiherr von Stein, the director of the National Office of Economics (in charge of paper alloca-

Fig. 4.4 Advertisement for Reclam's Portable Field Libraries, published in the firm's catalogue, 1916–1917.

tions), as well as to individual army corps to petition support for larger allocations. Many of the letters would have been familiar to readers of the book industry's trade journal, for Reclam had regularly used such documents throughout the war to advertise his editions. Arrayed in this form, they provided convincing proof of Philipp Reclam's assertion in his letter to Freiherr von Stein that his publishing house "had outgrown the parameters of a private business enterprise, and become a national institution" providing the nation with the "spiritual ammunition" needed for victory. These texts, skillfully assembled as a business advertisement, summarize the civilian and military expectations of the status of "the book at war," as well as the self-understanding of the publisher's mission in a *Kulturkrieg*.

Although Reclam editions were regarded highly even before the war, as a Lieutenant K. wrote to the firm, "it took the war to show us just how valuable they are"; inexpensive, easily sent through the mail, and "easy to pack comfortably in backpacks and carry them in pockets," they were ideally suited to the conditions of the war.

Several letters by soldiers and civilians reiterated the value of the volumes in terms of *Volksbildung*. A quotation from Paul Barth equated Reclam's enterprise with the gift of emancipation and sight: "Reclam's Universal Library is a lighthouse for the German people, for all those fellow citizens who yearn for the light of education to lead them from the desert, the storm, and the surge of the waves." The popular author Börries Freiherr von Münchhausen tied Reclam's "Promethean" activities to his own timely brand of cultural chauvinism: "Our cultural superiority over other nations is based on national education. National education is based on the inexpensive book. And in Germany, the inexpensive book has always been a Reclam book. I therefore consider the Reclam Publishing House an incalculable cultural institution." Professor Rudolf Eucken similarly related the cultural mission of the inexpensive book to the predisposition toward reading created by the war: "At no other time has this activity been as necessary as the present, when in our armies there exists a veritably insatiable hunger for good, affordable literature."

Reclam was judicious enough to cite several letters mentioning the role his inexpensive U-B could play in the nation's battle against *Schund*, a debate that will concern us later. "Unfortunately, a lot of trashy literature is being diffused out there, against which a collection such as your Reclam books is the most effective weapon," wrote a corporal, and another soldier was similarly quoted: "Your little editions are excellently suited to displace bad or bland literary products, something I have experienced often in the field." For the same reason, Professor Ludwig Geiger was incensed that Reclam's paper supplies might be cut: "It would be a shame, actually an unreplaceable loss, if the Universal Library were to suffer an interruption due to lack of paper; how much useless trash is out there that one could do without?" During the war, as was the case before, the fears unleashed by the *Schundkampf* (campaign against trashy literature) provided powerful ammunition for the sanctioned book industry.

For several letter writers who overlooked the legion of trashy literature ostensibly flooding the trenches, the hunger for "good" books produced by Reclam was proof of the "spiritual and moral superiority" of the German army. "The Universal Library," wrote Lieutenant General Metzler, "has been contributing its honest share to the cultural superiority of our people in arms, which, next to the achievements of our generals, have prepared the path to victories." A private stressed that it was this superiority that would determine victory or defeat: "Everybody who, if only for hours, has seen the misery of this war knows that it is only our spiritual and moral superiority that ensures us victory."

That letter writer explained how Reclam books and the activity of reading strengthened this moral capacity: "It is truly uplifting to see how all suffering is chased away and forgotten by good books." The suffering brought on by warfare was thus purged by Reclam, which provided an escape from the dull routine of trench warfare and the "emptiness of life in the trenches." Without the purging forgetfulness occasioned by reading—thus the logic of some twelve letters Reclam cited—the suffering brought on by terror and boredom might paralyze the capacity to continue fighting.

A letter published in the *Armeebuchhandlung der 4. Armee* explicitly raised the specter of military defeat, were Reclam not able to continue supplying its anodyne to the ailments of war: "Reclam's Universal Library belongs to the field book trade's most necessary stock: a slowdown in the provision of the German Army with good inexpensive reading material would not only cause serious damage to the general interest . . . it would have an extremely negative effect on the mood and the spiritual ability to resist among the soldiers who are hunger-ing for diverting and entertaining reading material." Without these books, it seems, the whole war machinery might come to a halt.

While invoking for his enterprise the humanistic, Enlightenment topos of education for all, Reclam also raised in his petition the specter of unmitigated individual suffering leading to national defeat. The combination was unbeatable.

"Im Felde unbesiegt" (Unbeaten on the battlefield) is the title of a revanchis-tic series published after the war arguing that not the military but rather the civilians and their parliamentary representatives had lost the war. The title would have been more accurate for a history of the Reclam publishing house during this period. Not only had the firm overcome the production difficulties of the war years, it had enjoyed its highest ever sales of books. Reclam solidified its reputation among cultural authorities, rendering ineffective any lingering resentment harbored by the book trade toward the "inexpensive book," and reached out to a new readership that remained grateful for the "education" and "forgetfulness" its books had provided. The war indeed ended with Reclam entrenched as a "a great national institution," as Philipp Reclam Jr. had written in his petition to von Stein in January 1918.

READING IN THE TRENCHES: LOADING
THE CAN(N)ON

Reclam contributed some of the first library books for what became known as front libraries. In 1917 alone, the publishing house donated three hundred of their portable field libraries for that purpose. Individual publishing houses providing books for the front was only one step, albeit an important one, in supplying the nation's "soldiers of culture" with books.

Early in the war, this broad movement to mobilize books had taken on many organizational forms. The movement to make books available to the fighting troops was initially—before governmental (that is, military) regulation set in—a broad action supported by numerous private agencies. The United Committee for the Distribution of Reading Material at the Front, consisting (by August 1914) of nineteen Protestant and Catholic publishers, libraries, and other groups organized War Book Weeks, supported by the German Book Trade Association. This function was later taken on by the Red Cross. The German Student Organization, meanwhile, created its own "Committee to Fund Mobile War Libraries at the Front," and in 1916, the Central Office for the Popular Book Trade equipped forty book wagons to carry their cargo of one thousand volumes virtually to the front lines.[31] By analogy to the field kitchens (called *Gulasch-kanonen* in soldier's slang), these book wagons became known in army newspapers as *Bildungskanonen* (education kitchens, but also education cannons).

By 1915, bookstores in the field had mushroomed along the fronts, but particularly in the west after the strategic stalemate following the Marne offensive. That same year, however, the military oversaw a distribution system along the western front that had hitherto been loosely administered. The Central Education Authority of the provisional general government in Brussels was founded to establish guidelines for the sale of books by individual distributors. Following debates in the Reichstag—specifically complaints that certain types of literature were not offered at the front and that caprice was causing patronization of some book distributors and publishers at the cost of others—the regulation of bookstores and libraries in the field was turned over directly to the authority of the quartermaster general.[32]

Thereafter the distribution of books was consolidated, with one or two major book distributors given highly coveted licenses to set up field bookstores and to help organize field libraries in the individual army corps. Military censors established lists regulating the types of books permitted for sale. Those army corps with soldier newspapers often assigned the editorial staff the task of implementing the censorship. In turn, the more elaborate and culturally minded army newspapers featured regular book review columns with purchase suggestions. Within the frontline jurisdiction of the Seventh Army, for example, some eighty field libraries were doing business by March 1918.[33] Various estimates placed the total number of field bookstores on the western front between nine hundred and one thousand.

These combined efforts brought about an enormously high level of book circulation. Several movements that had been gathering momentum before 1914 coalesced under the military's direction with impressive results: the popular education movement, the public library movement, and the triumph of the "inexpensive book."

As Ullstein's anniversary volume noted in 1927, only the lack of paper hindered higher circulations, as the demand was constant. Reclam claimed in January 1918 that fifty million copies from its Universal Library had been sold at the front, with high sales of the individual war series and topical books of all kinds. Of the eighteen most successful Ullstein books (as of 1927), only seven were not published during the war years.

By all accounts the war stimulated readership in Germany in an unprecedented manner. Numerous sources both in the war issues of the *Börsenblatt* and in published letters and diaries stress over and over the importance of reading at the front, and circulation figures available from contemporary publishers underline this fact. "In the field, every book was read that one could get hold of. . . . The unparalleled desire for reading is comparable to a spiritual famine." Descriptions of reading experiences are nearly as common in some of the German war literature as are depictions of corpses. Nearly half of the letters of fallen students, collected and edited by Witkop, include references to their readings: the New Testament, the works of Detlev Lilliencron, Goethe, Schiller, Keller, Johann Gottlieb Fichte, Kleist, and Nietzsche were often mentioned by students at the front. For a generation of student volunteers, schooled in the tradition of the *Bildungsroman* and prepared to experience the war as a *Bildungserlebnis* (formative, educational experience), the self-referentiality of reader's reading becomes as definitive as it had in *Werther, Don Sylvio,* and *Wilhelm Meister*.[34] Scores of autobiographical novels of authors who became canonical literary figures themselves after 1933 matter-of-factly inserted references to their prodigious reading on the front.

Wilhelm Hartung recalls reading chapters of *Zarathustra* between skirmishes at the front: "It was almost just a matter of good style to expect that *Zarathustra* would be found in a soldier's back pack. Between skirmishes, one took in a chapter just as one smoked a cigar."[35]

Franz Schauwecker, who wrote several best-selling war books after 1918, sprinkled his first-person accounts with notations about his and his comrades' reading. Schauwecker's reading list indicates the contours of a literary canon, which when read while threatened by cannon fire informs his obtainment of a correct worldview. The relation between the two is important, as the soldiers'

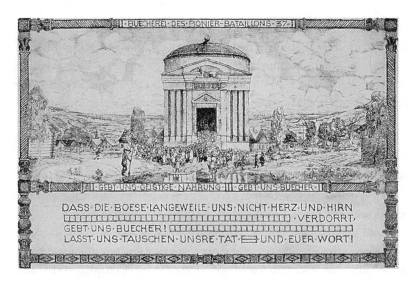

BUECHEREI · DES · PIONIER-BATAILLONS · 37.

GEBT · UNS · GEISTIGE · NAHRUNG ‖ GEBT · UNS · BUECHER ‖

DASS · DIE · BOESE · LANGEWEILE · UNS · NICHT · HERZ · UND · HIRN · VERDORRT,
GEBT · UNS · BUECHER!
LASST · UNS · TAUSCHEN · UNSRE · TAT ⊟ UND · EUER · WORT!

Fig. 4.5 Postcard produced by an army unit targeting potential contributors to its military library. "Give us spiritual nutrition, give us books!"

devotion to reading legitimated the claims of intellectual superiority by nationalistic veterans during the Weimar Republic. While confronting the possibility of death, Schauwecker reported, soldiers found succor in and learned the true meaning of these works: "the Bible, Goethe's *Faust*, Nietzsche's *Zarathustra*, Schopenhauer's *World as Will and Representation*, Hackel's *World Mysteries*, Rohrbach's *The German Idea in the World* and his *Touring Book of the World's Politics*, Chamberlain's *Foundations of the Nineteenth Century*, a selection of German poetry, a volume of Shakespeare's plays, Dickens's novels, Platonic wisdom. . . . These are the books of the front."[36] Even Ernst Jünger, the apologist for battle in the definitive *Bildungserlebnis*, was careful to include references to his acts of reading in *Storm of Steel*; he described his reading of *Simplicissimus* and *Ariost*, the latter while "stretched out on the grass, with great pleasure." In *Das Wäldchen* 125, he twice refers to his reading of Hermann Löns.[37]

Nowhere is the inherited *Bildungsroman* tradition of incorporating reading as an element of narrative structure so evident as in Walter Flex's *Der Wanderer zwischen beiden Welten*, a work that gained a cult following in the *Wandervogel* movement after its 1917 publication.[38] In Flex's eulogy to Ernst Wurche, the literary references and discussions far outnumber depictions of war dead. Flex's narrative self-consciously reenacts the self-referentiality of reading that was similar to the tradition of the *Bildungsroman* by constructing and imitating a literary reality between the two friends. Before they ever exchanged words, Flex was drawn to Wurche because his presence conjured images in Flex's imagination of Zarathustra ("he who comes from above") and of Goethe's *Wanderer* (page 8). The first discussion between the narrator and this young "wise man" is occasioned by Wurche's unpacking of three books—a field edition of the New Testament, *Zarathustra,* and a volume of Goethe's poems—during a shared train ride (8).

Their discussion of these works in the novel opens a dialogue on aesthetics and ethics, interspersed with Flex's and Goethe's poetry, which the narrator relates through the period of Wurche's death in battle. Flex's maxim that the war should be fought for its own sake, regardless of the outcome, is reflected in the virtual absence of any combat scenery or tactical analysis. Rather, the war becomes an almost inconsequential setting for the more essential ethical and aesthetic concerns animated through reading at the front.

Although *Der Wanderer zwischen beiden Welten* harvested lavish praise from reviewers for its depiction of the erudition and idealism of Germany's student-soldier, numerous contemporary observers also pointed to the development of new readers whose reading was facilitated by the war. As the *Börsenblatt* gleefully noted, "many a soldier now reaches for a book who previously had no interest in reading."[39]

Published letters of students often related such incidents that greatly affected them: "In attendance were a factory worker, a fieldhand, etc., but they could not get enough of Goethe, and what astonished me most: not Goethe's youthful love poetry was the most effective, but rather fine, quiet, mature songs like *An den Mond.* What a mood there was in our bunker; I have never witnessed such an enthusiasm for Goethe."[40]

Such texts fueled the hopes of many wartime *bürgerliche* thinkers: with various social classes thrown together in close-knit military units, the war might eliminate class warfare. If a mechanism for reading and education could be established and properly administered, the aesthetics of Weimar classicism (as interpreted by the established proponents of *Volksbildung*) might, after all, overcome the teachings of Marx.

The so-called *Arbeiterdichter* (worker poet) Max Barthel markedly profited from such hopes, as his poem "Goethe" became an oft-cited example of the class-surmounting educational possibilities the war afforded.[41] The opening verses of the poem create an atmosphere of desperation while under fire. Trapped in "our murky hiding place," comrades "scream like animals," and grenades explode, mixing "blood and brain to dirt." The poet's horror is ameliorated by his discovery of a "worn, thin book," a volume of Goethe's *Songs of Spring,* and reading the poems he experiences an epiphany:

I don't know what now swelled in me
    around me broke all feelings of constraint,
I don't know what yearned within me
    in wondrous exuberance.
From within me screamed out the air of life
    and jubilantly called out its Gloria,
To rise a thousandfold up high
    while never yet so near to death.
I found here, in these wild currents
    out of all the agony and rage
The resurrection of the new Man
    noble, helpful, good.

The working-class soldier who escapes a deadly bombardment to write this poem finds comfort and guidance not in a literature that would indict those responsible for subjecting his comrades to such horror, but rather in an Enlightenment vision of aesthetic education. For proponents of popular education efforts during the war, the so-called worker-poets offered tangible evidence that their efforts would dissolve the artificial barriers sustained by class hatred and activate a new community born in the trenches. They envisioned war as a *Bildungserlebnis* that would inspire the formation of a particularity-surmounting Frontgemeinschaft that would overcome the differences of class, region, and religion out of which an authentic national identity would be forged.[42]

Field minister Ludwig Hoppe actively participated in the movement to bring free books to the trenches, underlining (to potential contributors) the opportunity afforded by trench conditions to promote reading while emphasizing what was no doubt the most compelling motivation for the military's interest in these activities: "He who serves at the front knows how heavily the monotonous and boring life of trench war burdens the soul of a thinking person."[43] The High Command realized that upholding morale in a war whose Western front had unexpectedly turned into seemingly interminable trench warfare could become an issue of central importance. For most of the war, trench life alternated between moments of acute terror and extensive periods of boredom. Both sensations accompanied soldierly routine on the eastern front as well, albeit under different operating parameters. It was believed that boredom was dangerous to morale, and before the widespread inception of cinema and theater in the war zone during the last two years of the war, books were the most convenient anodyne to the problem. Reclam's petition to the army in 1918 astutely appealed to this sentiment. Philipp Witkop's organization of higher education was another similarly inspired initiative. Creating reading facilities might provide the necessary diversion from monotony. Although the army was therefore happy for its own reasons to endorse the lofty aspirations of pedagogues to enact a program of aesthetic education, military authorities were equally worried about the effects of the loosening of morality in wartime. Writing about the army's administration of educational facilities in a semiofficial postwar history, professor and captain (A. D.) Melchoir von Hugo emphasized reading as a means to sublimate the drive for instinctual pleasure: "The war necessitates loosening here and there the framework of moral law that we are accustomed to. To recognize this necessity and to limit it as far as possible requires the most severe self-discipline and responsibility . . . and it must be built upon a foundation of spiritual or intellectual values."[44]

The unspoken object of von Hugo's reference is the military's establishment and administration of bordellos, which, however, did not completely diminish alarming rates of battle-incapacitating gonorrhea and syphilis affecting the troops.[45]

For this reason too the establishment of reading and educational facilities became a military priority. The army's commitment to the program, somewhat passive in the early months of the war, gained in intensity and focus as the war stalemated, and particularly so once Ludendorff became quartermaster general. By 1916, Ludendorff was no longer content to leave the administration of reading to well-intentioned civilians.

INTERLUDE

These organized efforts to direct reading between 1914 and 1918 did not stop signifying with the end of the war. Apart from studying their consequences for the institution of literature during the war, interwar military historians and social scientists began reassessing this branch of the war effort to determine what lessons could be derived from them for the benefit of National Socialist cultural politics. Although it would be inappropriate to view all German history before 1933 as a prelude to National Socialism (as the "new revisionists," reacting to the continuity thesis underlying the writings of the Bielefeld school of historiography have stressed) the military efforts to direct wartime reading did establish a mechanism as of 1918 that appears to have prefigured similar efforts thereafter.[46] Just as National Socialism came to represent the *Frontgemeinschaft* of the First World War as a prearticulation of an ideal *Volksgemeinschaft*, its cultural overseers derived great profit from other "lessons" taught by the Great War, including the insights on how to utilize reading for total national mobilization.

Most commentators during the Third Reich felt that the attempt to generate interest in reading had indeed fallen on fertile ground, and there was some symbolic capital to be collected in self-portrayals by reader-veterans who had since become National Socialists. Some believed, however, that the military had not thoroughly exploited this possibility of influencing the troops. The most expansive assessment of the subject of wartime reading, *Die Lektüre unserer Frontsoldaten im Weltkrieg,* written in 1941 and thoroughly imbued with a racist National Socialist ideology, is interesting as an example of how the inherited symbolic legacy of wartime reading was interpreted and appropriated for National Socialism by its social science. The author, Inge Ehringhaus, concluded after 136 pages of evidence that reading had taken a quantitative leap during the First World War: "At no other time did the book find such diffusion as during the war, and at no other time was the possibility of influencing the masses and gaining a wide readership so advantageous as during the war. It is repeatedly emphasized that so many were introduced to good books then for the first time."[47]

Ehringhaus's stress on the word *possibility* suggests that she is about to lament the squandering of a unique opportunity. Indeed, although acknowledging the devoted organizational work of many private and state agencies in distributing books, her conclusion was that not enough steps had been taken to oversee their selection. She believed, as had many wartime observers, that the opportunities afforded by war to solidify specific values through the organization of reading facilities were unique and essential; thus she concluded that greater care should be taken to exclude all works that paralyzed the "spirit of the troops in regard to their fighting strength, discipline, and strength of resistance," particularly all Jewish authors and trashy literature (141).

Ehringhaus was harsh in her appraisal of military efforts during the First World War. Although no effort was undertaken to sequester Jewish authors from the bookstores—even after the *Judenzählung*—most of her other "lessons" had in fact been institutionalized belatedly under Ludendorff's command. The movement to provide troops with literature in the Second World War needed only to perpetuate the organizational forms put into practice by the end of the First World War. Field libraries, portable field libraries, and field bookstores that were centrally organized and administered, whose book selections were strictly supervised, soldiers that had "Nietzsche, Hölderlin, and *Faust* in the rucksack," were all experiences that were lived through and written about twenty-five years before National Socialism established a mechanism for their return. What did change in some cases during the Second World War were the titles and authors made available to soldiers, not the mechanism of control set in place by 1918. Ehringhaus's criticisms, encountered also in the official military historiography written between the wars, has validity in reference to the Imperial Army's unpreparedness to deal with such matters in 1914.[48] The army, however, made prodigious strides by the end of the war to solidify its control over the activity of reading by soldiers.

The organization of book distribution during the war is a telling chapter in the issue of government control of reading matter, the lessons of which were ready to be applied twenty years later in Germany under National Socialism.

THE *VOLKSBILDUNG* MOVEMENT
AND MILITARY LIBRARIES

As soon as it was clear that this war would not consist of a single sweeping campaign but would continue for some time, numerous nonmilitary organizations attempted to relieve the boredom of the front by sending books on a massive scale to both the eastern and western fronts. Foremost among these efforts was the collection undertaken by the German Book Trade Association following appeals to publishers and booksellers by its director Karl Siegismund. By October 27, 1914, the *Börsenblatt* reported that more than 250,000 books and 600,000 magazines had been donated by members of the book trade for this purpose.[49]

Simultaneously, regional book trade organizations, such as the Hamburg-Altonaer Book Trade Association, joining forces on September 3 with the Hamburg War Library Committee and the Freiburg Book Trade Assortment Association, initiated independent collections. By October, 50,000 volumes had been distributed to hospitals and ships by the Hamburg group alone (pages 13–14).

The book trade was joined in this movement by a number of organizations concerned with popular education. Efforts to create a certain type of broad reading culture logically flowed into this "mobilization" of books for the front. As soldier-readers would be unable to frequent their local libraries, new, and in some cases mobile, libraries needed to be established at the front.

Thus, the annual report of the *Gesellschaft für Verbreitung von Volksbildung* in 1914 noted that a major portion of its activities had been directed to provide soldiers on active duty and in hospitals with 100,000 volumes of "good" literature. The People's Library in Frankfurt a.M., mentioned in the same issue, had reassigned its thirteen "traveling libraries" for usage by army hospitals (page 186).

The *Deutsche Dichter-Gedächtnis-Stiftung* (German poet memorial endowment) had by October donated 74,141 books and 31,175 magazines to hospitals and regiments, and several other popular education agencies similarly contributed their experience and services to the "book mobilization" effort (page 51). The Prussian Ministry of Cultural Affairs, in reminding the public-library movement of its special task regarding the "spiritual education of the people," spoke from experience in January 1915 remarking that "in many cases, it will be possible without great difficulties to make the libraries directly available to the armies (field hospitals, etc.), but in other ways too, they will be especially useful in the current situation."[50]

The various groups soon overcame their differences and consolidated into a Central Committee for the Supply of Reading Material to the Troops. In addition to the above-mentioned groups, established organizations like the Central Association for the Foundation of People's Libraries, and confessional groups such as the Catholic Borromäus-Association and the Central Committee for the Inner Mission of the German Protestant Church joined forces in this new, overarching Central Committee. Infantry General von Pfuel served as honorary chairman of the organization, which appealed to the public to send "biographies, war stories, travel accounts, geographical depictions, suitable novels, and illustrated magazines," to be forwarded to the various collection centers (page 201).

By the beginning of December 1914, the Central Committee had collected one million books and an equal number of magazines; by the end of December, 3,200,000 volumes had been forwarded (page 201). This reading material was sorted into subject categories and forwarded to various field hospitals under the supervision of the Prussian War Ministry. Each library unit consisted of 50 percent "entertaining books for the general public," 10 percent "entertaining books for more mature tastes," 10 percent each of military science, "uplifting works," history, and geography, magazines, and finally, some "works about moderation" and games.

These categories marked a shift from those the army had encouraged—or rather permitted—in the past. Earlier libraries had consisted almost exclusively of works of military science and journals directly related to military life and published under the supervision of the military (such as the *Deutscher Soldatenhort* and the *Unteroffizier Zeitung*). Belletristic works had been all but excluded from these libraries that were in any case quite modest in scope and number, despite the initial involvement of the Society for the Spread of People's Education as early as 1904.[51] With the beginning of trench warfare, however, and its effects on morale, the War and Cultural Ministries encouraged these efforts to supply a variety of books not only to hospitals but regiments on the front as well. Because of the support of civilian agencies concerned with popular education, there were many willing volunteers to help stock libraries.

In principle, augmenting army libraries with the reading material provided by volunteer efforts fit nicely within the conceptual framework of the army as an *Erziehungsschule der Nation* (educational school of the nation). For proponents of this theory, whose origins in Germany go back at least to the Napoleonic wars, the army was to mold not only the body of the soldier but the mind and spirit of the citizen as well.[52]

The intersection of this idea with the popular education movement at home was easier once the war began, because the politics and aesthetics of the prominent library organizations were unquestionably patriotic and antimodernist in orientation. The sentiment underlying their efforts is suggested in an article reprinted in the central organ of the popular education movement, the *Blätter für Volksbibliotheken und Lesehallen* (edited by the director of the Landesbibliothek in Wiesbaden, Professor E. Liesegang). The article, written by the poet and author Julius Hart, joyfully embraced the transformation wrought by the war on the institution of German literature: "[We sense] that this spirit of the war has whisked away with one fell swoop the whole poetry of fashion, perversities and decadence, wild eroticism and snobbish entrepreneurship, and formal and technical emptiness. Finally, we will liberate ourselves from the aping of a foreign mentality and no longer be so totally devoted to admiring it. This art of play, of appearance, and overly refined luxury must make way again for an earnest, manly, inner art, which will suck its strength from the blood of the battlefield."[53] Hart conjectured that the war had freed Germany from the "pernicious" influence of literary modernism and replaced its decadent focus with a "manly" and national art. These are the implicit criteria that had characterized the book reviews of the association's journal before 1914, and they similarly mark the journal's reading suggestions throughout the war. It was characteristic for the journal's reviewers to award their highest praise to books on the ongoing war published by the notoriously chauvinistic Deutsche Verlagsanstalt and Mittler in Berlin, the semiofficial publishing house of the Prussian officer corps. In the realm of lyric poetry, no volumes were as fulsomely praised by the journal as those by Rudolf Herzog, the fellow townsman of Walter Bloem and the author of *Vom Stürmen, Sterben, Auferstehen* and *Ritter, Tod und Teufel.*[54]

By March 1917, the journal reported, the Central Committee had distributed ten million volumes to soldiers. As far as possible, the aesthetic principles voiced in the journal were employed in selecting "suitable" reading matter for the front. Consequently, in all the accounts about front libraries published in the Börsenblatt or in army newspapers, one will find little mention of the authors whom literary historians today associate with early modernism.

The literary education that the mobilization of books made available after 1914 was profoundly chauvinistic and antimodernist in orientation. This is a key point for reflection on the war's impact on the reading culture of the 1920s and 1930s. Apart from banning a critical or pacifist literature published primarily in neutral countries, the army (and the cooperating institutions) were likewise compelled to prevent Germany's soldiers' contamination by a literature that Julius Hart had labeled a "faddish poetry of perversion and decadence."

As stated by Friedrich Schilling, author of an army "Memo Regarding Field Libraries" (1917) and an earlier pamphlet "Inexpensive Reading Materials for Hospitals and Troops in the Field" published by the *Dürerbund,* the central principle for selection was this: "Select what relaxes the front soldier and cheers his soul."[55] Equally clear was what should be avoided: "avoid all *Tendenz-* and *Problemschöpfungen* (literature with a bias and problematic literature)." *Tendenz* used this way is a by-word for socialist and other critical literature, while *Problemschöpfungen* is equated with modernism.

In place of such literature, Schilling recommended "beautiful" literature as the most suitable for soldier-readers, and he included two categories under this heading, "classical" and "good, entertaining" literature. These are in fact the two classifications most often encountered in the essays discussing reading facilities at the front. But which works were to be included in (or excluded from) the selection of classical or good entertaining literature? In a *Kulturkrieg,* which works would lend authority to the culture war? And were the bulk of Germany's soldiers, as Gerhard Hauptmann proclaimed, indeed avid readers of Goethe and Schopenhauer?

Whether or not Goethe was the author of choice for Germany's soldiers, cultural functionaries immediately utilized the movement to bring books to the front as ammunition in the propaganda war against the Allies. The thousands of letters of gratitude addressed to the *Society for Popular Education* for forwarding 800,000 books by 1917 were, at least for its president, evidence of the cultural superiority of the German nation. Speaking to the *Reichstag,* Prinz zu Schoenich Carolath told his listeners that the thank-you letters were "A sign of the elevated culture of our army. . . . I don't know whether this is the case in other armies, for instance the armies of the Entente, but I would tend to doubt it. I don't believe that the various military units of the Entente are being richly provided with books or have a desire for them. This too remains a title of distinction awarded to the German people and the German Army."[56]

INFANTRY REGIMENTAL LIBRARY 105

Although the activity of providing books for the front had considerable value in the campaign for foreign (and domestic) opinion, the question remains, what were the works most frequently read at the front libraries?

Schilling's memorandum itself provides an answer to these questions because it contains statistics on lender frequency culled from his on-site inspection of four front libraries. It is the only extant wartime document to provide such statistics, and while four libraries of the hundreds established by 1918 may be too few upon which to base a characterization, these statistics nonetheless indicate general trends. His observations were accepted as representative by the military authorities who reacted to his report. Schilling's findings provide revealing insights into the polemical usage of the concept of a *Kulturkrieg* in wartime propaganda and the actual workings of a field library on the western front. His documents demonstrate substantial discrepancies between the ideal "soldier of culture" stylized for propaganda purposes and the actual soldier reading in the trenches.

Schilling found that "good, entertaining literature" was by far the reading matter of choice at the front. Educational writings in the fields of philosophy, politics, and the natural sciences were often not borrowed at all. Furthermore, "classical" literature, although well represented in a two-thousand-volume library, was much less popular than entertaining literature. Ironically, cultural luminaries had previously pointed to these types of works to legitimate the cultural superiority of the German soldier.

The following statistics from the regimental library of Infantry Regiment 105 (Fifth Army Corps in Belgium) portray what types of literature made up a typical regimental library on the western front and reveal the actual borrowing habits of the soldiers:

Category	No. of volumes	No. read	% read
literary works	57	43	75.4
poetry	128	68	53.12
fairy tales, legends	53	38	71.7
novels and novellas	362	327	90.33
entertaining reading	738	738	100
humor	55	55	100
philosophy	36	23	63.89
literary history	22	6	27.27
art history	4	4	100
cultural history	19	12	63.16
general history	133	86	64.66
politics	60	33	55
geography	28	20	71.43
travel	21	17	80.95
natural science, medicine, and technology	206	137	66.50

The table shows that novels and novellas and popular literature were the categories with the largest number of volumes and the most often borrowed works. The limited offerings of works in philosophy, cultural history, and literary history found relatively little favor with the regiment's readers. Finally, the availability of general historical, political, and natural-scientific works far exceeded the demand for such literature.

Further statistics compiled by Schilling relate the number of volumes borrowed to the number of times each was borrowed. The three types of books most often read more than once belong to the categories of humor (6.25 readings per volume), novels and novellas (4.97), and "easy entertaining literature" (4.34). The types of books least likely to be widely circulated belong to the categories of literary history, poetry, political writings, general and cultural history, philosophy, and natural science.

These statistics plainly demonstrate that "entertaining" reading, along with novels and novellas, were the most popular at front libraries and "instructional" readings were much less popular. Not surprisingly—given this preference for entertaining literature—books published by Ullstein head the list of most frequently read works. On average, every copy of an Ullstein book was read ten and a half times, followed by Engelhorn (6), Fischer (5.5), Reclam (3), Dichter-Gedächtnis-Stiftung (nearly 3), Insel (2.5), Schaffstein (2), and *Kosmos* and *Natur* each once. No works published by the Kurt Wolff Verlag or the Dietz

Verlag were available in this library. Thus the two most prolific producers of what Schilling had labeled "Tendenz" and "problematische Literatur"—that is, socialist and expressionist authors—were not available.

Nineteenth-century realists, writers of *Heimat* literature, and to a lesser extent "classical" authors account for most of the offerings. The most popular author, however, was Wilhelm Busch, whose works were read 126 times. He was closely followed by Peter Rosegger, who was read 125 times. Hauff's works found sixty-eight readers, and Fontane's fifty-eight. Goethe was read only 36 times, less often than the comparatively unknown Ullstein authors Kurt Aram (58), Rudolf Bartsch (48), Walter Bloem (55), Paul Oscar Höcker (44), Richard Skowronnek (39), and Fedor Zobeltitz (45). The Friedrich Schiller volumes were read less often than Bölsche (33) or Rudolf Herzog (24).

Schilling's statistics also showed how often individual works of any given author were read. Within the category labeled poesy, Wolfgang Goethe's *Faust I. Teil* found the most readers (9), followed by Friedrich Hebbel's *Die Nibelungen* (8), Richard Wagner's *Götterdämmerung*, and Goethe's *Faust in ursprünglicher Gestalt* (7 each). Other works read at least five times included Wagner's *Tristan und Isolde* (6), Esaias Tegner's *Frithjofssage* (7), Wagner's *Tannhäuser*, Goethe's *Götz von Berlichingen*, and *Hermann und Dorothea* (each five times). Of works from that same category, Wagner's *Der fliegende Holländer*, Gottfried Kinkel's *Otto der Schütz*, and Alfred Tennyson's *Enoch Arden* were not read a single time.

The discrepancy between available reading matter and actual borrowing was greatest in the category of poetry. No volume was read more often than Nicolaus Lenau's *Gedichte* (7), while Ludwig Arnim's *Des Knaben Wunderhorn* and Gregori's *An goldenen Tischen* were each read six times. Ludwig von Beethoven's *Briefe*, Matthias Claudius's *Aus dem Wandsbeker Boten*, Joseph von Eichendorff's *Gedichte*, Karl Vollmöller's *Parcival*, Eduard von Mörike's *Gedichte*, and the anthology *Deutsche Lyrik seit Liliencron* were each read five times.

The number of poetry volumes never read at all is more extensive than the number read at least five times. The list of ignored works includes anthologies of the poems of Ernst Moritz Arndt, Gottfried Bürger, Annette von Droste-Hülshoff, Theodor Körner, Eduard von Mörike, Fritz Reuter, Friedrich Schiller, Ludwig Uhland, and Walter von der Vogelweide. Volumes of poetry, along with works in history and the natural sciences, generated the least interest among the library's readers. In Schilling's analysis, these statistics "regarding the abundance of precious works not being read" underlined the need to appoint competent, permanent librarians to regimental libraries. Instead of limiting the choice of candidates to those not suited to combat duty, as was the War Ministry's custom, Schilling wrote a memo imploring the army to appoint the best qualified candidate to this essential post: "Only a man of education and authority who serves continuously in that post, can administer with understanding the spiritual treasures of our people."

Although cultural functionaries had a vision of an "ideal" reader who supposedly read voraciously from among the works that follow, the regiment's statistics reveal that these "treasures" were not borrowed a single time: *Bismarck's Speeches,* Johann Gottlieb Fichte's *Address to the German Nation,* Friedrich Jahn's *German Folk Customs,* Martin Luther's *To the Christian Nobility of the German Nation,* Thomas Mann's *Friedrich and the Grand Coalition,* Ernst Treitschke's *The Ordensland Prussia,* and Wilhelm I's *Letters, 1870–71* and *Letters to Bismarck.* The discrepancy between the actual reading interests of soldiers and what the proponents of cultural superiority believed the soldiers were reading is sharply acute in light of these statistics. Even as various cultural functionaries continued to imagine the trenches as a kind of "moral institution" (borrowing Schiller's language) in which class differences were surmounted through popular education, the books provided by army and popular education agencies did not interest the soldiers. Although the authorities could exclude a socially critical and modernist type of literature from field libraries, they could hardly force soldiers to ingest the normative canon of the Second Reich.[57]

Given the limited interest in either didactic writings or Weimar classicism, belletristic works were the most popular in the regiment's library, and a list of the works most often read by the soldiers is revealing. As documented by Schilling, every one of the available volumes of entertaining and humorous literature found readers, as did most of the novels and novellas. Many of the most frequently read works were by authors who are virtually forgotten today. Others are as familiar today as they were during the war. Again, it is essential to keep in mind when considering the reading habits of soldiers that two extensive categories of German literature—"biased and problematic writings"—were from the beginning kept from the front libraries. On the other hand, despite national attempts by some circles to discourage the availability of "enemy" writings, a fair sampling of Russian, English, and French literature was available in translation to regimental readers as late as 1917, and several of the works by Leo Tolstoi, Feodor Doestoevsky, Paul Verlaine, Victor-Marie Hugo, Émile Zola, Thomas Carlyle, and Charles Dickens found interested readers.[58]

For Schilling, the fact that the overall lender frequency for novels and

Fig. 4.6 Poster encouraging the reading of "our thinkers and poets. The book offers joy and consolation."

novellas was higher than that for entertaining literature was reason for joy: "It is especially pleasing for the level of education in the regiment that percent-agewise, the more valuable literature (novels and novellas) is being read more frequently than the lighter entertaining literature." This fact is misleading, however, as the total available number of works labeled "entertainment litera-ture" was more than double that of the other category, and every single such volume was read at least once, which cannot be said of numerous novels and novellas kept by the library.

More fundamentally, the aesthetic values underlying Schilling's differentia-tion between the two categories, although certainly mirroring the notions regarding the canon upheld by the Dürer Association and echoing a familiar polarity in post-enlightenment German literary history, invite other questions concerning the standards employed in distinguishing between the two. A contemporary reader of German literature might find it curious to discover such canonical works as Joseph von Eichndorff's *Aus dem Leben eines Tau-*

genichts, Franz Grillparzer's *Der arme Spielmann,* or a collection of Adelbert Stifter's *Erzählungen* categorized as entertaining literature, given the simultaneous presence of forgotten works by Herman Bang and Henryk Sienkiewicz in the higher category. Given this mode of categorization, another pertinent question is what exactly separates "good entertaining literature" from "trashy literature"?

The category of entertaining literature included many works whose authors are largely unknown today.[59] If, however, Schilling's statistics are representative of other field libraries as well, these largely unknown works overwhelmingly constituted the reading diet of Germany's soldiers while at war. Furthermore, if the war schooled a new generation of readership, it is with these works that soldiers "went to school." In terms of lender frequency, these works by little-known authors are—to subvert Franz Schauwecker's phrase—the actually read "Books of the Front." Although sufficient evidence exists to support the view that a new generation of readers had been stimulated by conditions at the front, it is quite an exaggeration to claim that Germany's soldiers reentered civilian society immersed in Weimar classicism. A consideration of the most widely read works from the available selection at the front, by contrast, provides a good sense of what notions about literature veterans may have carried over into the Weimar Republic. The "good, entertaining literature" of Walter Bloem, Rudolf Herzog, Fedor von Zobeltitz, and others schooled soldiers in a culturally affirmative literature that prevented a positive reception of the critical and avant-garde war novel and favored literature that perpetuated expectations developed during the war.

THE ADMINISTRATION OF
FELDBUCHHANDLUNGEN: ARMY POLICY,
SCHUND, AND REICHSTAG DEBATE

Trench bookstores were also entangled in the ever tightening web of book control, which extended to regulation of the books available for purchase in trench bookstores. In legitimating this mechanism of control, the debates surrounding the pernicious influence of *Schund* played a decisive role. United in their opposition to its dissemination, the army, the established book trade, and organizations concerned with *Volksbildung* created a pretext for a network of control that would regulate not only purported trash but other objects as well.

Before General Quartermaster Ludendorff took matters in hand in November 1916, a number of outlets for the sale of books had flourished in the occupied territories. Some army corps had given permission to several smaller paper goods and book stores to do business in individual towns under their jurisdiction. In early 1915 the *Börsenblatt* encouraged book vendors to undertake "the systematic cultivation and exploitation of such markets, which promise the book industry good success." Other army corps granted that privilege to a single large entrepreneur, often to a firm that already possessed a license to operate stores in train stations. By late 1915, such publishing empires as Ullstein, Hilger, and Stilke had established virtual monopolies in many sectors of the front, leading to vociferous complaints from other publishers who felt locked out from this lucrative market. General headquarters, after discussions with the publisher's society, addressed the complaints by sending out the following directive to all army commands: "In consideration of repeated complaints, a new unitary regulation is required. In it, institutions which have proven themselves should be protected provided they make allowance for participation by all native publishers. This later provision presupposes, of course, that their presence is warranted and justified in respect to the genres they publish and the content of these works."[60]

Even as a systematic unification of policy was begun, not all publisher's series were to be handled by the field bookstores; rather, the thrust of the decree was to ensure more access to the market for those firms considered acceptable. Subsequent complaints directed to the quartermaster general by various groups who felt their products were being treated with prejudice (notably Catholics and Socialists) continued to express dissatisfaction with existing arrangements.[61] Ludendorff, however, ensured full support for his measures from the established book trade in a series of meetings with the heads of the German Book Trade Association, the Retail Book Association, and the German Publishers' Association. A directive from his office in November 1916 summarized the suggestions and complaints received by that office since centralizing control over the establishment of bookstores in the field on January 3, 1916:

Primarily, there are complaints that the field bookstores are under the control of just a few bookstore companies. Monopolization by select individual publishers must be decisively opposed. By January 15, 1917, submit documentation to this office that states 1) the present occupant of the bookstore, 2) suggestions for change in the organization of the book trade in the field, 3) a statistical breakdown of the percentile participation of the individual publishing houses in the sale of books. In addition, there have been repeated complaints about the display of undeniably trashy and sensational literature. There is also a lack of inexpensive and well-written books and magazines that are popular with the men.

Instruct the officers charged with the supervision of field bookstores to pay greatest attention to the selection of reading material and to take care that the field book trade becomes an institution truly benefiting the men.[62]

The attention that Ludendorff devoted to the issue reflects his increased preoccupation with the influence of reading on his troops. The activity of reading was important in maintaining morale after two years of war, and Ludendorff sought to ensure that only "suitable" literature would perform this function. Recognizing the importance of maintaining good relations with the organized book trade, the decree reflects that organization's concerns about "trashy" literature and competition for the book market in the occupied territories, much discussed in the pages of the *Börsenblatt.*

Ludendorff's decree also addressed concerns that were voiced in several Reichstag debates on the merits of bookstores and libraries in the field. In these debates, the major political parties expressed support for establishing facilities making books accessible to soldiers.

Protocols of the legislative year 1917, for example, indicate just how pervasive the idea of the army as an educational institution had become. Representative Heinrich Schulz from Erfurt spoke on behalf of the Social Democrats in praising "the good start made in enabling soldiers the possibility of developing their mental capacities alongside normal military training and activity."[63]

Schulz, the author of *Arbeiterbildung und Bildungsarbeit* had been active before the war in planning and enacting a program of worker's education, and the educational potential presented by the establishment of field bookstores was of great interest to him: "The field bookstores, along with some other opportunities, offer the possibility to conduct a share of valuable cultural-politics, not only during the war in general, but actually in the midst of battle conditions themselves" (3147).

Schulz continued that although he did not believe that every German soldier had marched off to war "with Goethe's 'Faust' in his backpack," he could document "how strong the need was felt for reading and education in worker's circles." Schulz judged the situation, "therefore we have the duty to do what we can from here, the homeland, to feed them intellectual nourishment as much and often as possible" (3150).

Schulz's optimism for the educational potential of the situation was dampened, however, by the monopolistic control of the three largest publishing houses: "Right away, a number of larger publishing houses immediately entered this newest arena of capitalistic exploitation. The main companies who to this day hold the business firmly and almost exclusively in their hands are the well-known railroad station book vendor Stilke and the publishing firms of Hilger and Ullstein" (3148).

Because a monopoly's policies are dominated by a "purely profit driven interest," there were several pernicious effects, according to Schulz: "Less-established firms had been precluded from reaching an audience at the front, the larger publishing houses sold works [*Ladenhüter*, unsalable items] at the front which otherwise would not find buyers, and these conditions finally had encouraged the production of literary war trash" (3149).

One finds an uncanny agreement between Schulz's remarks and Ludendorff's decree, even if for different reasons. Both decry the monopolistic control exercised by the above-named firms, who for their part had stimulated remarkable levels of circulation. But Ludendorff had little interest in promoting the specific presses—such as the Dietz Verlag—that Schulz felt were being disadvantaged. Indeed, Ludendorff continued to support the Stilke enterprise, taking pride in the firm's success in his autobiography. Although a common concern about the prevalence of "trashy literature" underlies both documents, the authors' opinions of what constituted such literature would have varied in many instances, particularly after the implementation of the Patriotic Instruction propaganda campaign. As the war entered its final year, Ludendorff increased his intensity in directing officers overseeing the selection of books to avoid socialist literature. The type of literature deemed to be "trashy" could also include those with a socialist bent.

On the other hand, the examples of *Kriegschund* cited by Schulz were also included in the lists of forbidden trashy literature periodically issued by Ludendorff's office. Foremost among them were publications of the Verlagshaus für Volksliteratur und Kunst, which sold mildly erotic books. Their titles—*Kriegsbräute* (War Brides), *Die Schwester des Franktireurs* (The Sister of the Partisan Fighter), *Deutsche Hiebe, Deutsche Liebe* (German Thrashing, German Loving)—provoked laughter in the Reichstag (page 3151), but their existence was a bane to dozens of organizations concerned with *Volkserziehung*, including the Social Democrats.

The *Schundkämpfer* (trash combatants) uniformly condemned the Nick Carter novels and the series "Wanda von Brannburg," "Pat Conner, Master Detective," and "Nat Pinkerton: The King of Detectives," but such programmatic appeals seemed to presuppose that the standards constituting "good" literature (like morality?) were self-evident.

Rudolf Schenda has suggested that the vehemence with which the antitrash debate was waged had much to do with the economic interests of publishers affiliated with the German Book Trade Association who felt threatened by the unwanted competition the so-called trashy literature posed: "Hiding behind the opposition of the teachers to trashy literature are the massive economic interests of publishers who recognized the strongest possible threat to the sale of their own merchandise in the mass production of their trashy literature competitors."[64]

My research for the period 1914–1918 would support that view. Although the established publishing houses also regarded the book production of the independent *Volksbildung* organizations with suspicion, they were united with them—for differing reasons—against publishers deemed to be purveyors of trashy literature. Groups as disparate as the "German Poet's Memorial Foundation," which was interested in promoting "good" literature, and the publishers who belonged to the German Book Trade Association, who were upset that the firms producing "trash" did not belong to the association and thus did not abide by the organization's rules, in this case shared a common purpose.

The issue of literary trash continued to play an important role during the war years, as such journals as Karl Brunner's *Die Hochwacht* and Ferdinand Avenarius's *Dürerbund* agitated to protect readers from the dangers of pernicious literature. Frustrated by the lack of a uniformly enforced policy before the war, the antitrash combatants convinced individual army corps to enforce statutes in earnest. A policy was thus inaugurated that took advantage of the state of siege legalized by the war.

The Seventh Army Corps in Münster and the Eleventh Corps in Kassel were the first, in late 1915, to establish lists numbering several hundred volumes of "trashy" literature, which thereafter were prohibited from sale within their jurisdiction. In March 1916, the Berlin army corps revised the earlier lists and created a policy model that most other army corps followed. A most significant change in directives affected the traveling book vendors and "the stationary trade" as well.

The army enforced the new law with some vigor. In Württenberg's Thirteenth army corps, for example, the army and local police threatened a year's imprisonment for any book dealer that sold volumes like *Red Napoleon* or *Ten Years in the Foreign Legion*. Responsible officers in Stuttgart filed periodic reports attesting that all bookstores had been inspected and whenever necessary their owners had been warned or punished.[65]

Brunner and Avenarius specifically exempted those series that treated the war in a patriotic fashion from the category of trash. This, it seems, was an issue too thorny for them to broach: for what did the word *patriotic* denote, and was its meaning identical in all literary uses?

Still, so long as the triad "God, Kaiser, Fatherland" was upheld, *Börsenverein* publishers generally had no need to fear the ire of the moralists. The much-heralded German Poet's Memorial Foundation, for example, was quick to add the series *Der Eichenkranz* to its publications in 1915 (the first volume by Fritz Müller was entitled *Mirthfulness from the War*) to complement its offerings of *Heimatliteratur* (literature about home), among them works by Otto Ernst, Hermann Löns, Peter Rosegger, Herman Stehr, Ernst Zahn, and selected fiction of nineteenth-century realism.

"Hesse's Popular Library," published by Hesse and Becker, another series often recommended (along with that of the German Poet's Memorial Foundation) by the library association journal, the *Blätter für Volksbibliotheken und Lesehallen,* had added dozens of war books to its offerings by 1917. Their titles suggest little difference from those published by the producers of so-called *Schund: The Spy and Other Tales, The Navy Cruiser's Last Distress,* and *Heroes and Comrades* were three of the many recommended by the library journal. The onerous designation "trash" often seemed to have less to do with the story than with who published it.

If for ultimately different reasons than those motivating the bourgeois combatants of "trashy literature," Heinrich Schulz's reasoning would seem to place him securely in the tradition of Social Democracy that embraced German Classicism as the source of its aesthetic judgment. For it is the inexpensive volumes of German classicism produced by publishers such as the German Poet's Memorial Foundation, Reclam, Teubner, and Wiesbadener Volksbücher that for Schulz legitimate their reputation as publishers of "good" books, even though each firm's offerings also included volumes that one could at best describe as "entertaining literature."[66]

Schulz overlooked, however, how easily any unwanted type of literature could be labeled as trash. His socialist colleague, Dr. Haas from Baden, was more sensitive to the implications of the debate in the Reichstag for censorship, but he too advocated restriction of "trashy" literature: "Gentlemen, we certainly don't want to impose a kind of censorship that authorizes the army commands to regulate the reading wishes of soldiers like schoolmasters; however, what is clearly trash ought not be permitted entrance to the field bookstores."

But precisely such a "schoolmaster's hand" was increasingly evident at the front once Patriotic Instruction began in earnest, and the specter of "trashy literature" provided the conceptual basis from which to implement it. For Haas, what constituted trash was self-evident. (He uses the "Kino library" series as his example.) But how could "trashy" literature be contained? Could all "reasonable people" agree on what was and was not trash?

Before considering the intersection of the trash debate with literary depictions of heroism, a last ingredient mentioned by Schulz within the constellation of popular education issues merits attention. It is the question of affordability and the status of the "inexpensive book" within the book industry.

Reclam and other like-minded publishing enterprises merited praise in Schulz's eyes because they packaged affordable books. "A soldier wants to have precisely those inexpensive books. He is able to afford twenty pfennigs for a book, and once in a while forty or sixty pfennigs; but he can never afford to pay three or four marks."[67] Of course, Schulz reminded his listeners, most firms preferred selling expensive books: "When I sell a book for four marks, I profit much faster then if I sell twenty books for twenty pfennigs each! . . . But the soldier cannot afford to buy a book for four marks. For the soldier, for the soldier's intellectual invigoration, it is much more important that the twenty books for twenty pfennigs stem from the Reclam collection or from the *Wiesbadener Volksbüchern* or from another collection than from a book for four marks" (3149).

Those firms that had committed their resources before the war to the production of inexpensive books benefited from these calls for reform. Although the movement toward the "inexpensive book" had been resisted for obvious economic reasons by various members of the established book industry before 1914, many firms—for example, Cotta, Teubner, Insel, DVA—now began their own "Tornister-Bibliotheken" (backpack libraries), using the production principles pioneered by Reclam, to take advantage of the situation. Producing inexpensive books had become a patriotic duty. A hardcover previously distinguished a "good book"—distinguished, that is, from mere *Kolportage-Literature* (works hawked by traveling salesmen) in softbound volumes with flimsy paper—but now a book could no longer be judged by its cover. This industry wide shift to inexpensive books is one of the war's lasting legacies.

WAR TRASH AND HEROICISM

Perhaps the most lucid criticism offered by an antitrash combatant on the difficult subject of trashy war literature was Paul Samuleit's essay *Trashy War Literature*. In contrast to most of his compatriots (including Brunner and Avenarius) Samuleit indeed described an unholy alliance between patriotism and "trash." When several established firms began producing trashlike volumes on patriotic themes, Samuleit's concern with protecting the nation's youth focused on youth at home who were "tremblingly and vicariously experiencing the momentous events." Greedy publishers, he warned, are quick to capitalize on the psychological state of these youths and their yearning for adventure.[68] Worse yet, the same immoral scribblers who enticed young souls before the war were also quick to abuse the "natural" interest of these easily excitable youngsters: "We face the fact that our youth devours incredible amounts of trashy war literature, which because of its mass appearance surely is not without effect. The same speedy pens that week for week before the war threw out onto the market the products of an impure, unbridled imagination in endless criminal and adventure swindles (stories would be much too kind a name) have thrown themselves with astonishing swiftness and unanimity onto the war events in order to reduce and mint this lofty and tragic content into a desperate meaningless tickling of the nerves and senses" (8). His criticisms, however, which could easily apply to many of the volumes labeled "good entertaining literature" by others, were instead directed solely at the same publishing houses he and his colleagues had opposed before the war—for example, Mignon Publishers and the Publishing House for Popular Literature and Art. Thus, the list of "trashy literature" he sent to regional army commanders included not a single volume produced by any member of the *Börsenverein.* Yet almost all of the Ullstein and Reclam war books shared the characteristics of the "adventure swindles" he held up to ridicule.

It is the exaggerated heroicism of the protagonists of the Mignon series, however, that most upset Samuleit. The fictional characters Heinz Brandt, who joins the Foreign Legion, Horst Kraft, a boy scout, and Konrad Götz, a member of the *Wandervögel,* are all portrayed as heroes whether their adventure transforms them into artillerymen, fliers, or cavalrymen—they all share "the unfailing assuredness with which they conduct themselves in all situations of supreme danger from which they emerge unscathed and in all the characteristics of their wondrous deeds." Furthermore, the settings for their deeds and the representations of geography and tactics are all "hazy and indistinct" (page 18).

According to Samuleit, this war was characterized by lengthy and massive battles, and these "trashy" representations inevitably portrayed limited *Raufereien* (brawls) of smaller groups "because only in such a setting does the superhuman hero have the opportunity to enact his wondrous deeds" (18). Samuleit further claimed that their celebration of individual heroism on the part of enlisted men cultivated disrespect for authority and the military leaders because it did not acknowledge the tactical genius of Ludendorff and Hindenburg as the font of victory.

Samuleit had identified this heroic archetype, whose characteristics were the same in city streets, suburbs, or the front. These criteria match characteristics of protagonists in several of the most popular volumes of Ullstein's war series—as in the adventures recounted in Manfred von Richthofen's autobiography or Plüschow's *Der Flieger von Tsingtau*—and serve equally well in Ernst Jünger's *Storm of Steel*, based on his wartime diary, published in several editions after 1922. Jünger read such "trash" as an adolescent before joining the French Foreign Legion. Further, at least one contemporary English reader of Jünger's war diary echoed Samuleit's complaint about the geographical and tactical "haziness of trashy literature" and wondered in print whether this topographical inexactness perhaps resulted from too many head injuries sustained by the author.[69]

Samuleit's criticism, flawed as it is, was limited to easy targets because both the military itself (whose responsibility was to prevent "trash") and the publishing trade had a great deal of interest in promoting the atavistic heroism so severely rejected by Samuleit, and a great deal to lose if definitions of trash became too precise.

In their attempt to create images of heroic soldiers, for example, individual army corps collected and kept files of "heroic deeds," which were regularly published in local and army newspapers. Military reporters writing for major publishing houses regularly filled their columns with accounts of individual feats of derring-do that belied the subordination of the individual to modern war machines. It is surely the army's continuing valorization of the hero that led the writers of the official army communiqués to focus increasingly on the deeds of particular "supermen," for example, the flying aces Oswald Boelke, Max Immelmann, and von Richthofen. Certainly it was unnecessary for strategic purposes to mention each new air victory by these "knights of the sky." The presence of these accounts in the communiqués in the last years of the war indicates the need to sustain the language of heroism, using the best suitable carriers for its expression.

Samuleit's insistence that the war was a "gigantic battle," lasting weeks and months and involving the artful coordination of thousands of individuals over vast expanses of terrain, was quite correct, but such portrayals did not sell books.

In any case, as a library journal article called "War Books for Our Youth" defensively noted, it was extremely difficult to apply rigid standards to stories depicting the war. What mattered most, wrote Johanna Mühlenfeld, were "purity of character, strict observance of historical facts, faultless German," and the "plausibility of the fictive plot."[70]

Her point, which pleaded leniency in judging books that, after all, were serving a good cause, was underlined in the *Dürerbund*'s literary *Kriegsratgeber* (War adviser, 1915–1916), intended to aid both the layman and the professional librarian in selecting reading material. Taking stock of the prolific appearance of war chronicles, the journal praised the production of popular treatments by the established book trade: "To the honor of the German book trade, publishers, and writers, it must be said that truly worthless, tasteless, and bad quality is hardly to be found among them." The slight hesitation implied by the qualifying modifier "hardly" is clarified by his explanation "that of course one must not measure these entertaining books by the same yardstick as one would serious works of instruction and science."[71]

The *War Adviser* found much to praise in its wartime issues. Presumably, it influenced the purchase policies of German libraries and thus helps to account for the thousands of such volumes one still finds today. A perusal of several hundred of these volumes reveals an affirmative publishing industry interacting with the state and military. The collaboration manifests most of the traits that Adorno and Horkheimer attributed to the culture industry.

ARMY-ADMINISTERED FIELD BOOKSTORES
UNDER THE AEGIS OF "PATRIOTIC
INSTRUCTION"

Public responses to the *Schund* debate provided the military with a conceptual framework legitimating its subsequent control of book distribution and the organization of libraries during the rest of the war. Ludendorff's solution to end monopolies, discussed in the *Reichstag* and alluded to in his own decree, was to establish book stores run by the army itself. The general quartermaster established "guidelines for the establishment of bookstores in the combat zone," intended to direct the establishment of a "purely military operation."[72] The antidote to monopolization was, as Ludendorff saw it, to accord strict control over the sale of books to the army itself. Once assuming command, Ludendorff could build on preexisting arrangements with the publishing trade. After his decree of January 3, 1916, any new bookstores were, whenever possible, run by soldiers who had been engaged in the book trade in their civilian life. The German Book Trade Association in Leipzig cooperated with the army's policy by compiling lists of appropriate personnel.

The final selection of books to be made available for sale to the troops was left to the approval of an individual officer. Lists of forbidden books and trashy literature were periodically amended to assist the supervising officer, and notices of new works considered especially suitable for consumption by soldiers, like the earlier-mentioned *Wir Marokko-Deutschen in der Gewalt der Franzosen* published by Ullstein, were circulated.

In compliance with Ludendorff's decree all military bookstores periodically provided tables listing the percentage of books sold in each store by publisher. Lists still extant from 1917 for individual, "purely military-run operations" show the following statistical breakdown: Reclam (10 percent), Ullstein (9 percent), S. Fischer (8 percent), Hesse and Becker (7 percent), Insel (7 percent), and Hilger (6 percent). Both the *Deutsche Verlagsanstalt,* with its overwhelming production of military chronicles, Teubner Publishers, with its war series, and G. J. Goeschen each accounted for 4 percent of the market. Albert Langen accounted for 3 percent of the books sold, while Enßlin's inexpensive adventure stories from the series "Bunte Bücher" and Callweg, the Dürer Association's publishing house, each accounted for 2 percent of total sales. The field bookstore in Cirey, which had a more extensive selection, reported simultaneously that the above firms, along with Cotta, Georg Müller, Grethlein, Piper, and Fleischel enjoyed equal shares of the market.[73]

It seems that the beneficiaries of Ludendorff's centralization polices were those firms that had inaugurated inexpensive series (with volumes costing one mark and less) that were in tune with the desired nationalist proclivities. Although after 1916 firms such as Ullstein and Hilger could no longer determine which books would be sold in most *Feldbuchhandlungen,* their publications that met these two desiderata continued to sell briskly under the army's stewardship.

One officer entrusted with overseeing the supply of books in one area of the front was the well-known author Richard Dehmel, who had accepted the post with high expectations of the possibilities for popular education. But Dehmel, who as an author had been the subject of a censorship trial, discovered with dismay that his duties reduced the position to that of a censoring functionary:

> My office as "book-examiner"—God forgive—has metamorphosed into a subdivision of the censorship police. I had hoped that here one could at least attend to the distribution of good books; but instead the office deals only with avoiding the introduction of bad books, and "bad" not from a pedagogic but from a military-bureaucratic viewpoint. In fact, we have virtually nothing to examine. The examination is undertaken in Leipzig by a supposedly liberal staff of critics. We receive only lists of applications from book vendors, administration offices, custom offices, etc., regarding the books to be imported.[74]

Dehmel's remarks, contained in a war book that Samuel Fischer had urged him not to publish, disclose the ever-tighter web of book control practiced under Patriotic Instruction, initiated in autumn 1917.

The aim of the program, as enunciated by the "Guidelines for Patriotic Instruction," was to promote "strength to fight" and "belief in victory."[75] The organizational forms judged to be best suited to induce this morale were comprehensive and diverse: lectures by civilian speakers, the expansion of the scope of army newspapers, increased control over field bookstores, introduction of reading rooms where "good" literature was available, and the proliferation of field theaters and cinemas. As we have seen before, Philipp Witkop, administrator of a series of university courses at the front, Walter Bloem, director of the *Feldpresse Stelle*, and Anton Kippenberg, a regional director, were three individuals involved in executing this program. The common content of this patriotic instruction, regardless of the organizational means employed, was to solidify an undiminished "determination to gain victory, which cannot be shaken by the whispering of any rumors from outside our ranks. . . . Our men should not become soft as a result of the solicitude and infiltration in their spiritual condition, but on the contrary, should become hardened. Patriotic Instruction is to orient him to the inexorable facts of today. Fate has decreed the difficult path as the one that our nation must now take. Recalcitrance and grumbling strengthen the hopes of the enemy and lengthen the path to peace. The strength to fight and belief in victory shorten that path."

Appropriate guidelines were added as the war continued and as the individual programs became more elaborate. Each army corps was assigned its own regional director. One of his most important tasks was to oversee the supply of books in his area of the front. As we have seen, it was believed that reading had become an indispensable inspiration to better morale on the front, and Ludendorff meant to ensure that only the "right" kind of literature was made available to the troops. His task was facilitated by the establishment of centralized military bookstores in most corps, a process that began in 1916. As Ludendorff had intended, this centralized form of book distribution gradually eliminated most private civilian bookstores. Within the army corps where the process was successfully installed, an individual army bookstore could request only those books and newspapers that were on order at the central bookstores. Direct contact between a bookstore and a publisher was not permitted. Thus, only those works approved of by the overseers of the central bookstores (the regional directors of Patriotic Instruction) would be available for sale in the field. Local supervisors, like Richard Dehmel, were thereby markedly curtailed in influencing the selection of books; hence his frustration.

Even where earlier contracts allowed the firm Stilke to provide its services to a region, the firm did so under the ever-stricter supervision of the regional director. By the end of the war, Stilke and Schmitt (the firm that had garnered a contract with the Bavarian First Army Corps) ordered reading material only as directed by the supervising military officers.

The Chief of Informational Services (IIIb) Nicolai stressed in his meetings with regional army corps commanders that book commerce in war zones is "inseparable from Patriotic Instruction," and in 1918 he encouraged them to expand the number of book outlets in each army corps.[76]

The director of the Eighth Army Corps's campaign, Captain Leonhard, in underlining that same point, noted that the well-documented desire for education by the troops provided a unique opportunity to influence the hearts and minds of soldiers: "Every expressed hunger for education offers an excellent opportunity to influence the mentality of the men in the sense of Patriotic Instruction through the assignment of suitable reading material." Regional directors were told also that they should not hesitate to forbid any pernicious reading material: "Field bookstores in the war zone operate under the jurisdiction of Supreme Army Command. Of course it is quite impossible that reading material will be distributed by this service organ, which has been judged by Army Command to be damaging to the spirit of the troops. We need not in any way tread too gingerly with the prohibition against distributing certain books and newspapers."[77]

The newspapers *Vorwärts* and the *Berliner Tageblatt* were most immediately affected by these measures. Soldiers were precluded from purchasing "undesirable" newspapers unless they were willing to be marked—via regular military mail supervision—as a direct subscriber. At the same time, as discussed in Chapter 2, Nicolai and Bloem were taking steps to replace civilian newspapers and upgrade the scope and circulation of the army newspapers within the jurisdiction of army corps. Similarly, unless a soldier could acquire books while on leave or find civilians willing to send books to him through the mail, he was compelled to choose his reading materials from the army's preselection. Though far from a hermetical seal, these steps undertaken in the last stage of the war tightened the flow of production and consumption. To the extent that literature contributed to individual and public memory of the war, this tightening of the line between production and consumption constitutes an important dimension of our understanding of systematic censorship. Freud remarked that the presence of memory, regardless of how displaced, is indicative of the limits of censorship. The system described here could not proscribe all memory in the direction of Patriotic Instruction, but this institutional setting, mediating between *Aufklärung* and everyday life, left traces that are evident in later commemorizations of "die große Zeit."

Because army bookstores were convenient, their turnover was brisk. "Sales rates rise constantly," the representative of Army Corps A, Captain von Johnston, told Nicolai in June 1918. The forty bookstores in that area, situated in a section of the western front, reported an income of 80,000 marks a month as of February 1918.[78] Rittmeister Goertz, representing Army Corps C, reported the existence of seventy bookstores in its section of the western front, with monthly receipts of 200,000 marks. Goetz noted that 50,000 marks monthly was pure profit, used by the army corps to finance Patriotic Instruction.[79]

Thus a remarkable economy, feeding in part on soldiers' desire for education and entertainment, funded a program whose aim was to perpetuate the psychological preparedness to continue the war at all costs. In light of subsequent developments in Germany between 1933 and 1945, the intertwining of state, capital, and military interests after 1916 marks a significant and portentous chapter in the bureaucratization of culture. Furthermore, by actively representing the war as being winnable until the last week before the truce was signed, and by preselecting a specific type of literature for soldiers intended to sustain that belief, the campaign promulgated the myth that the war had not been lost on the battlefield.

The interaction of the military with selected publishing houses and the *Volksbildung* movement combined to foster an unprecedented circulation of books. As I have shown, this activity was motivated by many factors, none of which were innocent. An impression remains in the popular imagination of *die große Zeit* of idealistic young soldiers reading Goethe and Nietzsche. That image rests in part on a rhetoric generated during the war for specific reasons, and also on such textual evidence as the *War Letters of Fallen Students,* which as we have seen are no less disinterested. The image needs to be broadened with reference both to the institutions that fostered reading culture and to the kinds of books that schooled a nation at war.

Chapter 5 Publishing the War: Cotta and the "Spirit of 1914"

The collaboration between the organized book trade and the military has not yet been fully documented, partially because of the general absence of archival materials pertaining to the wartime activities of most publishing houses. Most firms were never interested in preserving records, and many of the records they did keep were destroyed in the bombings of Munich, Leipzig, Stuttgart, and Berlin during the Second World War. The self-validating histories commissioned by the publishing houses themselves have usually been the authoritative source for literary historians interested in the role of publishers in establishing and perpetuating any given canon of literature.

Perusing recent histories of publishing firms, one wonders how the tens of thousands of affirmative war books produced between 1914 and 1933 came to fill libraries in Germany and elsewhere. Previous scholarship focusing on the period from 1900 to 1933 in publishing activity has centered on firms that are thought to have laid the groundwork for National Socialism.[1] This analysis has led to an encapsulation of "bad" Nazi or Nazi-sympathetic firms, separating them sharply from the "good" (bourgeois) mainstream. In Germany, however, ugly expressions of cultural chauvinism and enthusiastic affirmation of the war do not belong exclusively to the camp of acknowledged prefascist publishers. They are also part of the mainstream literary marketplace, which, along with the myth of an undefeated army, entered the troubled period of the Weimar Republic.

Like history, the literary text is a construction, the product of the interaction of a host of mediating agencies and institutions. German literary and historical prose written before 1945 about the First World War recalls explicitly the relation among authority, the state, and narration, which Hegel had cited as the precondition of historical writing more generally. Examining the practices that framed production in publishing houses offers an insight into these relations in a specific context. It also serves to displace the authority grounding textual meaning from the author, as traditionally assigned by literary criticism, to the institution of literary culture, as the agency in which the characteristics defining mass culture and the literary marketplace effectively intermingle to produce semantic meaning. The theoretical point of my interest in Reclam, Ullstein, and now Cotta is, therefore, not to replace the author as the originating agent of discourse with a new originator (that is, the publisher) nor to affirm the benign role often attributed in commissioned histories of publishing houses to the publisher as a heroic handmaiden of the author's work. Instead, joining the noun *literature* to another—*institution*—reformulates the aim of literary analysis as a social process.[2]

From this social-historical perspective, it is unhelpful to treat individual works as if they were autonomous from the mediating agencies that ultimately made them social products. Nor is it useful to ground the meaning of a text by reading the author as its source and defining principle, or, alternatively, by the volition to see in that work a mirror of any particular sociopolitical *Zeitgeist*. On the other hand, it is highly useful to see the institution of literature as one of many social and economic institutions engaged in the contentious process whereby political and social discourse is produced and disseminated. Writers, and their intentions, form only one part of this social process. There are many other agencies that also mediate this process: publishers, booksellers, book reviewers, and, as a good deal of recent literary theory (particularly reader-response criticism) has argued, the actual readers of imaginative literature. Roland Barthes, who profoundly influenced the turn toward reader-response criticism as well as poststructuralism, discerned in the "death of the author" a reopening of the work against the closure of signification which the concept of the author had imposed upon literature. He wrote: "The reader is the space on which all the quotations that make up a writing are inscribed without any of them being lost; a text's unity lies not in its origin but in its destination." The text is not a fixed entity, indifferent to those who read it. In Barthes's view, the polymorphous nature of the work cannot be contained by any single reader. The reader, however, cannot be held up as a transcendental grounding for the reception of meaning. Readers, like texts, are not outside of history, but are themselves subject to the "incessant movement of recontextualization," which Jacques Derrida has offered as one definition of deconstruction.[3] Readers too are constituted—by educational practices, class, race, and gender—and to transfer interpretative authority from the author to the reader simply displaces the "author-function" to the reader in order to continue to assign intentionality. Paradoxically, this may ascribe a sovereignty to the reader that borders on volunteerism as much as had the sovereignty attributed the author.

Such volunteerism is limited, however, by consideration of the necessity of the work to appear as an object to be read. Between 1914 and 1918 in Germany, a work or text typically would have been written by an author (perhaps upon solicitation), accepted by a particular publishing house, reviewed by state and military censors, and printed in numbers deemed acceptable by authority (given the limitations of paper and glue rationing) before it was presented to readers. Roger Chartier has therefore urged that "it is essential to remember that no text exists outside of the support that enables it to be read; any comprehension of a writing, no matter what kind it is, depends on the forms in which it reaches its reader." Consideration of this material process undermines the possibility both of a traditional reading of the "text itself" and one that postulates "a direct immediate relationship between the 'text' and the reader, between the 'textual signals' used by the author and the 'horizon of expectation' of those he addresses."[4]

To seek out the workshop origins of a text or series of texts is not to reinstate origination as the linchpin of meaning but to consider any textual "presentation" as being already a mediated re-presentation constituted by the play of institutional forces described throughout this study. In the language of formalism it is belatedly to "bare the device" in a manner that conjoins a linguistic analysis with consideration of the institutional forces that prefigure a work's presentation. Within this conceptual space beyond origins and "authorship," the publishers appear as privileged readers, who on a very fundamental level determine literary value because they determine what will be published and available for reception. The limits to that privilege during the war became apparent when the work accepted by the editorial board was submitted to the military censors, and the commodity thereafter was purchased by enough readers to make a profit.

The activities of Cotta, Ullstein, and Reclam during the war highlight different facets of the interaction between the publishing industry and the military in enlarging a reading public and in creating and disseminating "knowledge" about the ongoing war. The types of manuscripts solicited and published by each firm bespeak an active role in affecting public opinion about war events and a constant interpretation on their part of how to structure the events and facts in the "unprocessed historical record" into a narrative. Although individual (his-)story tellers similarly structure the historical record by including some events and excluding others, stressing some and subordinating others, the publisher ultimately selects or rejects from the plethora of possible arguments, emplotments, and ideological implications submitted to them to determine what will be made available to the reading public.

As expressed in Chapter 2, a general assumption behind my analysis is the consideration that in the long run, the normative, paradigmatic view of battle-field conditions that was created and disseminated through wartime accounts conditioned many readers during the Weimar Republic to reject the antiwar novels of the late 1920s in favor of a type of literature (Beumelburg, Schau-wecker, Wehner) that continued the narrative and thematic strategies of representation patterned during the war itself. Cotta's publishing efforts contributed to this pattern by actively creating a particular war aesthetic in this vein, thus confirming what had been well documented as early as the eighteenth century: publishing houses can be thought of as an institution where aesthetic, political, and economic forces commingle to produce textual meaning.

Although suitable archival records about individual publishing house activity during the war are extremely scarce, substantial records do exist for Cotta. I will focus on the firm's role in disseminating a view that has been labeled "the spirit of 1914." This discussion augments consideration of Ullstein as a site where the war book as best-seller emerges, and the analysis of Reclam in relation to the role that reading came to assume on the front.

As the war began, Cotta could look back at what was no doubt the most illustrious publishing heritage in Germany. In the view of Adolf Kröner, the firm's owner, the prestige derived from having been the publisher of Goethe and Schiller was enhanced by becoming the publisher of Bismarck's *Thoughts and Memories*. The progression Goethe–Schiller–Bismarck, itself an indication of the direction taken by the firm during the Wilhelmine era, also suggests Cotta's turn to memoiristic, historical, and political prose, while its contemporary belletristic offerings were dominated by the likes of Jacob Christoph Heer, Rudolf Herzog, and Rudolf Stratz. At the beginning of the war Cotta was controlled by Robert Kröner, who immediately assumed command as a captain training recruits in nearby Ludwigsburg. His proximity to Stuttgart allowed him to continue directing the firm, with the assistance of editors Eduard von der Hellen and Karl Rosner. Rosner, who later became an official war correspondent and a confidant of Crown Prince Wilhelm, suggested a policy in mid-September 1914 that would guide the firm's interest in literature about the war. Despite the uncertainties of the literary marketplace, he advocated active solic-itation of war books: "It would surely be a great source of joy were Cotta able to harvest as rich a crop as possible from this time of war." Foremost among Rosner's recommendations in this letter was the suggestion to approach high-ranking military and diplomatic figures to convince them to write either mem-oirs or popular histories of the military's tactics and exploits. Although the High Command reserved the prerogative of writing a "total history of the war," Rosner speculated that regional army or navy commanders might be persuaded to undertake works limited in scope but "offer[ing] the promise of large sales."[5]

The firm consequently approached a number of officers and was successful in stimulating the interest of Admiral Kurt von Maltzahn, General Friedrich von Bernardi, and the Prussian war minister Hermann von Stein. The pub-lisher's expectations for the ideational content of such works is apparent in Cotta's letter to Kurt von Maltzahn (October 8, 1914) in which Kröner in-formed the admiral that he intended to publish "a patriotic work about the German Fleet" and asked for his cooperation in the expectation that such a work could be expected to "exercise a strong recruiting power on behalf of the German Navy."[6] Von Maltzahn reacted with enthusiasm, and subsequent correspondence reflected their anticipation of the war's victorious conclusion. When the war ended without the anticipated victory, both parties agreed to forgo publication, with Kröner writing on November 22, 1918: "We too cannot presume that now and during the next few years an interest in a book about the German Navy (which indeed no longer exists) will be as strong as it would have been in the case of a fortunate conclusion to the war."[7]

This episode reveals the policy adopted by Cotta regarding the war. Cotta approached only senior officers as potential authors for its war histories. Cotta's adaptation of the perspective of the High Command is confirmed by the list of authors whose unsolicited manuscripts were rejected between 1914 and 1918. All of the war prose submitted by soldiers below the rank of captain was summarily rejected, most without even being read by an editor. Further, it was evident that Cotta was not interested in publishing the perspective of the frontline combatant, even if that of a field officer.[8]

The parameters of any account that would bear the firm's insignia were clearly set by Cotta's expectation of a narrative extolling the tactical superiority of a victorious High Command. In 1918, faced with the factual reality of an unavoidable military collapse, Cotta left the war open-ended by refraining from encoding defeat in its publications. Instead, in the decade after the Armistice the firm continued to sell those works that incarnated the "spirit of 1914" that characterizes the wartime championing of the poetry of Rudolf Herzog, Otto König, and Gustav Schüler, the war fiction of Thea von Harbou and Friedrich Loofs (writing under the name Armin Steinart), and the essays of Friedrich Meinecke.[9]

Cotta's publishing of war books by these writers between 1914 and 1918 attests to the nationalistic and cultural-conservative policy adopted by the firm throughout the war. The firm's best-selling war book, actually published before hostilities began, was one of three written by Thea von Harbou entitled *War and Women* (1913).[10]

This collection of short stories depicting the reactions of several idealized women to the war remarkably anticipated the enthusiastic public affirmation of the declaration of war in August 1914. The virtues celebrated by von Harbou's heroines—a commander's wife who is transformed from a pacifist to an ardent patriot, a mother who encourages her youngest son to join the navy even though his brother has drowned in a submarine, a nurse who stays at her station in a surgery ward even though it means losing a last chance to visit her mortally wounded brother—propelled her book to best-seller status and frequent reprintings in both civilian and military newspapers.

The story "Three Days' Leave" prophetically anticipated the carnivalesque atmosphere of July and August 1914, effectively capturing the "spirit of 1914." As a regiment's commander prepares to leave for the front, his wife (previously a "passionate champion on behalf of the idea of world peace" [23]) is caught up in the outburst of emotion generated by the pealing of bells and the singing of patriotic songs. The "conversion" of Brigitte von Wasdorff is described by the omniscient narrator as a religious rebirth: "As a wave spills over everything that comes close to it, thus the holy inspiration of this hour carried her away without resistance as well. And she allowed herself to be carried by it and looked and listened as if she had been born blind and deaf and suddenly had been healed" (34).

Her experience culminates in a sensation of ego-dissolution that permits her to become a "part of the whole," a member of a totality "which is of one blood." Buoyed by the enthusiastic reception of the book, Kröner encouraged von Harbou to cease her work on other projects and write additional war books. Cotta published two other works by her despite von der Hellen's reservations regarding their literary merit. The promise of financial success for such topical works ultimately outweighed the editor's aesthetic reservations.

Although von Harbou's stories skillfully evoked the "spirit of 1914" for wartime readers, Friedrich Meinecke gave that sentiment a political-historical founding in *Die deutsche Erhebung von 1914* (The German uprising of 1914). This volume of essays resulted from Kröner's direct appeal to Meinecke (September 30, 1914) to submit a manuscript that would render the political-historical meaning of "this time of greatness" for the German public.[11]

The essays that Meinecke submitted for publication subsequently were often quoted during the first years of the war, and since that time have been used as singular examples of the "spirit of 1914." The work combines a certitude regarding the ultimate rationality of an orderly historical process with Meinecke's faith that the spirit of the German nation was destined to triumph over the materialism incarnated by the West: "In the midst of the most terrible war in human memory . . . the German people raises itself to its old faith in the meaning and reason of human history, in the victory of spirit over brute force, and in the victory of the ideas that affect this spirit."[12]

These essays provide a potent and often-repeated rhetoric elevating Germany's war effort to the status of an all-encompassing idea, and they also mark Cotta's editorial guidelines regarding its publication of war books. Manuscripts that adhered to an analogous interpretation of ongoing events in the form of poetry, like Gustav Schüler's religiously colored poems in *Gottessturmflut* or Otto König's *Glocken im Sturm* were assured a sympathetic reading by Cotta's editors. Indeed, Cotta's publication of König's war poems, which valorized in equal measure the spirit of the German and the Austrian war efforts, garnered him an invitation to the Austrian High Command and to the front as an official war correspondent.

It is again telling that Cotta summarily rejected any war poetry submitted by actual combatants. Similarly, prose that did not convey either nationalism or a sense of the spiritual essence of the conflict was rejected. Thus, in April 1915, Cotta rejected F. M. Kircheisen's proposal for his war books because of the concern that the author intended to devote too much attention to neutral and enemy countries in his account. Karl Rosner (April 26, 1915) wrote: "I worry somewhat that Herr Kircheisen, perhaps because of his permanent residence in Geneva, seems to think more objectively and more neutrally about our war than will be stomachable for every German thinking man. We don't need books that above all else are timidly concerned not to hurt any Frenchmen, Englishmen, or Belgians."[13]

The absence of traditional heroicism led to Cotta's rejection of Curt Moreck's collection of short stories, *Men in Battle* (submitted in August 1915). These stories bespoke an accurate military analysis of trench conditions in that phase of the war, as reflected in the work's motto that "to hold out and be patient, this is modern heroism." As with his own war books, Rosner insisted that narrative representations of the war be infused with traditional, not passive, heroicism and a sense of the "higher" spiritual mission motivating the German war effort. Although Cotta published other works by Moreck before 1914, both Rosner and von der Hellen believed that his wartime prose was no longer "timely."[14]

In rejecting yet another of Moreck's submissions (January 26, 1915), *Combat and Peace,* Rosner again raised the issue of heroicism in arguing that the war constituted a watershed in literary taste: "The passive heroes of the past who allowed themselves to be borne by life will presumably not recapture the preferred spot in narrative literature they previously occupied. The new hero of the novel will be an active person, who masters life."[15] By inference, Rosner was predicting an end to the preeminence of naturalism and certain forms of expressionist modernism, and the rebirth of heroic literature.

In 1916, Rosner finally agreed to publish a war novel set at the front. Friedrich Loofs, a medical officer, had written a novel (*Der Hauptmann*) that was influenced by his admiration for Theodore Fontane. Loofs envisioned the work as a counterpoint to the "dreadful" volumes of the Ullstein war series. Unlike the Ullstein books, he claimed that his was a story that "realistically" depicted events on the front.[16] Impressed by the manuscript, Eduard von der Hellen wrote Kröner that it was the finest story about war he had ever read; his enthusiasm was subsequently shared by Rosner and Kröner.

Each of these readers was enthusiastic about the manuscript because it transferred the "spirit of 1914" into the trenches. Enlivened by predictable depictions of enemy misconduct and atrocities, the narrative focuses on a company of soldiers who, in trying to rescue their much-admired commanding officer, incarnate idealism, self-sacrificing bravery, and optimism. Von der Hellen admired the "excellent psychological observations" depicting "the genuine human being, as he *must* develop in the most varied directions due to war."[17]

The title figure of *Der Hauptmann* is the first servant of his company, and like all the other officers (including an army doctor), he is motivated by an acute sense of duty. The soldiers never reflect on the reasons for the war; the condition of being at war is simply accepted by all as given. There is neither any suggestion that peace will arrive through any means save a German military victory. The "necessary" character development of the "genuine human being," to which von der Hellen alluded in his editorial evaluation, is the willing affirmation of the inevitability of death in defense of the nation. The student volunteer Loos embodies this affirmation: following a display of cowardice, he gladly accepts his death on the battlefield at the end of the story.

Although the story's plot and character portrayals fit nicely into Cotta's editorial policy, its depictions of battle did in fact cause problems with the regional military censors. The numerous excised passages share one common feature—a depiction of trench violence—that readers would not encounter in any war books published in Germany before 1919. The sanctioned conception of this war as being fundamentally a spiritual conflict of ideas, as Meinecke had paradigmatically written, did not allow for a depiction of the corporeal violence wrought by modern warfare.

The most explicit depictions of battle carnage—heads smashed opened by shovels, soldiers literally blown up by mortar fire, the blood of bayonetted soldiers pouring over their killers—were excised, along with the passages in which (anticipating Remarque's similar language) warfare was depicted as not elevating soldiers in the manner of an educational experience but rather transforming them into frenzied animals.[18]

Typical of such passages is the moment when the field doctor Bornemann lets loose his fury: "Bornemann didn't think for a moment longer about the Red Cross armband which he had worn on his left arm. . . . There was only one will in him and one thought: kill. . . . Here murder jubilated, here people had become animals who wanted to tear each other up, to maim and mash."[19] A graphic depiction of the physical results of this will to kill was available only in manuscript form, because it too was censored: "The butt of the soldier's weapon mashed down and smashed a skull into a bloody mess. That was not enough to still the rage of the others. He turned the bloody weapon around: twice, three times, he drilled the bayonet into the body, pressed the dirty boot against the lifeless corpse and pulled it out again. Then he stabbed it again" (201). A later description of a trench battle was similarly censored, specifically limiting the omniscient narrator's voice describing the "hellish fight from man to man": "Accompanied by moaning of rage, the mangling and mashing causes lust.

Only one will expresses itself any longer: Kill! Only one thought any longer: Kill! Only one last craving, which drives both weapon and arm toward the life of the enemy"(261).

More than ten years later, Remarque described a scene similar to this that astonished readers, and the realism of Jünger's portrayal of the effect of battle on bodies in his *Storm of Steel* misled at least one commentator into believing his to be writings opposed to war. Both events attest to the later effects of wartime censorship. But the first-time (and thus dependent) author Loofs and the Cotta editorial board were more than happy to accommodate this type of censorship, with Loofs in fact complimenting "the most literate censor" for his "editing" suggestions.[20] Cotta's most recent house history notes that the firm had little difficulty with censoring agencies during the First World War. This is undoubtedly correct, but primarily so because the firm pursued an editorial policy with which the wartime government, increasingly dominated by military leadership, felt most comfortable. When problems occurred, as with *Der Hauptmann* or Rolf Lauckner's collection of vignettes, *The Detour to Death*, Cotta's editors required each author to remove any even *potentially* (in Lauckner's case) offensive material.[21] The firm that had published Goethe, Schiller, and Bismarck fully endorsed the war effort through November 1918 and sought to perpetuate the idealism that characterizes the "spirit of 1914."

In November 1916, after the book was cleansed of objectionable passages, Cotta wrote Loofs that the Central Office for Foreign Service wished to translate *Der Hauptmann* into several languages for its propaganda activity abroad.[22] The work harvested lavish praise from such organs as Avenarius's Dürer Association, with the "Literary Adviser" of the organization proclaiming *Der Hauptmann* "to be unquestionably the most powerful of all previous war tales," truly authentic and realistic.[23]

Cotta's concerted efforts in late 1914 to secure manuscripts by leading military figures finally failed to result in publications because of the "unhappy outcome" of the war. The firm did, however, take consolation in its publication of a memoir which de facto (if belatedly) offered Cotta's interpretation of the war's "meaning." The memoir was that of Crown Prince Wilhelm, and its release in 1922 created a sensation in the book market. In all, 400,000 copies of *Erinnerungen* were sold.[24] Cotta's success in soliciting Wilhelm's manuscript was a direct result of the close relationship that Karl Rosner had developed with the prince while Rosner was a war correspondent with the Crown Prince Army Corps.

It was Rosner who suggested to the Prince that he write his memoirs, and he quickly confirmed Kröner's and von der Hellen's interest in the project.[25] In order to provide Wilhelm with a veil of deniability, Rosner was credited as the memoir's editor. Any subsequent controversy of the "sketches, documents, diaries, and discussions" upon which the memoir was explicitly purported to be based could be attributed to the editor and not to the author.

Given the impossibility of ascribing the war with the narrative structure (and comic ending) of a successful military campaign as initially intended by Cotta's editorial staff, the firm had thus selected an authorial voice that reappraised the unforeseen circumstances in memoir form. As an indication of publishing policy, it is noteworthy—if not surprising, given the firm's choice of wartime authors—that Cotta chose the perspective of a monarchist from which to analyze recent events.

Equally symptomatic is Cotta's preference for the memoir rather than a fictional novel or play as the genre best suited to the war. Like virtually all belletristic publishers in Germany, Cotta showed no interest in fictional renderings of the war until the late 1920s.

The publication of Wilhelm's *Memories* thus marks Cotta's most significant contribution to the highly charged debate regarding the war's causes and meanings that dominated the Weimar Republic. The work also displays a number of affinities with the Cotta's wartime volumes by Meinecke, von Harbou, and Loofs, evidence of a continuity of editorial policy even after military defeat had altered the manner in which the war could be represented.

Wilhelm's memoir concludes with an affirmation of the same "spirit of 1914" that animated the works of Meinecke, von Harbou, and Loofs. In opposition to both the Allies' "criminal strangling treaty of Versailles" and the "rat catcher's melodies of a world brotherhood in a paradise of internationalism," Wilhelm implored his readers to "be above all Germans, once, and then once again!"[26] The essence of that Germanness is, as with Meinecke, primarily a question of *Geist:* "I call up the German spirit, let it be strengthened; for the spirit creates the deed and fate, and the tool (through which it operates) is meaningless without it. Perhaps this sentence is the key to that fate through which we have passed for a generation—and to that other one into which we will stride as people who have overcome all enemies if we husband our best strengths" (347).

Wilhelm's prophecy, formulated with the cadence of biblical language, calls upon the passing of time to recast a narrative that historical events have defined as tragic into an open-endedness in which November 1918 can be seen as but one of a series of phases through which an ultimately victorious German *Geist* must pass.

Wilhelm assigned the same transcendent meaning to the categories of history and German *Geist* as had Meinecke's Cotta publication; Wilhelm's analysis of specific wartime events would additionally become familiar with much of the antidemocratic war fiction published later in the Weimar Republic. The core of that analysis is his assertion that the war was lost not on the battlefield but at home by the combination of an inept civilian leadership and a population unwilling to match the sacrifices of the soldiers and military leaders. The work presents an early articulation of the "stab-in-the-back theory," an interpretation that is constitutively tied to the agitation of the antidemocratic Right during the 1920s.

Wilhelm believed that Germany began the war "with the best army in the world" (131). The obstacle to victory was an inept civilian government led by Bethmann-Hollweg that eventually compelled the military leadership ("they did so pressured by circumstances") to assume control over civilian affairs. Ludendorff was "forced to intervene because of the inaction and weakness of the administration and personalities who by right and duty had been called to the implementation of the tasks" (151).

Although front soldiers struggled against increasingly desperate odds, the homeland degenerated into—in Wilhelm's words—a "seat of putrification, from which an ever new mud-river of agitation, subversion, and rebellious elements who urged overthrow wallowed toward the front and poisoned it" (232). The antinomy between homefront and war zone, never alluded to pejoratively in prose between 1914 and 1918, became frequently employed in representations of the war published in the 1920s. Indeed, when after 1933 a National Socialist perspective framed all narratives published about the war, that antinomy, presented as an explicit antagonism between front soldiers and corrupt, self-serving civilians became a nearly ubiquitous element of post-1918 front mythology. Ultimately, writes Wilhelm, this "defeatism" succeeded in poisoning even the front. He was appalled to discover through conversations with troops in September 1918 that the *Frontgeist* of his troops had so degenerated that "a primitive, unsublimated self-preservation drive had become master over the insight in the necessity to stand fast" (238). The prince's language, opposing the virtues of intellect, duty, and necessity to the unsublimated (*hemmungs-los*) egoism of lowly corporeality and self-preservation, perpetuates and valorizes the same spiritual qualities characteristic of all of Cotta's publications about the war. The "ending" assigned the war in this, the firm's most significant postwar publication, comes as close to fulfilling the editorial intent formulated in 1914 by Rosner and Kröner as the "unfortunate" events of 1918 would allow.

There is an affinity between all the war works published by Cotta that cannot be accounted for solely with reference to the individual authors. The published works share this affinity by virtue of the continuity of editorial policy embedded in the publishing house, whose editors consciously directed a specific framing of the war.

Chapter 6 "Nevertheless!":

Long Live War!

On May 10, 1919, a number of publishers, including Eugen Diederichs, Karl Siegismund, Walter de Gruyter, Gustav Kilpper (of the publishing firm Deutsche Verlags Anstalt), and the new president of the Association of the German Book Trade, Anton Meiner, met in Leipzig with representatives of the academic world and the Foreign Ministry to inaugurate the German Society for Foreign Book Trade. The assembly elected Anton Kippenberg, the director of Insel Publishing who had spent most of the war devoting his services to the war effort in Belgium, as the organization's first president. Kippenberg's fusion of culture and politics, displayed in the rhetoric he used in the mission of the new organization, indicates a continuation of the goals promoted during the war years, albeit with tactical adjustments dictated by the war's outcome.

Kippenberg's election followed a warmly received speech that summarized the laudatory efforts of the publishing industry during the war and pointed to its special task in preserving the "soul" of German culture during the difficult times ahead. Kippenberg's little-known speech warrants closer inspection as a symptom of the self-understanding of mainstream publishing in Germany following the "catastrophe" of November 1918.[1] It should not, however, be viewed in isolation from manifestos and essays written by other bourgeois publishers in Weimar's early years. In many such texts, the general sense of societal crisis brought on by the lost war serves as a reference point for discussions of the specific malaise affecting the book trade.[2] Thus, inflation, paper shortages, a shrinking marketplace abroad and at home, changes in reading habits, and competition from other media (most notably film) frequently coalesce in essays written in the 1920s as the material facts indicative of a larger economic and spiritual crisis.

At the same time, such manifestos retained the concept of the special cultural mission of the book trade by invoking a redemptive hope that promised to bridge what is ultimately cultural (not material) despair. In this rhetoric, crisis is ultimately spiritual crisis, and the answer to the implied question—who shall save the Reich?—is posited as bourgeois German culture and its guardians, the publishing industry.

As previous chapters have shown, such a self-understanding had been actively fostered by the industry's instrumentalization during the war years. The mobilization of German society for war in August 1914 was matched by a cultural mobilization by the German publishing industry. The imperative to quench the thirst for reading at the front with the "right" books, institutionalized later by Ludendorff in accordance with the propaganda campaign of Patriotic Instruction, was matched by an effort at home to legitimate the war as a *Kulturkrieg,* for which the nation's most precious literary icons were pressed into service. In this context, self-proclamations by publishers and the established book trade, which portrayed themselves as the cultural guardians of the nation during the First World War and the Weimar Republic, resonate with intentions that are far from neutral or innocent.

Kippenberg's address continued in this vein by wedding the industry's mission to the foreign policy of the state. Although the traumatic defeat of the German military forces as well as the loss of foreign book markets demanded a change in publishing strategy, the publisher's mission remained unchanged. In another pertinent sense, an unchanged dynamic of crisis continued to saturate the self-presentations of the industry as it had during the war. Defeat had merely replaced war as the reference point of this crisis dynamic.

Kippenberg at first recalled the tragic events of the present: "We take on our task in the darkest day of a German history that has known its share of tragedies, in a time of deepest humiliation, greatest material and spiritual deprivation, and the most extreme shakeup of our state structure. . . . But our spirit, the soul of our people, cannot be stolen. They will, so we deeply hope, come forth enriched deeper and purer by the trials of this era and manifest themselves in new creations." His language, portraying German history as a series of crises of which the present disaster is merely the most traumatic, simultaneously names the vehicle of its redemption—German *Geist*. The genius of this spirit transcends even the bleakest momentary setback. Kippenberg's rhetoric emplots November 1918 not as the dismal conclusion of a failed national narrative but instead as an unquiet and fecund model point.

The language of rebirth used by Kippenberg also resonated in countless welcoming speeches by university presidents to returning soldiers and in the nationalist literature about the lost war that flooded the marketplace, particularly after 1928 in reaction to Remarque's *All Quiet on the Western Front*.[3] Kippenberg's implicit recourse to the parable of Job—who remained faithful to "the Word" despite all disasters that befell him—is also echoed in the promise contained in the works of nationalist war book authors who frequently employed the same rationale of national "purification" used by Kippenberg.[4] What had begun in August 1914 as a war of culture remained precisely that even in defeat, and the German book industry was prepared to play a special role in this campaign as it had during the war. Kippenberg assured his audience that the publishing industry had achieved much in disseminating German culture during the war: "For the previously allied nations and occupied territories, the work of German bookstores in the field and individual book vendors proved to be invaluable in Romania, Bulgaria, Turkey, Belgium, Poland, the Baltic, the Ukraine, and Finland. Even if the structure that was initiated by them is now destroyed, we can hope that the seeds they have strewn around Germany's borders will sprout and bear fruit in the future."

Kippenberg's geopolitical mapping of the German book industry's sphere of influence retains the promise of a harvest in the organic metaphor of "seed" and "planting," albeit one that had been deferred. Kippenberg had firsthand knowledge about these efforts to establish the German book trade in the occupied territories. As a captain and regional director of Patriotic Instruction in occupied Belgium, he had overseen the establishment of sixty-five army-administered bookstores. He had worked closely in that capacity with *Insel* author Rudolf Alexander Schröder, who had been assigned to the district's office for "Literary and Artistic Propaganda," one of whose tasks was to create a climate that would enable "the German book industry to win [the region] as a market, while displacing French and Dutch competition."[5] Furthermore, Kippenberg had provided advice to his fellow regional directors stationed in all of the above-mentioned occupied territories.[6]

The war's conclusion had temporarily ended these promising activities. The bookstores established outside the nation's borders were dissolved, and Germany's enemies seemed intent upon weaning the populations of the formerly occupied territories; indeed, the territories now forcibly separated from the German *Reich,* from German culture. Consequently, the most immediate post-war mission of the German book trade, particularly given the anticipated outcome of the Versailles Treaty, was to help these populations (including the "Millions of Germans," our "unredeemed brothers") to counter the pressures that the Allies would apply to distance them from German culture: "To preserve their German heritage in the midst of all seductions of an economic and cultural nature, in spite of the powerful means our enemies will ruthlessly apply in order to suppress the German language and German essence is the task above all for the German book and German publishing, because therein lies the only, but perhaps also the strongest, propaganda, which the enemies will be unable to shut down."

Even though the German army had failed, the German book trade retained a latitude in which it might succeed. Kippenberg called for a second wave of mobilization in the continuing worldwide battle for readership; Kippenberg urged his fellow publishers to remember their political mission: "First and foremost, we will want to distribute German spirit, German literature, science, and art abroad through the medium of the printed word. . . . This is an extremely important political task and at the same time an important service on behalf of the German word that we shall be undertaking."

This was not the first time Kippenberg had offered such an assessment of the "political task" of German letters. He had used this argument, including his vision of a book trade society fostering contacts abroad, in appealing to Eberhard von Bodenhausen to use his influence to have him be appointed to his position in Belgium. He wrote von Bodenhausen in May 1915 that regardless of whether Germany meant to keep Belgium or make it into a protectorate, it would be necessary to create cultural ties there—"as, by the way, with other countries as well"—particularly through the book trade, "which in this regard should become much more politicized" in order to provide such export "a real foundation; . . . thus, I dream of a book trade society for foreign countries that would create channels for the distribution of German books and German ideas (newspapers too)."[7]

After Germany's defeat, talk of annexing territories was irrelevant. On the other hand, although military defeat had closed some opportunities, others now suggested themselves. Speaking to the newly founded organization, Kippenberg postulated a special role for German publishers, particularly given the army's defeat. In light of current discussions of a League of Nations, he foresaw that role in the building of bridges between the nations. In order for the peoples of the world to learn more about each other, German, as an international language, would serve as the medium of translation to make the best and most characteristic of the world's literature available to all.

Kippenberg was in essence describing his own aspirations, which were soon put into practice for Insel, whose success continued to reap him praise after the Second World War.[8] Implicit in his positively charged conception of the German *Sonderweg* (particular path), destined by the nation's unique spiritual and geographical position to mediate the meaning of social reality for the world is a conception of culture, and specifically language, as a weapon. Even if Germany had been thwarted as a major military power, the German language itself was a powerful means of influence. His argument for Germany's special status is couched cautiously but optimistically. Kippenberg stated that the work would begin not because "the sick world needs German essence alone in order to become healthy," but rather that just as the Germans "have made the spiritual treasures of all nations and times" their own, they had "indispensable gifts to bestow." Kippenberg believed that the spiritual struggles of the times had "their origin in Germany, and must be brought to a close there," and Germany's publishers had an obligation to share their "gifts" with other cultures.

Kippenberg's address was warmly praised by the other speakers that evening, including the representative of the Foreign Ministry, Legationsrat von Hahn. Von Hahn told Kippenberg that the Foreign Ministry intended to financially subsidize the work of the German Society for Foreign Book Trade. He also proposed a motto for the organization; reminding his audience that the French defeat in 1871 had spawned the phrase "Quand même" (nevertheless!), von Hahn proposed to use the same motto ("Dennoch!"): "I believe if this spirit and this volition rules in the entire German Fatherland, then we will not want for success. For the leaders of the Entente will never succeed in beating down this volition."

In the self-understanding of both Kippenberg and his colleagues, as well as the Foreign Ministry, the book trade was to continue the war through other means. The nation's defeat in 1918 had not ended the cultural war but rather forced a change of tactics, in which the mobilization of the publishing industry, begun in August 1914, would continue.[9]

REMEMBERING THE BODY: BRUNO VOGEL'S
ES LEBE DER KRIEG! EIN BRIEF

Even while the four-to-one ratio between war-affirmative and antiwar books published as of 1933 suggests the unequal footing of political-aesthetic forces, the government's role in guiding the representation of the war during the Weimar period, though much diminished compared with its role of 1916–1918, cannot be discounted. Although the Republic had proclaimed that "censorship does not take place," the controversy over Bruno Vogel's war book *Es lebe der Krieg! Ein Brief* (Long live war! A letter) shows that it in fact did.[10] Vogel describes the war legacy as he saw it in 1924, and consequently the commemoration of the war as a matter of contestation emerged as the central issue.

In writing about *Long Live War!* I am explicitly directing attention to a work that is one of a number of forgotten First World War narratives, whose unfamiliarity today is indicative of the outcome of the contest regarding the war's representation in Weimar and Nazi Germany. Vogel's work was made *unschädlich* (innocuous), as the Nazis might have said, both by the trials in which it became embroiled following its appearance in 1925 and by the appropriation of specific aspects of the war legacy by National Socialism and the regime's simultaneous burning and prohibition of critical war literature, which left no place for Vogel's writing in post-1933 Germany.

The text bears witness to the conditions in Germany affecting the literary representation of the war in three distinct phases: the war years, the Weimar Republic, and post-1933 Germany. First, Vogel reflects upon the intervention of the imperial state and its institutions in generating an affirmative war aesthetic between 1914 and 1918. Through his genre of choice, the letter, he accords the character of such war-sustaining thought both thematic treatment and a formal focus.

Second, the text itself is an attempt to intervene in the process of remembrance undertaken by various authors between 1919 and 1932. Like other war books, *Long Live War!* can be perceived as being engaged in a wider interdiscursive battle for control over the war's events, dates, and symbols. What these signs were to signify was at stake in the charged reception of war literature during the 1920s. Finally, the fate of Vogel's book during Weimar foreshadows National Socialism's purge of undesirable war representations and the regime's elevation of a "correctly understood" war legacy to its pantheon of canonical cultural artifacts. Thus, like other books about the war, Vogel's book must be understood not simply as a "mirror" of any given individual's war experience but also as a participant in an interdiscursive process of memory-formation. Each is embedded in a changing social context that influences what is written (and read) in any given period, and how a topic is approached (by author and reader).

Few works of fiction published during the early years of the Weimar Republic offered as damning a critique of the coercive, war-affirmative state and social structures of late Wilhelmine Germany as can be found in *Long Live War!*[11] Vogel's interpretation of the war was based on impressions gathered both as a combatant and as a survivor who had witnessed the spirit of resentment and revenge gathering strength in the early Weimar Republic. Like Erich Marie Remarque, Vogel, born in 1898, had left high school to participate in the last two years of the fighting on both the eastern and western fronts. He received an Iron Cross (second class, as he laconically noted) for his valor at Cambrai in 1917. Vogel's work predates *All Quiet on the Western Front* by three years. Unlike Remarque's book, *Long Live War!* was not an overwhelming popular success as measured against other contemporary war treatments (the 1929 reissue lists a printing of 26,000–35,000) but its volatile reception fully presaged the violent antipathy that the political right accorded *All Quiet on the Western Front.*

Upon its publication in 1925, *Long Live War!* became the subject of an extended court dispute. Both the author and its publisher Arthur Wolf were accused of violating paragraph 184 (distribution of lewd publications) as well as paragraph 166 (blasphemy) of the constitution. Following trials in Leipzig and Dresden, testimony in support of the book provided by Thomas Mann, Fritz von Unruh, Käthe Kollwitz, Kurt Hiller, and Magnus Hirschfeld, among others, a five-day incarceration in prison for the publisher Arthur Wolf, house searches to uncover unsold copies of the forbidden book, and the assessment of a four-hundred-mark fine for the publisher (paragraph 28 of the press law), the work was permitted to be reprinted, albeit without the two episodes that the court had declared lewd.[12] The resulting edition, disdainfully referred to by Vogel as the "castrated edition," was issued in 1926 and 1929. Arthur Wolf appropriately characterized the published trial proceedings as itself a telling "cultural document" of Weimar: the trials amply indicate that the state censorship of works dealing with the First World War was indeed continuing after the abdication of the Kaiser and Germany's surrender in November 1918.

The trials adversely affected the dissemination of this powerfully antimilitaristic work. They also help to account for the continuing reluctance of Weimar publishers to publish works about the war that transgressed the paradigmatic codes perpetuated during the war itself. This episode thus augments the discussion of previous chapters that offered an institutional understanding of the links between the periods 1914–1918 and 1933–1940 by suggesting a link between the administration of an information-production and censorship apparatus during the *Kaiserreich* and its immediate aftereffects for the Weimar Republic. Surely it must have given publishers pause to consider what awaited them at the hands of the state if they published a work such as Vogel's that portrayed, as its author wrote, "facts . . . that, however, contrast obviously with words like field of honor, patriotic rapture, national culture, moral renewal."[13] It is not only the fact that Vogel wrote about army-administered bordellos and communicable sexual diseases, which lead to a soldier killing his diseased wife and child and committing suicide ("The Hero's Death of Private Müller III"), or that, given the imperatives authorized in the name of God he equated the spirit of Jesus with the devil ("Phosphorous"), or that he assembled decaying corpses in order to reflect upon the meaning of their deaths ("Those Without a Future"). These episodes provided the grounds for the trial of the book. The perspective on the war's meaning, however, which led to its being put on trial, infuses the entire work and is not limited to those three episodes. The strategy animating the succession of episodes exposes the tension between the efforts of the state and its institutions (religion and education) to imbue the war with moral and ideal meaning on one hand, and certain "facts" on the other.

Vogel's work is written in the same epistolary form (signaled by the work's subtitle, *A Letter*) that characterized a great deal of the prose published about the war during its first years. The work thus explicitly offers its critique in the guise of that same voice of subjectivity that had been used under conditions of wartime censorship to legitimate the appearance of a unified will speaking with one voice in affirmation of the war. Throughout the First World War, the imperial army had collected letters written by soldiers and encouraged their dissemination in newspapers and book form—so long as they legitimated in the "authentic" voice of the front soldier the desired virtues of the fighting hero. Explicitly excluded in such published letters, as we saw in Chapter 3, were accounts that transgressed the ever-growing censorship code relating, for example, to depictions of combat violence, or narratives that questioned the national purpose animating the war effort. Moreover, as the process of war commemoration began during Weimar, such letters written at the front under conditions of censorship were often enough upheld by the political right as the legitimate conveyers of *Frontgeist* over and against the belated and fictitious reorderings undertaken by the mere *Literaten* (scribblers). Vogel's choice of genre (letter) with which to write his critique is thus strategic in contesting the use of soldiers' letters for the war effort. Vogel's organization of his subject matter via a selection of letters from the war years addressed to a contemporary citizen of a Kaiserreich become a republic communicated "facts" that wartime censorship codes had explicitly suppressed.

Long Live War! is also a letter in this second sense. As its opening chapter, "Dear Mrs. Privy Counsellor" indicates, the ten episodes that follow are assembled as a form of communication to the mother who had hosted a birthday party for her sixteen-year-old son, Werner, and on that occasion expressed the hope that he would become a "capable soldier." The narrative situates this opening event in a postwar, contemporary Weimar setting. The work's final chapter, "The Scream," ends with the word *mother* followed by an exclamation point, a reiteration of the last word screamed by a soldier before his nighttime death on the battlefield. Given the structure of the entire work, *mother* both underscores the author's indebtedness to expressionism and functions as a final appeal to the addressee of Vogel's postwar letter—that is, Werner's mother—that she now will (hopefully) have reflected upon what her wish for her son would mean. As such, this work also refers to its precondition, the undiminished difficulty besetting communication in the postwar era between those who have experienced war in the manner testified to in Vogel's narrative and those for whom "the next war" has already become a tenable topic of discussion.

In the following pages, I discuss four of the work's episodes to further illustrate Vogel's narrative strategy.[14] The first one, "Dear Mrs. Privy Counsellor," recalls as its point of departure that during Werner's recent birthday celebration, phrases familiar from the beginning of the previous war resonated among the guests: "God-willed unavoidability of war," "toughening up of our youth," "sole salvation from the swamp of immorality and lewdness," and "eternal laws of historical occurrences." For the letter writer who recollects these exchanges, the question becomes "How can people who experienced and survived Verdun, Ypres, the Somme, Isonza, and the Carpathians long to become used as battlefield manure?" (7–8). The narrator allows that he can certainly understand how it might be possible for servants of God to prove that the religion of love makes it an ethical duty to participate in organized mass murder, or how drunken youths can praise the ethical value of war, or finally, that high school students would want to escape the pedagogical whip of their teachers. What does not make sense to him, however, is that such students would see their only salvation in being shoved into the barbed wire of the trenches, or that workers, whose exploited labor currently pays for the last war, could wish for a return of "die große Zeit." Vogel takes Kaiser Wilhelm's proclamation of a domestic truce one step further by reminding his reader that the war "no longer recognized differences between political parties" but only "dummies" and "sly ones," and workers must know that, just as during the First World War, they will again belong to the "dummies" (8).

Against this clear danger, the narrator envisions a coming total war that does not respect the distinction between civilians and soldiers, and consequently will envelop everyone equally in the horror of an unbounded front, thereby prohibiting any rebirth of a war-affirmative ideology. For apparently the First World War had not been perceived as horrible enough to the nation to prevent such recklessness. Perhaps the survivors of this total war "will tell their children, if they have any, what they suffered, will tell them in a way that people will never forget" (9). The rest of Vogel's narrative can be understood precisely as an attempt at provoking memories of the raw destruction of human beings for the benefit of the few, which, for Vogel, is the war's meaning.

The next story in *Long Live War!* embarks upon this strategy of remembrance by deepening the contrast between the sheer violence wrought upon the individual body and the ideals/ideology that mask or legitimate this violence. In juxtaposing two perceptions of the war's meaning, "Son and Father" again uses the form of the letter to jarringly convey the inconsistency between the front and a civilian perception of it.

The letters portray a failed communication between a father and son, nameless in order to give the relationship archetypical force. The father, upon reading his son's letter from the field while riding in a train, throws it away and storms off with the comment, "That swine is my son" (11). His compartment neighbor (the episode's narrator) retrieves the crumpled letter from which he reconstructs their miscommunication.

After years of silence, the father had written his socialist son following the outbreak of war in 1914. As recalled in the son's letter, the father had expressed his hope that the "grand sublimity of the thought of being permitted to join the fight for the highest and holiest goods of every individual German, for throne and altar, had healed [the son] (from [his] prior state) and led [him] to become a capable and serious-minded human being, having recognized the unworthiness of [his] crazy and damnable ideas on the field of honor" (11). The father thus expresses a line of thinking familiar from official proclamations and their recycled expressions in newspapers, journals, and poems of the literary main-stream in late Wilhelmine Germany: the awakening of the sense of German national purpose effected by the war has obviated the misguided class struggle that had marred the internal unification of the *Reich* that was proclaimed but not realized following the Franco-Prussian War. For the father, following the like-minded sentiments much celebrated during the First World War, the exercise of duty at the front in solidarity with those at home had fostered the recognition of a higher national cause.

The son's letter from the field denounces the father's reasoning with an alternative logic and language that wartime censorship regulations prohibited from entering public discourse. The son contrasts his father's image of an euphemistic "field of honor" with an actual place of combat, albeit one that is unnamed in the letter. The letter writer's abbreviations conform to wartime censorship regulations discussed in Chapter 3 that prohibited the naming of specific places for reasons of military security.[15]

The son then describes the dread that comprises the soldier's daily routine fighting the elements, exhaustion, fear, hunger, and lice during a relatively quiet period at the front. When this "calm" ends as his unit prepares to go into battle, he notices the dreamlike sense of unreality that accompanies their activity. The inability to comprehend what awaits them escalates into pure shock as the unit's members are decimated by enemy bullets. The letter writer recounts surprise at stumbling into a ditch and noticing a boot above him containing bones and torn up flesh. A memory of a Christian Morgenstern poem ("The Knee") is rekindled before the son realizes that the boot is his own. He relates the effects of battle in one long expressionistic sentence whose combination of exact and visceral depiction would have been censored in Germany between 1914 and 1918: "Ungraspable violent orgy of sadism: millions of pain-wincing nerves under yawning wounds, despair-muffled will to live, chopped muscles from which blood oozes slowly or pumps out in small fountains, parching thirst tortures gasping thoughts, in vain, destroyed lungs fight for air, brain porridge and skull shards swirl through the dancing mud, out of turning, slit-open corpses surge slimy intestines over the field of honor whose shame is covered by stinking, dense fumes, like humid dark gray coffin sheets, embroidered with gloomily glowing sparks" (18).

The "field of honor" is revealed as a place of infamy whose violence, analo-gous to the violence of misrepresentation in operation with such euphemisms as "field of honor," has been covered over. The jarring contrast to the father's idealistic image of battle, congruent with the information disseminated by the censored press, is further underlined with the question now asked by the letter writer: "Perhaps you presume, dear father, that now the heroic sons sang with defiantly proud lips 'Deutschland, Deutschland über alles!' and then with teary eyes shouted a final 'Long live the Kaiser!' as it so often was reported in the newspapers" (18). The conjecture is not entirely unfair, since following the official Army Communiqué report about Langemarck from November 11, 1914, it had become commonplace to invoke the singing of the song by troops under fire as a sign of their unbending will.[16] Instead, the son reports having heard cries of "Me—dic, Me—dic" and "Comrade, shoot me dead, please, please shoot me dead," and "Help!" (18–19).

The son further describes how as the smoke cleared, other grotesque apparitions came into view: an officer carrying his own severed hand, beyond shock and singing "Life is so beautiful, one only needs to understand it," scorched bodies described as "humanlike," and random limbs still twitching. In this inferno, the mercy killing of a mortally wounded comrade becomes an act of salvation.

Such are the "facts of battle," the understanding of which prohibits the son from accepting the euphemisms of the father, and as a final irony he conveys the fact that the attack had been misplanned by a general still intoxicated from the night before. Unlike those under his command, he would not suffer any consequences; military honor and justice are served by holding a subordinate officer accountable.

The next segment of *Long Live War!* to be considered here, "The Reformation," takes its title from the name of an orthodox Protestant religious journal containing an article written by a minister, which becomes one of three events leading to a reformation in a different sense.[17] A soldier's letter relates the entire story, describing the text that was read by the few survivors of a battalion that once numbered 394, 191, and finally 19 men: "I can no longer suffer hearing the whimpering and howling about war caused misery and despair. The war is not Germany's misfortune, but rather her fortune. Thank God that we have the war; it alone can still save our nation if that is still possible, which we piously trust. War is the great surgical knife, with which the grand doctor of nations cuts open terrible, all-poisoning abscesses. The wounds would otherwise close again too quickly and the evil would become worse than before" (25–26).

Such sentiments—minus the personification of God as surgeon—arguing the beneficial results of war for the community, pointed to a genealogy that included Kant and Hegel. In the "Analytic of the Sublime" in the *Critic of Judgment*, Kant argues that "even war, when it is conducted with order and a sacred attention to civil rights, has something sublime about it; and it makes the thinking of a people conducting it in this manner all the more sublime, the more dangers said people had to face in order to bravely persevere. A long peace, on the other hand, merely tends to cultivate a spirit of commerce, but with it, makes dominate lowly egoism, cowardliness, and effemination, and it tends to lower the mentality of a people." The fact that the technological capacities harnessed by the First World War had dramatically unsettled categories such as order and courage did not deter contemporaries from invoking Kant as part of the war mobilization effort. The point here, however, is the legitimation of war as a condition periodically necessary to prevent the ossification of a mere "spirit of commerce" or "effemination" and its self-centered, unheroic virtues. It is a position given a context of nation-forging by Hegel, who in both *Philosophy of Right* and *Phenomenology of Spirit* sees war as a positive antipode to the dangers presented to the ethical life of the family, civil society, and the state engendered by the divisions of bourgeois society. Forcefully confronting the individual with his finiteness, war reminds citizens of their larger, collective purpose, thus forging identity through combat with and against the Other.[18]

Not only are the losses to the decimated battalion thereby legitimated, the pastor's message in "The Reformation" suggests the advisability of an unending war to prevent a return to the "diseased" conditions afflicting the nation. Two other events figure in the action that ends the episode. A dying soldier tells members of his unit about the corpse nailed by comrades to a cross at the front to protest battlefield tactics. No one ever found out who was responsible. Secondly, the division commander, who is said to be unable to control his "appetite" for the *Pour le merite* medal, issues a proclamation declaring that he would not tolerate "cowardliness and dereliction of duty."

Returning from their most recent engagement, which reduced the battalion to less than twenty men, the soldiers pass by division headquarters, where its commanders make plans from the safety of an underground bunker. Gramophone music is heard from below and a guard remarks that "wine and women" are always part of this "underworld." The differences between the conditions experienced by the combatants and those who command their destruction in the name of God, the Nation, and the Kaiser finally leads to rebellion and revenge. Key sentences of each of the three earlier events are rearranged by montage to portend a new order and logic:

One soldier from the Battalion says: "I won't tolerate cowardliness or dereliction of duty!"
Another voice: "War is a terrible surgical knife. Cut open the abscesses!"
Another: "They never learned which of the comrades had done it."

Grenades are then thrown down the chimney and voices are heard chortling "Reformation festival." No one ever learned who was responsible (26).

In another of the book's chapters, "An Inconsequential Experience," an uninvited soldier on leave visits a "German Patriotic" youth group, where he tells the story that gives the chapter its name. Following a stressful night, the military unit to which he belonged discovered that the source of the noise that has kept them all awake is a mortally wounded Russian soldier whose every attempt at movement causes him to scream. The uninvited speaker asks his audience: "If any of you knew for a fact that you must die tomorrow or at any time in your life the way that Russian did, would you still uphold war as the necessity of the hour?" (23). In contrasting the individual's suffering with the nationalistic abstraction underpinning cultural mobilization, the speaker's argumentation draws its force from a mode of argumentation similar to the one Freud found to explain the phenomenon of battlefield heroism: "Such heroism is mostly propelled by the narcissistic belief in one's own immortality."[19]

The final story to be discussed here in the context of war representation and commemoration is titled "Those Without a Future," one of the chapters that brought the book, its author and publisher to trial. An introduction identifies the text as the remains of a play written on toilet paper. The characters in this remarkable play are unburied decaying corpses of all nations who have assembled at night to exchange stories about life and their battlefield deaths. The place in Carpathia where they gather is marked by a cross that commemorates their death (39):

> Here rest 122 brave heroes of the allied Austrian-Hungarian and German Armies.
> Be faithful unto death and I will give you the crown of life.

The inscription represents a typical form of commemoration for the fallen warrior of the First World War. The dead are brave heroes who "rest" in the assurance of eternal life promised by their fidelity and by the Christian God. The depiction of the unshakeable loyalty unifying the German–Austria–Hungarian coalition is underscored as a matter not of diplomatic expediency but as an alliance to the death.

By contrast, the stories exchanged by the corpses disturbingly contrast the disparities between such forms of commemoration and the decaying corpses in order to undermine the easy harmonies contained by the inscription. Each corpse describes his physical and emotional suffering brought about by tactical stupidity, vaingloriousness, and, equally important, by the ideological apparatus of the state and its institutions that have legitimated this suffering and violence. The dead did not die willingly, the corpses do not "rest" comfortably, and the Russian dead who lie underneath but are unmentioned by the inscription are portrayed as comrades of the allied dead rather than those who caused their deaths.

The contrast between the language employed by the state and the language of pain emanating from the tortured individual body is expressed in the recurring image of the war as a form of cannibalism organized for the benefit of society's rulers with common soldiers as the victims. Soldiers are portrayed as the victims of a morality that "prepares" them to be cooked and eaten. (One might think of this relation as a twist on Bertolt Brecht's contemporaneous popularization of the phrase—"first comes eating, then morality": Vogel's credo would read "First came morality, then being eaten.") Metaphors of appetite and hunger, already employed in earlier sections of *Long Live War!* saturate this play. A commanding officer's "hunger" for a medal leads to the annihilation of a battalion. Russian soldiers chased into impenetrable German artillery fire are transformed into "human marmalade" and "soldier salad." As recounted by Corpse Number 4, yet another tactical blunder occasioned by a sadistic officer—"a man from the old school" who organized the slaughter and masturbated while watching his troops being killed—will be covered up by rewarding the few survivors with Iron Crosses, and this "as plentifully as with kitchenware" (44). Of course, Corpse Number 5 tells his comrades that none of these facts were mentioned by the war reporter in his newspaper account of the events. From the perspective of its victims—these decaying corpses—war is represented as organized slaughter, sustained furthermore by a "recipe" as recited by Corpse Number 5: "Well, you take equal amounts of the Fatherland's honor and culture, add the usual ideals and several of the highest goods of the nation, spice it lightly with historical necessity and allow the entirety to stew for a while in previously stirred up enthusiasm. *Gourmands* achieve a special peccant aroma by adding Bible quotations. To be served in a sauce of heroism" (41). Human beings are no more than meat for the High Command, who in turn are no more attached to their troops than butchers are to cattle. Corpse Number 4 explains that they died so that the generals, the munitions, and the leather manufacturers could profit. "We died a wretched death so that others can stuff their bellies" (44).

Vogel's devastating critique of the war thus was a frontal assault on the ideological apparatus that represented it as a noble and ethical pursuit. Reacting to one corpse's story of having been wounded and then eaten alive by rats for three days, another responds with the eternal "truth" perpetuated in school: "It is sweet and honorable to die for the Fatherland. As one already learned in school" (46). The mobilizing power of this war-affirmative ideology, moreover, seemed not to lose its force despite the carnage. The decaying corpse, which for Vogel in 1924 was the truest emblem of the war's meaning, was again suppressed by the form of commemoration the state's ideological apparatus found to represent the war. The violence rendered upon the body by this warfare was being perpetuated by monuments that celebrated the unwilling heroism of its victims, a form of commemoration designed to inspire the next generation to submit to the same slaughter: according to Corpse Number 5, "The gratitude of the Fatherland is guaranteed us. . . . They will erect monuments for us, and on the anniversary of this or that important *Schlachtfest* [meal consisting of fresh homemade pork, also a battle celebration], they will gather here and will remember our putrification with words of honor. And they will jointly swear fidelity to remain steadfast toward us and to also slaughter our children" (50).

These words of Corpse Number 5 are joined by the wish of Corpse Number 21: "We millions of corpses should all fall in at the sixth hour, just as we are now, torn into pieces and eaten up, in order to go before those who gave birth to us" (50).

In the introduction to this book, I alluded to the harmony staged by soldier cemetery landscapes, disingenuous because of their spatial structurings as well-ordered symmetries where identity is seemingly preserved. By speaking in the name of the suffering body and the decaying corpse—whose proper name has been wedded to a supra-individual entity, the nation—Vogel's work intervenes against the possibility of such a commemorative aesthetic. Vogel's work can thus be seen as an effort to prevent the war's horror from being passively accepted. His is a story of refuse, of that, which like the son's letter, has been discarded as worthless, in order to enjoin the reader to refuse, to decline acceptance, consent, or compliance.

During the trials of *Long Live War!* Vogel defended his book by asking the following question: "What is the state (and its prosecuting attorney) doing to avoid the immoral conditions against whose repetition this book is fighting? What is the state (and its prosecuting attorney) undertaking against the nationalistic war agitators who would like to drive humanity and their own people into a new similar bath of steel?"[20] The answer to Vogel's question, as we have seen, was to censor the book and fine its publisher. There is perhaps no better proof of how astutely Vogel had framed his critique and why his book, as a book of remembrance, deserves consideration by scholars of the Weimar Republic.

Conclusion

Returning from army duty during the Franco-Prussian War, the period that Walter Bloem commemorated in *Die Schmiede der Zukunft*, Friedrich Nietzsche had occasion to link the aspirations of a "political reunification" to his disturbing analysis of the value that both education and history had assumed. In *The Use and Abuse of History for Life*, Nietzsche diagnosed a number of symptoms of an all-pervading "historical disease," one of which related directly to the issue of warfare and its representation in literature: "The war hasn't even ended yet, and already it has been turned over a hundred thousand times on pressed paper, and already served up as the newest excitant for the tired palate of those greedy for history."[1] The veteran of the Franco-Prussian War was witness to an early phase of a constellation that blossomed fully during the First World War.

The Franco-Prussian War and the First World War are both installments of the framing of war, mass-circulated narration, nationalism, and a near satiation of the senses in the name of a monumental, if not sublime, notion of history. Beginning in autumn of 1914, the hunger for literature about the ongoing war led to circulation figures previously unheard of in the publishing industry. Ullstein's war books, glorifying in equal measure the heroes and technologies of the war while also providing valuable geopolitical instruction, achieved sales levels that fully mark the arrival of the popular best-seller in a contemporary sense. The war accelerated a particular commodification of literary culture in Germany, commented upon by Nietzsche, by defining the efforts associated with the popular education movement, the public library movement, and the marketing of the inexpensive book as national imperatives. The modernization of the publishing industry, however, was independent of the modernist movement in literary history. On the contrary, the innovations in the publishing world contributed to the development of a sense of collective identity and national culture that would solidify the ideal of nationhood proclaimed in 1871.

The reunified Reich quickly stylized the ongoing war as *die große Zeit,* and numerous individuals and institutions embarked upon a multilayered enterprise to preserve its greatness. The activities of the Imperial Army were of central importance to constructing public memory about the war. Defeating the enemies on the battlefield was the primary but not exclusive aim of the military and the state. Forging a collective national identity that would transcend boundaries, particularly of class, and that would commemorate and monumentalize the political and social order that had achieved victory were manifestations of the same imperative in the social and historical realms.

After establishing the authorial prerogative of the High Command to write the definitive depiction of the war, the military early instituted measures to frame the events of the war into a particular narrative. Buttressed by the collection of authentic letters, stories, and diaries, the dissemination of war prose through army war reporters and army newspapers, the enactment of censorship norms, and paper supply restrictions, the OHL displayed a regulative interest not only in the flow of wartime information but also in the value that such regulated information would acquire in the later writing of the war's history. Had the German war effort ended in victory and the army truly remained "unbeaten on the battlefield," a ready-made history awaited dissemination that would have confirmed the *Sendungsbewußtsein* (conviction of the mission) articulated in unguarded language by Wilhelm II in 1905 when he proclaimed that Germans are "the salt of the earth."[2] Germans had long been immersed in an educational curriculum that confirmed this belief and its virtues of "discipline, order, reverence and religiousness," love of "the German Fatherland as it is, and not in accord with impossible strivings," the necessity "to keep at a distance what has been dragged in by foreign people and customs," and the consciousness that God would not have done so much for Germany "if he had not destined [Germany] for greatness." Through the tangible proof of victory and the documentation of a unified collective will that achieved it, the German empire would have inherited the seamless effect of the inevitable, the natural, and the true. The very ability to analyze the effects of numerous institutions in generating such martial and national practices and discourses as *Frontgeist*, the "spirit of 1914," and later, the idea of being "unbeaten on the battlefield" is predicated upon the fissure of 1918 that interrupted the creation of this national epic. Although damaged by Germany's defeat, wartime portrayals nonetheless remained "history making."

A remarkable hubris pervades the rhetoric of the cultural and literary figures encountered in this study, but it is perhaps more generally symptomatic of a culture participating in the historical illness diagnosed by Nietzsche. Efforts to create a monumental style of Wilhelmine culture and politics by recourse to historical legitimation infused the discursive parameters depicting the war as a time of greatness. As we have seen, preparation for producing the history to be written about the war included the gathering and selection of authentic evidence that corroborated an affirmative stance, to be spoken by "the voice of the people." Soldiers and civilians were bombarded with advertisements for diaries in which they could keep a record of their personal experiences during the war. The title page of such diaries bore the inscription "My experience during the time of greatness" with a conveniently preprinted line for the individual to enter his name, profession, or rank. Irrespective of the individual makeup of such experience—whether on land, at sea, or in the air—the prescription of the war as a time of "greatness" places beyond doubt the nature and treatment of the experience to be ordered.

Encouraging the diaries, however, was only one sign of a larger effort undertaken by the military leaders, publishers, academics, and authors to produce evidence of the "greatness" of this time. The First World War was a *Kulturkrieg* not only in the rhetoric of cultural superiority professed by German chauvinists, but also in the sense that the cultural sphere was an essential component that was instrumentalized for the war effort. It is appropriate to consider this instrumentalization in conjunction with the meaning that Adorno and Horkheimer, in *Dialectic of the Enlightenment*, ascribed to the concept of the culture industry, albeit with qualifications. These authors largely overlooked the precedent of a state/military role in mediating the creation of an affirmative mass reading culture, and their analysis of a culture industry does not focus sufficiently on emergent proclivities already in evidence in Wilhelmine Germany and the First World War. By contrast, I have demonstrated a multilayered bureaucratization of culture, and the standardization and rationalization of culture that were articulated during the war years in the interaction of the state, the military, and private institutions disseminating a particular form and content of reading culture.

I have examined aspects of the reading, writing, and circulation of war books during and after the war. I have placed the literature that was produced and read in the context of a social and political order in which the texts participate. As we have seen, during the war numerous individuals, institutions, and agencies joined in a literary mobilization to produce and support the affirmation of the German war effort. Though these prodigious activities did not result in the desired aim of military victory, they left traces that decidedly affected the ways in which survivors would belatedly be able to think about the war.

The overall effect of this wartime cultural mobilization was to severely curtail the possibility of reordering of the war in order to lend support to the Weimar Republic. In making this assessment, one need not resort to an all-too-functionalist understanding of hegemony wherein the subjugation of the subject by a dominant order dispersing messages uncritically received is taken as given ("doomsaying prophecy"). On the other hand, ignoring the power of the state and its institutions in structuring experience and memory lapses into an understanding of reading as undetermined and unrestricted (then and now) that ignores the unequal footing available to critics of the war ("cheerleading").

Viewed hegemonically, the victories that conspire to seal the fate of subsequent victims depend substantially on a tradition given force by the appearance of the seamless, the natural, and the inevitable. Hegemonic cultural practices always seem to attempt to fix the meaning of history and tradition, arranging any number of particularities and singular events into a manifold unity: the one story, the one identity, and the one nation. This certainly holds for early twentieth-century Germany. Whether as a prearticulation so weighted that its fulfillment is "destined" to arrive thereafter, or ex post facto as a selective ordering of past events that "necessarily" demonstrate the present as a causal link in a past-future teleology, both of these dominant cultural strategies are discernible in the forging of collective identifications as national identity. Study of *die große Zeit* in Germany permits us to examine the dense cultural capital at stake in the articulation of the political between 1914 and 1940, and furthermore, the extent to which normative culture, however unactualized for anti-hegemonic purposes, has been a strategic site for the orchestration of the political. The resulting understandings may perhaps contribute to a more general assessment of historical-spatial movements as potential horizons of disarticulation, where, once unframed in Walter Benjamin's sense, tradition can be actualized as what it always potentially is: "thoroughly alive and extremely changeable." Thus, in place of a view of hegemony which is seen in everyday parlance as a type of relation in totality (telos, structure, identity), the present study contributes to an understanding of it as a "hiatus that had opened in the chain of historical necessity," a "response to a crisis" rather than the "majestic unfolding of an identity." If so, recognition of the force exercised in the cultural realm in forging identifications may appropriately, as Max Horkheimer offered in his 1931 essay "The Present Situation of Social Philosophy and the Tasks of an Institute for Social Research," address "the philosophical interpretation of the vicissitudes of human fate—the fate of humans not as mere individuals . . . but as members of a community."[3]

The authority bequeathed by the state to narrate the history of the war was never in the hands of the left. As we have seen, a reordering did occur in the late 1920s, but within five years most of the paradigmatic elements of a war narrative prestructured during the war itself returned in National Socialism's canonization of its "correctly" understood lessons. The history of the reception of Philipp Witkop's various collections of student letters is indicative of this. Such war book authors of the Weimar Republic period as Bruno Vogel, Ludwig Renn, and Edlef Köppen, who sought to contest the nationalist rendering of the war, consequently took aim at the symbols that a wartime propaganda had generated, precisely in recognition of their continued powerful presence. Köppen's *Army Communiqué*, which sold fewer than ten thousand copies between its publication and prohibition, aimed directly at the mask of objective history prefigured by the OHL's prerogative to write the definitive account of the war. Köppen begins his novel with the 1915 censorship decree reserving that authority for the OHL. Vogel, whose 1925 *Long Live War! A Letter* contrasts the slogans generating (and belatedly celebrating) the unwilling "heroism" of the war's victims with the violence rendered upon the individual body, was brought to trial on charges of immorality. The prohibition of both books, along with those by Remarque, Renn, and others followed in 1933.

When I began my study of the legacy of the First World War, I was puzzled that so few books written about the war were critical about anything but its outcome. I understand better now that I have studied the institutional forces that conjoined to make such a critique so fragile. German publishers were either personally disinclined to produce or were censored from producing a nonaffirmative war literature. The military embarked upon a collection effort of "authentic" materials as well as actively producing prose whose ultimate narrative function was predetermined as evidence of a *Frontgeist* that remained a lasting legacy. Equally portentous was the relation between narration and authority established by the prerogative of the OHL to write the definitive history of the war. Finally, the efforts of individuals and organizations to bring education to the trenches, enveloped in a rhetoric of cultural superiority, exposed readers to an aesthetic that was overwhelmingly chauvinistic and antimodernist. With few exceptions, authors writing about the war after 1918 did so again in terms of a war aesthetic constructed between 1914 and 1918. That aesthetic is itself largely premised on nineteenth-century ideas about nationhood and narration.

My study, consequently, has centered on the efforts of nationalist and conservative representatives of literary culture in constructing their particular understandings of what the war should come to signify. This has been necessary given the lack of attention that such efforts have been accorded by scholarship. Furthermore, an understanding of how these efforts congealed in institutionalizing a particular war aesthetic brings into sharp relief those other efforts that literary history more fondly associates with the Weimar Republic. The modernist and new objectivist aesthetics that emerged in Germany in the 1920s and were associated with the names Bertolt Brecht, Alfred Döblin, Marieluise Fleisser, Robert Musil, and others took hold despite the intentions of the agencies forging the war aesthetic. It may be valuable, however, also to read their works with a consideration of the makeup and role of the literary institutions that existed during the First World War.

An institutional critique of literature is helpful in explaining deferred continuities in the cultural sphere in Germany between 1914 and 1933. The force exercised in shaping a particular framework for rendering the war's "events" as historical and literary narratives established a context that proved difficult for the political left to contest. National Socialism, on the other hand, profited immensely from an inherited arsenal of slogans, codes, and historical evidence generated to represent *die große Zeit*. A significant element of the party's appeal was its ability to portray their policies as "movement" toward the full presence promised in 1914—a powerful and unified nation purged of particularities or contradictions—but deferred by the "unhappy outcome" of the First World War. In this, National Socialism completed the tautology prefigured by the propaganda work of a wartime culture industry.

Notes

INTRODUCTION

1. Köppen's book and Vogel's book are again in print, following their limited reception and silencing trial, respectively, during the Weimar Republic. *Heeresbericht* is discussed in Chapter 2, *Es lebe der Krieg! Ein Brief* in Chapter 6. As books of remembrance, both merit translation into English, particularly to widen the scope of "representative" German narratives of the war available to non-German readers today—beyond, for example, Erich Maria Remarque's *All Quiet on the Western Front* or the various war writings by Ernst Jünger.

2. See in particular White, *The Content of the Form.*

3. The most extensive collection of these printed materials is to be found in the *Bibliothek für Zeitgeschichte* in Stuttgart.

4. Helpful contributions to the German genres of the war novel and, to a lesser extent, war poetry that map the terrain have been written. See in particular Bridgewater, *The German Poets of the First World War;* Anz and Vogl, *Die Dichter und der Krieg: Deutsche Lyrik 1914–1918;* Korte, *Der Krieg in der Lyrik des Expressionismus;* Marsland, *The Nation's Cause;* Müller, *Der Krieg und die Schriftsteller;* Prümm, *Die Literatur des soldatischen Nationalismus der 20er Jahre;* Gollbach, *Die Wiederkehr des Weltkrieges in der Literatur;* Theweleit, *Männerphantasien;* Travers, *German Novels on the First World War;* Stickelberg-Eder, *Aufbruch 1914;* Hüppauf, *Ansichten vom Krieg;* and Bornebusch, *Gegenerinnerung.*

5. The tautological effect of the category as a producer of social meaning, powerfully legitimating and sustaining any given order, has been persuasively argued in the early work of Foucault, notably in *The Order of Things: An Archeology of the Human Sciences* and *The Archaeology of Knowledge and the Discourse on Language,* trans. A. M. Sheridan Smith (New York: Pantheon, 1972); see also White, *Tropics of Discourse;* Attridge, Bennington, and Young, *Poststructuralism and the Question of History;* and Natter and Jones, "Identity, Space and Other Uncertainties," in Benko and Strohmayer, *Space and Social Theory.*

6. On soldier cemeteries as purposeful conveyers of cultural meaning, see Mosse, *Fallen Soldiers.* On the painstaking efforts after 1918 by western European governments to overcome the "anxiety of erasure" by naming all the war's fallen, see Thomas Laqueur, "Names, Anxiety, Erasure," in Schatzki and Natter, *The Social and Political Body.* A comparative European approach toward the attachment of memory and mourning to privileged cultural sites is found in Winter, *Sites of Memory, Sites of Mourning.*

7. See Rainer Nägele, "Belatedness: History after Freud and Lacan," in his *Reading after Freud,* 174, who on that same page also characterizes *Nachträglichkeit* as "the transformation and rewriting of experiences, impressions, and memory traces on the basis of later experiences and in the context of a new phase of development."

8. My later discussion of the transformations that the various editions of Philipp Witkop's *Kriegsbriefe gefallener Studenten* (War Letters of Fallen Students) undergo is intended as an illustration of the process whereby individual texts—the letters—are edited, rearranged, or suppressed in order to belatedly reconfigure the "meaning" of the war between 1916 and 1942.

9. The fate of Bruno Vogel's *Es lebe der Krieg! Ein Brief,* however, offers a noteworthy caution in this regard. Although the Weimar Constitution had proclaimed that censorship would not occur, Vogel's powerfully antimilitaristic work was put on trial in 1925 for having violated paragraphs 184 (dissemination of lewd writings) and 166 (blasphemy), with the result that the publisher was fined and the book censored. As I discuss in Chapter 6, *Es lebe der Krieg!* has become one of a number of narratives of the First World War that have been forgotten due to the outcome of the contest over the war's representation in Weimar and Nazi Germany.

10. I am suggesting here an analogy between the dream as the "grounds" of hermeneutic interpretation, which is given to the analyst in only this form, and the prose written and published during the war that I consider in light of the mechanisms of censorship and mediation that attempt to structure their content. See Weber, "The Blindness of the Seeing Eye," in *Institution and Interpretation,* 78: "For the dream 'itself' is already an *Entstellung* [displacement]: not merely by virtue of what Freud describes as 'secondary elaboration (or revision)' *(sekundäre Bearbeitung),* but also because the specific mechanisms of articulation that constitute the distinctive language of the dream are all forms of *Entstellung.*" See also Weber, *Return to Freud: Jacques Lacan's Dislocation of Psychoanalysis.*

11. Sigmund Freud, *Die Traumdeutung* (Frankfurt: S. Fischer, 1984), 127, reprinted from *Gesammelte Werke,* vols. 2–3 (Frankfurt: S. Fischer, 1942). English translation based on James Strachey, *The Interpretation of Dreams* (New York: Avon, 1965), 175–76.

12. Sigmund Freud, "Zeitgemäßes über Krieg und Tod," in *Gesammelte Werke,* vol. 10 (London: Imago, 1949).

13. Sigmund Freud, *Die Traumdeutung* (Frankfurt: S. Fischer 1984), 227.

14. Freud's remarks on censorship and memory have been joined to a lengthy list of fundamental concepts of psychoanalysis that may be productively employed such that presumed binary oppositions between individuals and societies can be recast for historical analysis. That list, as Dominick LaCapra has recently underscored in his revisitation of the *Historikerstreit* (historian's debate), includes the concepts of transference, resistance, denial, repression, acting-out, and working-through. See LaCapra, "Revisiting the Historians' Debate: Mourning and Genocide," (*History and Memory* 9, no. 1/2 (1997):80–112), itself a revisitation of his argument in *Representing the Holocaust*. As LaCapra insists—in part against Freud himself—these concepts offer not merely a matter of analogy between individual and society but rather an orientation toward these concepts that sees them as referring to modes of interaction, mutual reinforcement, and orientation toward others, such that their relative individual or collective status should not be prejudged. Mourning and melancholia, for example, as forms of memory and forgetting might be better understood as consistently operating at various scales—from the individual to the collective—enabling and reinforcing various displacements of traumatic experience. In "Archive Fever: A Freudian Impression," Jacques Derrida extends the above list of concepts to see in psychoanalysis both a theory of memory and a theory of the archive. (*Diacritics,* 25(2): 18). As I discuss further below and in Chapter 2, the relation between the *arkhe,* the hermeneutic authority of the *archons,* and the institutional passage between "public" and "private" memory are intimately bound to the question of narration, authority. and nationhood in the contentious debate in Germany regarding the lost war's meaning.

CHAPTER 1: WHAT IS WAR LITERATURE AND WHY DOES IT MERIT STUDY?

1. This phrase is an extension of Anderson's *Imagined Communities,* which, in addition, reflects on Walter Bloem's *Die Schmiede der Zukunft* (The Forgers of the Future), discussed in Chapter 2.

2. Within the context of British labor history, see Woollacott, *On Her Their Lives Depend.* Woollacott stresses a view of women's work during the war not as an aberration but as the locus of women's participation in the war: "For Tommy's sister, munitions making was just as much an experience of war as being in the armed forces was for Tommy" (15). Such a recasting of war experience remains to be fully articulated in a German context, perhaps in part due to conditions that Ute Daniels has ascertained—namely, that for women in Germany, the First World War did not "emancipate" nor "modernize" the workplace—the number of women who joined the work force for the first time after 1914 is not quantitatively significant—despite the seeming pressures of a war economy. Furthermore, the halting steps toward integrating women's service more fully into the war economy following Paul von Hindenburg and Erich Ludendorff's assumption of command foundered on residual disrespect within the military hierarchy and its highly ambivalent expectations toward social outcomes portended by a gendering of the economy. See Daniels, *Arbeiterfrauen in der Kriegsgesellschaft,* for their reasons. The fostering of women for service as trench diggers and the news service is an outgrowth of

the Hindenburg Plan, which was initiated in the summer of 1916. This plan recognized the desirability of upgrading the employment of women as part of the total mobilization. Regarding the changes in the war economy wrought most broadly by Hindenburg and Ludendorff, see Gerald Feldman's classic study, *Army, Industry, and Labor in Germany,* as well as *The Great Disorder.* In fact, as Ursula von Gersdorff shows, the German High Command's anticipation of a short war in 1914 also relegated women's service to a limbo state of volunteerism (Women's National Service). Even with the reorganization via the Hindenburg Plan toward the "Auxiliary Service Law," the High Command shied away from instituting a year of war service for women. Thus the volunteer trench-digger corps of women did not see service until 1917, and the group of what would have been the first service-initiated women in the Germany military—as news information relayers (telephone and telegraph operators)—received training only in late summer 1918 before the war ended. See von Gersdorff, *Frauen im Kriegsdienst,* 15–33. Von Gersdorff argues that the war provided women with new work and significant responsibility. As noted above, however, Ute Daniels does not believe that this and other evidence is qualitatively sufficient to warrant the conclusion that the war introduced a major step toward women's social emancipation.

3. The situation in Germany appears to differ from that of Britain, where, as Sandra Gilbert's analysis of war writings shows, access to front lines as nurses, ambulance drivers, doctors, and messengers was sufficiently frequent so as to provide a larger number of women authors the material—and nearly incontestable "credentials"—for a great deal of literature centered at the front. See Gilbert and Gubar, *No Man's Land: The Place of the Woman Writer in the Twentieth Century,* vol. 2, ch. 7. As Claire Tylee remarks, however, even in the areas occupied and defended by the British, what one might call "zonal thinking" retained an absolute material basis in the general prohibition of women from combat areas. See Tylee, *The Great War and Women's Consciousness.* As Klaus Theweleit has shown, the German situation makes a number of war books ideal objects of investigation for the various pathologies of male fantasy. See Theweleit's *Männerphantasien,* particularly vol. 1.

4. Beyond equating the front and the workplace and their respective dangers, from a late-twentieth-century perspective mindful of the continuities and ruptures in cultural experience premised to some extent on the memory of the First World War but more so on the reshaping of our understanding of the separation of combat and noncombat zones between 1939 and 1945, it should be no longer as problematic to assert that modern wars (including the First World War) can be interpreted as belonging to the realm of experience for all whose lives are changed by them, an understanding that animates the essays collected in Cooke and Woollacott, *Gendering War Talk,* and Higgonet, Jenson, Michel, and Weitz, *Behind the Lines.* For German cultural history, see the primary documents in Brinker-Gabler in *Frauen gegen den Krieg,* which include essays and proclamations by Hedwig Dohm, Bertha von Suttner, Clara Zetkin, Helene Stöcker, Lida Gustava Heymann, and Rosa Luxemburg. For English literature, see Tylee, *Great War.*

5. See Eley and Blackbourn, *The Peculiarities of German History* for an exploration of particular peculiarities relevant to this study.

6. See Angelika Tramitz, "Vom Umgang mit Helden," in *Kriegsalltag* (Stuttgart: Metzler, 1989) for a valuable characterization of the ideal subject called forth in middle-class

women's writing about the war. Further characterizations of normative subject positions that emerge in rereading women's writings published during the war can be found in several of the essays in *August 1914: Ein Volk zieht in den Krieg*, Berliner Geschichtswerkstatt (Berlin: Verlag Dirk Nishen, 1989), particularly Christiane Eifert, "Wann kommt das 'Fressen,' wann die 'Moral,'" 103–14, Herrad-Ulricke Bussemer, "Weit hinter den Schützengraben," 136–46, Rosemarie Dülm and Gudrun Wedel, "Aber darüber nachzudenken, machte es alles nur noch schlimmmer," 203–11, and Jutta Schulze, "Berlin im Kriege," 242–54. These useful contributions point to a smaller but valuable body of war literature whose full import awaits further scholarship, toward which I hope to contribute.

7. See again Tramitz, "Vom Umgang mit Helden," in which she postulates a resulting split consciousness, in which the public and private faces of pain and pride, sadness and joy have become inseparable—whenever the "ideal good and German woman" appears in print.

Harbou's Cotta books are discussed in Chapter 5. Bäumer's Cotta book, *Der Krieg und die Frau*, like the others published by the firm, stressed the "spirit of 1914" in characterizing War Welfare, a group that linked women's organizations of numerous religions and parties, as "one of the first structures in which the subsumption of the political parties into a great domestic folk community is being realized" (27). In the same work, she generalizes a (national) spirit of self-sacrifice beyond its sexed particularity by equating the value and danger of childbirth with that of trench fighting so long as both occur in the national cause.

8. Claire Tylee, in *Great War*, notes a similar dynamic at work in more recent secondary literature about the cultural memory of the war. In particular, Paul Fussell's enormously important and influential book *The Great War and Modern Memory*, which portrays the war as the birthplace of a modern, that is, ironic, consciousness and culture, likewise centers on the front as the site where such a consciousness is brought into being, thus precluding women from its formation or development. In short, the equation of combat soldier and modern consciousness suggests that "for an understanding of 'modern understanding' we remain dependent upon men" (Tylee, *Great War*, 7). As valuable as his reading of a select group of Great War poets is, the German context also offers other reasons to doubt Fussell's general positing of a modernist sensibility—or, more accurately, the content of that sensibility—given birth by the First World War. In short, the question of how and on what grounds "representative" works are constituted remains of central import in reflecting upon the canonical perpetuation of modern memory.

9. Examples of books that differentially employed the (spatially) broader narrative frame described here include Arnold Zweig's *Der Streit um den Sergeanten Grischa* (1927), Ernst Glaeser's *Jahrgang 1902* (1928), which narrated the war experiences of Germans too young to enlist in the army, and Edlef Köppen's *Heeresbericht* (1931). *Heeresbericht*, discussed in Chapter 2, uses montage to critically interlink the war experience of numerous social classes, groups, and occupations within Germany with a range of combat experiences on the western and eastern fronts. Doing so between 1914 and 1918 would have been impossible in Germany, for reasons I explore later. In film, G. W. Papst's direction of *Westfront 1918* pointedly linked the (male) suffering at the front with that by (female) civilians forced to extreme measures by starvation.

10. See Michel Foucault, *The Archaeology of Knowledge and the Discourse on Language* (New York: Pantheon, 1972), 23. As Foucault stressed, the book's "unity" (like that of the author's oeuvre) is variable and relative, a principle of categorization that quickly loses its sovereignty under epistemological scrutiny. See also the essay by Roland Barthes, "From Work to Text," in *Image, Music, Text,* ed. Stephen Heath (New York: Hill and Wang, 1977), 155–64, for its conception of the *Text* (in counterdistinction to an understanding underpinning "the work") as a methodological field. In this writing, Barthes stresses the fundamental openness of "the text." It is "that *social* space which leaves no language safe, outside, nor any subject of the enunciation in position as judge, master, analyst, confessor, decoder" (164). By contrast, hegemony functions to reduce and stabilize language's inherently polymorphous character to a uni-accentuality supporting the dominant order. On reading support systems: Roger Chartier, "Texts, Printings, Readings," in Hunt, *New Cultural History,* 161.

11. In significant part because of the technological developments fostered by the war, aesthetics dramatically shifted toward new media and new aesthetic programs that remark, in Derrida's sense in *Of Grammatology,* not only the "end of the book" but also "the beginning of writing." See, as an example, Virillio, *War and Cinema,* for examples developed within the domain of technologies of light (e.g., cinema, spotlights, nightscapes). Kern's *Culture of Time and Space* has broadly sketched the confluence of scientific, aesthetic, and technological developments during the war that deeply affected European experiences of time, space, and—for present purposes—the book. Although other media also became objects of cultural mobilization during the war—notably film after 1916, and theater throughout—the intermedia competition between literature, film, radio, and other aesthetic forms fostered by new technologies continued to be articulated throughout the Weimar Republic, as documented in Kaes, *Manifeste.* Literary critics caustically wrote "why bother buying books, buy gramophone records instead," while critics of traditional theater like Bertolt Brecht celebrated sporting events as the harbingers of a new kind of audience with new aesthetic demands ("Mehr guten Sport" [More good sporting events], in *Bertolt Brecht: Schriften,* vol. 5, 27–30. Astute observations of the interlinkage between technology, capital development, and aesthetics are recorded throughout Walter Benjamin's interwar writings, most notably in extant parts of the *Passagenwerk* project.

12. Yet the fervor with which the majority of Germany's writers greeted the outbreak of war should profit from consideration of this phenomenon as participating within the generalized late-nineteenth-century context of a crisis of "the book" and "the author"; the war importantly reasserted the spiritual mission of the author "transcending" the commodification of book culture.

13. Baron and Müller, "Weltkriege und Kriegsromane," 14. It in turn echoes the earlier observation made by Margrit Stickelberger-Eder in her study of Ernst Glaeser's *Jahrgang 1902,* 16. For a depiction of Ernst Glaeser's curious intellectual odyssey from the Weimar Republic to his death in 1963, see my entry on him in Lutz, *Metzler Autoren Lexikon,* 192–94.

14. See Whalen, *Bitter Wounds,* on combat injury during the war and for the social and

political repercussions of the walking wounded and widowed for social policy during the Weimar Republic.

15. See Karin Hausen, "The German Nation's Obligations to the Heroes' Widows of World War I," in Higonnet et al., *Behind the Lines,* 126.

16. Benjamin, "Theorien des deutschen Fascismus," in *Gesammelte Schriften,* 238–50. For an explanation of Benjamin's ambivalent reaction to the war, see Martin Jay, "Walter Benjamin: Remembrance of the First World War," forthcoming.

17. On the debates surrounding the designation of commemorative anniversaries, sites, and rituals during the Weimar Republic, see Whalen, *Bitter Wounds,* ch. 1. A comparative selection of essays on the general topic of like-minded "wars over memory" in Germany and elsewhere during this century can be found in Gillis, *Commemorations.* Such contentiousness, echoing positions from the period, continues today among scholars on the issue of how to even date the beginning of the Weimar Republic. See Peukert, "Die Weimarer Republik in der Kontinuität der Deutschen Geschichte," in *Die Weimarer Republik,* 13–32, particularly p. 15 on these periodization difficulties: "On the level of political history, the Weimar Republic therefore has neither a clear beginning nor a clear end. Viewed historiographically, this is a result of the interpretation-dependence of all acts of chronology, as well as the still-bitter competition between extant historical interpretations of the period."

18. A cross section of these reactions can be found in Gollbach, *Die Wiederkehr des Krieges in der Literatur,* 275ff; in an excellent short book by Rüter, *Remarque,* 150–74, and in Müller, *Der Krieg und die Schriftsteller.*

19. Ernst Jirgal, *Die Wiederkehr des Weltkrieges in der Literatur* (Vienna: Reinhold Verlag, 1931). The situation of Germanistics would be dramatically altered by the early 1930s, when a "middle generation" of Germanists—such as Hermann Pongs, Herbert Cysarz, and Walter Linden laid the groundwork for a "properly understood" canonization of war literature acceptable to the new regime. See Pongs, "Krieg als Volksschicksal im deutschen Schriftum I," Cysarz, *Zur Geistesgeschichte des Weltkrieges,* and Linden, "Volkhafte Dichtung von Weltkrieg und Nachkriegszeit," *Zeitschrift für Deutschkunde* 48(1934):1–22. A selected reprint of the writings of Germanists under National Socialism can be found in Gilman, *NS-Literaturtheorie.*

20. See, for example, Hitler's foreword to Zöberlin, *Der Glaube an Deutschland.* Eberhard Jäckel in his standard work, *Hitlers Weltanschauung,* 21, succinctly states that the Nazi Party, founded in 1919, was a product of the German defeat in the First World War. See also Mason, *Arbeiterklasse und Volksgemeinschaft,* as well as his "Legacy of 1918 for National Socialism," in Mattias and Nicolls, *German Democracy and the Rise of Hitler.* A paradigmatic rendering of the nationalist war experience is of course to be found in Hitler's *Mein Kampf* in chs. 5–7. The central concepts inscribed by Zöberlin and a host of other authors of "soldierly nationalism" are in place in these chapters, entitled "The World War," "War Propaganda," and "The Revolution." Hitler's catalog of salient elements is to be found in his descriptions of *Aufbruchstimmung* (mood of awakening), Langemarck's spirit of sacrifice, comradeship, debilitating enemy (both allied and domestic, that is, "Marxist" and "Jewish") "propaganda," and rage at the Kaiser's abdica-

tion and the subsequent revolution, all emplotted in a narrative whose synergistic lesson is the stab-in-the-back thesis.

21. Akademie der Künste, "Das War ein Vorspiel nur . . . ," 196, 212. The Berlin ceremony on the same day singled out only Remarque's book: "In protest against the literary betrayal of soldiers of the war; toward the education of the nation [Volk] in the spirit of its self-defense, I place on the pyre the writings of Erich Maria Remarque." As documented in the above-mentioned book, the names singled out stand for dozens of others whose war books were thereafter put on the forbidden index of libraries and bookstores. On the film version of Remarque's book, see Eksteins, "War, Memory, and Politics."

22. A "schoolbook" example of such curricular canonization is the series titled "Die Deutsche Folge: Dichtung der Gegenwart in Schulausgaben," published by Langen-Müller. In addition to offering a selection of the war letters edited by Philipp Witkop (see Chapter 3), half of the thirty-volume series published as of 1938 consisted of selections from the firm's war books by such authors as E. G. Kolbenheyer, Paul Alverdes, K. B. von Mechow, J. M. Wehner, Ernst Wiechert, H. F. Blunk, Richard Euringer, Georg Britting, Heinz Steguweit, and Joachim von der Goltz. Several of these authors were also represented in the contribution of the firm of Friedrich Schöningh to the field that appeared in its series "Der Deutsche Quell," discussed below. The central publishing organ of the NSDAP began a series titled "Soldaten-Kameraden" (Soldiers-Comrades), which by 1944 numbered over seventy volumes. Earlier volumes featured writing selections from party-approved veterans of the First World War (for example, Hans Zöberlin, Heinz Steguweit, Tüdel Weller), while later volumes offered writings by World War Two "soldier poets" writing with a similar aesthetic. The extent of the series' dissemination is suggested by Friedrich Joachim Klähn's "ghostly" novel of the First World War, *Das Gastmahl,* which was in its tenth (and last) edition with a printing of 226,000–285,000 in 1944, while Luis Trenker's *Hauptmann Ladurner* was in its ninth edition with a printing of 161,000–180,000 that same year. As Trenker explained in his preface, it told the tale of the "Fighting and suffering of unknown soldiers of the Great War between 1914 and 1918, about the dire need and despair through which they simply had to pass in order that their faith in the reassertion of German courage and German strength could become a certainty." In both works, the necessary reorientation of the war's meaning and temporality is consistent with the exegesis by Helmut Hoffmann, quoted below. Lastly, a full account of *Germanistik* under National Socialism has yet to be written, partially due to the unavailability or inaccessibility of sources that would permit a thorough institutional analysis of the discipline's operation. Such an account, however, will find Holger Klein's "Weltkriegsroman und Germanistik, 1933–1938," Lundgreen, *Wissenschaft im Dritten Reich,* and several of the essays included in Allemann, *Literatur und Germanistik nach der Machtübernahme* useful. A long-overdue comprehensive disciplinary history of *Germanistik* in Germany is underway on several fronts. See, for example, Fohrmann and Voßkamp, *Wissenschaftsgeschichte der Germanistik im 19. Jahrhundert,* Hermand, *Geschichte der Germanistik,* and Rosenberg, *Zehn Kapitel zur Geschichte der Germanistik.* Peter Uwe Hohendahl, in assessing the developments toward a disciplinary history, notes that an answer to the big question—what the aims are that currently drive (in reference to a national project) interest in reconstructing the development of the

discipline—remains unsettled ("Germanistik als Gegenstand der Wissenschaftsgesch-ichte"). Since Germanistics is practiced worldwide, future study of the discipline would also benefit from worldwide consideration of various colonial and postcolonial settings.

23. Pröbsting, *Weltkrieg und deutsche Dichtung.*

24. Walter Benjamin quote from preface to *Das Kunstwerk im Zeitalter seiner technischen Reproduzierbarkeit.*

25. Hildegard Brenner, "Die Republikaner beugen sich dem Wort der Obrigkeit," in Akademie der Künste, *Das War ein Vorspiel,* 65–80. Other newly elected members of the German Academy of Poesy who had written war prose or poems include Heinrich Lersch, Börries von Münchhausen, and Will Vesper. Two other authors prominent in any discussion of war literature, Ernst Jünger and Hans Carossa, were nominated to join but declined.

26. According to Richards, *German Bestseller,* Werner Beumelburg's *Sperrfeuer um Deutsch-land* (1929) sold 328,000 copies by 1940, his *Die Gruppe Bosemüller* (1930) sold 170,000 copies by 1939, his *Mit 17 Jahren vor Verdun* (1931) sold 142,000 copies by 1940, and, finally, his *Douaumont* (1923) had sold 135,000 copies as of 1940.

27. Ziegler, *Wie die Pflicht es befahl,* 6–7.

28. See Baird, *To Die for Germany,* particularly ch. 9 for a wider treatment of the myth of death and its public rituals in Germany during the Second World War.

29. For an early example, see Ziesel, *Krieg und Dichtung.* Although it falls outside the purview of the present study, an analysis of this "new" war literature in Germany would demonstrate the great extent to which most of this post-1940 writing replicates models established by those authors of the First World War canonized by National Socialism. One might suggest also that these models carry over further, if only as a code to be negated, in the antifascist writing strategies of the late forties and fifties.

30. See the bibliography to Chapter 12 that chronicles this process in Owen, *Erich Maria Remarque.* A systematic reassessment of Remarque's activities, currently being under-taken by the Remarque archive in Osnabrück, will likely change this situation for the better. Also, some more recent scholarship, conducted with implicit attention to ques-tions raised by reader response criticism, has widened the scope of interest by starting with the novel's best-seller status in order to then differentiate its varied reception by contemporary readers. Such a view permits a richer reading of the work by viewing it as a screen upon which multiaccentual and overdetermined social interests are projected. The case of Remarque is, of course, only one in the post-Enlightenment history that characterizes the "great divide" between popular and high culture in German aesthetics. Important historical insights on their agonistic and symbiotic relationship are provided by Huyssan, *After the Great Divide,* Bürger, Bürger, and Schulte-Sasse, *Aufklärung und literarische Öffentlichkeit,* and Bürger and Bürger, *The Institutions of Art.* In a number of humanistic and social scientific disciplines, *postmodernism* has stood for a greater interest in cultural phenomena and documents hitherto pejoratively contained by the category of popular culture. On the differentiated arrival and force of postmodernism in the scholarship of the humanities and social sciences, see Jones, Natter, and Schatzski, *Postmodern Contentions.* As I suggest here, the war book (in both senses used here) is involved in the path taken by book culture (and its supporting institutions) in Germany

during the first half of the twentieth century. In terms of what Sam Weber has labeled the "demarcation of disciplines," I note in passing that social historians of Germany have proven to be more likely than literary critics to touch upon questions related to war literature and recommend consideration of this assessment as part of a general questioning of the relation between "the aesthetic," "the social," and "the political" as divided and managed for the purpose of scholarship within the university.

31. No doubt due in part to his longevity, Ernst Jünger's various war writings—whether set at the front or in other topographies—gained in renown and interest in the 1980s and 1990s. A recent issue of *New German Critique* (no. 59, Spring 1993) addresses the phenomenon and the writings. Regarding the overloud praise of Jünger's aesthetic achievements (for example, *Die Aesthetik des Schreckens* by Karl Heinz Bohrer and the more recent "rediscovery" of Jünger as postmodern avatar), see the essay by Andreas Huyssen, "Fortifying the Heart—Totally: Ernst Jünger's Armored Texts," *New German Critique* 1993, no. 59: 3–23. Beyond Huyssen's critique of Bohrer's interpretative move—separating aesthetics from ethics and experience—Bohrer's attempt to situate Jünger's wartime writings (including *Storm of Steel*) in the company of Baudelaire, Flaubert, and other modernists also suffers from his lack of familiarity with the copious body of aesthetically similar literature written by unheralded combat veterans in Germany between 1914 and 1940. Had he contextualized Jünger's war writings in terms of other (unread) war book authors Bohrer might have found less uniqueness to celebrate and more evidence suggesting Jünger's affinity to nineteenth-century popular literature—despite certain traits of, for example, magical realism and the "end" of the subject, which have been highlighted in order to mark Jünger's affinity to aesthetic modernism. Of course, the varied understandings of what describes literary "modernism" in German and other literatures in part support the slippage of definition permitting Jünger's in- or exclusion from "its" camp.

32. This lacuna is signaled by the title essay collection edited by Wette, *Der Krieg des kleinen Mannes.*

33. Important elements of that critique, drawing upon the early and later Frankfurt school, are differentiated in Bürger, *Vermittlung—Rezeption—Funktion,* and in Bürger et al., *Aufklärung und literarische Öffentlichkeit,* which qualifies aspects of the argument for the relation between literature and the emerging public sphere during the Enlightenment (and thereafter) put forward by Jürgen Habermas in his paradigm-making *Strukturwandel der Öffentlichkeit,* in particular regarding the status of art as the medium purportedly prearticulating the exercise of civic, political activity. In an essay entitled "The Institution of Art as a Category of the Sociology of Literature" (Bürger and Bürger, *Institutions of Art*), Peter Bürger points to the contradictory institutionalization of art in civil society that is enacted in the premier text of aesthetic education, Schiller's *Letters on the Aesthetic Education of Mankind:* "For education *by means* of aesthetics presupposes recipients who are [already] capable of the kind of interaction with works of art that Schiller has in mind" (8). Moreover, as Mark Redfield has stressed in *Phantom Formations,* drawing upon the work of Jean-Luc Nancy, Philippe Lacoue-Labarthe, and Paul de Man, it is not a matter of aesthetics repeatedly unable to "transcend" the purposeful machinations of power, a proposition that actually reinforces such machinations through the very pretense of transcending them. Analyses of formative writings of Jena romanti-

cism and by Kant and Schiller demonstrate the inherent politicality of the entire discourse rather than the unwitting and occasional instrumentalization of aesthetics. As Lacoue-Labarthe has read it, "this problematic of the subject unpresentable to itself, [and with it] this eradication of all substantialism" became "the most difficult and perhaps insoluble question of Jena romanticism and literature, instituted in its wake." See Lacoue-Labarthe and Nancy, *Literary Absolute*, 30. One might say that the presumed regulative status of the "as if" in Kant's and Schiller's aesthetics acquires something approaching constitutive force following the act of instituting literature as the medium enabling the education of humanity through its "practiced teleology" of "representative" works. Regarding the apparent contradiction between literature's autonomy and instrumentalization—which has been of great cogency for the present study—Bürger points to the resolution offered by the theory itself: "The apparent contradiction between autonomous art and instrumentalization of the work of art in the process of upbringing dissolves when one considers that it is precisely by virtue of its autonomous status that the work of art can be made into an instrument of upbringing" (182).

34. The war and interwar periods are chapters in a complicated post-Enlightenment history of issues regarding literature's institutionalization, its supporting institutions, and the process of literary canonization. A kindred theoretical presentation attuned to various dimensions of the concept of literary institution and the agencies through which that norm has been practiced in Germany is Hohendahl's *Literarische Kultur im Zeitalter des Liberalismus*.

35. Benjamin, *Das Kunstwerk im Zeitalter seiner technischen Reproduzierbarkeit*, 29.

36. As will be detailed in Chapter 4, *Dialektik der Aufklärung*. For an account of the developments of the various institutions of literature within the time frame indicated by its title, see Hohendahl, *Literarische Kultur im Zeitalter des Liberalismus, 1830–1870*, particularly 303–410. For cultural developments within Social Democracy, see Langewische, "Arbeiterbibliotheken und Arbeiterlektüre," and Lidtke, *The Alternative Culture*.

37. As also identified by Bornebusch in *Gegen-Erinnerung* and by Müller in *Der Krieg und die Schriftsteller*.

38. On war memorials, see vol. 3 of Lurz, *Kriegsdenkmäler in Deutschland;* also R. Kosseleck, "Kriegerdenkmale als Identitätsstiftungen der Überlebenden," in Marquard and Stierle, *Identität*, and Winter, *Sites of Memory, Sites of Mourning*, ch. 4; on cemeteries, see Mosse, "Deutsche Soldatenfriedhöfe," in Vondung, *Kriegserlebnis*, 241–61, and Mosse, *Fallen Soldiers*, chs. 5 and 6. First World War Tombs of the Unknown Soldiers, a special case of the politics of commemoration, have been examined in an Allied context by Tom Laqueur ("Names, Bodies, and the Anxiety of Erasure," in Schatzki and Natter, *Social and Political Body*, 123–41), and Ken Inglis in particular in "Entombing Unknown Soldiers: From London and Paris to Baghdad," *History and Memory* 5(Fall/Winter 1993):7–32. No true (that is, neither the Tannenberg Memorial nor the *Neue Wache*) Tomb of the Unknown Soldier was dedicated in Germany during the Weimar Republic.

39. See Lange, *Marneschlacht und deutsche Öffentlichkeit*, for a day-by-day account of military disinformation following the Marne offensive.

40. Hitler, *Mein Kampf*, 180–81. In this passage, Hitler does not mention a specific place in

Flanders, that is, Langemarck, a nonnaming that I take to represent his attempt to equate that one specific incident with the *Frontgeist* imbuing the army throughout the 1914 autumn campaign.

41. Ludwig Renn, "Deutschland, Deutschland über Alles!," in Kläber, *Der Krieg,* 36.

42. See Bakhtin, *Dialogic Imagination.* On Russian Formalism more broadly, see Lemon and Reis, *Russian Formalist Criticism,* and Bennett, *Formalism and Marxism.*

43. See his "Narrativity in the Representation of Reality," in *Content of the Form,* 19.

44. White, "Narrativity in the Representation of Reality," 14. Derrida, who offers that there is no political power without control of the archive (11), has recently characterized the play of temporality and force (*Gewalt*) in a manner that is consistent with the epistemology of archive employed in the present study: "The technical structure of the *archiving* archive also determines the structure of the *archivable* content, even in its very coming into existence and in its relation to the future." See "Archive Fever," *Diacritics,* 17. Of further application to study of the archives generated during the war are Bonnie Smith's reflections on the gendered characteristics of the archive in relation to the professionalization of history since Leopold von Ranke. See Smith, "Gender, Objectivity, and the Rise of Scientific History," in Natter, Schatzki, and Jones, *Objectivity and Its Other,* 51–66.

45. See for example Franz Schauwecker, *Aufbruch der Nation* (Berlin: Frundsbergverlag, 1930): he ends this novel with precisely these words. An entry under the heading "Kriegsliteratur" (war literature) in the 1933 edition of *Der große Herder,* an encyclopedia compiled by a publishing house linked to the Catholic center, lists twenty-eight contemporary books as being antiwar and ninety-nine as being patriotic. Although one might want to question the bluntness of these categories, it is telling that the issue was framed in this way, and the numerical relationship between the two groups is, in any case, indicative.

46. The major texts documenting the positions of historians in reaction to the Habermas-Nolte exchange can be found in Augstein, *Historikerstreit.* The debate has fostered a slew of commentaries, of which Charles Maier's *Unmasterable Past* is one of the first that is sensitive to broader methodological and epistemological questions pertinent to the depiction of this history. See in particular Chapter 2, "Habermas among the Historians." For an equally useful account more informed by the attempt to relate the dispute with *Tagespolitik* in the Federal Republic, see Evens, *In Hitler's Shadow,* and Diner, *Ist der Nationalsozialismus Geschichte?* Several of the essays collected in Friedlander, *Probing the Limits of Representation,* explicitly address the historians' debate of the question of representation after the Shoah. Lastly of note, essays by Dominick LaCapra that have read the debate in terms of both epistemology and disciplinary politics through analytical categories provided by psychoanalysis, most recently "Revisiting the Historians' Debate." Volker Berghahn renders the methodological significance of the Fischer controversy in "Die Fischer-Kontroverse," as does Fritz Fischer himself in "Twenty-Five Years Later: Looking Back at the 'Fischer Controversy' and Its Consequences." For Fischer's most recent rendering of the continuities that result from his understanding of the aggressive, risk-taking strategy practices in Wilhelmine Germany and the exercise of power by National Socialism, see his *Hitler War Kein Betriebsunfall.* To my knowledge, no German historian has yet undertaken for Germany the kind of broad disciplinary

self-scrutiny (linking intellectual, institutional, and social analysis) attempted by Peter Novick's *That Noble Dream* on the changing practices of U.S. academic history, but see the valuable historiographical studies by George Iggers on historians who have practiced in Germany, including *The German Conception of History, The Social History of Politics,* and *Leopold von Ranke and the Shaping of the Historical Discipline.* Such studies rekindle the reminder that in Germany the linkage of history and national identity is not new to the *Historikerstreit;* after all, nineteenth-century governments paid for state theory and history, with some discernible interest in the process.

47. Saul Friedländer, in Diner, *Ist der Nationalsozialismus Geschichte?* 43. This passage as a whole might be taken as suggesting the possibility of an "endpoint" of the dialogical process (the fifth or tenth generation?) finally permitting closure.

48. See White, *Tropics of Discourse,* "The Fictions of Factual Representation," 125, and "Historical Emplotment and the Problem of Truth," 37–53. While White here is principally speaking of nineteenth-century historians, he clearly feels this description is still relevant as a characterization of the continued practice of the discipline. An insightful analysis of the contribution of this and his two other major books toward a cross-disciplinary dialogue among literary, political, and historical theory, books whose aim is a rethinking of our connections to the past beyond objectivism and relativism, is Roth's *The Ironist's Cage,* particularly ch. 7, and Wulf Karsteiner's cogent "Cultural Criticism and Political Theory: Hayden White's 'Critique of the Writing of History,'" in *History and Theory* 32/33(1993):273–95. On "documentary history," see LaCapra, *History and Criticism,* 18–19, and for his reading of psychoanalysis as a tool for analysis of the dispute, see "Representing the Holocaust: Reflections on the Historians' Debate," 108–27, in Friedlander, *Probing the Limits of Representation.* See too Samuel Weber's "The Blindness of the Seeing Eye: Psychoanalysis, Hermeneutics, *Entstellung,*" 73–84, in *Institution and Interpretation* for an additional account of the value of psychoanalysis for social science and the humanities. See too Natter, Schatzki, and Jones, "Contexts of Objectivity," pp. 1–17, as well as the other contributions to Natter, Schatzki, and Jones, *Objectivity and its Other,* for essays that address various dimensions of the "objectivity question" spanning the social sciences and humanities. Linking these essays is a cognizance not only of the dangers that accompany a rigid formulation of objectivity but also of those that lurk in its facile rejection.

49. Yet it can be said that they participate in the fragmentary status as ruins that might be applied more generally to efforts to "preserve" twentieth-century German history. Archives and their materials incarnate the discontinuities that warfare generates. Once-extant records, which, for example, still existed in the 1930s and which would have been helpful for the analysis, were destroyed or dispersed during and after the Second World War. This applies, for example, to the archives of major German publishing houses (such as Ullstein and Reclam) or to the numerous holdings of wartime letters and diaries ardently collected between 1914 and 1918 that mostly exist now in the selected and edited form presented in interwar military histories and anthologies or to some extent in the postmodern effort to re-collect them, as I discuss in Chapter 3. A theoretical understanding of public memory (and tradition) as marked by gaps, erasures, and changes is thus materially substantiated in the condition of the archives.

50. A mode of analysis that typifies, for example, Momber's *'S ist Krieg!*

51. See Weber's introduction to *Demarcating the Differences,* ix–x, which thus characterizes "the other side of the coin" of Derrida's project: "It is the highly ambivalent *making* of such *facts* that has increasingly imposed itself upon and throughout the more recent writings of Derrida as well as upon the field of problems and of practices associated with his work." Thus one effect of what Derrida was describing as the metaphysics of presence is precisely the "obfuscation of institution as an indispensable, but also inevitably problematic part of the articulation of meaning."

52. Horkheimer, *Dialektik der Aufklärung,* 76. The value of this line of thought and the work's understanding of the culture industry have undergone considerable and geographically varied reception contexts since 1944, recently broadly mapped by Hohendahl, *Prismatic Thought,* particularly 3–20 and 119–48. As incisive and important as the *Dialectic of the Enlightenment* is to the present study, the timeframe of the essay on the "culture industry" neglects its operation as evidenced for the Wilhelminian period (and the First World War) as well as the manifest force of the hybrid of state and military structures presented here. This latter point might have been of interest in developing and refining the theory of state capitalism articulated in the late 1930s onward (for example, by Friedrich Pollack, Franz Neumann, and Otto Kirchheimer). For a general overview, see Jay, "The Dialectical Imagination," and for an overview of critical theory in the 1930s, see Kellner, *Critical Theory, Marxism, and Modernity.* I also intend to contribute to a reevaluation of *Dialectic of Enlightenment's* critique of culture in relation to the state and economy of interwar Germany and by reference to the military and economy during the First World War. In particular, the presentation of cultural production and reception in Germany between 1914 and 1940 may better help avoid the schematic categorization of popular, mass, and elite culture, which in recent years has permitted the too-easy dismissal of Adorno's purported mandarin elitism and his and Horkheimer's singular focus on production—rendered monolithically—rather than reception in the cultural realm.

CHAPTER 2: ESTABLISHING THE PARADIGM

1. On the general topic of censorship and its evolution in Germany, see Breuer, *Geschichte der literarischen Zensur in Deutschland.* Chapters of its history between the Enlightenment and the 1930s are discussed in McCarthy and von der Ohe, *Zensur und Kultur,* conceptually in particular in the essay by Wolfram Siemann, "Normenwandel auf dem Weg zur 'modernen' Zensur: Zwischen Aufklärungspolizei und politischer Repression," 63–86, and in the still-remarkable H. H. Houben, *Verbotene Literatur von der klassischen Zeit bis zur Gegenwart.* For the First World War, see Fischer, *Pressekonzentration und Zensurpraxis im ersten Weltkrieg,* Koszyk, *Deutsche Presse,* and Deist, *Militär und Innenpolitik im Weltkrieg,* for the most complete documentary history of the evolving agencies and institutions guiding censorship policy during the war. Bearing in mind significant differences between the situation in 1914 and that of 1918, one can concur with Fischer's assessment (as it applies to 1918) that the state control of communication during the war "in this thickness and concentration represent an absolute novelty in Germany" (9). See Barkhausen, *Filmpropaganda für Deutschland im ersten und zweiten Weltkrieg* for an

overview of the reactive and proactive regulation of film images and their production, and Rother, *Die letzten Tage der Menschheit* for its copious reproductions of war-affirmative representations produced during the war in film and other visual and popular media (such as photography, poster art, painting, and monuments).

2. A succinct and probing introduction to the phenomenon can be found in Reinhard Rürup, "'Der Geist von 1914' in Deutschland," in Bernd Hüppauf, *Ansichten von Krieg*, 1–30. An excellent casting of key aspects of the spiritual mobilization, exemplified by Stefan George, Thomas Mann, Rainer M. Rilke, Ernst Troeltsch, and Sigmund Freud, is Philippi, *Volk des Zorns*. Klaus Vondung cites and analyzes numerous pertinent contemporaries in *Die Apokalypse in Deutschland* and in the edited essay collection *Kriegserlebnis*, particularly in "Propaganda oder Sinndeutung," 11–40, as does Eckart Koester in *Literatur und Weltkriegsideologie*. For a telling of the story from the perspective of European intellectual history, see Stromberg, *Redemption by War*, and Eksteins, *Rites of Spring*. Böhm, *Aufrufe und Reden deutscher Professoren im ersten Weltkrieg*, includes a helpful introduction and interesting documentation of academic mobilization. See also Schwabe, *Wissenschaft und Kriegsmoral*, for an analysis of the generally chauvinistic involvement of German university professors. On the number of war poems produced, see Bridgewater, citing Julius Bab among others in "German Poetry and the First World War."

3. The uproar provoked in the 1960s by the so-called Fischer controversy attests to what extent this belief had been accepted and perpetuated by German historians, and to the level of shock provoked when Fritz Fischer asserted that on the German side the outbreak of the First World War, far from being a defensive war, was a preplanned offensive strategy just waiting for the right occasion to be set in operation.

4. On expressionism, see Korte, *Der Krieg in der Lyrik des Expressionismus*. For reasons the present study details, these expressionists have been overly represented in literary and cultural history as emblematic of the "experience" of the war. On the Pan-Germans, see Chickering, *We Men Who Feel Most German*. On confessional expectations and practices in the context of governmental policy, see Nipperdey, *Religion im Umbruch*, Besier, *Religion—Nation—Kultur*, and Heath Spencer, *Church Politics, Periodicals, and Modern Theology: German Cultural Protestant Zeitschriften and Their Constituencies, 1890–1918*, dissertation, University of Kentucky, 1997. As Egmont Zechlin, Stephen Magill, George Mosse, and others have pointed out, Jewish-German responses in August 1914 were similar to those of other social segments; the so-called *Judenzählung* undertaken by the High Command in October 1916 therefore was a deep shock to German Jews, questioning as it did the assumption of Jewish assimilation, on a model that preserved difference "merely" in religious terms. See Zechlin, *Die deutsche Politik und die Juden im ersten Weltkrieg*, Mosse, *Toward the Final Solution*, chs. 10 and 11, and Stephen Magill, "Defence and Introspection: German Jewry 1914," in Bronson, *Jews and Germans from 1860 to 1933*, 209–33. Student letters are explored in detail in Chapter 3. Hitler, *Mein Kampf*, 176–77.

5. On Social Democracy's response to the war, see Müller, *Burgfrieden und Klassenkampf*, Schorske, *German Social Democracy*, and Groh, *Vaterlandslose Gesellen*. Vignettes spanning social and confessional reactions to the war's outbreak can be found in Berliner Geschichtswerkstatt, *August 1914* (Berlin: Verlag Dirk Nishen, 1989). Reminders of the spirit are ubiquitous in war novels published between 1915 and 1918, employed as a

presumed reference point in the narration. The very need to re-present August 1914 as part of these later narratives is quite suggestive as regards its passage into memory, but it is also suggestive of the ongoing mobilization power that this spirit would assume in the development of future war memories.

6. The series as a whole receives attention in Chapter 4.

7. Although much more readable in terms of the political than generally assumed, evocations of "the days of August" leave virtually unreflected the kind of politics required to enact the political visions to be found in them. On the distinction between the two terms, see Mouffe, *Return of the Political,* and my commentary on her project, "Radical Democracy: Hegemony, Reason, Time and Space," *Society and Space* 13(1995):267–74.

8. These civilian hardships are vividly described by Laurence Moyer in chs. 5 and 7 in *Victory Must Be Ours.* For a detailed assessment of the nutritional changes and effects on well-being caused by the serious rationing that began in 1915, see Offer, *The First World War.*

9. See Lange, *Marneschlacht und Kriegsöffentlichkeit,* 14–19, and Wallach, *The Dogma of the Battle of Annihilation.* The consequences in generating an understanding of *Langemarck* are explored in Bernd Hüppauf, "Langemarck, Verdun, and the Myth of a New Man," and Uwe-K. Ketelsen, "'Die Jugend von Langemarck': Ein Poetisch-Politisches Motiv der Zwischenkriegszeit," in Koebner, Janz, and Trommler, *"Mit uns zieht die neue Zeit."*

10. The presentation of this aspect of the war is sympathetic to the analysis of Fritz Fischer and his students. See *Griff nach der Weltmacht, Der erste Weltkrieg und das deutsche Geschichtsbild,* and the essays in *Hitler war kein Betriebsunfall.* See too Geiss, *Das deutsche Reich und der erste Weltkrieg.*

11. In *Mein Kampf* the two categories of identity are explicitly overlain in Hitler's repudiation of the *Burgfrieden:* he concludes the narration of his war experience, which he claims was his motivation to become a politician, with the following lesson learned from the *Dolchstoßlegende:* "As the first Kaiser to do so, Wilhelm II extended his hand in reconciliation, unable to anticipate that slackers have no honor. Even while holding the Kaiser's hand in one of their own, they searched with their other one for a blade. One cannot come to terms with the Jews, there can be only a simple yes or no" (225). On National Socialism, anti-Semitism, and the war experience, see the well-documented essay by Steven T. Katz, "1918 and After: The Role of Racial Antisemitism in the Nazi Analysis of the Weimar Republic," in Katz, *Anti-Semitism in Times of Crisis.* On the positions academic historians have taken on this issue, see Jäger, *Historische Forschung und politische Kultur in Deutschland,* and Heinemann, *Die verdrängte Niederlage.* Weimar historians, mandarins with weak (if any) allegiance to the Republic, largely failed to undertake the writing of a history that would have dispelled the myth's explanatory power and therewith provided the Republic with an alternative understanding legitimated by social science. Groundbreaking in explaining the contemporaneous orchestration of the stab-in-the-back thesis is Petzold, *Die Dolchstoßlegende.* In characterizing Ludendorff's activities, Petzold reports on a conference on September 29, 1918, at which Ludendorff advised the Kaiser to name new ministers to government: "They should [be the ones to] make the peace that now must be made. They should eat the bread which they have crumbled in our soup" (32).

12. *Mein Kampf,* 224. Though Hitler and National Socialist propaganda efforts generally

continued to rhetorically summon the "lessons" of the war and mark it as the genealogical birthplace of "the movement," its lessons at the time of *Mein Kampf*'s publication include the need for a total eradication of the spirit of *Burgfrieden* (domestic truce) while preserving most of the other elements associated with the "spirit of 1914."

13. On that date, High Command (OHL) was ordered to seek approval for its decisions and regulations from the Reichschancellor or his designated representatives. "Only then was finally actualized what the Social Democrats and the Progressive People's Party had striven toward in the censorship debates of 1915–1916—namely, the government's assumption of overall responsibility for the censorship measures taken by the military" (Kurt Koszyk, "Entwicklung der Kommunikationskontrolle zwischen 1914 und 1918," in Fischer, *Pressekonzentration und Zensurpraxis im ersten Weltkrieg,* 180). On Patriotic Instruction, see Wilhelm Deist, *Militär und Innenpolitik,* for an overview and documentation of its design, and Günther Mai, "'Aufklärung der Bevölkerung' und 'Vaterländischer Unterricht' in Württemberg," for the application of it within one affected region.

14. Breuer, *Geschichte der literarischen Zensur in Detuschland,* 212.

15. See Kurt Koszyk, "Entwicklung der Kommunikationskontrolle," 152–210.

16. See Generalstabbestimmungen (General Staff Decrees) in *Hauptstaatsarchiv* Stuttgart (HSA), M635 Cluster 934.

17. On the organizational competencies entrusted with censorship issues, see Deist, *Militär und Innenpolitik im Weltkrieg, 1914–1918* (Düsseldorf: Droste, 1970), liv. On censorship in Bavaria, see Fischer, *Die Münchner Zensurstelle während des ersten Weltkrieges.* There are three separate "blue books" in the *Kriegsarchiv,* Stuttgart, Bestand M731.

18. Decree dated October 10, 1914.

19. On voluntary precensorship, see "Bericht der (Württembergischen) Presseabteilung über ihre Tätigkeit von Anfang des Krieges bis zum 31 Mai 1916," HSA, M77/2 14a. (The report was updated until the end of the war). For Hoffmann, see HSA, M77/2 Cluster 14.

20. See "Begründung der bestehenden Präventivzensur" in HSA, M77/2 Cluster 14, which also quotes the Chief Censor Office (Oberzensurstelle [OBZ]), of October 31, 1915, that it is not possible "to sharply distinguish between political, military, and economic questions [for which reason] it is left to the judgment of the authorities authorized to enforce the decree from the Head Censor Office of September 6, 1915, to decide which writings they wish to view as political. Therein is given a justification for the resolution [of the situation] which was found here from the [war's] beginning."

21. Koszyk, *Deutsche Presse* and *Zwischen Kaiserreich und Diktatur.*

22. For example, the *Kriegsarchiv* Stuttgart, Press Office section, has a substantial file listing for all war years of those newspapers in Württemberg that were fined and warned, with the reason for each action. On cooperation, see "Denkschrift von Sonnenburg" quoted by Doris Fischer, *Die münchner Zensurstelle,* 31–33. In February 1918, the crown prince urged the kaiser to prohibit the publication of *Vorwärts, Berliner Tageblatt,* and the *Frankfurter Zeitung* because of the "mischief that they have created in the heads of our troops during the previous months." Although the censors agreed to warn each paper, their publication was not suspended—again a telling limit of governmental censorship predicated on maintenance of a fragile domestic truce. See Koszyk in *Pressekonzentration und Zensurpraxis im ersten Weltkrieg,* 150. As I discuss in Chapter 4, it was another matter

entirely whether the military needed to permit these newspapers to be sold within its territorial jurisdiction on the eastern and western fronts.

23. Richards, *German Bestseller*, 64, 90. All together, Bloem published over forty titles, principally novels and plays. The 1941 figure is listed in the *Deutsches Bücherverzeichnis*.

24. Bloem, *Vormarsch*, 3–10.

25. Walter Bloem's diary, written after 1945 and given the working title "Werk und Tat" (Work and Deed), was intended for publication, but to his great surprise, he was unable to find a publisher.

26. In "Werk und Tat," 158, Bloem offers his own opinion on why he became a best-selling author shortly before the First World War. He points to a fundamental shift in audience expectations as a result of the changing political situation from which he benefited: "Midway into 1911, *Das eiserne Jahr* began selling briskly. . . . What had happened? An uncanny transformation of the world's political atmosphere had begun. The Morocco Conference of Agidir had revealed Germany's complete isolation with one fell swoop. The German reading public began to realize that the forty-year period of peace that had been bequeathed our people following centuries of eternal wrestling would perhaps not be perpetually guaranteed."

27. Bloem, *Die Schmiede der Zukunft*, 514.

28. Hitler's hate of "Parlamentarier," for example, is amply documented in vol. 1 of *Mein Kampf*, 182, which he subtitled "A Reckoning." "I hated these blathermouths; back then I hated all these politicians and had it been up to me, a parliamentary ditch-digging battalion would have been formed; then they could have blathered away to their heart's content without angering or damaging [the interests of] decent and honest people."

29. Although recognizing the unacceptability of the view of 1914–1918 and modernity that makes the First World War into the time when "'modern memory' replaced something else," Jay Winter accounts for the "enduring appeal of many traditional motifs" by recourse to their definition as "an eclectic set of classical, romantic, or religious images and ideas" in his corrective of Paul Fussell, *Sites of Memory, Sites of Mourning*, 5. Winter continues: "The multifaceted sense of dislocation, paradox, and the ironic could express anger and despair, and did so in enduring ways; it was melancholic, but it could not heal." In my study, which is limited to circumstances in Germany, the persistence of certain images and ideas (and not others) is less unrestrictedly and more socially understood in relation to institutional processes that generated and perpetuated them. Though thoroughly "traditional"—in the postromantic sense of defining individual identity in terms of a supra-individual collectivity, they too, because of the telos of national reformation inscribed in their production, could not offer healing following Germany's defeat. Benjamin's recognition of how substantial the loss was in the lost war is at issue here. Thus Germany's defeat probably made a "universal problem of grief and its social expression" (Winter, 224) different in its contents from those observable in England and France.

30. A thorough depiction of its reception in a book that is generally centered on Bloem's Weimar years and on a reading of *Bruderschaft* is Morris, *From Weimar Philosemite to Nazi Apologist*. For Bloem's broadening of temporal focus, see in particular his *Unvergängliches Deutschland*.

31. Bloem drew upon his experiences in Belgium in writing the second volume of his *Kriegserlebnistrilogie,* entitled *Sturmsignal,* also published by Grethlein. See Anton Kippenberg's unpublished letter of May 31, 1915, to Eduard von Bodenhausen, *Deutsche Literaturarchiv* (DLA), Marbach, A: Kippenberg. Bodenhausen had previously been instrumental in placing R. A. Schroeder in the Political Department there.

32. A full-scale account of the men of letters who were mobilized in this effort and the history of its scope has not yet been written. A recent valuable contribution that asks many of the right questions with regard to the cultural mobilization of expressionism in Belgium is edited by Rumold and Werckmeister, *The Ideological Crisis of Expressionism.* As underscored by many of the contributors to the volume, the task of writing this history is hampered by the apparent loss of many relevant archival materials. On the planned journal within the context of the Political Department, see "Plan einer Zeitschrift über Belgien," Bayerisches *Kriegsarchiv,* Munich, HS 1592, papers of General von Harrich. Another prominent man of letters with strong ties to Insel who worked on the journal and in the Press Office of the Political Department is Wilhelm Hausenstein. Further discussion of the efforts undertaken by Hausenstein, Schroeder, and some of the conflicting imperatives marking their activities can also be found in Rumold and Werckmeister, *Ideological Crisis of Expressionism.* On Schroeder's responsibilities, see "Arbeitsbegrenzung der politischen Abteilung und der Zivilverwaltung in Sachen der Pressepropaganda," Bayerisches *Kriegsarchiv,* HS 1592, Harrich. Under Graf Harrach's supervision, Schroeder was in charge of "literary and artistic propaganda." One of his tasks was to create a climate that would enable "German book production to conquer Flanders as a market while displacing the competition from France and Holland."

33. Kippenberg's success in stimulating the sale of war bonds among the troops earned him a commendation from the commander of the Fourth Army: "The brilliant success, which the seventh loan subscription had among the members of the Fourth Army, is thanks first and foremost to the tireless work of advertisement and information directed by the office of Patriotic Instruction. I applaud your services as director of Patriotic Instruction and pronounce my particular thanks and my recognition for the successful services that you have contributed to the Fatherland." in DLA, A: Kippenberg, November 25, 1917. Kippenberg's wartime activity and that of the Insel Verlag between 1914 and 1918 warrant a full-length study. The conclusion of this investigation will return to Kippenberg's political-aesthetic agenda. Literary criticism has not sufficiently acknowledged the consequences for literary production that his political engagement for the war effort imply. Additionally, these activities during the First World War may be important in further contextualizing the "Paul de Man Affair," occasioned by the revelation of his pro-German, anti-Semitic wartime journalism in Belgium. I hope to address this subject matter in greater detail in a future study.

34. Cincinnatus, *Der Krieg der Worte,* 8. The work received the support of the Foreign Ministry, which commissioned Cotta to do several editions. For a cross section of the many memoirs that chronicle the sentiment that the German informational services were always a step behind the propaganda wings of the Allied governments, see the contemporary citations used by Klaus Vondung in his essay "Propaganda oder Sinn-

deutung" (Propaganda or Interpretation of Meaning), in *Kriegserlebnis*, 11–40. One of the most portentous commentaries on the "lessons" to be drawn from these "failures" is presented in Hitler's *Mein Kampf*, ch. 6 ("War Propaganda").

35. "Feldzeitungen und Feldbuchhandlungen: Eine Forderung des modernen Stellung- krieges," *Generallandesarchiv*, Karlsruhe, 456/EV2.

36. "Aufzeichnung aus der Pressebesprechung von 10.4.1916," HSA, M635/934.

37. Bloem, *Das ganze, halt!* 139. The three books published as a single volume enjoyed a revival, with a printing of 205,000, by 1939, according to Richards, *German Bestseller*, 60.

38. Bloem, *Das ganze, halt!* 139–40. Bloem makes the same points in his "Notizen über die Tätigkeit der Feldpressestelle des Generalstabes des Feldheeres, Charleville, 1916–18," *Bundesmilitärarchiv* Freiburg, Bloem, *Nachlaß* (unpublished works), N 31/8.

39. Höcker to *Kommandantur Lille*, November 16, 1916, Bayerisches *Kriegsarchiv*, AOK 6 Bestand 214.

40. These papers provided several well-known authors of the 1920s their first exposure to a wider audience. The papers themselves were much in demand as memorabilia in Germany, although the more serious ones were viewed with suspicion by the larger presses as undesirable competition.

41. "Besprechung der Leiter der Armeezeitungen am 23.3.1916 im Großen Hauptquartier," *Bundesmilitärarchiv* Freiburg, PH 3/93.

42. As reported by Nicolai in "Feldzeitungen und Feldbuchhandlungen—eine Forderung des modernen Stellungkrieges," *Generallandesarchiv* Karlsruhe, 456/EV 2; "Besprech- ung der Leiter der Armeezeitungen am 23.3.1916." *Bundesmilitärarchiv* Freiburg, PH 3/93.

43. Ibid. Bloem's "Notizen über die Tätigkeit der Feldpressestelle" depicts a reluctant audi- ence on this occasion: "The gentlemen were a bit miffed at the beginning, because they feared a cutting down to size of their independence. Soon, however, they realized that the arrangement was purposeful, and that it would ensure them a dependable source of material regarding the most important questions of the day." Even a personal friend of Bloem's, Paul Oscar Höcker, editor of the important *Lillier Kriegszeitung*, complained in his autobiography that as a result "the input of the combat zone during the last year became ever weaker. . . . The [army] newspapers became ever more alike in their output" (Höcker, *Gottgesandte Wechselwinde*). On the recognition of their importance, see further General Hauptquartier (Gr. H. Qu.), February 3, 1918, Chef des General- stabes des Feldheeres No. IIIb 15127/II Mob, "An Heeresgruppen und Armee- oberkommandos des Westens," 456, *Generallandesarchiv* Karlsruhe, AOK7. The quota- tion continues: "I therefore request that the army corps direct effort to ensure that a redistribution of the extant army newspapers across the entire front occur, so as to also provide those army corps with a field newspaper that are without one."

44. And was linked to it in Gr. H. Qu. Chef des Generalstabes des Feldheeres M.J. No. 2737, Zr. January 1, 1916, "An Oberbefehlshaber Ost, Oberkommando Mackensen, alle A.O.K.'s, alle Kriegsministerien, Generalquartiermeister, Stellvertr. Generalstab." *Generallandesarchiv* Karlsruhe, GLA 456.

45. I discuss the collection efforts of war letters in this vein extensively in Chapter 3.

46. M.J. No. 2737, Zr. January 1, 1916.

47. Gr. H. Qu. December 28, 1914, Chef des Generalstabes des Feldheeres M.J. No. 12073; "An das Oberkommando der 1.–9. Armee pp" (To the Higher Command of the First Through Ninth Armies), *Generallandesarchiv*, Karlsruhe, GLA 456. "Zensurverfügungen des Generalstabes vom 3.10.1914," HSA, M635/934.

48. *Reichtag Protokol*, Session 172 (June 6, 1918): 3402–3; ibid. 3403.

49. Ibid., 3403. In order to refute Haas's remarks, the *Kriegspressedienst* subsequently published in pamphlet form a defense written and signed by the war reporter attacking his claims.

50. M.J. No. 2737, Zr. January 1, 1916.

51. *Fünfzig Jahre Ullstein,* "Die erfolgreichsten Kriegsbücher." I depict Ullstein's war series in Chapter 4.

52. M.J. No. 2737, Zr. January 1, 1916.

53. Cotta, for example, on August 24, 1914, sent out such letters to both Admiral Curt von Maltzahn and General of the Cavalry Friedrich von Bernardi, who had already become a Cotta author before 1914, with his *Deutschland und der nächste Krieg* (Germany and the Next War): "We hope we are not misguided in assuming that your excellence has been deliberating over a plan to offer a literary treatment of the ongoing war, its prehistory, its manifestations, and consequences. We probably hardly need to provide assurances of how pleasurably we would greet the appearance of your work about the war in our publishing house. . . . In consideration of the fact that works about the World War of 1914 probably can be expected in great numbers, it would be of great value to appear among the first of these and at an appropriate time to announce this happy circumstance to the public as soon as possible." DLA, A: Cotta, *Autorenkorrespondenz.* Unlike von Maltzahn, Bernardi did not plan such an undertaking. On the prerogative of the OHL, see Gr. H. Qu. January 28, 1914, Chef des Generalstabes des Feldheeres M.J. No. 12073. "An das Oberkommando der 1.–9. Armee pp." *Generallandesarchiv,* Karlsruhe, GLA 456.

54. H. Qu. August 15, 1917, "Heeresgruppe Deutscher Kronprinz Nachrichtenoffizier J. No. 6115 Geheim!" Verteilung: A.O.K. 1, 3, 5, 7, Feldpressestelle, Chef IIIb II, GLA 456 *Generallandesarchiv* Karlsruhe. For an authoritative account of press monopolization in the early twentieth century, see Koszyk, *Deutsche Presse.* The information access policy of the government may have further accentuated an antagonism that finds expression in the dualism "Berlin vs. Provinz," notably in literary criticism of the early twentieth century. For some of the implications of this antagonism, see Meyer, *Berlin-Provinz.*

55. Bloem, *Das ganze, halt!* 146.

56. "Dienstanweisung für den Offizier-Kriegsberichterstatter" (Service Regulations Affecting Officer War Reporters), *Bundesmilitärarchiv* Freiburg, Rm. 5, No. 3842: "In dealings with the civilian war correspondents it is particularly important to observe that the information given the Officer War Correspondents be kept confidential. . . . Officer War Correspondents should nonetheless never permit the civilian correspondents to feel that they are disadvantaged because the officers will generally have access to better information."

57. Bloem, *Das ganze, halt!* 151.

58. "Verteilungsübersicht der O.K.B. Arbeiten für die Heimat- und Auslandspresse vom January 1, 1918–January 7, 1918." Quoted by Deist, *Militär und Innenpolitik,* 868. Deist

is doubtless correct in presuming that the success of the O.K.B.s in getting published was probably even greater, because "experience shows that not all newspapers would have sent in their printed copies." The 1982 film *Das Boot* portrayed an example of how Bloem's idea blossomed in the Second World War for the navy. Of course, the *Wehrmacht* also continued the practice established by the OHL, while Bloem himself, then seventy-one years old and a major, went to the *Luftwaffe* to serve as a war correspondent, lecturing and writing articles and plays.

59. Bloem, "Notizen über die Tätigkeit der Feldpressestelle."

60. In my reading of Bloem's unpublished diary "Werk und Tat" (which he wrote after 1945), I see far greater continuities with the author of the war books analyzed here than with the person who briefly complains in the diary that Verdun "was the most colossal military insanity [without specific attribution of *whose*] that has ever been undertaken" or with the author of *Brüderlichkeit*, who, as Morris argues, was a philosemite and a critic of some of the leading figures of the Wilhelmine military hierarchy, rues in the diary that he had not made more and earlier contributions to "the movement." Also, his pleasure at being in the Kaiser's company (and to some extent having his ear), additionally may mitigate against stressing too much Bloem's "questioning" of "the rightness of the Wilhelmine order." See Morris, *From Philosemite to Nazi Apologist*, 10.

61. "Dienstanweisung für den Offizier-Kriegsberichterstatter," *Bundesmilitärarchiv*, Freiburg, Rm. 5, No. 3842. Deist, *Militär und Innenpolitik*, also quotes part of the document under its old signature number, 867–68.

62. Corporal Hitler learned this lesson from its efforts: "All propaganda must be popular and its mental level set according to the absorbing capacity of the most limited amongst those for whom it is being directed. . . . If, however, the goal is to draw an entire people into its sphere of activity, as in the scenario of conducting propaganda to see a war through to the end, then the care taken to avoid too-elevated mental presuppositions can hardly be great enough" (*Mein Kampf*, 197).

63. This and the next two quotations are from "Dienstanweisungen für den Offizier-Kriegsberichterstatter."

64. By mid 1916, shortages in food supplies had become so acute that black humor treatments of the topic needed to be forbidden: "Those newspaper firms that also publish *Witzblätter* (joke magazines) are requested to do what they can to ensure that the scarcity of food goods is not made the butt of jokes. One magazine published two proletarians in conversation, who tell one another how much dog meat they have processed. Such manifestations are tasteless, and affect both foreign and domestic audiences (who see how far some people are willing to go in mocking the poorer elements of the population) equally badly." See "Pressebesprechungen," HSA, No. 151, v. July 21, 1916, O.Z. in Cluster M77/2.

65. H. Qu., August 15, 1917, "Heeresgruppe Deutscher Kronprinz, Nachrichtenoffizier, Geheim!" *Generallandesarchiv*, Karlsruhe, GLA 456.

66. For a good impression of just how "insignificant" these sacrifices demanded of civilians had become by then, see Moyer, *Victory Must be Ours*, Daniel, *Arbeiterfrauen in der Kriegsgesellschaft*, and Offer, *The First World War*. See additionally, the essays in Mai, *Arbeiterschaft in Deutschland*. Offer, however, provocatively states that an issue during

the rationing and subsequent food riots of the final two years was the unwillingness of Germans to convert to vegetarianism—essentially what the war economy had forced upon civilians. For an important depiction accenting the effects for the civilian population, see Kocka, *Klassengesellschaft im Krieg.* Ullrich depicts everyday hardship in *Kriegsalltag,* and Bellon offers a significant interlinked regional and industrial focus in *Mercedes in Peace and War,* particularly in ch. 4, "World War One at the Daimler Motoren Gesellschaft."

Civilian complaints, which reached the front in the form of letters, were, wrote Hitler, poison that thoughtless women concocted at home without realizing that this was the primary means of strengthening the enemy's belief in victory while at the same time prolonging and sharpening the suffering of their loved ones at the front. Hitler's personification of *die Heimat* as that which betrays, often takes on a misogynist tone, generating a mental economy of "good" and "bad" women / *Heimat.* See also Theweleit's *Männerphantasien,* vol. 1, ch. 1, for an analyis of the characteristics of "good" and "bad" women in *Freikorps* (private militia) literature. Hitler's account of (female) complaints ends with the assertion "that in their wake, the senseless letters of German women cost the lives of hundreds of thousands of men" (*Mein Kampf,* 208).

67. The O.K.B. reports by Loofs, Goltz, and Hollander are stored (along with all others on Bavarian troops) in Bayerisches *Kriegsarchiv,* Stv. Generalkdo I. AK, Vol. 1714. Many, including two I quote from, do not list the specific author and they are not all paginated.

68. See Goltz, *Der Baum von Clery.*

69. After the war, other German commentators saw cultural difference and superiority in the layout and makeup of cemetery landscapes. The "tragic-heroic" spirit of Germanic cemeteries was contrasted with the mere "dress parade of the dead" and the "sea of flowers" used by the Allies. See Mosse, *Fallen Soldiers,* 112. Here the covered body continues to be an object of signification, even after death.

70. Bayerisches *Kriegsarchiv,* IAK, No. 1714, January 18, 1918, from the War Ministry, communiqué No. 2938A.

71. See for example their usage in Foerster, *Wir Kämpfer im Weltkrieg,* and another official series, *Deutsche Regimenter im Weltkrieg,* whose two hundred volumes were overseen by the Reich archive. Hollander's literary career skyrocketed after the war. Some of his works of the period include *Grenze der Erfüllung: Ein Novellenkreis, Der Eine und der Andere, Das fiebernde Haus,* and *Schicksale gebündet.* He continued publishing after 1933, mostly with the Scherl-Verlag. Goltz published two collections of his work during the war: *Deutsche Sonette,* reprinted in 1944 by Langen-Müller, and *Eiserne zehn Gebote an die deutschen Krieger.* His greatest publishing success, however, was the war book *Der Baum von Clery.* Langen-Müller issued a chapter of the novel as a volume of its "kleine Bücherei," of which 21,000–30,000 copies had been printed that same year. Johann Bubendey was mostly known as a dramatist before the war (*Der Backfisch,* 1910, *Liebesboycott,* 1911), but he also published several novels thereafter. Hans Fritz von Zwehl subsequently wrote several plays dramatizing the war. See his *Nach Troyas Fall, Aufruhr in Flandern,* and *Frühlingsschlacht.* Friedrich Loofs, who also used the pseudonym Armin Steinart, saw his literary career flounder in the late 1920s after a falling out with Cotta. He spent the last years of his life practicing psychoanalysis in Berlin.

72. The list of medals and commendations that Bloem compiled for his *Nachlaß* fills one
and a half pages. (*Nachlaß* Bloem, *Bundesmilitärarchiv* Freiburg.) Nicolai (and Moltke)
became favorite whipping boys in postwar technical military writing. Nicolai's private
papers, regrettably, are presumed lost. For Bloem's remarks, see *Das ganze, halt!* 140. One
other reason Bloem gave for his conflict with Nicolai, which one finds reformulated
(more bluntly) again in his diaries, was perhaps as telling: for Nicolai, "co-workers were
subordinates, whose right to express opinions, critique, and resistance toward misguided
notions of the leadership was banished into very narrow confines by the prerogative of
soldierly obedience."

73. As discussed in Chapter 1.

74. Bloem joined the party in 1938. In his diary, which was written after 1945, he maintained
that he had done so for solely literary reasons, "in order to garner a true understanding
about the character, value, and forceful fate of Hitlerism," 451. At other times, however,
he mentions wishing that he had done more earlier to support the party. On soldierly
nationalism, see Prümm's *Die Literatur des soldatischen Nationalismus der 20er Jahre* for
both his scholarly justification of the term and his discussion of Jünger's war books of the
1920s. Another work that discusses Jünger that has aided my understanding of his war
books was Böhme, *Fassungen bei Ernst Jünger,* for his insightful presentation of the
different versions of Jünger's war books between 1920 and 1970. Despite the numerous
demonstrable revisions of this diary and also of his war diary in light of subsequent
Tagespolitik, the various *Fassungen* (editions) maintain a narrative voice invoking authenticity, immediacy, and experience. Noteworthy treatments of Jünger can also be
found in Müller, *Der Krieg und die Schriftsteller;* Theweleit, *Männerphantasien; New
German Critique* 59(1993); Barnouw, *Weimar Intellectuals and the Threat of Modernity;*
Herf, *Reactionary Modernism;* and Volmert, *Ernst Jünger.* On best-sellers, see the lists
compiled by Richards in *German Bestseller,* which despite incomplete reliability is highly
informative in this regard. The number of war books mentioned there that belong to
this category of best-selling literature is a forceful reminder of the discrepancy between
works that literary critics read today as indicative of the period and those that were read
in bulk by a contemporary audience.

75. See Lübbe, *Politische Philosophie in Deutschland,* and Sontheimer, *Antidemokratisches
Denken in der Weimarer Republik,* for a good general orientation to these currents.

76. Eberhard Jäckel, who has written a number of important studies on National Socialism,
including *Hitler's Weltanschauung,* ultimately finds two irreducible elements that define
Hitler's politics, the drive for "Lebensraum" in the East, and his radical anti-Semitism.
"The zero hour"—1945—can be thought to have abruptly terminated cultural development leading up to and including 1933–1945. But one should not forget that despite its
destructiveness, the period of National Socialist control in Germany lasted only thirteen
years. To some extent, the National Socialist "movement" was a porous vessel into which
a number of currents flow. Based on an analysis of National Socialist electoral strategy, it
is practical to think of National Socialism's appeal as a "catchall party of protest," which
directed its agitation to carefully chosen audiences, often promising and proclaiming
different things to different groups. For that reason too it is difficult to strictly differentiate the movement's ideology (or ideologies) from its competitors. See Childers,

The Nazi Voter, "The Limits of National Socialist Mobilization: The Elections of 6 November 1932 and the Fragmentation of the Nazi Constituency," in his *Formation of the Nazi Constituency,* and "The Social Language of Politics in Germany." A major reason for National Socialism's stunning electoral victories in the late Weimar period was the party's successful self-presentation as a political interest group speaking on behalf of the "forgotten veterans" of the war. Campaign literature promised immediate reform of the pension and injury compensation system. Hitler was portrayed as the embodiment of the unknown or forgotten soldier of the war, the party as an extension of the Frontgeist of the trenches. During the final years of the Republic, most of the major veteran organizations—*Kyffhäuser Bund, Deutscher Offiziersbund,* and the *Reichsverband deutscher Kriegsopfer* allied themselves with the Nazi Party. The *Reichsbund* (founded by the Social Democrats) and the *Internationaler Bund* (allied with the Communist Party) were dissolved in spring 1933. For a useful account of the legal situation and political motives of German war veterans in the 1920s and the fate of these veteran organizations, see Whalen, *Bitter Wounds,* 155–81; also Bessel, *Germany and the First World War,* on the return of the soldiers and their war legacy, chs. 3 and 9; and 1914–1939. See also Mosse, *Nationalization of the Masses.*

77. Bloem, *Das ganze, halt!* 151. Theweleit, *Männerphantasien,* 114, makes an appropriate connection in his examination of *Freikorps* novels: "Fathers are not in demand in these books. [These authors] write as sons who have outlasted Wilhelm II, the pitifully abdicated father whose mistakes they aim to rectify. The father is a failure, they have taken up the battle to take his place with Mother Germany."

78. Bloem, as mentioned earlier, never added the category "Jew" to his litany of those culpable.

79. A more detailed discussion of these matters follows in Chapter 4.

80. Additional continuities are suggested in my "Nachricht, Botschaft, Verheißung: Der (veröffentlichte) erste Weltkrieg," in Althaus, Cancik-Lindemaier, Hoffmann-Curtius, and Rebstock, *Der Krieg in den Köpfen,* 141–49.

81. Ernst Jünger, who gloried in the war, ends his narration of *Storm of Steel* with the protagonist being awarded the "Pour le Merite" commendation, a distinctly upbeat conclusion that avoids any reflection on or mention of the war's outcome. But such nonclosure is true also for novels like *All Quiet on the Western Front,* which ends with the protagonist's death while the war continues.

82. HSA, MI/11 Bestand 982.

83. See my entry, "Edlef Köppen," in Lutz, *Metzler Autoren Lexikon,* 376–77.

84. Axel Eggebrecht, "Heeresbericht und Heldentod," *Tagebuch* (May 24, 1930):819–21. Other noteworthy reviews were written by Kurt Pinthus and Ernst Toller; an example of its negative reception is the review by Wilhelm Westecker in *Neue Literatur* 32 (1931): 214–18, who critiques Köppen for his "liberal worldview," which of necessity fails to appreciate the "historical meaning" of the war experience.

85. Köppen's novel receives further treatment in Michael Gollbach's introduction to a reissue of the novel (Kronberg: Scriptor Verlag, 1977) and his *Die Wiederkehr des Weltkrieges in der Literatur.* See also Bornebusch, *Gegenerinnerung,* and Travers, *German Novels of the First World War,* ch. 6.

86. In addition to the works cited at the beginning of this chapter on the ramifications of the "Fischer Controversy," see the proceedings of an international conference held in Stuttgart in August 1985 organized and published under the title *Neue Forschung über den ersten Weltkrieg* (Freiburg: Militärgeschichtliches Forschungsamt, 1986), as well as Rohwer, *Neue Forschungen zum ersten Weltkrieg*, particularly Bruno Thoß, "Weltkrieg und Systemkrise: Der erste Weltkrieg in der westdeutschen Forschung, 1945–1985," 31–80. See also Blackbourn and Eley, *Peculiarities of German History*, 28–32, for its linkage to the *Sonderweg* debate.

CHAPTER 3: THE USE AND ABUSE OF *FELDPOSTBRIEFE* FOR CULTURAL LIFE

1. This seems to be particularly true of newspapers outside of Berlin. See, for example, issues of the *Schwäbisches Tageblatt* 1914–1915.

2. Führen, *Lehrer im Krieg*, vol. 2, 17.

3. Deist, *Militär und Innenpolitik*, 73.

4. Lange, *Marneschlacht und deutsche Öffentlichkeit*, 83. Lange describes the adventurous history accompanying the publication of Stegemann's *Geschichte des Krieges*. Volume I deals with the period up to September 15, 1914, and thus with the forbidden subject of the Marne. It was impossible to get the manuscript from Switzerland (where Stegemann was living) into Germany because of censorship regulations. Stegemann was forced to smuggle the manuscript over the border on a trip to Berlin. Nonetheless, the manuscript remained unpublished for over a year until January 1917, when Ludendorff decided he would permit the publication. Once published, Stegemann's history was a frequently cited reference for journalists and was also recommended by the *Oberpressestelle*, thus offering a salient wartime exemplification of the process of belatedness introduced earlier.

5. Zu UıK No. 7995 UIGI, *Landesarchiv* Koblenz, Bestand 475/1182, *Landratsamt* Neuwied. "Sammlung der Briefe und Tagebücher aus Kriegszeiten, 1912–1936." In addition to the decree itself, the file details the organizational resolution of the initiative at the local (*Neuwied*) level.

6. Ibid.

7. Buddecke, *Die Kriegssammlungen*. Lieutenant Colonel Buddecke's list, the result of an army-commissioned survey, names 217 collections. Not all of them, however, collected *Feldpostbriefe*.

8. The poster, dated December 1914, is part of Bestand RH 6 I/58, *Militärarchiv* Freiburg.

9. Decree V 8675, Kriegsministerium Berlin No. 841/1115.Z.1 (December 3, 1915), *Landesarchiv* Koblenz, Bestand 475/1182.

10. "Zusammenstellung von Zensurverfügungen des Kriegsministeriums, des Stellv. Generalstabs und der Oberzensurstelle des Kriegspresseamts Berlin 1916," HSA, M635 Bestand 934.

11. Ibid. Virtually none of the Prussian government's collection survived the Second World War bombings of Berlin.

12. Fritz Schlawe, preface, *Die Briefsammlungen des 19. Jahrhunderts*.

13. My experience in the 1980s attempting to find letter holdings described in various First World War era publications confirmed what Peter Knoch discovered in his effort: "In

the archives of the Federal Republic, they appear for the most part nominally. . . . Only a portion of this material has found its way into the archives or in the hands of private collectors." See the introduction to his edited collection, *Kriegsalltag*, 2–3. Recent attempts described in the volume by Peter Knoch, Wolf-Dieter Mohrmann, and Edith Hagener to create an archive of war letters by appealing to the general population are commendable and to be encouraged, but also wage a losing battle against time and interest—not to mention attic or cellar clearings, as Knoch notes. Several methodological questions arise in considering the contemporary value of these belated non-state-sponsored collections. For now, note that my study proceeds in recognition of the unavoidably fragmentary character of historical context, for reasons both material and conceptual, rather than from an effort to resuscitate history's wholeness.

14. Höcker, *Gottgesandte Wechselwinde*, 376.

15. Hesse, *Brief ins Feld*, 11. Walter von Holländer, "Die Entwicklung der Kriegsliteratur," *Die neue Rundschau* (1916):1274. Holländer viewed the direction that war literature had taken quite critically, criticizing the fact that the war had "set into motion far too many people (not authors)."

16. Imhoff, preface to *Der deutsche Krieg in Feldpostbriefen*, 5–6. As noted in Chapter 2, the military at this time began to collect depictions of heroic deeds, as requested by Kaiser Wilhelm, in order to validate and disseminate heroes and heroic virtues.

17. This and the next three quoted censorship decrees are found in "Zusammenstellung der zur Zeit noch in Geltung befindlichen Bekanntmachungen des stellv. Generalkomandos April 25, 1915," HSA M77/2 Bestand 15.

18. Letter writers, both at home and in battle zones, who complained or expressed their concern over wartime conditions, were thus equally positioned as risk factors in disrupting the national cause. The ideal narrative voice for both civilians and combatants, by contrast, was one that suffered quietly and heroically. For women at home, as Angelika Tramitz suggests, part of the burden associated with the virtue of quiet suffering is that communicating genuine cares and troubles may subsequently have become blameworthy should anything happen to the letter's recipient. See her "Vom Ungang mit Helden," in Knoch, *Kriegsalltag*, 97. Certainly Hitler's judgment in *Mein Kampf* cited earlier should be read as evidence underscoring the validity of this concern, just as its occurrence provided "tangible" causes for and a holy purpose to his misogyny. A wartime statement released by the War News Office regarding the dangers of such letters is reprinted in the appendix to Bernd Ulrich, "Feldpostbriefe im Ersten Weltkrieg: Bedeutung und Zensur," in Knoch, *Kriegsalltag*, 81–83.

19. Sigmund Freud, *Die Traumdeutung* (Frankfurt: S. Fischer 1984), 227.

20. Bernd Ulrich is right in pointing to the demand by the sailors who revolted and penned their Kiel-program of November 4–5, 1918, to immediately suspend letter censorship (item number 3) as a sign of how effective its threat had been to inhibit unwanted expressions of discontent for writers and readers networked by this circuit right until the final days of the war: "In the face of the billions of letters from and to the field, an airtight system of control could only fail. Nonetheless, many soldiers were made quite cognizant of the dangers of a censoring intervention, with its possible legal ramifications." See "Feldpostbriefe im Ersten Weltkrieg," 49.

21. Imhoff, *Der Deutsche Krieg in Feldpostbriefen,* 5.

22. The language of heroism—as in heroic deed, book, grave, grove—is ubiquitous in the wartime language of newspaper accounts, poetry, and narrative prose.

23. *Kriegsarchiv* Stuttgart, unnumbered.

24. See, for example, the Foerster's multivolume *Das Württembergische Heer im Weltkrieg* or the numerous publications of the Reichsarchiv during the 1920s such as Foerster, *Wir Kämpfer im Weltkrieg.*

25. The signator of the early army communiqués, Adjutant von Stein, was in fact awarded several honorary doctorates in recognition of his "contributions to the German language." It is not unlikely that due to its neutral presentation, particularly in counterdistinction to the all-too-spirited manifestos evoking the significance of *die große Zeit,* this terse and nonspeculative style of writing inspired allegiance on the part of many veterans who were writing in the 1920s.

26. Imhoff, *Der deutsche Krieg in Feldpostbriefen,* 8.

27. As noted earlier, many of the social sciences and humanities are presently engaged in a form of disciplinary self-scrutiny, a self-examination of the operating assumptions that underlie the production of knowledge over time in any given discipline. Besides situating the *Kriegsbriefe gefallener Studenten* within institutional parameters, my discussion of Philipp Witkop's academic career is intended as a contribution to the disciplinary history of one such field in the twentieth century, *Germanistik* in Germany.

28. Numerous war-letter anthologies were published during the Second World War, and after the war, a volume bearing Witkop's title appeared. See Bahr, *Kriegsbriefe gefallener Studenten, 1939–1945.* The preface notes the "shock" caused by Witkop's anthology. A noteworthy resurfacing of the genre is the 1960 republication of *Kriegsbriefe jüdischer Soldaten* (Stuttgart: Seewald, 1961), which was issued to all *Bundeswehr* recruits with a foreword by then-defense minister Franz Joseph Strauss of West Germany. A noteworthy example of post-1945 books joining writings from the First and Second World Wars is *Den Gefallenen.* This curious volume, with a foreword by Theodor Heuss, includes excerpts from texts by Josef M. Wehner, Joachim von der Goltz, Hans Grimm, Georg Britting, and Karl Bröger, among other authors of the First World War.

29. Private *Nachlaß* Witkop, correspondence.

30. Witkop, *Arbeiterbildung.*

31. Witkop, *Arbeiterbildung,* 19.

32. Chapter 4 continues the examination of this aesthetic ideology in discussing the role of reading at the front.

33. "Deutsche Dichtung im Weltkrieg," *Kriegszeitung der 7. Armee* 243 (June 3, 1917).

34. Private papers of Witkop, carbon copy of letter dated November 1913.

35. The following are the works by Witkop not elsewhere cited in this study, which are known to me: *Die deutschen Lyriker von Luther bis Nietzsche, Deutsches Leben der Gegenwart, Goethe: Leben und Werk, Heinrich von Kleist, Die neuere deutsche Lyrik, Tolstoi, Frauen im Leben deutscher Dichter, Volk und Erde: Alemannische Dichterbildnisse.*

36. Witkop definitely did not belong to the NSDAP. See "Personalakten Witkop" at the university archive of Freiburg. The stories of the pressure upon him came from his

widow, Anna Witkop, and his last assistant, Professor Erwin Rupprecht, in conversations with me August 12, 1985.

37. Writing to Karl Henckell from Freiburg on April 24, 1916, Witkop reported the intense sadness he felt anthologizing war letters regarding "these unreplaceable losses" and noted a sinking mood in Freiburg due to the ubiquity of the war marked by an increase in the number of hospital stations, threat of airplane attack, and the "cannon thunder from the Vogese Mountains that frequently causes our windows to tremble." The letter can be found under Karl Henckell's correspondence, one of about fifty in the *Handschriftenabteilung der Stadt und Landesbibliothek,* Dortmund. Parts of Witkop's correspondence with Henckell (and Dehmel) are also preserved in Witkop's private papers. The Thomas Mann Archiv in Zürich has 120 letters from Witkop, many of which are printed in Mann, *Thomas Mann Briefe, 1889–1936.*

38. *Kriegszeitung der 7. Armee,* Nos. 295, 315, 323, 349, 385.

39. Chapter 5 includes a detailed examination of the organization of such bookstores in the war zone.

40. Mann, *Briefe,* 144.

41. Witkop, *Kriegsbriefe deutscher Studenten* (1915).

42. Witkop, "Die Dichtung," *Der Kampf des deutschen Geistes im Weltkrieg* (Gotha: Perthes, 1915), 103.

43. Witkop, "Der Deutsche Unterricht" in *Der Weltkrieg in Unterricht* (Gotha: Perthes, 1915), 105. Witkop was able to express this hope because he communicated frequently with Thomas Mann about Mann's wartime writing, including the first stages of the project that became *Der Zauberberg.* I hope to address a reading of that work with reference to this Mann-Witkop correspondence in a future study.

44. Witkop, "Der deutsche Unterricht," 58.

45. Witkop, "Die Dichtung," 113.

46. Hegel, *Aesthetic III,* 134.

47. Witkop, "Die Dichtung," 119.

48. Hegel, *Aesthetic III,* 121.

49. Witkop, "Der deutsche Unterricht," 62–63.

50. Hegel, *Aesthetic III,* 121–22.

51. Witkop, "Die Dichtung," 119.

52. Witkop, "Der deutsche Unterricht," 64.

53. Witkop, *Kriegsbriefe deutscher Studenten* (1915), 2.

54. Witkop, *Kriegsbriefe deutscher Studenten* (1916), vi.

55. Witkop, *Kriegsbriefe deutscher Studenten* (1916), 2.

56. On the demands of "objective" narration, particularly with reference to actual events— as given by historical representation—see Barthes, "To Write: An Intransitive Verb?" in his *Rustle of Language,* and White, "The Value of Narrativity in the Representation of Reality," in White, *The Content of the Form,* 3, and his "Historical Emplotment and the Problem of Truth," in Friedlander, *Probing the Limits of Representation,* 37–53.

57. Witkop, *Kriegsbriefe deutscher Studenten* (1916), vii.

58. Witkop, *Kriegsbriefe deutscher Studenten* (1915), 7.

59. Philipp Witkop, letter to Professor Fuchs, July 20, 1915, *Universitätsarchiv* Tübingen, *Korrespondenz* Fuchs.

60. Dr. Willi Warstat, preface, *Das Erlebnis unserer jungen Kriegsfreiwilligen.*

61. Böhm, *Aufrufe und Reden deutscher Professoren im ersten Weltkrieg.*

62. Chancellor Bethmann-Hollweg, letter to Philipp Witkop, December 28, 1916, private *Nachlaß* Witkop.

63. Pfeilschifter, preface, *Kriegsbriefe katholischer Soldaten.*

64. Witkop, *Kriegsbriefe deutscher Studenten* (1916), 42–43.

65. Typewritten copy of letter in private *Nachlaß* Witkop.

66. Correspondence, private *Nachlaß* Witkop. See also Spengler, *Sechs aus einem Dorf* and *Wir waren drei Kameraden.*

67. Contract dated 1943, private Witkop *Nachlaß,* suggests 210,000 as the number sold as of 1943.

68. Stark, *Entrepreneurs of Ideology,* 242.

69. Axel Eggelbrecht, "Gespräch mit Remarque," *Die Literarische Welt* 5, no. 24 (December 6, 1929).

70. Private *Nachlaß* Witkop, 1929.

71. Hans Reichmann, "Nationalistische Bücher und ein Buch der Nation," *C.V. Zeitung,* October 3, 1930.

72. Karl Schwendemann, "Die Deutsche Jugend im Weltkrieg," *Deutschland* (February 1929): 51–54. See also Schwendemann's letter to Philipp Witkop, November 22, 1928, private *Nachlaß* Witkop. In a subsequent letter (March 20, 1929) Schwendemann wrote Witkop, "By the way, the book is being zealously ordered by our foreign missions."

73. Anonymous review of *Kriegsbriefe gefallener Studenten* in *Der Gral* 6 (1929): 390.

74. Konrad Kern, review of *Kriegsbriefe, Akademische* in *Monatsblätter* (February 1929): 171–175.

75. Anonymous review of *Kriegsbriefe gefallener Studenten* in *Vom Frohen Leben* (March 1929): 253.

76. Theodor Maus, review of *Kriegsbriefe* in *Deutschkunde* (1929):302.

77. Wehner, *Langemark.* Wehner's title leaves out the "c" in the city's standard German spelling.

78. Visually and textually rendered, for example, in the opening prelude of Leni Riefenstahl's document of the 1934 party congress, *Triumpf des Willens.*

79. Philipp Witkop, letter to Georg Müller Verlag, November 23, 1932, Bayerische *Staatsbibliothek,* Ana 381, III (Witkop, Philipp).

80. In contrast to the case of Karl Peterson, who disappeared as a letter writer following this exchange, (excerpts from) several other of Friedel Oehme's letters were retained, the last of which recounts an episode now emblematic of how readers would remember Oehme's attitude toward the war. He recounts listening to a recitation of Homer and thereupon sending his former Greek instructor a greeting. Without the eliminated letter, these other letters could only highlight an understanding of the war as being a valued educational institution. See *Kriegsbriefe gefallener Studenten* (1933), 242–43.

81. Pfeiler, *War and the German Mind,* 102.

82. Hafkesbrink, *Unknown Germany,* 71.

83. With sympathy for the importance of contemporary efforts to collect whatever un-published war letters remain, perhaps in the hope that such letters might provide the material from which authentic histories might finally "reveal the truth," it may place too great a burden upon their presumed "authentic," "immediate," and "nonliterary" status. See Knoch, *Kriegsalltag*, who contrasted the "actual experience" to be found in war letters with (primarily literary) depictions, "which only retrospectively took shape, that is, long after the experience itself" ("Einleitung," *Kriegserlebnis*, 9). As with Pfeilschifter and Hafkesbrink, however unintended, such an epistemology reinscribes a highly suspect aesthetic and historiography witnessed following both the First and Second World Wars. To begin with, as Knoch also mentions (p. 12), some letter writers exercise self-censorship, and other contributors (such as Bernd Ulrich, "Feldpostbriefe im Ersten Weltkrieg: Betiding und Zensur," 40–83), describe aspects of state censorship. Further, the out-of-timeness of such documents presents interesting questions regarding their value vis-à-vis traditions of reception that require fuller theorization than otherwise would permit their employment as documentary evidence. Lastly, as I argue here, beginning with my discussion of the dual notions attached to the word *Geschichte*, the privileging of immediacy as "authenticity," which then operates to denigrate the (non)truth value of something called literary, is epistemologically misguided.

84. Zöberlin, *Der Glaube an Deutschland*. Hitler's unpaginated endorsement reads "Auf den Weg!" (A Signpost Toward Our Goal). Zöberlin's book had 521,000–550,000 copies in print by 1941.

85. The following scholars have meritoriously contributed in other respects to uncovering aspects of a body of evidence that had previously been forgotten or marginalized, but they also provide example of such continued usage: Martin Travers, *The German War Novel* (Stuttgart: Akademischer Verlag, 1982); Hubert Rüter, *Remarque: Im Westen nichts Neues* (Paderborn: Schöningh, 1980); Margrit Stickelberger-Eder, *Aufbruch 1914: Kriegsromane der späten Weimarer Republik* (Zurich: Artimus, 1983); Eric Leed, *No Man's Land: Combat and Identity in World War One* (Cambridge: Cambridge University Press, 1979); Robert Whalen, *Bitter Wounds* (Ithaca: Cornell University Press, 1984); Ulrich Linse, "Das Wahre Zeugnis: Eine Psychohistorische Deutung des Ersten Weltkrieges," and Angelo Bazzanella, "Die Stimme der Illiteraten," both in Klaus Vondung, ed. *Das Kriegserlebnis: Der erste Weltkrieg in der literarischen Gestaltung der Nationen*.

CHAPTER 4: LITERATURE AT WAR

1. Sombart, *Händler und Helden*; Plenge, *Krieg und Volkswirtschaft*; Meinecke, *Die deutsche Erhebung von 1914*; Thomas Mann, "Gedanken im Krieg," in Mann, *Politische Schriften und Reden*; Ringer, *The Decline of the German Mandarins*; Schwabe, *Wissenschaft und Kriegsmoral*; Vondung, "Deutsche Apokalypse 1914," in Vondung, *Das Wilhelminische Bildungsbürgertum*; Reinhard Rürup, "Der Geist von 1914 in Deutschland: Kriegsbegeisterung und Ideologisierung des Krieges im Ersten Weltkrieg," in Hüppauf, *Ansichten vom Krieg*, 1–30; Kocka, *Bildungsbürgertum im 19. Jahrhundert*.

2. Zentralstelle für Volkswohlfahrt, *Deutsche Reden in schwerer Zeit*, 116.

3. Böhm, *Aufrufe und Reden deutscher Professoren*, 51.

4. *Börsenblatt für den deutschen Buchhandel,* No. 248 (October 24, 1914).
5. Böhm, *Aufrufe und Reden deutscher Professoren,* 53.
6. Ibid., 49. On wartime objectivity, *Die geographische Zeitschrift* 1914, 603.
7. Hauptmann, *Sämtliche Werke,* 846. Originally published August 26, 1914, in the *Berliner Tageblatt.*
8. *Börsenblatt,* No. 55 (1915).
9. Meiner, *Der deutsche Verlegerverein, 1886–1935,* 144.
10. *Börsenblatt,* No. 71 (1915).
11. The Ullstein series of Kriegsbücher (war books) contained, among others, the following authors and titles:

   - Paul Oscar Höcker, *An der Spitze meiner Kompagnie* (1914).
   - Ludwig Ganghofer, *Die Front im Osten* (1915).
   - Ganghofer, *Reise zur deutschen Front* (1915).
   - Heinz Tovote, *Aus einer deutschen Festung im Krieg* (1915).
   - Otto von Gottberg, *Die Helden von Tsingtau* (1915).
   - Hans Fischer, *Nach Siberien mit Hunderttausend Deutschen* (1915).
   - Ernst Ludwig von Wolzogen, *Landsturm im Feuer* (1915).
   - Emil Zimmermann, *Meine Kriegsfahrt von Kamerun zur Heimat* (1915).
   - Fedor von Zöbeltitz, *Kriegsfahrten eines Johanniters* (1915).
   - Rudolf Hans Bartsch, *Das Deutsche Volk in Schwerer Zeit* (1916).
   - Paul Grabein, *Im Auto durch Feindesland* (1916).
   - Goerg Forstner, *Als UBoots Kommandant gegen England* (1916).
   - Karl Strobl, *Der Krieg im Alpenrot* (1916).
   - Friedrich von Kühlwetter, *Skagerrak* (1916).
   - Gustav Fock, *Wir Marokko Deutschen in der Gewalt der Franzosen* (1916).
   - Paul König, *Die Fahrt der Deutschland* (1916).
   - Karl Dönitz, *Die Fahrten der Breslau* (1917).
   - Max Valentiner, *300,000 Tonnen Versenkt!* (1917).
   - Manfred von Richthofen, *Der rote Kampfflieger* (1917).
   - Werner Otto Hentig, *Meine Diplomatenfahrt ins verschlossene Land* (1918).
   - Walter Klinkmüller, *Ein deutscher Offizier im revolutionären Russland* (1918).
   - Hans Grimm, *Der Ölsucher von Duala* (1918).

12. Höcker, *Gottgesandte Wechselwinde,* 229–30.
13. *Fünfzig Jahre Ullstein,* 90–91.
14. On Ullstein's role in developing an "urbane" *Unterhaltungsliteratur* in the 1920s, exemplified by Vicki Baum, see King, *Bestseller by Design.*
15. For a then-contemporary "scientific" rendering of this notion, see Artur Dix, "Das verkehrsgeographische Grundproblem des Weltkrieges: Die eurasische Hochstraße, ihre Bedrängung und ihre Ausstrahlungen," *Die geographische Zeitschrift* 1917, 1–9.
16. Ratzel, a veteran of the 1870–1871 war, is a founding figure of modern cultural and political geography, most remembered today as the academic who gave the term *Lebensraum* a geopolitical stamp. See Woodruff Smith's chapters on Ratzel in *Politics and the Sciences of Culture in Germany, 1840–1920* (New York: Oxford University Press, 1991). I

am currently at work on a study of Ratzel's writings and career in the context of theories of space and representation.

17. Felix Lampe, "Der erdkundliche Unterricht,", *Der Weltkrieg im Unterricht,* 141–75.

18. See Livingstone, *The Geographical Tradition,* for an excellent general account. For Germany, particularly for the Wilhelmine period, see Schultz, *Die deutschsprachige Geographie von 1800 bis 1970,* and for the years 1918–1945, see Herb, *Under the Map of Germany.* See also Godlewska and Smith, *Geography and Empire,* and Benko and Strohmayer, *Space and Social Theory,* for recent critical reevaluations of nineteenth- and twentieth-century geographies.

19. Lampe, "Der erdkundliche Unterricht," 147. On military-geographic strategy, see Kern, *The Culture of Time and Space,* particularly the final chapter. R. Langenbeck, "Welchen Nutzen kann der erdkundliche Unterricht aus dem großen Kriege ziehen," in *Die geographische Zeitschrift* 1916, 277–78.

20. Alfred Hettner, "Unsere Aufgabe im Kriege," *Geographische Zeitschrift* 1914, 601–3. He explains, anticipating Lampe's remarks, that the war could be counted on to expand public recognition of geography's pedagogical necessity and the discipline's utility in answering questions about the likely outcome of the war based on spatial, ethnic, and economic conditions, as well as contributing to the question of how to divide affected territories following the war's conclusion.

21. *Fünfzig Jahre Ullstein,* 89.

22. Ullstein, letter to Presseabteilung des Admiralstabs, November 2, 1917, *Bundesmilitärarchiv* Freiburg, Rm. 5, v. 3763.

23. A complete list is available in DLA, A: Petzold, *Nachlaß.*

24. Heymann, *Kriegsgedichte und Feldpostbriefe.*

25. Were enough primary materials available to support such research, it would be quite informative to consider continuity and transitions in the publication of war literature between 1914 and 1933 on the basis of their continued editorial activity.

26. For a complete listing of the series (and other related war books) see Johann, *S. Fischer Verlag: Vollständiges Verzeichnis aller Werke, Buchserien und Gesamtausgaben mit Anmerkungen zur Verlagsgeschichte.* For an interesting if overly benign account of Fischer's war involvement see de Mendelssohn, *S. Fischer und sein Verlag.*

27. *Börsenblatt für den deutschen Buchhandel,* No. 90 (1915):556.

28. *Kriegsratgeber des Dürerbunds* (1915–1916):26.

29. Advertisement of the Reclam Verlag (n.d.), preserved by the firm in Ditzingen near Stuttgart. Brought to my attention by Diedrich Bode.

30. Mentioned in the cover letter sent by Philipp Reclam to Freiherr von Stein, director of the *Reichswirtschaftsamt,* in January 1918, as part of his petition to ensure continued allocation of paper supplies for the firm. The entire prospectus can be found in the *Bayerisches Hauptstaatsarchiv,* Section IV, War Archive, 1. Armee Korp, No. 1750. The prospectus is not paginated or titled. All references to individual quotations on the following five pages of the chapter refer to this document.

31. On the organization of wartime book weeks, see *Börsenblatt,* No. 129 (1915):854 and No. 115 (1916):637. On the movement to organize mobile front libraries, see Ludwig Hoppe,

Felddivisionsgeistlicher im Hauptquartier des Oberbefehlhabers Ost, "Die Bildungs-kanone: Ein Gruß an die Freunde und Gönner des Ausschusses für fahrbare Kriegsbüchereien," (Berlin, n.d.); also his *Feldpredigerfahrten*. Also relevant to the complex of libraries in the war zone discussed in the present chapter are "Welche Vorteile bieten fahrbare Kriegsbüchereien," Bericht des Kriegsministeriums (Berlin), November 21, 1915, and "Denkschrift über Feldbüchereien, bearbeitet von Direktor Dr. Friedrich Schilling," both in HSA, M730 Cluster 78 and M 1/11 Cluster 1086.

32. On the restructuring of education and reading organizations in occupied Belgium, see *Börsenblatt*, No. 9 (1916):37. For a listing of the numerous debates regarding libraries in the war zone, see *Verhandlungen des Reichtages: Sachregister, 1914–1918, Stichwort* "Feld-buchhandlungen."

33. *Kriegszeitung der 7. Armee*, Rubric "Der Bücherwagen," March 18, 1918.

34. On the sociology of reading, mass culture, and the literary marketplace, see Schenda, *Die Lesestoffe der kleinen Leute*, special issue on mass culture, *New German Critique* 29 (1983), particularly the articles by Russell Berman, "Writing for the Book Industry: The Writer under Organized Capitalism," 39–56; and Frank Trommler, "Working Class Culture and Modern Mass Culture before World War I," 57–70; Dieter Langewiesche and Klaus Schönhoven, "Arbeiterbibliotheken und Arbeiterlektüre im Wilhelmi-nischen Deutschland," *Archiv für Sozialgeschichte* 16 (1976):135–204; Dieter Lange-wiesche "Politik-Gesellschaft-Kultur: Zur Problematik von Arbeiterkultur und kul-turellen Arbeiterorganisationen in Deutschland nach dem 1. Weltkrieg," *Archiv für Sozialgeschichte* 23 (1982):359–402; Vernon Lidtke, *The Alternative Culture*, 159–92. Reinhard Wittmann's valuable *Geschichte des deutschen Buchhandels* is unable to provide much coverage of the book trade's mobilization during the First World War. On the spiritual hunger for books, see *Börsenblatt*, No. 235 (1915):1358. On self-referentiality in reading, see Kurth, *Die zweite Wirklichkeit*.

35. Hartung, *Großkampf, Männer und Granaten*, 41.

36. Schauwecker, *Das Frontbuch*, 103.

37. Jünger, *In Stahlgewittern*, 156, and *Das Wäldchen 125*, 151.

38. Flex, *Der Wanderer zwischen beiden Welten*. Judging by the circulation figures reported by Richards in his *German Bestseller*, Flex's book was one of the ten most widely read works in Germany before 1945.

39. *Börsenblatt*, No. 296 (1915):1650.

40. Witkop, *Kriegsbriefe Gefallener Studenten*, 4th ed. (München: Georg Müller, 1928), 242.

41. Barthel, *Verse aus den Argonnen*, 44–45. The poem also appeared individually in a number of army newspapers and civilian journals. It is reprinted in Volkmann, *Deutsche Dichtung im Weltkrieg*, 178–79. This influential volume is the National Socialist canon of First World War poetry. Volkmann comments on the poem: "Just as the field book editions of Faust and Goethe's poems were coveted backpack goods and loyal compan-ions in the trenches, one could also put together a small harvest of war poems written about Goethe" (310). He is probably correct, though to my knowledge no one has yet undertaken the task.

42. These wartime aspirations can reasonably be placed in relation to those discussed in Chapter 1 on the institution of literature beginning in the 1790s. As such, it is irrelevant

to see the events of 1914–1918 as "evidence" of the "politicization of aesthetics" (or for that matter, the aesthetization of politics), thus leaving intact a purer "nonexceptional" separation of the two, because analysis of the 1790s discussion shows that the aesthetic education is constitutively political. The First World War serves as a particular, illustrating a general condition. This may not perhaps, as Martin Jay cautions, be grounds for the wholesale condemnation of the general. See " 'The Aesthetic Ideology' as Ideology: Or What Does It Mean to Aestheticize Politics," in Jay, *Force Fields,* 71–83. Other so-called *Arbeiterdichter* (worker-poets) include Heinrich Lersch, Karl Bröger, and Alfons Petzold. Volkmann, in the introduction to his collection *Deutsche Dichtung im Weltkrieg,* accounted for their success with the statement: "Already in 1914, the workers, who had surmounted artificially cultivated class hatred and in the spirit of national comradeship had grown into the roles of contemporary poets, were greeted particularly warmly" (17). Volkmann's formulation is also an example of the National Socialist representation of wartime *Frontkameradschaft* (comradeship of the trenches) as a first working-through of the later *Volkskameradschaft* or *Volksgemeinschaft.* As I discuss in Chapter 2, for nationalist veterans following Germany's defeat, that Gemeinschaft in turn was remembered as the prearticulation of a general Volksgemeinschaft, which the rest of German (civilian) society, however, had not adequately embraced between 1914 and 1918.

43. Hoppe, *Feldpredigerfahrten an der Westfront,* 133.
44. A useful cultural exploration of the impressions of German soldiers on the Eastern Front that notes the differences in settings and hence memory of the war is Liulevicious, "War Land: Peoples, Lands, and National Identity on the Eastern Front in World War One." On intellectual pleasure, see Melchoir von Hugo, "Die geistige Führung des Krieges," Schwarte, *Der große Krieg,* 123.
45. One of the few works of literature published about the war that thematized their existence is Vogel's 1924 *Es lebe der Krieg!* discussed in Chapter 6.
46. The most sustained and sharply focused presentation of the "new revisionist" position is found in Blackbourn and Eley, *The Peculiarities of German History.* See also Evans, *Rethinking German History.* With great acumen Tom Childers cogently summarized the stakes of the debate between them and the Bielefeld school while simultaneously proposing a linguistic ground upon which one might move beyond the impasse. See his "Social Language of Politics in Germany: The Sociology of Political Discourse in the Weimar Republic," *American Historical Review* 95, No. 2 (1990):331–58.
47. Ehringhaus, *Die Lektüre unserer Frontsoldaten im Weltkrieg,* 137.
48. See *Klassiker in finsteren Zeiten,* which includes a brief description of reading at the front during the Second World War. On her criticisms, see Ehringhaus, *Die Lektüre unserer Frontsoldaten im Weltkrieg,* 147.
49. *Börsenblatt,* October 27, 1914: 250.
50. "Kundgebung vom 15ten Januar, 1915," cited in *Blätter für Volksbibliotheken* (1915):83.
51. Ellis, "Army, State, and Politics in the Grand Duchy of Baden 1866–1920," 82–88.
52. Höhn, *Die Armee als Erziehungschule der Nation.*
53. *Blätter für Volksbibliotheken* (1915):18.
54. Herzog, *Ritter, Tod und Teufel* and *Vom Stürmen, Sterben, Auferstehen,* were reviewed with fulsome praise by the *Blätter* (1917):73–74.

55. Friedrich Schilling, "Denkschrift über Feldbüchereien," HSA, M1/II Cluster 1086.

56. *Reichtagsprotokol* (1918):3151. Of course, other combatant nations also had a stake in providing books to the troops. The U.S. context, for example, is mapped by Wayne Wiegand in *An Active Instrument for Progaganda.*

57. Soldier newspapers were another matter, and there, as in the *Kriegszeitung der 4.ten Armee* (the newspaper edited by Anton Kippenberg), each of the prominent unread authors mentioned above figured as a source for quotation or cultural feuilleton.

58. The following works, situated by Schilling in the category of "novels and novellas" were borrowed at least thirteen times by members of the regiment: James Fenimore Cooper, *Der rote Freibeuter* (The Red Pirate) (15 times); Ernst Wichert, *Die Schwestern* (15); Ernst Zahn, *Der Schatten* (26); Joseph von Eichendorff, *Aus dem Leben eines Taugenichts* (19); Max von Eyth, *Der blinde Passagier* (17); Gerhard Hauptmann, *Bahnwärter Thiel* (25); Jonas Lie, *Auf Irrwegen* (13); Karin Michaelis, *Treu wie Gold* (14); Theodor Fontane, *Gesammelte Werke* (21); Friedrich Friedrich, *Die Frau des Arbeiters* (17); Paul Heyse, *Der verlorene Sohn* (14); E. T. A. Hoffmann, *Berliner Novellen* (16); Rudolf Binding, *Der Opfergang* (13); Franz Grillparzer, *Der arme Spielmann* (13); Arnold Zweig, *Brennendes Geheimnis* (18); Heinrich von Kleist, *Die Verlobung in St. Domingo* (16); Eduard von Mörike, *Maler Nolten* (14); Emil Ludwig, *Zwischen Himmel und Erde* (16); Charles Dickens, *Die Pickwicker* (15); Peter Rosegger, *Als ich noch der Waldbauernbub war* (18); Theodor Storm, *In der Sommermondmacht* (13); Sienkiewicz, *Quo Vadis* (19); and Leo Tolstoi, *Anna Karenina* (16). Less frequently read, but still above or equal to the ten-to-one ratio of the Ullstein books, were Thomas Mann, *Tonio Kröger* (12); Detlev von Liliencron, *Eine Sommerschlacht* (12); Dickens, *Der Kampf des Lebens* (12); Klara Viebig, *Simson und Delila* (11); Rosegger, *Waldheimat* (11) and *Allerhand Leute* (11); Walter Scott's *Ivanhoe* (10) and *Die Braut von Lammermoor* (12); Eduard von Keyserling, *Beate und Mareile* (11); Hoffmann, *Kriegsgeschichten* (11) and *Musikergeschichten* (11); and Herman Bang, *Hoffnungslose Geschlecter* (10) and *Die vier Teufel* (12). The only Heinrich Heine text available, *Die Harzreise,* was read eight times, a collection of Edgar Allan Poe's stories seven, and a volume of Guy de Maupassant novels nine times.

59. The following works were read at least thirteen times by regimental readers: Paquet, *Seegeschichten* (15); Robert Bennet, *Das Gespenst* (14) and *Lebendig begraben* (15); Charles de Berkeley, *Die Alte Geschichte* (20) and *Zwischen Lipp und Kelchesrand* (20); Blicher-Clausen, *Inga Heine* (14); Matthias Bodkin, *Verschwindende Diamanten* (15) and *Paul Becks Gefangennahme* (14); Lucy Clifford, *Ein sonderbarer Stellvertreter* (A Wild Proxy) (16); Paul Oscar Höcker, *Die indische Tänzerin* (19); Molot, *Daheim* (22) and *Lieutenant Bonnet* (21); Margarete von Oertzen, *Irrlichter* (26); Ernst von Wolzogen, *Der Thronfolger* (26); Fedor von Zobeltitz, *Aus Tiefem Schacht* (24), *Die herbe Gräfin* (28), and *Krach* (26); Antonie Gubalke, *Zweierlei Liebe* (20); Mór Jókai, *Die unsichtbare Sängerin* (14); Malten, *Nur eine Magd*; Ivan Turgenev, *Der Raufbold Kukerja* (13); and *Erste Liebe* (18); Karl Weiser, *Ein genialer Kerl* (17); Gertraut Beaulieu, *Großstadtoriginale* (14); Berezik, *Ehestandsgeschichten* (19); Pötze, *Kriminalhumoresken* (15); Friedrich Schlicht, *Militaria* (14) and *Schöne Theaterluft* (13); Julius Rosen, *Der deutsche Lausbub in Amerika* (15); Adelbert Stifter, *Erzählungen* (15); Friedrich Gerstäcker, *Ein sonderbares Duell* (17); Kurt Aram, *Violett* (18) and *Kusine aus Amerika* (28); Rudolf Hans Bartsch, *Der Flieger*

(25); Franz Beyerlein, *Similde Hegewald* (15) and *Ein Winterlager* (15); Walter Bloem, *Das lockende Spiel* (31) and *Komödiantinnen* (15); Helene Böhlau, *Sommerbuch* (13); Albert Brachvogel, *Die große Gauklerin* (17); Rudolf Herzog, *Zum weissen Schwan* (21); Höcker, *Verbotene Frucht* (26) and *Sonne von St. Moritz* (18); Felix Holländer, *Charlotte Adutti* (16); Wilhelm Jensen, *Unter heisser Sonne* (19); Gottfried Keller, *Die Heimat* (18); Max Kretzer, *Der Mann ohne Gewissen* (16); Victor von Kohlenegg, *Die drei Lieben der Dete Voss* (20); Fritz Mauthner, *Der letzte Deutsche von Blatera* (19); Fritz Reuter, *Ins neue Land* (17); Klara Viebig, *Dillettanten des Lebens* (13); Richard Voss, *Das Mädchen von Anzio* (13); Wolff, *Der Krieg im Dunklen* (14); Ernst von Wolzogen, *Mein erstes Abenteuer* (15) and *Das Kuckucksei* (13); Zobeltitz, *Das Vorschnell Vermählte Ehepaar* (19) and *Gasthaus zur Ehe* (19); and finally, Ernst Wichert, *Der Wilddieb* (20). In sum, these authors and titles open a highly suggestive window on the world of reading at the end of the Wilhelmine period.

60. GQM 1a No. 33340, December 5, 1915, *Generallandesarchiv* Karlsruhe 456 EV2.

61. See for example GQM 1a No. 16419, June 2, 1916, *Generallandesarchiv* Karlsruhe: "The Association of the German Catholic Book Trade has brought up the fact that Catholic texts with either entertaining or religious contents are virtually shut out of bookstores in the field. Requests from Catholic publishers to at least offer one or another of their books for sale, have reportedly had little success. . . . Insofar as the complaints are justified, I leave it in your hands to rectify the problem."

62. GQM 1c No. 35611, November 30, 1916, *Generallandesarchiv* Karlsruhe.

63. *Reichstagsprotokol* (May 8, 1917):3150.

64. Schenda, *Die Lesestoffe der kleinen Leute,* 7.

65. "Presse Angelegenheiten," and HSA, M77/1 Bu 60.

66. See Kratzsch, *Kunstwart und Dürerbund.* On the "Deutsche Dichter-Gedächtnis-Stiftung," see Heinrich Müller, "Die Deutsche Dichter Gedächtnis Stiftung," *Archiv für die Geschichte des Deutschen Buchhandels* (1986):131–215.

67. *Reichstagsprotokol* (1917):3149.

68. Samuleit, *Kriegsschundliteratur,* 7.

69. In a certain sense, those 1920s writings of Jünger's that bring the war back to the city complete a cycle between 1914 and the Weimar years from city to front and from front to city. On the transport of the war to the urban landscape by Jünger and others, see Bernd Hüppauf, "Die Stadt als imaginerter Kriegsschauplatz," *Zeitschrift für Germanistik* 2(1995):317–36.

70. *Blätter für Volksbibliotheken* (1917):43.

71. *Kriegsratgeber des Dürerbundes* (Munich: Callwey, 1916), 9. The Dürerbund published two similar annual reports during the war.

72. "Leitsätze für die Einrichtung von Buchhandlungen auf dem Kriegsschauplatz," *Bundesmilitärarchiv* Freiburg, 1916.

73. "Versorgung der Truppen mit Lesestoff," September 9, 1917, Armee OK 5, *Bundesmilitärarchiv* Ph 5 IV.

74. Dehmel, *Zwischen Volk und Menschheit,* 453.

75. "Leitsätze für den vaterländischen Unterricht," *Bundesmilitärarchiv* PH 5 IV, No. 2.

76. "Leitsätze für den vaterländischen Unterricht" *Bundesmilitärarchiv* Freiburg, PH5 IV, No. 2. See also "Aufzeichnung über die Besprechung mit den Leitern des Vaterlän-

dischen Unterrichts an der Westfront," (June 27, 1918), Bayerisches *Kriegsarchiv* 456/ EV8 XIV A.K. 8819. During June and July, Nicolai visited with regional directors on the *Westfront* and the *Ostfront.*

77. "Aufzeichnung der Besprechung des Chefs IIIb mit den Leitern des Vaterländischen Unterrichts auf dem Balkan und in der Turkei" (July 13, 1918). Nicolai made the same point at all three regional meetings.

78. Aufzeichnung über die Besprechung des Chefs IIIb mit den Leitern des Vaterländischen Unterrichts auf dem Balkan und in der Türkei (July 13, 1918), Bayerisches *Kriegsarchiv,* 456/EV8 XIV A.K. 8819. Also AOK 6, 214, which contains a ledger of accounts for the *Schmittsche Buchhandlung,* which had garnered the privilege of administrating book sales within the territory of the Bavarian army. Schmitt paid for this privilege by returning a percentage of its profits back to the army, which in turn used it to help finance the propaganda campaign.

79. Aufzeichnung der Besprechung des Chefs IIIb mit den Leitern des Vaterländischen Unterrichts auf dem Balkan und in der Turkei (July 13, 1918).

CHAPTER 5: PUBLISHING THE WAR

1. See for example Gary Stark's study of the neoconservative publishers in Germany, *Entrepreneurs of Ideology.*

2. As suggested in Chapter 1's discussion of Enlightenment aesthetics, *institution* not only functions as a noun, it also refers to the *process* generating the noun, as in the institution of the institutions of literature.

3. On historians' use of literature, see Stark, "Von Nutzen und Nachteil der Literatur," 25–26. Barthes, *Image, Music, Text,* 148. Derrida, *Limited Inc.,* 136.

4. Roger Chartier, "Texts, Printings, Readings," in Hunt, *New Cultural History,* 161. He goes on to argue that "a sorting out of two types of apparatus becomes necessary, between those entailed by the putting into text, the strategy of writing, the intentions of the 'author,' and those resulting from the manufacture of the book or publication, produced by editorial decision or through workshop procedures, which are aimed at readers or readings that may not be at all like those the author intended."

5. Karl Rosner, letter to Robert Kröner, September 17, 1914, DLA, Rosner: Cotta *Korrespondenz.* Rosner himself contributed extensively to the "harvest" of literary works about the war. His first such work was a collection of poems entitled *Wir tragen das Schwert!* (We Bear the Sword) published by Cotta in 1914. Once he became a *Kriegsberichterstatter* (war reporter), he compiled a number of further volumes: *Der graue Ritter: Bilder von Kriege in Frankreich und Flandern* (Berlin: Scherl, 1916), *Vor dem Drahtverhau: Bilder aus dem Grabenkriege in Frankreich und Flandern* (Berlin: Scherl, 1916), *Mit der Armee v. Falkenhayn gegen die Rumänen* (Berlin: Scherl, 1917), *Die Feindin: Kriegsbilder aus Frankreich und Flandern* (Leipzig, Reclam, 1917), and *Die große Frühlingsschlacht 1918: Tagebuchblätter von Karl Rosner* (Berlin: Scherl, 1918).

6. DLA, Cotta, *Korrespondenz* Robert Kröner.

7. Ibid.

8. DLA, Cotta, *Gutachten: 1914–1918.* This observation comes from having read through

the twelve volumes that constitute the firm's official correspondence regarding solicited and unsolicited authors during the war.

9. Schüler, *Gottessturmflut;* Otto König, *Glocken im Sturm: Gedichte aus dem Krieg* (Stuttgart: Cotta, 1915). Citations for the other works will be given as they are discussed below.

10. Her other war books published with Cotta are *Der unsterbliche Acker* (1915) and *Die Flucht der Beate Hoyermann,* (1916). Her most famous work is probably *Metropolis* (Berlin: Scherl, 1926). *Der Krieg und die Frauen* enjoyed a printing of 100,000 by the end of the war, very high numbers for a Cotta book of the period.

11. Cotta, *Autorenkorrespondenz,* 1914. The volume of essays appeared in print before the end of the year.

12. Meinecke, *Die deutsche Erhebung von 1914.*

13. Cotta, *Gutachten,* 1915.

14. Ibid.

15. Ibid.

16. Friedrich Loofs, letter to Cotta, February 27, 1916, DLA.

17. Cotta, *Gutachten,* 1916.

18. The same censorship restrictions that Chapter 2 and 3 examined, particularly with reference to the publication of *Feldpostbriefe,* apply equally here.

19. Cotta, galley proofs, "Der Hauptmann," 196, 199.

20. Friedrich Loofs to Cotta, March 25, 1916, DLA, Cotta-Loofs.

21. Cotta, *Autorenkorrespondenz.* The editor's letter informed Lauckner there might be a problem with his story "Brüsseler Spitzen" and suggested the removal of the passage. Unfortunately, the galley proofs that would reveal the specific offense are not extant.

22. DLA, Cotta: Loofs.

23. *Literarischer Jahresbericht des Dürerbundes* (1917–1918): 127. Philipp Witkop also numbered himself among the work's admirers, writing Karl Henckell in a letter dated May 17, 1917, "It is the best big story to have come out." Henckell-Korrespondenz, Stadt und Landesbibliothek, Dortmund.

24. Wilhelm, *Erinnerungen des Kronprinzen Wilhelm.*

25. Cotta: Rosner-Kronprinz Wilhelm.

26. Wilhelm, *Erinnerungen,* 346.

CHAPTER 6: "NEVERTHELESS!"

1. "Bericht über die Gründungsversammlung der Deutschen Gesellschaft für Auslandsbuchhandel zu Leipzig, den 10. Mai 1919" (Report on the founding meeting in Leipzig of the German Society for the Foreign Book Trade). The speech exists apparently only as a part of the recorded proceedings of that day's meeting. Thanks are due Gerhard Schuster, DLA Marbach, for alerting me to its existence.

2. A sampling of them can be found in print in Kaes, *Manifesten der Weimarer Republik* and Hans Widmann, ed., *Der deutsche Buchhandel in Urkunden und Quellen* (Hamburg: Dr. Ernst Hausedell, 1965).

3. See, for example, "Begrüßung der aus dem Kriege Heimgekehrten Studierenden am 16.

Februar 1919, Rede des Rektors Professor Dr. Johannes Haller 'Von Tod und Auf-
erstehung der Deutschen Nation,'" (Tübingen: Mohr, 1919).

4. See, for example, the speech by Josef Magnus Wehner (author of *Sieben vor Verdun* and
   other war prose) commemorating *Langemarcktag* in 1932: "The German nation had not
   been morally mature enough during the war to realize the hopes associated with *die
   große Zeit.* The sacrifice of Germany's soldiers, however, who had gone to their deaths at
   Langemarck singing 'Deutschland über Alles' provided the assurance and the basis of a
   solemn covenant with the war's survivors to realize this promise." Josef Magnus Wehner,
   "Vorrede," in *Langemarck* (Munich: Georg Müller, 1932).

   This volume also appeared as part of Langen-Müller's series of *Schulheften* (1933–
   1945), nearly half of which consisted of excerpts from war books published by the firm by
   such war book authors as Paul Alverdes, Joachin von der Goltz, Hans Grimm, K. B. von
   Mechow, and Heinrich Zillich. As such, the series, whose individual volumes appeared
   only after being authorized by the state, is literally a schoolbook example of the National
   Socialist canonization of a "correctly rendered" war literature.

5. See "Arbeitsbegrenzung der Politischen Abteilung und der Zivilverwaltung in Sachen
   der Pressepropaganda," Bayerisches *Kriegsarchiv,* HS 1592, Harrich.

6. As documented by the "Aufzeichnung über die Besprechungen Chefs IIIb mit den
   Leitern des Vaterländischen Unterrichts auf dem Balkan und in der Türkei," July 13,
   1918, in Bayerisches Staatsarchiv IV, 456/EV8 XIV A.K. 88, 19.

7. Letter to von Bodenhausen in Zeller, *Die Insel,* 175.

8. See Bernhard Zeller, "Vorwort," in his *Die Insel,* 6: "In the course of very few years, an
   impressive program of world literature was built up, which gave equal consideration to
   Russian and Chinese, Romanesque and Flemish, Anglo-Saxon and northern literatures."

9. Under the weight of the war-guilt question, the state department did not limit its efforts
   to the book trade, though this is an important chapter of that story. Efforts were made to
   "export" German science as cultural goods in the battle for world opinion, with physics
   promoted as a particularly prestigious example of German culture. See Foreman, "Weimar
   Culture, Causality, and Quantum Theory," and "The Financial Support and Political
   Alignment of Physicists in Weimar Germany."

10. On the complex of Weimar censorship with specific reference to the crystallization of
    the "Gesetz zur Bewahrung der Jugend vor Schund und Schmutz" (Law for the protec-
    tion of youth against trash and dirt) in 1926, see Detlev Peukert, "Der Schund- und
    Schmutzkampf als 'Sozialpolitik der Seele,'" in Akademie der Künste, *Das War ein
    Vorspiel nur . . . ,* 51–63.

11. A reprint of the 1925 first edition was published in Berlin by the Klaus Guhl Verlag in
    1978. The quotations used in this chapter follow the 1978 reissue of the 1925 edition and
    not the 1929 (*kastrierte* [castrated]) edition. I hope to find a publisher that would enable
    me to translate Vogel's book for readers of English.

12. Schütte, "Ein Vergessener Schriftsteller,"

13. As just one example of publishers' hesitations, remember that Remarque experienced
    considerable difficulty in finding a press before Ullstein bought the manuscript (after
    much internal debate). Likewise, the hundreds of novels that "suddenly" appeared in
    print once Remarque's book opened the floodgate bespeak less the phenomenon of a

reflective hiatus necessary for authors to organize their thoughts than a case of authors taking out of their closets manuscripts that they had been led to believe were unpublishable. Bruno Vogel, quoted by Schütte, "Ein Vergessener Schriftsteller," 54.

14. A forthcoming essay discusses the entire text in greater detail.

15. See Chapter 3 for the exact language of the relevant censorship decrees.

16. Including, as I discuss in Chapter 1, by Hitler in *Mein Kampf,* 180–81.

17. An overview of the journal is provided by Gunther Brackelmann, *Der deutsche Protestantismus im Epochenjahr 1917.* On the matter of war chauvinism, liberal Protestant theology could be just as righteous. See Heath Spencer, "Church Politics, Periodicals, and Modern Theology: German Cultural Protestant Zeitschriften and Their Constituencies, 1890–1918," Ph.D. diss., University of Kentucky, 1997.

18. Kant, *Kritik der Urteilskraft,* 163. See too the numerous references to Kant in the supplement sections of wartime soldier newspapers, where he and most canonical figures of German idealism and romanticism were interpreted as avatars of the German effort during the First World War. For a short but useful amplification of Hegel's position on war, influenced by Shlomo Avineri and Charles Taylor, see Elshtain, *Women and War,* 73–82.

19. Sigmund Freud, "Zeitgemäßes über Krieg und Tod" in *Gesammelte Werke,* 10; *Werke aus den Jahren 1913–1917* (London: Imago, 1949): "The rational justification of heroism is based on the judgment that one's own life is not as valuable as certain abstract and general goods. More often, however, I believe instinctual and impulsive heroism dominates, which ignores such a motivation, and simply acts following the assurance offered by the Steinklopferhanns character in Anzengruber: Nothing can harm you, who spits at danger" (350).

20. Quoted by Schütte, "Ein Vergessener Schriftsteller," 49.

CONCLUSION

1. Friedrich Nietzsche, "Vom Nutzen und Nachteile der Historie für das Leben" (The use and abuse of history for life), in his *Friedrich Nietzsche Werke I,* 238.

2. From Kaiser Wilhelm II, March 22, 1905, in Bremen: "Wir sind das Salz der Erde," Pollman, *Lesebuch zur deutschen Geschichte,* 67–68.

3. Walter Benjamin, "The Work of Art in the Age of Mechanical Reproduction," in *Illuminations,* ed. H. Arendt (New York: Schocken, 1969), 223. A further elaboration of the import of these points for the study of culture, which draws on the works of both Benjamin and Chantal Mouffe, are my "Radical Democracy"; "Disciplining Boundaries," in McCarthy, *The Future of Germanistik in the USA,* 111–21; and "German Cultural Studies: A Review," *Transculture* Vol. 1, No. 2 (1996). See LaClau and Mouffe, *Hegemony and Socialist Strategy,* 7. English translation in Horkheimer, *Between Philosophy and Social Science,* 1.

Works Cited

UNPUBLISHED SOURCES

The primary unpublished materials cited in this study are housed in the collections noted in the acknowledgments, and they are marked individually with each note. These archives are the *Generallandesarchiv* Karlsruhe, the *Hauptstaatsarchiv* Stuttgart (HSA), the *Bundesmilitärarchiv* Freiburg, the private papers *Nachlaß* of Bloem in the *Stadtarchiv* Wuppertal, the *Deutsche Literaturarchiv,* Marbach (DLA), the archive of the University of Tübingen, the Bayerisches *Hauptstaatsarchiv* IV (*Kriegsarchiv*), the Stadt und Landesbibliothek Dortmund, and the private papers (*Nachlaß*) of Philipp Witkop in Freiburg, now moved to *Deutsches Literaturarchiv,* Marbach.

PUBLISHED SOURCES

Akademie der Künste, Berlin. *"Das war ein Vorspiel nur. . . .* Berlin: Akademie der Künste, 1983.

Akademischer Gemeinschaftsverlag. *Den Gefallenen: Ein Buch des Gedenkens und des Trostes.* Munich, 1952.

Alleman, Beda. *Literatur und Germanistik nach der Machtübernahme.* Bonn: Bouvier, 1983.

Althaus, Hans-Joachim, Hildegard Cancik-Lindemaier, Kathrin Hoffmann-Curtius, and Ulrich Rebstock. *Der Krieg in den Köpfen: Beiträge zum Tübinger Friedenskongreß "Krieg-Kultur-Wissenschaft."* Vol. 73, *Untersuchungen des Ludwig-Uhland-Institutes der Universität Tübingen,* 1988.

Amburger, Waltrud. *Männer, Krieg, Abenteuer.* Frankfurt: R. G. Fischer, 1985.

Anderson, Benedict. *Imagined Communities: Reflections on the Origin and Spread of Nationalism.* London: Verso, 1983.

Anz, Thomas, and Joseph Vogl, eds. *Die Dichter und der Krieg: Deutsche Lyrik, 1914–1918.* Munich: Hanser, 1982.

Attridge, Derek, Geoff Bennington, and Robert Young, eds. *Poststructuralism and the Question of History.* Cambridge: Cambridge University Press, 1987.

Augstein, Rudolph. *Historikerstreit: Die Dokumentation der Kontroverse um die Einzigartigkeit der nationalsozialistischen Judenvernichtung.* Munich: Piper, 1987.

Avenarius, Ferdinand, ed. *Kriegsratgeber des Dürerbunds.* Munich: Callwey, 1915–1917.

Bahr, Walter, and Hans Walter, eds. *Kriegsbriefe gefallener Studenten, 1939–1945.* Tübingen: R. Wunderlich, 1952.

Baird, Jay. *To Die for Germany.* Bloomington: Indiana University Press, 1990.

Bakhtin, Mikhail. *The Dialogic Imagination: Four Essays.* Ed. Michael Holquist. Austin: University of Texas Press, 1985.

Barkhausen, Hans. *Filmpropaganda für Deutschland im ersten und zweiten Weltkrieg.* Hildesheim: Georg Olms, 1982.

Barnouw, Dagmar. *Weimar Intellectuals and the Threat of Modernity.* Bloomington: Indiana University Press, 1988.

Baron, Ulrich, and Hans Harro Müller, "Weltkriege und Kriegsromane," *Zeitschrift für Literaturwissenschaft und Linguistik* 75 (1989):14–38.

Barthel, Max, ed. *Verse aus den Argonnen.* Jena: Eugen Diederichs, 1916.

Barthes, Roland. *The Rustle of Language.* Trans. Richard Howard. Berkeley: University of California Press, 1989.

———. *Image, Music, Text.* Ed. Stephen Heath. New York: Hill and Wang, 1977.

Bartsch, Rudolf Hans. *Das deutsche Volk in schwerer Zeit.* Berlin: Ullstein, 1916.

Bathrick, David, and Anton Kaes, eds. *New German Critique* 59 (1993). Special issue on Ernst Jünger.

Bäumer, Gertrud. *Der Krieg und die Frau.* Stuttgart: Cotte, 1915.

Bellon, Bernard. *Mercedes in Peace and War: German Automobile Workers, 1903–1945.* New York: Columbia University Press, 1990.

Bendele, Ulrich. *Krieg, Kopf, und Körper: Lernen für das Leben—Erziehung zum Tod.* Frankfurt: Ullstein, 1984.

Benjamin, Walter. *Gesammelte Schriften.* Vol. 3. Frankfurt: Suhrkamp, 1972.

———. *Das Kunstwerk im zeitalter seiner technischen Reproduzierbarkeit.* Frankfurt: Suhrkamp, 1977.

Benko, Georg, and Ulf Strohmayer. *Space and Social Theory: Geographical Interpretations of Postmodernism.* Oxford: Blackwell, 1997.

Bennett, Tony. *Formalism and Marxism.* New York: Methuen, 1979.

Berghahn, Volker. "Die Fischer Kontroverse: 15 Jahre Danach." *Geschichte und Gesellschaft* 6(1980):207–23.

Berman, Russell. "Writing for the Book Industry: The Writer under Organized Capitalism." *New German Critique* 29(1983):39–56.

———. *The Rise of the Modern German Novel*. Cambridge: Harvard University Press, 1986.

Besier, Gerhard. *Religion—Nation—Kultur*. Neukirchen-Vluyn: Neukirchener, 1992.

Bessel, Richard. *Germany after the First World War*. Oxford: Oxford University Press, 1993.

Blackbourn, David, and Geoff Eley. *The Peculiarities of German History: Bourgeois Society and Politics in Nineteenth-Century Germany*. Oxford: Oxford University Press, 1984.

Bloem, Walter. *Die Schmiede der Zukunft*. Leipzig: Grethlein, 1913.

———. *Vormarsch*. Leipzig: Grethlein, 1916.

———. *Brüderlichkeit*. Leipzig: Grethlein, 1922.

———. *Das ganze, halt!* Leipzig: Grethlein, 1934.

———. *Kriegserlebnistrilogie*. Leipzig: Grethlein, 1936.

———. *Werk und Tat*. Manuscript. *Stadtarchiv* Wuppertal.

Böhm, Karl, ed. *Aufrufe und Reden deutscher Professoren im ersten Weltkrieg*. Stuttgart: Reclam, 1975.

Böhme, Ulrich. *Fassungen bei Ernst Jünger*. Meisenheim: Hain, 1972.

Bornebusch, Herbert. *Gegen-Erinnerung: Eine formsemantische Analyse des demokratischen Kriegsromans der Weimarer Republik*. Frankfurt: Peter Lang, 1985.

Börsenverein der Deutschen Buchhändler. *Börsenblatt für den deutschen Buchhandel*. Leipzig, 1914–1918.

Brackelmann, Gunther. *Der deutsche Protestantismus im Epochenjahr 1917*.

Brecht, Bertolt. *Schriften*. 2nd ed. Berlin: Aufbau, 1975.

Breuer, Dieter. *Geschichte der literarischen Zensur in Deutschland*. Heidelberg: Quelle and Meyer, 1982.

Bridenthal, Renate, Atina Grossmann, and Marion Kaplan, eds. *When Biology Became Destiny: Woman in Weimar and Nazi Germany*. New York: Monthly Review, 1984.

Bridgewater, Patrick. "German Poetry and the First World War," *European Studies Review* 1(1971):147–86.

———. *The German Poets of the First World War*. New York: St. Martin's, 1985.

Brinker-Gabler, Gisela, ed. *Frauen gegen den Krieg*. Frankfurt: S. Fischer, 1980.

Bronson, David, ed. *Jews and Germans from 1860 to 1933*. Heidelberg, 1979.

Bubendey, Johann Friedrich. *Der Backfisch*. Berlin: Theater Verlag Eduard Bloch, 1910.

———. *Liebesboycott*. Berlin: G. Lehmann, 1911.

Buck-Morss, Susan. *The Dialectics of Seeing: Walter Benjamin and the Arcades Project*. Cambridge: MIT Press, 1989.

Buddecke, Albert. *Kriegsliteratur: Eine Systematische Zusammenstellung ausgewählter Bücher und Schriften über den Weltkrieg*. Leipzig: Gustav Fock, 1917.

———. *Die Kriegssammlungen: Ein Nachweis ihrer Einrichtungen und ihres Bestandes*. Oldenburg: G. Stalling, 1917.

Bullivant, Keith, ed. *Culture and Society in the Weimar Republic*. Manchester: Manchester University Press, 1977.

Bürger, Christa, Peter Bürger, and Jochen Schulte-Sasse, eds. *Aufklärung und literarische Öffentlichkeit*. Frankfurt: Suhrkamp, 1980.

Bürger, Peter. *Vermittlung—Rezeption—Funktion*. Frankfurt: Suhrkamp, 1979.

Bürger, Peter, and Christa Bürger. *The Institutions of Art.* Trans. Loren Kruger. Lincoln: University of Nebraska Press, 1992.

Chickering, Roger. *We Men Who Feel Most German: A Cultural Study of the Pan-German League.* Boston: Allen and Unwin, 1984.

Childers, Tom. *The Formation of the Nazi Contituency.* London: Croom Helm, 1986.

———. "The Social Language of Politics in Germany: Society and Political Discourse in the Weimar Republic." *American Historical Review* 95, No. 2 (1990):331–58.

———, ed. *The Nazi Voter: The Social Foundations of Fascism in Germany, 1919–1933.* Chapel Hill: North Carolina Press, 1983.

Cincinnatus (J. Lettenbauer). *Der Krieg der Worte.* Stuttgart: Cotta, 1916.

Conrad, Claus. *Krieg und Aufsatzunterricht.* Frankfurt: Peter Lang, 1986.

Cooke, Miriam, and Angela Woollacott. *Gendering War Talk.* Princeton: Princeton University Press, 1993.

Cysarz, Herbert. *Zur Geistesgeschichte des Weltkriegs: Die dichterischen Wandlungen des deutschen Kriegsbilds.* Halle/Salle: Max Niemeyer, 1931.

Daniels, Ute. *Arbeiterfrauen in der Kriegsgesellschaft.* Bielefeld: Vanderhoeck and Ruprecht, 1989.

Dehmel, Richard. *Zwischen Volk und Menschheit.* Frankfurt: S. Fischer, 1919.

Deist, Wilhelm. *Militär und Innenpolitik im Weltkrieg, 1914–1918.* Düsseldorf: Droste, 1970.

Deist, Wilhelm, Manfred Messerschmidt, Hans-Erich Volkmann, and Wolfram Wette, eds. *Ursachen und Voraussetzungen der Deutschen Kriegspolitik.* Stuttgart: Deutsche Verlags-Anstalt, 1979.

Delbruck, Hans, ed. *Der deutsche Krieg in Feldpostbriefen.* Vol. 1. Munich: Georg Müller, 1915.

de Mendelssohn, Peter. *S. Fischer und Sein Verlag.* Frankfurt: S. Fischer, 1970.

Denkler, Horst, and Karl Prümm, eds. *Die deutsche Literatur im Dritten Reich.* Stuttgart: Reclam, 1976.

Derrida, Jacques. *Of Grammatology.* Trans. Gayatri Spivak. Baltimore: Johns Hopkins University Press, 1976.

———. *The Postcard from Socrates to Freud and Beyond.* Chicago: University of Chicago Press, 1987.

———. *Limited Inc.* Evanston: Northwestern University Press, 1990.

———. "Archive Fever." *Diacritics* 25, no. 2 (1995): 9–63.

Diner, Dan, ed. *Ist der Nationalsozialismus Geschichte? Zur Historisierung und Historikerstreit.* Frankfurt: Fischer, 1991.

Dönitz, Karl. *Die Fahrten der Breslau.* Berlin: Ullstein, 1917.

Druckenmüller, Alfred. *Der Buchhandel in Stuttgart seit Erfindung der Buchdruckerkunst bis zur Gegenwart.* Stuttgart: J. B. Metzlerische Buchhandlung, 1908.

Eberhard von Bodenhausen, Harry Graf Kessler: Ein Briefwechsel, 1894–1918. Marbacher Schriften. Ed. Hans-Ulrich Simon. Marbach a.N.: Deutsches Literaturarchiv, 1978.

Ehringhaus, Inge. *Die Lektüre unserer Frontsoldaten im Weltkrieg.* Berlin: Junker und Dünnhaupt, 1941.

Eksteins, Modris. "War, Memory and Politics: The Fate of the Film *All Quiet on the Western Front,*" *Central European History* 13/1(1980):60–82.

————. *Rites of Spring*. Boston: Houghton Mifflin, 1989.

Ellis, John. *Eye Deep in Hell: Trench Warfare in World War I*. Baltimore: Johns Hopkins University Press, 1976.

Ellis, Larry. "Army, State and Politics in the Grand Duchy of Baden 1866–1920." Ph.D. Diss. Johns Hopkins University, 1986.

Elshtain, Jean. *Women and War*. New York: Basic, 1987.

Evans, Richard. *Rethinking German History: Nineteenth-Century Germany and the Origins of the Third Reich*. London: Evans, Unwin, Hyman, 1987.

————. *In Hitler's Shadow: West German Historians and the Attempt to Escape from the Nazi Past*. New York: Pantheon, 1989.

Faulenbach, Bernd. *Ideologie des deutschen Weges: Die deutsche Geschichte in der Historiographie zwischen Kaiserreich und Nationalsozialismus*. Munich: C. H. Beck, 1980.

Feldman, Gerald. *Army, Industry and Labor in Germany, 1914–1918*. Princeton: Princeton University Press, 1966.

————. *The Great Disorder: Politics, Economics, and Society in the German Inflation, 1914–1924*. Oxford: Oxford University Press, 1993.

Fetzer, Günther. *Wertungsprobleme in der Trivialliteraturforschung*. Munich: Wilhelm Fink, 1980.

Fischer, Doris. "Die Münchner Zensurstelle während des Ersten Weltkrieges: Alfons Falkner von Sonnenburg als Pressereferent im Bayerischen Kriegsministerium in den Jahren 1914 bis 1918/19." Ph.D. Diss. Munich, 1972.

Fischer, Fritz. *Griff nach der Weltmacht: Die Kriegsziele des Kaiserlichen Deutschland, 1914–1918*. Düsseldorf: Droste, 1961.

————. *Der erste Weltkrieg und das deutsche Geschichtsbild: Beiträge zur Bewältigung eines historischen Tabus*. Düsseldorf: Droste, 1977.

————. "Twenty Five Years Later: Looking Back at the 'Fischer Controversy' and Its Consequences." *Central European History* 21(1990):207–23.

————. *Hitler war kein Betriebsunfall*. München: C. H. Beck, 1992.

Fischer, Hans. *Nach Siberien mit hunderttausend Deutschen*. Berlin: Ullstein, 1915.

Fischer, Heinz Dietrich, ed. *Pressekonzentration und Zensurpraxis im ersten Weltkrieg*. Berlin: Volker Spiess, 1973.

Flex, Walter. *Der Wanderer zwischen beiden Welten*. Munich: Beck, 1917.

Fock, Gustav. *Wir Marokko Deutschen in der Gewalt der Franzosen*. Berlin: Ullstein, 1916.

————, ed. *Das Württembergische Heer im Weltkrieg*. Stuttgart: Verlag Berger's Literalisches Buro, 1921–1925.

Foerster, Wolfgang, ed. *Wir Kämpfer im Weltkrieg: Feldzugsbriefe und Kriegstagebücher aus dem Material des Reichsarchivs*. Berlin: Neufeld & Henius, 1929.

Fohrmann, Jürgen, and Wilhelm Voßkamp, eds. *Wissenschaftsgeschichte der Germanistik im 19. Jahrhundert*. Stuttgart: Metzler, 1994.

Foreman, Paul. "Weimar Culture, Causality, and Quantum Theory, 1918–1927: Adaptation by German Physicists and Mathematicians to a Hostile Intellectual Environment." *Historical Studies in the Physical Sciences* 3(1971):1–115.

————. "The Financial Support and Political Alignment of Physicists in Weimar Germany." *Minerva* 12(1974):39–66.

Forstmann, Walter. *U39 auf Jaad in Mittelmeer*. Berlin: Ullstein, 1918.

Forstner, Georg Günther. *Als UBoots Kommandant gegen England*. Berlin: Ullstein, 1916.

Foucault, Michel. *The Order of Things: An Archeology of the Human Sciences*. New York: Pantheon, 1970.

————. *The Archaeology of Knowledge*. New York: Pantheon, 1972.

Freud, Sigmund. *Gesammelte Werke*. London: Imago, 1949.

Friedlander, Saul, ed. *Probing the Limits of Representation*. Cambridge: Harvard University Press, 1992.

Fuchs, Werner. *Todesbilder in der Modernen Gesellschaft*. Frankfurt: Suhrkamp, 1969.

Führen, Franz, ed. *Lehrer im Krieg*. 2 vols. Leipzig: Kommisionsverlag, G. Kummer, 1936.

Fünfzig Jahre Ullstein, 1877–1927. Berlin: Ullstein, 1927.

Fussell, Paul. *The Great War and Modern Memory*. New York: Oxford University Press, 1975.

Ganghofer, Ludwig. *Die Front im Osten*. Berlin: Ullstein, 1915.

————. *Reise zur deutschen Front*. Berlin: Ullstein, 1915.

Geiss, Imanuel. *Das deutsche Reich und der erste Weltkrieg*. Munich: C. Hanser, 1978.

————. *Das deutsche Reich und die Vorgeschichte des ersten Weltkrieges*. Munich: C. Hanser, 1978.

Die geographische Zeitschrift. Wiesbade: F. Steiner, 1914–1918.

Gersdorff, Ursula von. *Frauen im Kriegsdienst*. Stuttgart: Deutsche Verlags-Anstalt, 1969.

Gilbert, Sandra, and Susan Gubar. *No Man's Land*. Vols. 1–3. New Haven: Yale University Press, 1988–1994.

Gillis, John, ed. *Commemorations: The Politics of National Identity*. Princeton: Princeton University Press, 1994.

Gilman, Sander, ed. *NS-Literaturtheorie: Eine Dokumentation*. Frankfurt: Athenäum, 1971.

————, ed. *Antisemitism in times of Crises*. New York: New York University Press, 1991.

Godlewska, Anne, and Neil Smith, eds. *Geography and Empire*. Oxford: Blackwell, 1994.

Gollbach, Michael. *Die Wiederkehr des Weltkrieges in der Literatur: Zu den Frontromanen der späten zwanziger Jahre. Theorie-Kritik-Geschichte Band 19*. Kronberg, Sweden: Scriptor, 1978.

Goltz, Joachim von der. *Der Baum von Clery*. Munich: Langen-Müller, 1934.

Gottberg, Otto von. *Die Helden von Tsingtau*. Berlin: Ullstein, 1915.

Grabein, Paul. *Im Auto durch Feindesland*. Berlin: Ullstein, 1916.

Groh, Dieter, and Peter Brandt. *Vaterlandslose Gesellen. Sozialdemokratie und Nation, 1860–1990*. Munich, 1992.

Grupp, Peter. "Harry Graf Kessler als Diplomat." *Vierteljahrshefte für Zeitgeschichte* 40(1992):61–78.

Haarmann, Hermann, and Walter Huder, eds. *Das war ein Vorspiel nur . . . .* Berlin: Medusa, 1983.

Habermas, Jürgen. *Strukturwandel der Öffentlichkeit: Untersuchungen zu einer Kategorie der bürgerlichen Gesellschaft*. Berlin: Zuchterhand, 1965.

Hafkesbrink, Hanna. *Unknown Germany*. New Haven: Yale University Press, 1984.

Harbou, Thea von. *Die Flucht der Beate Hoyermann*. Stuttgart: Cotta, 1915.

————. *Der Krieg und die Frauen*. Stuttgart: Cotta, 1913.

————. *Der unsterbliche Acker.* Stuttgart: Cotta, 1915.

Hardt, Fred B., ed. *Kulturdokumente zum Weltkrieg I: Die Deutschen Schützengraben- und Soldatenzeitungen.* Munich: R. Piper, 1917.

Hartcup, Guy. *The War of Invention: Scientific Developments, 1914–18.* London: Brassey's Defence Publishers, 1988.

Hartung, Wilhelm. *Großkampf, Männer und Granaten.* Berlin: W. Kolk, 1930.

Hauptmann, Gerhard. *Sämtliche Werke.* Berlin: Propylüen, 1974.

Hegel, Georg Wilhelm. *Aesthetic III: Die Poesie.* Ed. R. Bubner. Stuttgart: Reclam, 1971.

Heinemann, Ulrich. *Die verdrängte Niederlage: Politische Öffentlichkeit und Kriegsschuldfrage in der Weimarer Republik.* Göttingen: Vandenhoeck and Ruprecht, 1983.

Hentig, Werner Otto von. *Meine Diplomatenfahrt ins verschlossene Land.* Berlin: Ullstein, 1918.

Herb, Henrik. *Under the Map of Germany: Nationalism and Propaganda 1918–1945.* London: Routledge, 1995.

Herberg-Rothe, Andreas. *Militärgeschichte als Friedenforschung? Einführung in die Dialektik der Wissenschaft von Krieg und Frieden.* Studienreihe: Militärgeschichte, Friedensforschung, Militärpolitik. Band 1. Frankfurt am Main: R. G. Fischer, 1981.

Herman, Jost. *Geschichte der Germanistik.* Reinbeck: Rowohlt, 1994.

Herman, Jost, and Frank Trommler. *Die Kultur der Weimarer Republik.* Munich: 1982.

Herzog, Rudolf. *Ritter, Tod und Teufel.* Leipzig: Quelle und Meyer, 1915.

————. *Vom Stürmen, Sterben, Auferstehen.* Leipzig: Quelle und Meyer, 1916.

Hesse, Hermann. *Brief ins Feld.* Munich: K. A. Müller, 1916.

Heymann, Walter. *Kriegsgedichte und Feldpostbriefe.* Munich: Georg Müller, 1915.

Higonnett, Margaret Randolph, Jane Jenson, Sonya Michel, and Margaret Collins Weitz, eds. *Behind the Lines: Gender and the Two World Wars.* New Haven: Yale University Press, 1987.

Hitler, Adolf. *Mein Kampf.* Munich: Franz Eher, 1925.

Höcker, Paul Oscar. *An der Spitze meiner Kompagnie.* Berlin: Ullstein, 1914.

————. *Ein Liller Roman.* Berlin: Ullstein, 1917.

————. *Gottgesandte Wechselwinde: Lebenserinnerungen eines Fünfundsiebzigjährigen.* Bielefeld: Velhagen & Klasing, 1940.

Hohendahl, Peter Uwe. *Building a National Literature: The Case of Germany, 1830–1870.* Trans. Renate Baron Franciscono. Ithaca: Cornell University Press, 1982.

————. *Literarische Kultur im Zeitalter des Liberalismus, 1830–1870.* Munich: Beck, 1985.

————. *Prismatic Thought: Theodor W. Adorno.* Lincoln: University of Nebraska Press, 1995.

————. Germanistik als Gegenstand der Wissenschaftsgeschichte. *Internationales Archiv für Sozialgeschichte der deutschen Literatur.* Vol. 21 (1996):143–61.

Höhn, Reinhard. *Die Armee als Erziehungsschule der Nation: Das Ende einer Idee.* Bad Harzburg: Verlag für Wissenschaft, Wirtschaft und Technik, 1963.

Holländer, Walter V. *Deutsche Sonette.* Berlin: B. Cassirer, 1916.

————. "Die Entwicklung der Kriegsliteratur." *Die neue Rundschau* (1916):1274.

————. *Eiserne zehn Gebote an die deutschen Krieger: In Worte gebracht von einem Infanterieoffizier.* Leipzig: Panther-Verlag, 1915.

————. *Schicksale Gebündet: Ein Menschenpanorama von Heute.* Berlin: Ullstein, 1929.

Hoosen, David, ed. *Geography and National Identity.* Oxford: Blackwell, 1994.

Hoppe, Ludwig. *Feldpredigerfahrten an der Westfront.* Berlin: Ausschuss für Kriegsbüchereien an der Front, 1916.

Horkheimer, Max. *Between Philosophy and Social Science: Selected Early Writings.* Trans. G. F. Hunter, M. S. Kramer, and J. Torpey. Cambridge: MIT Press, 1993.

Horkheimer, Max, and Theodor W. Adorno. *Dialektik der Aufklärung.* Frankfurt: Fischer, 1969.

Houben, H. H. *Hier Zensur—Wer Dort? Antworten von gestern auf Fragen von Heute.* Leipzig: F. U. Brockhaus, 1918.

————. *Verbotene Literatur von der klassischen Zeit bis zur Gegenwart.* Berlin: Ernst Rowohlt, 1924.

————. *Der ewige Zensor: Mit einem Nachwort von Claus Richter und Wolfgang Labuhn.* Kronberg, Sweden: Atheneum, 1978. Reprinted from 1926 edition, Polizei und Zensur.

Hunt, Lynn, ed. *The New Cultural History.* Berkeley: University of California Press, 1989.

Hüppauf, Bernd, ed. *Ansichten vom Krieg: Vergleichende Studien zum ersten Weltkrieg in Literatur und Gesellschaft.* Königstein: Forum Academicum, 1984.

————. "Langemarck, Verdun and the Myth of a New Man in Germany after the First World War," *War and Society* 6, no. 2 (1988):70–103.

————. "Die Stadt als imaginerter Kriegsschauplatz." *Zeitschrift für Germanistik* 2(1995): 317–36.

Huyssen, Andreas. *After the Great Divide: Modernism, Mass Culture, Postmodernism.* Bloomington: Indiana University Press, 1986.

Iggers, George. *The German Conception of History: The National Tradition of Historical Thought from Herder to the Present.* Middletown: Wesleyan University Press, 1968.

————, ed. *The Social History of Politics: Critical Perspectives in West German Historical Writing since 1945.* Leamington Spa: Berg, 1985.

Iggers, George, and James Powell, eds. *Leopold von Ranke and the Shaping of the Historical Discipline.* Syracuse: Syracuse University Press, 1990.

Imhoff, General von. *Der deutsche Krieg in Feldpostbriefen.* Munich: Georg Müller, 1915.

Inglis, Ken. "Entombing Unknown Soldiers: From London and Paris to Baghdad." *History and Memory* 5(1993):7–32.

Insel Verlag. *Kriegs-Almanach 1915.* Leipzig: Insel, 1917.

Insel Verlag. *75 Jahre Insel Verlag: Eine Geschichte in Daten, Programmen und Dokumenten. Insel-Almanach auf das Jahr 1975.* Frankfurt am Main: Insel, 1974.

Jäckel, Eberhard. *Hitlers Weltanschauung.* Stuttgart: Deutsche Verlags Anstalt, 1981.

Jäckh, Ernst, ed. *Der große Krieg als Erlebnis und Erfahrung.* Gotha: Perthes, 1916.

Jäger, Wolfgang. *Historische Forschung und politische Kultur in Deutschland: Die Debate 1914– 1980 über den Ausbruch des ersten Weltkrieges.* Göttingen: Vanderhoeck Ruprecht, 1984.

Jay, Martin. *Force Fields: Between Intellectual History and Cultural Critique.* London: Routledge, 1993.

————. *The Dialectical Imagination.* Berkeley: University of California Press, 1973.

————. "Walter Benjamin: Remembrance and the First World War," lecture given at the University of Kentucky, September 1997.

Jirgel, Ernst. *Die Wiederkehr des Weltkrieges in der Literatur.* Wien-Leipzig: Reinhold, 1931.

Johann, Ernst. *S. Fischer Verlag: Vollständiges Verzeichnis aller Werke: Buchserien und Gesamtausgaben mit Anmerkungen zur Verlagsgeschichte 1886 bis 1956.* Frankfurt: S. Fischer, 1956.

Jones, John Paul, Wolfgang Natter, and Ted Schatzki, eds. *Postmodern Contentions: Epochs, Politics, Space.* New York: Guilford, 1993.

Jünger, Ernst. *Das Wäldchen 125.* Berlin: Mittler, 1930.

———. *In Stahlgewittern.* Berlin: Mittler, 1923.

———. *Sämtliche Werke.* Stuttgart: Klett, 1978.

Kaes, Anton, ed. *Manifeste und Dokumente zur deutschen Literatur, 1918–1933.* Stuttgart: Metzler, 1983.

Kansteiner, Wulf. "Hayden White's Critique of the Writing of History." *History and Theory* 32/33(1993):273–95.

Kant, Immanuel. *Kritik der Urteilskraft.* Stuttgart: Reclam, 1986.

Keegan, John. *The Face of Battle.* London: Jonathan Cape, 1976.

Kellner, Doug. *Critical Theory, Marxism, and Modernity.* Baltimore: Johns Hopkins University Press, 1989.

Kern, Steven. *The Culture of Time and Space, 1880–1918.* Cambridge: Harvard University Press, 1983.

King, Linda. *Bestseller by Design: Vicki Baum and the House of Ullstein.* Detroit. Wayne State Press, 1988.

Kippenberg, Anton. *Reden und Schriften.* Wiesbaden: Insel, 1952.

Kläber, Kurt, ed. *Der Krieg: Das erste Volksbuch vom grossen Krieg.* Berlin: Internationaler Arbeiter-Verlag, 1929.

Klassiker in Finsteren Zeiten. Marbach: Deutsche Schillergesellschaft, 1983.

Klein, Holger. "Weltkriegsroman und Germanistik, 1933–1938," *JEGP* (1985):467–83.

Klinkmüller, Walter. *Ein deutscher Offizier im revolutionären Russland.* Berlin: Ullstein, 1918.

Knoch, Peter, ed. *Kriegsalltag: Die Rekonstruktion des Kriegsalltags als Aufgabe der historischen Forschung und der Friedenserziehung.* Stuttgart: Metzler, 1989.

Kocka, Jürgen. *Klassengesellschaft im Krieg: Deutsche Sozialgeschichte, 1914–1918.* Göttingen: Vandenhoeck and Ruprecht, 1978.

———. *Bildungsbürgertum im 19. Jahrhundert.* 4 Vols. Stuttgart: Klett/Cotta, 1985–1989.

Koebner, Thomas, R. P. Janz, and Frank Trommler, eds. *"Mit uns zieht die neue Zeit": Der Mythos der Jugend.* Frankfurt: Suhrkamp, 1985.

Koester, Eckart. *Literatur und Weltkriegsideologie: Positionen und Begründungszusammenhänge des publizistischen Engagements deutscher Schriftsteller im ersten Weltkrieg. Theorie—Kritik—Geschichte Band 15.* Kronberg, Sweden: Scriptor, 1977.

König, Paul. *Die Fahrt der Deutschland.* Berlin: Ullstein, 1916.

Köppen, Edlef. *Heeresbericht.* Reprint ed. Kronberg, Sweden: Scriptor, 1976.

Korte, Hermann. *Der Krieg in der Lyrik des Expressionismus: Studien zur Evolution eines literarischen Themas.* Bonn: Bouvier, 1981.

Koszyk, Kurt. *Deutsche Presse, 1914–1945.* Berlin: Colloquium, 1972.

———. *Zwischen Kaiserreich und Diktatur: Die sozialdemokratische Presse von 1914 bis 1933.* Heidelberg: Quelle and Meyer, 1958.

Kratzsch, Gerhard. *Kunstwart und Dürerbund.* Göttingen: Vandenhoeck and Ruprecht, 1969.

Kraul, Margret. *Das deutsche Gymnasium, 1780–1980.* Frankfurt: Suhrkamp, 1984.

Krell, Max. *Das Alles gab es einmal.* Frankfurt: Heinrich Scheffler, 1961.

Kühlwetter, Friedrich von. *Skagerrak.* Berlin: Ullstein, 1916.

Kurth, Lieselotte. *Die zweite Wirklichkeit: Studien zum Roman des achtzenten Jahrhunderts.* Chapel Hill: University of North Carolina Press, 1969.

LaCapra, Dominick. *History and Criticism.* Ithaca: Cornell University Press, 1985.

———. *Representing the Holocaust: History, Theory, Trauma.* Ithaca: Cornell University Press, 1995.

———. "Revisiting the Historians' Debate: Mourning and Genocide," *History and Memory* 9, no. 1/2 (1997): 80–112.

Laclau, Ernesto, and Chantal Mouffe. *Hegemony and Socialist Strategy: Towards a Radical Democratic Politics.* London: Verso, 1985.

Lacoue-Labarthe, Philippe, and Jean-Luc Nancy. *The Literary Absolute.* Trans. Phil Barnard and Cheryl Lester. Buffalo: State University of New York Press, 1988.

Lange, Karl. *Marneschlacht und deutsche Öffentlichkeit, 1914–1939: Eine verdrängte Niederlage und ihre Folgen.* Studien zur Modernen Geschichte. Düsseldorf: Bertelsmann Universitätsverlag, 1974.

Langewische, Dieter. "Arbeiterbibliotheken und Arbeiterlektüre im Wilhelminischen Deutschland." *Archiv für Sozialgeschichte* 16(1976):135–204.

———. "Politik-Gesellschaft-Kultur: Zur Problematik von Arbeiterkultur und kulterellen Arbeiterorganisationen in Deutschland nach dem 1. Weltkrieg." *Archiv für Sozialgeschichte* 22(1982):359–403.

Leed, Eric. *No Man's Land: Combat and Identity in World War One.* Cambridge: Cambridge University Press, 1979.

Leitzen, Hans, ed. *Der große Krieg 1914–15 in Feldpostbriefen.* Wolfenbüttel: Julius Zwißlers, 1915.

Lemon, Lee, and Marion Reis, eds. *Russian Formalist Criticism: Four Essays.* Lincoln: University of Nebraska Press, 1965.

Lepenies, Wolf, ed. *Functions and Uses of Disciplinary Histories.* Dordrecht, Holland: D. Reidel, 1983.

Lidtke, Vernon. *The Alternative Culture.* New York: Oxford University Press, 1985.

Liulevicius, Vejas. "War Land: Peoples, Lands, and National Identity on the Eastern Front in World War I." Ph.D. Diss. University of Pennsylvania, 1994.

Livingstone, David. *The Geographical Tradition.* Oxford: Blackwell, 1992.

Loofs, Friedrich. *Der Hauptmann.* Stuttgart: Cotta, 1916.

Lübbe, Hermann. *Politische Philosophie in Deutschland.* Basel: Schwabe, 1963.

Lurz, Meinhold. *Kriegsdenkmäler in Deutschland.* Vols. 3 and 4. Heidelberg: 1984–1985.

Lutz, Bernd, ed. *Metzler Autoren Lexikon.* Stuttgart: Metzler, 1986.

Mai, Günther. *Arbeiterschaft in Deutschland, 1914–1918: Studien zur Arbeitskampf und Arbeitsmarkt im ersten Weltkrieg.* Dusseldorf: Droste, 1985.

———. " 'Aufklärung der Bevölkerung' und 'Vaterländischer Unterricht' in Württemberg,

1914–1918: Struktur, Durchführung und Inhalte der deutschen Inlandspropaganda im ersten Weltkrieg." *Zeitschrift für Württembergische Landesgeschichte* (1979).

Maier, Charles. *The Unmasterable Past: History, Holocaust and German National Identity.* Cambridge: Harvard University Press, 1988.

Mann, Erika, ed. *Thomas Mann: Briefe, 1889–1936.* Frankfurt: Fischer, 1961.

Mann, Thomas. *Politische Schriften und Reden.* Ed. Hans Bürgin. Frankfurt: Fischer, 1968.

Marcus, Thomas. *Buildings and Power: Freedom and Control in the Origin of Modern Building Types.* London: Routledge, 1993.

Marquard, Odo, and Karlheinz Stierle, eds. *Identität.* Munich: Wilhelm Fink, 1979.

Marsland, Elizabeth. *The Nation's Cause: French, English, and German Poetry of the First World War.* London: Routledge, 1991.

Mason, Timothy. *Arbeiterklasse und Volksgemeinschaft.* Opladen: Westdeutscher, 1975.

Mattias, Eric, and Anthony Nichols, eds. *German Democracy and the Rise of Hitler.* London: Allen and Unwin, 1971.

McCarthy, John, and Katrin Schneider, eds. *The Future of Germanistik in the USA.* Nashville: Vanderbilt, 1996.

McCarthy, John, and Werner von der Ohe, eds. *Zensur und Kultur: Censorship and Culture.* Tübingen: Niemeyer, 1995.

Meinecke, Friederich. *Die deutsche Erhebung von 1914: Aufsäze und Vorträge.* Stuttgart: Cotta, 1914.

Meiner, Annemarie. *Der deutsche Verlegerverein 1886–1935.* Leipzig: Kantate, 1936.

Mendelssohn, Peter de. *S. Fischer und sein Verlag.* Frankfurt: Fischer, 1970.

Meyer, Jochen. "Berlin-Provinz: Literarische Kontroversen um 1930." *Marbacher Magazine* 33(1985), 1–128.

Michael, Friedrich, ed. *Insel Almanach auf das Jahr 1974: Anton Kippenberg zum hundertsten Geburtstag.* Frankfurt: Insel, 1973.

Militärgeschichtliches Forschungsamt. *Neue Forschungen über den ersten Weltkrieg.* Freiburg, 1986.

Momber, Eckhardt. *'S ist Krieg! 'S ist Krieg! Versuch zur deutschen Literatur über den Krieg, 1914–1933.* Berlin: Das Arsenal, 1981.

Morris, Rodler. *From Weimar Philosemite to Nazi Apologist.* Lewiston: Edwin Mellen, 1988.

Mosse, George. *The Nationalization of the Masses: Political Symbolism and Mass Movements in Germany from the Napoleonic War through the Third Reich.* New York: Meridian, 1975.

———. *Toward the Final Solution: A History of European Racism.* New York: J. Fertig, 1978.

———. *Fallen Soldiers: Reshaping the Memory of the World Wars.* New York: Oxford University Press, 1990.

Mouffe, Chantal. *The Return of the Political.* Verso: London, 1993.

Moyer, Laurence. *Victory Must Be Ours: Germany in the Great War, 1914–1918.* New York: Hippocrene, 1995.

Müller, Hans-Harald. *Der Krieg und die Schriftsteller.* Stuttgart: Metzler, 1986.

Müller, Klaus Jürgen, and Eckardt Opitz, eds. *Militär und Militarismus in der Weimarer Republik: Beiträge eines internationalen Symposiums an der Hochschule der Bundeswehr Hamburg am 5. und 6. Mai 1977.* Düsseldorf: Droste, 1978.

Müller, Susanne. *Burgfrieden und Klassenkampf: Die deutsche Sozialdemokratie im ersten Weltkrieg.* Düsseldorf: Droste, 1974.

Nägele, Rainer. *Reading after Freud.* New York: Columbia University Press, 1987.

Natter, Wolfgang. "Literature at War: Reading and Writing in the Context of Institutions." Ph.D. Diss., Johns Hopkins University, 1990.

———. "Radical Democracy: Hegemony, Reason, Time and Space." *Society and Space* 13(1995):267–74.

———. "German Cultural Studies: A Review." *Transculture.* Vol. 1, No. 2 (1996):133–147.

Natter, Wolfgang, and John Paul Jones, "Identity, Space and Other Uncertainties." *Space and Social Theory.* Ed. Ulf Stroymayer and Georges Benko. Oxford: Blackwell, 1997.

Natter, Wolfgang, Ted Schatzki, and John Paul Jones, eds. *Objectivity and Its Other.* New York: Guilford, 1995.

Nietzsche, Friedrich. *Werke.* Ed. Karl Schlechta. Berlin: Ullstein, 1969.

Nipperday, Thomas. *Religion im Umbruch: Deutschland, 1870–1918.* Munich: C. H. Beck, 1988.

Offer, Avner. *The First World War: An Agrarian Interpretation.* Oxford: Oxford University Press, 1989.

Osborne, John. *Meyer or Fontane? German Literature after the Franco-Prussian War, 1870–71.* Bonn: Bouvier, 1983.

Otto, Ulla. *Die literarische Zensur als Problem der Soziologie der Politik.* Stuttgart: Ferdinand Enke, 1968.

Owen, C. R. *Erich Maria Remarque: A Critical Bio-Bibliography.* Amsterdam: Rodopi, 1984.

Petzold, Joachim. *Die Dolchstoßlegende.* Berlin: Akademie-Verlag, 1963.

Peukert, Detlev. *Die Weimarer Republik.* Frankfurt: Suhrkamp, 1987.

Pfeiler, Wilhelm. *War and the German Mind.* New York: Columbia University Press, 1941.

Pfeilschifter, Georg, ed. *Kriegsbriefe katholischer Soldaten.* Freiburg: Herder, 1918.

Philippe, Klaus-Peter. *Volk des Zorns: Studien zur 'Poetischen Mobilmachung' in der deutschen Literatur am Beginn des ersten Weltkriegs, ihren Voraussetzungen und Implikationen.* Munich: Wilhelm Fink, 1979.

Plenge, Johann. *Krieg und Volkswirtschaft.* Münster: Borgmeyer, 1915.

Pollmann, Bernhard, ed. *Lesebuch zur deutschen Geschichte.* Dortmund, 1984.

Pongs, Hermann. "Krieg als Volksschicksal im deutschen Schrifttum," *Dichtung und Volkstum* 35(1935):182–219.

Pressel, Wilhelm. *Die Kriegspredigt 1914–1918 in der evangelischen Kirche Deutschlands.* Göttingen: Vandenhoeck und Ruprecht, 1969.

Pröbsting, Agnes, ed. *Weltkrieg und deutsche Dichtung.* Paderborn: Schöningh, 1934.

Prümm, Karl. *Die Literatur des soldatischen Nationalismus der 20er Jahre.* Meisenheim: Scriptor, 1975.

Redfield, Marc. *Phantom Formations: Aesthetic Ideology and the Bildungsroman.* Ithaca: Cornell University Press, 1997.

Remarque, Erich M. *Im Westen nichts neues.* Berlin: Ullstein, 1928.

Richards, Donald Ray. *The German Bestseller in the 20th Century: A Complete Bibliography and Analysis, 1915–1940.* Bern: Herbert Lang, 1968.

Richthofen, Manfred Freiherr von. *Der rote Kampfflieger von Rittmeister Richthofen: Mit einer Studie von F. W. Korff.* Munich: Matthes and Seitz, 1977.

———. *Der rote Kampfflieger.* Berlin: Ullstein, 1917.

Ringer, Fritz. *The Decline of the German Mandarins: The German Academic Community, 1890–1933.* Cambridge: Harvard University Press, 1969.

Ritchie, J. M. *German Literature under National Socialism.* London: Croom Helm, 1983.

Rohe, Karl. *Das Reichsbanner schwarz rot gold: Ein Beitrag zur Geschichte und Struktur der politischen Kampfverbände zur Zeit der Weimarer Republik.* Düsseldorf: Droste, 1966, ed. by the Commission for the History of Parlimentarianism and Political Parties in Bonn.

Rohwer, Jürgen, ed. *Neue Forschungen zum ersten Weltkrieg.* Koblenz, 1985.

Rosenberg, Rainer. *Zehn Kapitel zur Geschichte der Germanistik, Literaturgeschichtsschreibung, Literatur und Gesellschaft.* Berlin: Akademie-Verlag, 1981.

Rosner, Karl. *Wir tragen das Schwert.* Stuttgart: Cotta, 1914.

———. *Die Feindin: Kriegsbilder aus Frankreich und Flandern.* Leipzig: Reclam, 1917.

———. *Mit der Armee v. Falkenhayn gegen die Rumänen.* Berlin: Scherl, 1917.

———. *Die große Frühlingsschlacht 1918.* Berlin: Scherl, 1918.

Roth, Michael. *The Ironist's Cage: Memory, Trauma and the Construction of History.* New York: Columbia University Press, 1995.

Rother, Rainer, ed. *Die letzten Tage der Menscheit: Bilder des ersten Weltkrieges.* Berlin: Deutsches Historisches Museum, 1994.

Rühl, Hohn. *Die Armee als Erziehungsschule der Nation.* Bad Harzburg: Verlag für Wissenschaft, Wirtschaft und Technik, 1963.

Rumold, Rainer, and O. K. Werkmeister. *The Ideological Crisis of Expressionism.* Columbia, S.C.: Camden House, 1990.

Rüter, Hubert. *Remarque: Im Westen nichts neues.* Paderborn: Schöningh, 1980.

Samuleit, Paul. *Kriegsschundliteratur.* Berlin: C. Heymann, 1916.

Schatzki, Theodore, and Wolfgang Natter, eds. *The Social and Political Body.* New York: Guilford, 1996.

Schauwecker, Franz. *Das Frontbuch.* Halle: Diekmann, 1927.

Schenda, Rudolf. *Die Lesestoffe der kleinen Leute: Studien zur populären Literatur im 19. u. 20 Jahrhundert.* Munich: Beck, 1976.

Schlawe, Fritz. *Die Briefsammlungen des 19. Jahrhunderts. 1815–1915.* Stuttgart: Metzler, 1969.

Schondorff, Achim. *Grundlegung einer volkswissenschaftlichen Lehre vom Menschen: Begründet auf Kriegsbriefen deutscher Studenten. Studien und Bibliographien zur Gegenwartsphilosophie.* Leipzig: S. Herzel, 1936.

Schorski, Carl. *German Social Democracy: The Development of the Great Schism.* New York: Wiley, 1965.

Schüler, Gustav. *Gottesturmflut: Religiöse Gedichte für die Kriegszeit.* Stuttgart: Cotta, 1915.

Schultz, Hans-Dietrich. *Die deutschsprachige Geographie von 1800 bis 1970.* Berlin: Selbstverlag des Geographischen Instituts der Freien Universität Berlin, 1980.

———. *Die Geographie als Bildungsfach im Kaiserreich.* Osnabrück: Selbstverlag des Fachgebietes Geographie der Universität Osnabrück, 1989.

Schütte, Wolfgang. "Ein vergessener Schriftsteller—Ein vergessenes Buch," *Marginalien: Blätter der Pirckheimer Gesellschaft,* No. 25 (1967):47–56.

Schwabe, Klaus. *Wissenschaft und Kriegsmoral.* Göttingen: Münsterschmidt-Verlag, 1969.

Schwarte, Max, ed. *Der große Krieg.* 10 vols. Leipzig: Johann A. Barth, 1923.

Smith, Woodruff. *The German Colonial Empire.* Chapel Hill, N.C.: University of North Carolina Press, 1978.

———. "The Colonial Novel as Political Progaganda: Hans Grimm's *Volk ohne Raum.*" *German Studies Review* 6(1983):215–35.

Sombart, Werner. *Händler und Helden: Patriotische Besinnungen.* Munich: Dunkler and Humbolt, 1915.

Sontheimer, Kurt. *Antidemokratisches Denken in der Weimarer Republik.* Munich: Nymphenberger, 1968.

Spengler, Wilhelm. *Wir Waren Drei Kameraden: Kriegserlebnisse.* With an introduction by Philipp Witkop. Freiburg: Herder, 1917.

———. *Sechs aus einem Dorf: Meine neuen Kriegserlebnisse.* Freiburg: Herder, 1919.

Stark, Gary. *Entrepreneurs of Ideology.* Chapel Hill: University of North Carolina Press, 1981.

———. "Von Nutzen und Nachteil der Literatur für die Geschichtswissenschaft: A Historian's View." *German Quarterly* 63(1990):19–31.

———, ed. *Essays on Culture and Society in Modern Germany.* College Station: Texas A&M University Press, 1982.

Stegemann, Hermann. *Geschichte des Krieges.* Stuttgart: Deutsche Verlags Anstalt, 1917–1921.

Steinart, Armin [Friedrich Loofs]. *Der Hauptmann.* DLA, Marbach.

Stickelberg-Eder, Margrit. *Aufbruch 1914: Kriegsromane der Späten Weimarer Republik.* Zürich: Artimus, 1983.

Stollmann, Rainer. *Ästhetisierung der Politik: Literaturstudien zum subjektiven Faschismus.* Stuttgart: Metzler, 1978.

Strobl, Karl. *Der Krieg im Alpenrot.* Berlin: Ullstein, 1916.

Stromberg, Roland. *Redemption by War.* Lawrence: University Press of Kansas, 1982.

Thauer, Wolfgang. *Die Bücherhallenbewegung: Beiträge zum Büchereiwesen.* Wiesbaden: Otto Harrassowitz, 1970.

Thauer, Wolfgang, and Peter Vodosek. *Geschichte der öffentlichen Büchereien in Deutschland.* Wiesbaden: Otto Harrassowitz, 1978.

Theweleit, Klaus. *Männerphantasien.* Reinbeck: Rowohlt, 1980.

Thoss, Bruno. "Weltkrieg und Systemkrise: Der Erste Weltkrieg in den Westdeutschen Forschung, 1945–1984." In *Neue Forschungen zum Ersten Weltkrieg.* Jürgen Rohwer, ed. Koblenz: Bernard and Graefe, 1986, 31–80.

Tovote, Heinz. *Aus einer deutschen Festung im Krieg.* Berlin: Ullstein, 1915.

Travers, Martin Patrick Anthony. *German Novels on the First World War and Their Ideological Implications, 1918–1933.* Stuttgart: Akademischer Verlag Hans-Dieter Heinz, 1982.

Trommler, Frank. "Working Class Culture and Modern Mass Culture before World War I." *New German Critique* 29(1983):57–70.

Tylee, Claire. *The Great War and Women's Consciousness: Images of Militarism and Womenhood in Women's Writings, 1914–1964.* Iowa City: University of Iowa Press, 1990.

Valentiner, Max. *300,000 Tonnen Versenkt!* Berlin: Ullstein, 1917.

Veeser, Aram, ed. *The New Historicism.* New York: Routledge, 1989.

Virilio, Paul. *Speed and Politics.* New York: Semiotext, 1986.

———. *War and Cinema.* Trans. Patrick Camiller. London: Verso, 1989.

Vogel, Bruno. *Es lebe der Krieg! Ein Brief.* 4th ed. "Castrated" ed. Leipzig: Wölfe, 1929. Reprinted in Berlin by Klaus Guhl, 1978.

Volkmann, Ernst, ed. *Deutsche Dichtung im Weltkrieg.* Leipzig, Reclam, 1934.

Volksbund Deutsche Kriegsgräberfürsorge, ed. *Den Gefallenen: Ein Buch des Gedenkens und des Trostes.* Munich: Akademischer Gemeinschaftsverlag, 1952.

Volmert, Johannes. *Ernst Jünger: In Stahlgewittern.* Munich: W. Fink, 1985.

Vondung, Klaus, ed. *Das Wilhelminische Bildungsbürgertum: Zur Sozialgeschichte seiner Ideen.* Göttingen: Vandenhoeck and Ruprecht, 1976.

———. *Kriegserlebnis: Der erste Weltkrieg in der literarischen Gestaltung und symbolischen Deutung der Nationen.* Göttingen: Vandenhoeck and Ruprecht, 1980.

———. *Die Apokalypse in Deutschland.* Munich: Deutsche Taschenbuch Verlag, 1988.

Wallach, Jehuda. *The Dogma of the Battle of Annihilation: The Theories of Clausewitz and Schlieffen and their Impact on the German Conduct of Two World Wars.* Westport, Conn.: Greenwood, 1986.

Wanderscheck, Hermann. *Weltkrieg und Propaganda.* Berlin: E. S. Mittler and Sohn, 1936.

Warstat, Willie. *Das Erlebnis unserer jungen Kriegsfreiwilligen.* Gotha: Perthes, 1916.

Weber, Samuel, ed. *Demarcating the Disciplines.* Minneapolis: University of Minnesota Press, 1986.

———. *Institution and Interpretation.* Minneapolis: University of Minnesota Press, 1987.

———. *Return to Freud: Jacque Lacan's Dislocation of Psychoanalysis.* Trans. Michael Levine. Cambridge: Cambridge University Press, 1991.

Wehner, Josef Magnus. *Langemark: Ein Vermächtnis.* Munich: Langen-Müller, 1933.

Werth, German. *Verdun: Die Schlacht und der Mythos.* Gladbach: Lübbe, 1979.

Wette, Wolfram, ed. *Der Krieg des kleinen Mannes: Eine Militärgeschichte von Unten.* Munich: Piper, 1992.

Whalen, Robert. *Bitter Wounds: German Victims of the Great War, 1914–1939.* Ithaca: Cornell University Press, 1984.

Whelan, Dolores. *Der Engel mausert sich: Das Bild der Frau in den Komödien von Eduard von Bauernfeld.* Bern: Peter Lang, 1978.

White, Hayden. *Tropics of Discourse.* Baltimore: John Hopkins University Press, 1978.

———. *The Content of the Form.* Baltimore: Johns Hopkins University Press, 1987.

Wicki, Hans. *Das königreich Württemberg im ersten Weltkrieg: Seine wirtschaftliche, soziale, politische und kulturelle Lage.* Bern: Peter Lang, 1984.

Widmann, Hans. *Tübingen als Verlagsstadt.* Tübingen: J. C. B. Mohr (Paul Siebeck), 1971.

Wiegand, Wayne. *"An Active Instrument for Propaganda:" The American Public Library During World War I.* Westport, Conn.: Greenwood, 1989.

Wiese, J. *Briefe der Feldgrauen.* Berlin: Globus, 1914–1915.

Wilhelm, Kronprinz. *Erinnerungen des Kronprinzen Wilhelm: Aus den Aufzeichnungen, Dok-*

umenten, Tagebüchern und Gesprächen Herausgegeben von Karl Rosener. Stuttgart: Cotta, 1922.

Winter, Jay. *The Experience of World War I.* New York: Oxford University Press, 1989.

———. *Sites of Memory, Sites of Mourning.* Cambridge: Cambridge University Press, 1995.

Witkop, Philipp. *Die Organisation der Arbeiterbildung: Eine Kritik und Verknüpfung sämmtlicher Arbeiterbildungsbestrebungen.* Berlin: F. Siemenroth, 1904.

———. *Die neuere deutsche Lyrik.* Leipzig: Teubner, 1910–1913.

———. *Der Krieg und die deutsche Dichtung.* Mannheim: *Badische neueste Nachrichten.* Reprint taken from the essay series "Der Kampf des Geistes," 1915.

———. "Der deutsche unterricht," in *Der Weltkrieg im Unterricht.* Gotha: Perthes, 1915.

———. *Heinrich von Kleist.* Stuttgart: Cotta, 1921.

———. *Deutsches Leben der Gegenwart.* Berlin: Volksverband der Bücherfreunde, 1922.

———. *Frauen im Leben deutscher Dichter.* Leipzig: Haessel, 1922.

———. *Die deutschen Lyriker von Luther bis Nietzsche.* Leipzig: B. G. Teubner, 1925.

———. *Tolstoi.* Wittenberg: A. Ziemsen, 1928.

———. *Volk und Erde: Alemannische Dichterbildnisse.* Karlsruhe: C. F. Müller, 1929.

———. *Goethe: Leben und Werk.* Stuttgart: Cotta, 1931.

———. *Volksausgabe: Kriegsbriefe gefallener Studenten.* Munich: Langen-Müller, 1933.

———, ed. *Kriegsbriefe deutscher Studenten.* Gotha: Perthes, 1916.

———, ed. *Kriegsbriefe gefallener Studenten.* Leipzig: Teubner, 1918.

———, ed. *Kriegsbriefe gefallener Studenten.* Munich: Georg Müller, 1928.

Wittmann, Reinhard. *Geschichte des deutschen Buchhandels.* Munich: Beck, 1991.

Wolzogen, Ernst Ludwig. *Landsturm im Feuer.* Berlin: Ullstein, 1918.

Woolacott, Angela. *On Her Their Lives Depend: Munitions Workers in the Great War.* Berkeley: University of California Press, 1992.

Württembergischen Landeskommandanten, ed. *Einzeldarstellungen der Geschichte der württembergischen Heeresverband: Württembergs Heer im Weltkrieg.* Stuttgart: Bergers Literarisches Büro, 1921.

Young, James. *The Texture of Meaning: Holocaust Memorials and Meaning.* New Haven: Yale University Press, 1993.

Zechlin, Egmont. *Die deutsche Politik und die Juden im ersten Weltkrieg.* Göttingen: Vandenhoeck and Ruprecht, 1969.

Zeller, Bernhard. *Autor, Nachlaß, Erben: Probleme der Überlieferung von Literatur.* Mainz: Akademie der Wissenschaft und der Literatur; Wiesbaden: Stein, 1981.

———, ed. *Die Insel: Eine Ausstellung zur Geschichte des Verlages unter Anton und Katharina Kippenberg.* Marbach: Deutsches Literaturarchiv im Schiller Nationalmuseum, 1965.

Zensurbuch für die deutsche Presse. Berlin: Oberzensurstelle des Kriegspresseamtes, 1917.

Zentralstelle für Volkswohlfahrt, ed. *Deutsche Reden in schwerer Zeit.* Berlin: C. Heymann, 1914–1915.

Ziegler, Mathes, ed. *Wie die Pflicht es befahl: Worte unserer Weltkriegsdichter.* Berlin: Nordland, 1940.

Ziesel, Kurt. *Krieg und Dichtung: Soldaten werden Dichter—Dichter werden Soldaten.* Vienna: A. Luser, 1940.

Zimmermann, Emil. *Meine Kriegsfahrt von Kamerun zur Heimat.* Berlin: Ullstein, 1915.

Zobeltitz, Fedor von. *Kriegsfahrten eines Johanniters.* Berlin: Ullstein, 1915.

Zöberlin, Hans. *Der Glaube an Deutschland: Ein Kriegserleben von Verdun bis zum Umsturz.* Munich: Franz Eher Nachfolger, 1931.

Zwehl, Hans Fritz von. *Nach Troyas Fall: Eine Novemberphantasie in einem Vorspiel und drei Akten.* Berlin: Oesterheld, 1923.

———. *Aufruhr in Flandern: Schauspiel.* Berlin: Oesterheld, 1935.

———. *Frühlingsschlacht.* Berlin: Oesterheld, 1935.

Index

Adorno, Theodor, 24, 168, 205, 222n52

Aesthetics: and war literature, 17–18, 21, 75, 177; categories of, 20; and Enlightenment, 24, 245n72; of Wilhelmine period, 26; and state power, 34, 218–19n33; and national identity, 36; of Witkop, 79, 93, 95–107; of immediacy, 119; and *Feldpostbriefe*, 120, 121; of *Volksbildungsbewegung*, 123, 152; and front's reading material, 146, 153, 158, 164, 208; aesthetic education, 147, 148, 218–19n33; and Cotta, 180; and politics, 192, 243n42; and commemoration, 202; and narration, 208; of modernism, 208, 218n31; and technology, 214n11

Archives: and literature as social process, 15; control of, 30, 74, 220n44; and *Feldpostbriefe*, 83, 234–35n13; and publishers, 174, 177, 221n49; theory of, 211n14

Army: and war literature, 1, 3, 25, 78, 194; and censorship, 8; and reading, 9, 135–36, 141, 150, 152; and meaning of war, 11–12; and Langemarck, 28; and academic institutions, 34; and Bloem, 49; regulation of war reporters, 60–61; and heroism, 89, 167; and Ullstein, 134–35; and *Feldbuchhandlungen*, 159–65, 168–73; and memory, 204; women's role in, 212n2

Army communiqués. *See Heeresbericht* (army communiqués)

Army field press agencies. *See Feldpressestelle* (army field press agencies)

Arndt, Karl Moritz, 55, 137

Aufklärung (enlightenment), 34, 92

Authenticity: and space, 12; and front, 12, 58, 75; and officer war reporters, 62; and *Feldpostbriefe*, 78, 85–90, 102, 105, 112, 114, 119, 194, 208, 239n83; of